D1593696

THE MACARTHUR NEW TESTAMENT COMMENTARY

LUKE 6-10

John MacArthur

MOODY PUBLISHERS/CHICAGO

All Scripture quotations, unless otherwise indicated, are taken from the *New American Standard Bible®,* Copyright © 1960, 1962, 1963, 1968, 1971, 1972, 1973, 1975, 1977, 1995 by The Lockman Foundation, Used by permission. (www.Lockman.org)

Scripture quotations marked ESV are taken from *The Holy Bible, English Standard Version.* Copyright © 2000, 2001 by Crossway Bibles, a division of Good News Publishers. Used by permission. All rights reserved.

Scripture quotations marked NKJV are taken from the *New King James Version.* Copyright © 1982 by Thomas Nelson, Inc. Used by permission. All rights reserved.

Cover Design: Smartt Guys design

Library of Congress Cataloging-in-Publication Data

MacArthur, John
   Luke 6-10 / John MacArthur.
     p. cm. — (The MacArthur New Testament commentary)
   Includes bibliographical references and indexes.
   ISBN 978-0-8024-0872-3
   1. Bible. N.T. Luke I-V—Commentaries. I. Title. II. Title: Luke six-ten.

BS2595.53.M33 2009
226.4'077—dc22

                       2009021035

We hope you enjoy this book from Moody Publishers. Our goal is to provide high-quality, thought-provoking books and products that connect truth to your real needs and challenges. For more information on other books and products written and produced from a biblical perspective, go to www.moodypublishers.com or write to:

Moody Publishers
820 N. LaSalle Boulevard
Chicago, IL 60610

5 7 9 10 8 6 4

Printed in the United States of America

To Grace Church missionaries Bruce Alvord, Brian Kinzel, and Greg White, on the occasion of the twentieth anniversary of Irpin Biblical Seminary. Over the last two decades, these faithful men have magnified the name of Christ through their tireless efforts in effectively training twelve hundred Ukrainian nationals in accurate Bible study and expository preaching. The current student body, representing two hundred national churches, gives evidence of the strength of this exceptional ministry. The fruit of their labors, the full extent of which cannot be known this side of heaven, is a legacy that will endure in the former Soviet Union for many generations to come.

Contents

CHAPTER   PAGE

Preface   vii

1. Lord of the Sabbath (Luke 6:1–11) — 1
2. Common Men, Uncommon Calling—Part 1: — 13
   Introduction (Luke 6:12–13)
3. Common Men, Uncommon Calling—Part 2: — 23
   Peter (Luke 6:14a)
4. Common Men, Uncommon Calling—Part 3: — 37
   Andrew, James (Luke 6:14b, c)
5. Common Men, Uncommon Calling—Part 4: — 45
   John (Luke 6:14d)
6. Common Men, Uncommon Calling—Part 5: — 53
   Philip, Bartholomew (Luke 6:14e, f)
7. Common Men, Uncommon Calling—Part 6 : — 63
   Matthew, Thomas, James the son of Alphaeus, Simon
   the Zealot, Judas the son of James (Luke 6:15–16a)
8. Common Men, Uncommon Calling—Part 7: — 73
   Judas Iscariot (Luke 6:16b)
9. The Popularity and Power of Jesus (Luke 6:17–19) — 83

10.	The Character of a True Christian (Luke 6:20–26)	91
11.	Kingdom Love (Luke 6:27–38)	101
12.	The Danger of Following the Wrong Spiritual Teacher (Luke 6:39–49)	111
13.	The Man Who Amazed Jesus (Luke 7:1–10)	121
14.	Jesus' Power over Death (Luke 7:11–17)	131
15.	Are You the Coming One? (Luke 7:18–23)	141
16.	The Greatest Man Who Ever Lived (Luke 7:24–30)	151
17.	The Parable of the Brats: Style Versus Substance (Luke 7:31–35)	161
18.	The Transformed Sinner (Luke 7:36–50)	169
19.	The Scope of Jesus' Ministry (Luke 8:1–3)	177
20.	Receptivity to the Gospel: The Parable of the Soils (Luke 8:4–15)	185
21.	Be Careful How You Listen (Luke 8:16–21)	197
22.	Calm in the Storm (Luke 8:22–25)	205
23.	The Maniac Who Became a Missionary (Luke 8:26–39)	215
24.	Jesus' Compassionate Power (Luke 8:40–56)	227
25.	A Profile of a Christian Messenger (Luke 9:1–9)	239
26.	The Compassionate Lord (Luke 9:10–17)	249
27.	Life's Most Important Question (Luke 9:18–22)	257
28.	A Portrait of True Discipleship (Luke 9:23–26)	265
29.	Previewing the Second Coming (Luke 9:27–36)	279
30.	The Significance of Faith (Luke 9:37–45)	287
31.	The Mark of True Greatness (Luke 9:46–50)	297
32.	A Mission of Mercy (Luke 9:51–56)	307
33.	Barriers to True Discipleship (Luke 9:57–62)	315
34.	Essential Elements for Evangelism (Luke 10:1–16)	323
35.	Joy at the Seventy's Return (Luke 10:17–24)	337
36.	Finding Eternal Life (Luke 10:25–37)	349
37.	The Christian's Priority (Luke 10:38–42)	361
	Bibliography	367
	Index of Greek Words and Phrases	369
	Index of Scripture	370
	Index of Subjects	380

Preface

It continues to be a rewarding, divine communion for me to preach expositionally through the New Testament. My goal is always to have deep fellowship with the Lord in the understanding of His Word and out of that experience to explain to His people what a passage means. In the words of Nehemiah 8:8, I strive "to give the sense" of it so they may truly hear God speak and, in so doing, may respond to Him.

Obviously, God's people need to understand Him, which demands knowing His Word of Truth (2 Tim. 2:15) and allowing that Word to dwell in them richly (Col. 3:16). The dominant thrust of my ministry, therefore, is to help make God's living Word alive to His people. It is a refreshing adventure.

This New Testament commentary series reflects this objective of explaining and applying Scripture. Some commentaries are primarily linguistic, others are mostly theological, and some are mainly homiletical. This one is basically explanatory, or expository. It is not linguistically technical but deals with linguistics when that seems helpful to proper interpretation. It is not theologically expansive but focuses on the major doctrines in each text and how they relate to the whole of Scripture. It is not primarily homiletical, although each unit of thought is generally treated as one chapter, with a clear outline and logical flow of thought.

Most truths are illustrated and applied with other Scripture. After establishing the context of a passage, I have tried to follow closely the writer's development and reasoning.

My prayer is that each reader will fully understand what the Holy Spirit is saying through this part of His Word, so that His revelation may lodge in the mind of believers and bring greater obedience and faithfulness—to the glory of our great God.

Lord of
the Sabbath
(Luke 6:1–11)

1

Now it happened that He was passing through some grainfields on a Sabbath; and His disciples were picking the heads of grain, rubbing them in their hands, and eating the grain. But some of the Pharisees said, "Why do you do what is not lawful on the Sabbath?" And Jesus answering them said, "Have you not even read what David did when he was hungry, he and those who were with him, how he entered the house of God, and took and ate the consecrated bread which is not lawful for any to eat except the priests alone, and gave it to his companions?" And He was saying to them, "The Son of Man is Lord of the Sabbath." On another Sabbath He entered the synagogue and was teaching; and there was a man there whose right hand was withered. The scribes and the Pharisees were watching Him closely to see if He healed on the Sabbath, so that they might find reason to accuse Him. But He knew what they were thinking, and He said to the man with the withered hand, "Get up and come forward!" And he got up and came forward. And Jesus said to them, "I ask you, is it lawful to do good or to do harm on the Sabbath, to save a life or to destroy it?" After looking around at them all, He said to him, "Stretch out your hand!" And he did so; and his hand was restored. But they

themselves were filled with rage, and discussed together what they might do to Jesus. (6:1–11)

The initial reaction to the Lord Jesus Christ was generally positive. Speaking of His early ministry in Galilee, Luke noted that when "He began teaching in their synagogues [He] was praised by all" (4:15). The Lord was so popular that when He "left [Capernaum] and went to a secluded place ... the crowds were searching for Him, and came to Him and tried to keep Him from going away from them" (4:42). After Jesus healed a leper, "the news about Him was spreading even farther, and large crowds were gathering to hear Him and to be healed of their sicknesses" (5:15). In the aftermath of His healing of a paralytic, the people "were all struck with astonishment and began glorifying God; and they were filled with fear, saying, 'We have seen remarkable things today'" (5:26). Even the religious leaders were unable to restrain their curiosity at first (5:17).

But curiosity eventually turned to hostility, which by the time the events in the sixth chapter of Luke's gospel occurred was escalating severely. The religious leaders had come to view Jesus as the most dangerous man in Israel, the biggest threat to their religious power and prestige. Their fears were well-founded. Jesus was the most powerful teacher the world had ever seen or ever will see, and He was assaulting their ritualism, legalism, and prideful hypocrisy. Even worse, while attacking them, the Lord was associating with the tax collectors, prostitutes, and other riffraff of society. When Jesus showed concern about their sins, since He came "to call ... sinners to repentance" (5:32), some of them responded with repentance and faith. But when He confronted the Pharisees and scribes, because they were the leaders of the religious establishment and the proud, unrepentant purveyors of the damning lie that God was pleased by self-righteousness, legalism, and ritualism, they found the Lord's discrediting of them to be intolerable and infuriating. They also found His choosing of common men instead of members of the religious elite as His apostles insulting.

The Lord did not escalate the conflict by being insensitive or ungracious, but by His uncompromising proclamation of the truth. The truth of God is the most important thing in the world (cf. Prov. 23:23). It is the message of sin, forgiveness, salvation, and the hope of eternal life. All the truth must be proclaimed no matter what the effects are, whether people embrace it, or are offended by it; whether they accept it and are saved, or reject it, and are eternally lost. There is no common ground between the truth and error.

Jesus spoke the truth in every situation, not under compulsion or against His will, but by His deliberate choice. By doing so, He exposed error both to those who taught it, and to anyone else who might have been attracted to it. The Lord never minced words when dealing with either false religion, or the wicked false teachers who purvey it (cf. Matt. 7:15–20; 23:1–36). His bold preaching of the gospel, which was incompatible with the Jewish religion of His day (Luke 5:36–39), forced people to choose between the gospel of grace and the works-righteousness system of contemporary Judaism.

At the heart of Jesus' conflict with the Pharisees and scribes was the Sabbath. Much of their self-righteous attempt to earn salvation by good works focused on keeping the Sabbath regulations. Because its observance was the mainstay or anchor of first-century Judaism, the Sabbath inevitably became a major point of contention between Jesus and the Jewish leaders. In this section of his gospel, Luke records two incidents in which Jesus boldly confronted their false view of the Sabbath, and established Himself as Lord over the Sabbath. The first incident took place in the grainfields; the second in a synagogue.

IN THE GRAINFIELDS

Now it happened that He was passing through some grainfields on a Sabbath; and His disciples were picking the heads of grain, rubbing them in their hands, and eating the grain. But some of the Pharisees said, "Why do you do what is not lawful on the Sabbath?" And Jesus answering them said, "Have you not even read what David did when he was hungry, he and those who were with him, how he entered the house of God, and took and ate the consecrated bread which is not lawful for any to eat except the priests alone, and gave it to his companions?" And He was saying to them, "The Son of Man is Lord of the Sabbath." (6:1–5)

The **Sabbath** was originally given by God in the Mosaic law (not before) to be a day of rest (the Hebrew word translated "Sabbath" comes from a verb that means, "to cease," "to desist," or, "to rest" [cf. Gen. 2:2]), refreshment, and worship for His people (Ex. 20:8–11). But by the first century, it had accumulated an enormous number of extrabiblical restrictions and regulations, so much so that it had become the most oppressive and burdensome day of the week.

The Talmud devotes twenty-four chapters to Sabbath regulations, describing in painfully exhaustive detail what was and was not permitted to be done. The result was a ridiculously complex system of external behavior restraints—so much so that one rabbi spent two and a half years studying just one of the twenty-four chapters.

For example, traveling more than 3,000 feet from home was forbidden. But if one had placed food at the 3,000 foot point before the Sabbath, that point would then be considered a home, since there was food there, and allow another 3,000 feet of travel. Similarly, a piece of wood or a rope placed across the end of a narrow street or alley constituted a doorway. That could then be considered the front door of one's house, and permit the 3,000 feet of travel to begin there.

There were also regulations about carrying items. Something lifted up in a public place could only be set down in a private place, and vice versa. An object tossed into the air could be caught with the same hand, but if it was caught with the other hand, it would be a Sabbath violation. If a person had reached out to pick up food when the Sabbath began, the food had to be dropped; to bring the arm back while holding the food would be to carry a burden on the Sabbath. It was forbidden to carry anything heavier than a dried fig (though something weighing half as much could be carried two times). A tailor could not carry his needle, a scribe his pen, or a student his books. Only enough ink to write two letters (of the alphabet) could be carried. A letter could not be sent, not even with a non-Jew. Clothes could not be examined or shaken out before being put on because an insect might be killed in the process, which would be work. No fire could be lit, or put out. Cold water could be poured into warm water, but not warm into cold. An egg could not be cooked, not even by placing it in hot sand during the summer. Nothing could be sold or bought. Bathing was forbidden, lest water be spilled on the floor and wash it. Moving a chair was not allowed, since it might make a rut in a dirt floor, which was too much like plowing. Women were forbidden to look in a mirror, since if they saw a white hair, they might be tempted to pull it out.

Other forbidden things included sowing, plowing, reaping, binding sheaves, threshing, winnowing, grinding, kneading, baking, shearing, washing, beating, dyeing, or spinning wool, tying or untying a knot, catching, killing, or skinning a deer, salting its meat, or preparing its skin. (For a detailed discussion of the rabbinic Sabbath restrictions, see Alfred Edersheim, "The Ordinances and Law of the Sabbath as Laid Down in the Mishnah and the Jerusalem Talmud," Appendix XVII in, *The Life and Times of Jesus the Messiah* [Grand Rapids: Eerdmans, 1974], 2:777–87.)

It was to people crushed by the unbearable burden (Matt. 23:4; Luke 11:46; Acts 15:10) of manmade, legalistic regulations that the Lord Jesus Christ said, "Come to Me, all who are weary and heavy-laden, and I will give you rest. Take My yoke upon you and learn from Me, for I am gentle and humble in heart, and you will find rest for your souls. For My yoke is easy and My burden is light" (Matt. 11:28–30).

This particular Sabbath found the Lord and His disciples **passing**

through some grainfields. *Sporimos* (**grainfields**) literally means, "sown fields"; the crop being grown in these particular fields was probably either wheat or barley. Since the grain was ripe enough to eat, it was probably spring or summer. As they walked along the paths between the rows of grain, the **disciples were picking the heads of grain, rubbing them in their hands, and eating the grain.** To do so was not wrong in itself; travelers were permitted by the Mosaic law to pick grain from their neighbors' fields to satisfy their hunger (though not, of course, to harvest it): "When you enter your neighbor's standing grain, then you may pluck the heads with your hand, but you shall not wield a sickle in your neighbor's standing grain" (Deut. 23:25).

But to do so on the Sabbath was a violation, not of the Mosaic law, but of the rabbinic restrictions described above. Specifically, the disciples were guilty in the eyes of the **Pharisees** of reaping (picking the grain), threshing (rubbing the husks together to separate them from the grain), and winnowing (throwing the husks away), and thus preparing food. The self-appointed guardians of the Sabbath were quick to pounce on the blatant violation of their silly regulations. **"Why do you do what is not lawful on the Sabbath?"** they demanded. Although they addressed their question to the entire group, the Pharisees' rebuke was directed primarily at Jesus, since His disciples were surely following His teaching and example. They viewed the incident as a direct attack on their whole religious system to which, as noted earlier, the Sabbath was central. Obviously, their presence in the grainfields indicates the constant scrutiny to which the religious leaders subjected Jesus, as they dogged His steps looking for an excuse to condemn Him.

Assuming responsibility for His disciples' actions, Jesus responded with a mildly sarcastic rebuke of the Pharisees' ignorance. They, of course, knew the history He was about to relate, but had ignored its true significance. As He frequently did (cf. 5:23; 10:26; 20:3–4, 24) **Jesus** answered their question with one of His own: **"Have you not even read** (cf. Matt. 19:4; 21:42; 22:31; Mark 12:10) **what David did when he was hungry, he and those who were with him, how he entered the house of God, and took and ate the consecrated bread which is not lawful for any to eat except the priests alone, and gave it to his companions?"**

The incident the Lord referred to is recorded in 1 Samuel 21:1–6. Fleeing Saul's relentless pursuit of him, David came to Nob, about a mile north of Jerusalem. David **was hungry,** as were **those who were with him.** Seeking food, they **entered the house of God** (the tabernacle), and asked Ahimelech the priest for five loaves of bread. The tabernacle, of course, was not a bakery, and the only bread available there was the **consecrated bread.** Also called the "bread of the Presence" (Ex. 25:30), it consisted of twelve loaves, placed each Sabbath on the golden table in the Holy Place. After the bread was replaced with fresh loaves, it could be eaten, but only by the priests (Lev. 24:9). Ahimelech was willing to give some of the consecrated bread to David and his men, on the condition that "the young men [had] kept themselves from women" (1 Sam. 21:4) (i.e., were ceremonially clean). After David assured him that they had done so, Ahimelech gave them the bread and they ate it.

The point of the account, which was lost on the Pharisees, was that mercy, compassion, and human need were more important than rigid adherence to even biblical ritual and ceremony. Mark 2:27 records that Jesus also said to them, "The Sabbath was made for man, and not man for the Sabbath," while Matthew records His rebuke, "But if you had known what this means, 'I desire compassion, and not a sacrifice,' you would not have condemned the innocent" (12:7). If a human priest could permit David to violate part of God's ceremonial law (perhaps even on a Sabbath, since the old bread being replaced had not yet been eaten by the priests), how much more could the Son of God allow His disciples to violate unbiblical human traditions?

Then Jesus stunned and outraged the Pharisees by declaring, **"The Son of Man is Lord of the Sabbath."** As such, He alone had the right to decide what behavior was appropriate on the Sabbath; He is the interpreter of God's will, law, and word. Since the Sabbath was established by God (Ex. 20:8–11), He, the Son of God, had authority over it. Thus, by claiming authority over a divinely instituted ordinance, Jesus was claiming full equality with God. Compare John 5:9–17, where our Lord was again confronted over His Sabbath activity and replied, "My Father is working ... and I Myself am working" (v. 17). Here again He clearly declared His equality with God, as evidenced by His sovereignty over the Sabbath.

IN A SYNAGOGUE

On another Sabbath He entered the synagogue and was teaching; and there was a man there whose right hand was withered. The scribes and the Pharisees were watching Him closely to see if He healed on the Sabbath, so that they might find reason to accuse Him. But He knew what they were thinking, and He said to the man with the withered hand, "Get up and come forward!" And he got up and came forward. And Jesus said to them, "I ask you, is it lawful to do good or to do harm on the Sabbath, to save a life or to destroy it?" After looking around at them all, He said to him, "Stretch out your hand!" And he did so; and his hand was

restored. But they themselves were filled with rage, and discussed together what they might do to Jesus. (6:6–11)

On another Sabbath, Jesus again confronted the Pharisees over the issue of the Sabbath. Luke does not specify when this incident took place, or the location of the **synagogue** (possibly Capernaum). However Matthew, Mark, and Luke all place it immediately after the incident in the grainfields, which suggests it happened soon afterward, perhaps on the next Sabbath. In keeping with the priority of His ministry, Jesus **was teaching** (cf. 4:14–15, 31, 44; 5:15, 17). The content of His message was not recorded, but He would have been preaching the gospel (3:18; 4:18; 7:22; 20:1; Mark 1:14)—the good news that the poor, prisoners, blind, and oppressed could be freed from their sin and the heavy burden of a false, damning, legalistic religion (4:18–21).

In the synagogue on that particular Sabbath **was a man . . . whose right hand** (only Luke, with his careful attention to medical detail, notes that it was his right hand) **was withered;** that is, atrophied due to paralysis. This man was the main object of Jesus' attention, and his healing was another assault on the Pharisees' restrictions for the Sabbath.

As always, the **scribes and the Pharisees** were there, hoping to find something for which they could condemn the Lord. As always, these zealous legalists **were watching** Jesus **closely. Watching closely** translates a form of the Greek verb *paratēreō*, which means, "to observe carefully," "to be on the lookout," or "to pay heed to." Often, as it does here, the word takes on a sinister tone, and could be translated, "to lurk," "to watch for an opportunity," or "to lie in wait" (cf. 14:1; 20:20; Mark 3:2). The scribes and Pharisees were by no means neutral observers, but rather spies.

Specifically, they were watching Jesus **to see if He healed on the Sabbath, so that they might find reason to accuse Him.** Ironically, these self-appointed guardians of the Sabbath system did not want to stop Jesus from breaking their Sabbath rules; they actually wanted Him to perform a healing, so they would have cause to indict Him. Christ's performing a healing would thus best suit their heinous hatred. Interestingly, never throughout His entire ministry did they doubt His ability to heal (cf. 5:17–26), which proved His ability to forgive sin (5:24). Yet the convoluted reasoning in their sinful, prideful, obstinate hearts was that if Jesus did heal, the consequence would be that they could charge Him with breaking the Sabbath.

Needless to say, ministering to a sick person was by no means a violation of the Old Testament regulations concerning the Sabbath (cf. Matt. 12:7). The rabbis, however, had decreed that no one, whether a physician, friend, or family member, could treat a sick person on the Sabbath.

To do so, they taught, would be work and hence a violation of the Sabbath. The only two exceptions they allowed were cases when a person might otherwise die before the Sabbath ended, or a pregnant woman who gave birth on the Sabbath. Other than those two situations, showing compassion and mercy to a suffering person made one a blaspheming lawbreaker.

As He had earlier done (5:22) and would later do (11:17), Jesus in His omniscience **knew what they were thinking.** The Lord was fully aware of their vicious, hateful thoughts toward Him; that they were waiting for Him to heal so they could accuse Him of breaking the Sabbath. Ignoring their legalistic, merciless regulations and intentions, Jesus **said to the man with the withered hand, "Get up and come forward!"** He was the perfect candidate to help the Lord stage His assault on their twisted view of the Sabbath. His condition was clearly not life threatening, so there was no possible justification under the death exception for helping him.

The crippled man **got up and came forward** and stood before the synagogue audience. It was a dramatic moment, as the people waited to see what Jesus was going to do. Addressing the scribes and Pharisees, who no doubt had front-row seats (11:43; 20:46; Matt. 23:6; Mark 12:39), Jesus asked the self-proclaimed experts on the law a pointed question. **"I ask you,"** He demanded, **"is it lawful to do good or to do harm on the Sabbath, to save a life or to destroy it?"** As was often the case, the Lord's question impaled His opponents on the horns of a dilemma. On the one hand, answering that it was lawful to do good on the Sabbath would officially authorize Jesus to heal the man. They could not then indict Him for breaking the Sabbath. On the other hand, answering that it was not lawful to do good would reveal their wicked, merciless hearts. That would tear down their veneer of self-righteousness and piosity and expose them as the hypocrites they were.

The scribes and Pharisees knew the correct answer to Jesus' question, which the book of Isaiah records. In two passages in Isaiah God indicted Israel for their superficial, shallow, false religion—the very issue Jesus was addressing:

> "What are your multiplied sacrifices to Me?" says the Lord. "I have had enough of burnt offerings of rams and the fat of fed cattle; and I take no pleasure in the blood of bulls, lambs or goats. When you come to appear before Me, who requires of you this trampling of My courts? Bring your worthless offerings no longer, incense is an abomination to Me. New moon and sabbath, the calling of assemblies—I cannot endure iniquity and the solemn assembly. I hate your new moon festivals and your appointed feasts, they have become a burden to Me; I am weary of bearing them. So when you spread out your hands in prayer, I

will hide My eyes from you; yes, even though you multiply prayers, I will
not listen. Your hands are covered with blood. Wash yourselves, make
yourselves clean; remove the evil of your deeds from My sight. Cease to
do evil, learn to do good; seek justice, reprove the ruthless, defend the
orphan, plead for the widow." (1:11–17)

Is this not the fast which I choose, to loosen the bonds of wickedness,
to undo the bands of the yoke, and to let the oppressed go free and
break every yoke? Is it not to divide your bread with the hungry and
bring the homeless poor into the house; when you see the naked, to
cover him; and not to hide yourself from your own flesh? Then your
light will break out like the dawn, and your recovery will speedily
spring forth; and your righteousness will go before you; the glory of the
Lord will be your rear guard. Then you will call, and the Lord will
answer; you will cry, and He will say, "Here I am." If you remove the yoke
from your midst, the pointing of the finger and speaking wickedness,
and if you give yourself to the hungry and satisfy the desire of the
afflicted, then your light will rise in darkness and your gloom will
become like midday. And the Lord will continually guide you, and satisfy your desire in scorched places, and give strength to your bones;
and you will be like a watered garden, and like a spring of water whose
waters do not fail. Those from among you will rebuild the ancient ruins;
you will raise up the age-old foundations; And you will be called the
repairer of the breach, the restorer of the streets in which to dwell. If
because of the sabbath, you turn your foot from doing your own pleasure on My holy day, and call the sabbath a delight, the holy day of the
Lord honorable, and honor it, desisting from your own ways, from seeking your own pleasure and speaking your own word, then you will take
delight in the Lord, and I will make you ride on the heights of the earth;
and I will feed you with the heritage of Jacob your father, for the mouth
of the Lord has spoken. (58:6–14)

As those two passages indicate, God rejected religious ritual divorced
from compassion, mercy, and doing good. The Sabbath above all days
was a day to express goodness; to show mercy and kindness to the
needy. But the rabbinic restrictions had so strangled the Sabbath as to
render such kindness forbidden.

The real issue was not the healing of the crippled man; Jesus was
not concerned primarily with their attitude toward him, or whether it
was right to do good to him. The deeper question was who was honoring
God: Jesus, who wanted to show mercy to a needy individual, or the
scribes and Pharisees, who wanted only to destroy Jesus? Sabbath observance was as they defined it—a litmus test of faithfulness to God. Paradoxically, these religious errorists scrupulously observed the minutiae of
their Sabbath laws while at the same time plotting to murder the Lord of
the Sabbath. As David Gooding observes,

The religious mind is a curious thing. It is not necessarily interested in common morality; still less in relieving human misery and affliction. It is interested in keeping rules; particularly the rules which spring from its own cherished interpretations of Scripture or tradition; and to these interpretations it will attribute the inflexible authority of God himself. Let God incarnate, contrary to its interpretations, interpose with a miracle of divine goodness to relieve human misery, then instead of revising its interpretations it will plan to stop such miracles happening again. (*According to Luke* [Grand Rapids: Eerdmans, 1987], 116)

There was a long pause while the Lord waited for a reply. But the scribes and Pharisees, shocked into silence, said nothing. Finally, **after looking around at them all** "with anger, grieved at their hardness of heart" (Mark 3:5), Jesus **said to** the crippled man, **"Stretch out your hand!" And he did so; and his hand was restored.** Jesus deliberately broke their Sabbath restrictions.

After witnessing this astonishing creative miracle, one would expect the next verse to read, "And the scribes and Pharisees believed." Such was not the case, however. Instead, **they themselves were filled with rage, and discussed together what they might do to Jesus** to destroy Him (Matt. 12:14). *Anoia* (**rage**) literally means, "folly," or "foolishness." It denotes in this context an irrational rage; they were out of their minds with fury at Jesus' direct assault on their hypocritical religion. Their reaction reflects the blindness and obstinacy of heart of those deeply involved in false religion. Amazingly, the Pharisees even enlisted the help of their bitter enemies the Herodians (Jews loyal to the Herodians) in their search for a way to eliminate Jesus (Mark 3:6). Such an alliance was highly unusual, since about the only thing the two parties had in common was their hatred of Jesus.

The Pharisees' irrational hatred of and fury toward Jesus was motivated by self-preserving fear. The Lord was striking monumental blows at the very heart of their religious system. Here, long before Passion Week, the religious leaders were already plotting Jesus' death. Their hatred would drive their continued opposition to Christ until they finally succeeded in having Him arrested and executed.

These two incidents bring out the stark contrast between Jesus and the Jewish religious leaders. It is the contrast between the representative of God's truth, and the representatives of false religion; between divine truth and human tradition; between profound knowledge and madness; between goodness and wickedness; between compassion and cruelty; between open honesty and hidden deception; between divine power and human impotence; between the kingdom of God and the kingdom of Satan.

Yet God's grace can penetrate even the most hardened heart. Not all of the Pharisees permanently rejected the Lord Jesus Christ. Acts 15:5 notes that there were "some of the sect of the Pharisees who had believed." One of those believing Pharisees, Saul of Tarsus, became the great apostle Paul. The self-proclaimed foremost of sinners (1 Tim. 1:15), he was called by the risen Lord to preach the gospel throughout the Roman world.

Common Men, Uncommon Calling— Part 1: Introduction (Luke 6:12–13)

2

It was at this time that He went off to the mountain to pray, and He spent the whole night in prayer to God. And when day came, He called His disciples to Him and chose twelve of them, whom He also named as apostles. (6:12–13)

Throughout redemptive history, God has chosen ordinary people to do extraordinary things, a truth that the apostle Paul emphasized in 1 Corinthians 1:20–29:

> Where is the wise man? Where is the scribe? Where is the debater of this age? Has not God made foolish the wisdom of the world? For since in the wisdom of God the world through its wisdom did not come to know God, God was well-pleased through the foolishness of the message preached to save those who believe. For indeed Jews ask for signs and Greeks search for wisdom; but we preach Christ crucified, to Jews a stumbling block and to Gentiles foolishness, but to those who are the called, both Jews and Greeks, Christ the power of God and the wisdom of God. Because the foolishness of God is wiser than men, and the weakness of God is stronger than men. For consider your calling, brethren, that there were not many wise according to the flesh, not many mighty, not many noble; but God has chosen the foolish things of

the world to shame the wise, and God has chosen the weak things of the world to shame the things which are strong, and the base things of the world and the despised God has chosen, the things that are not, so that He may nullify the things that are, so that no man may boast before God.

God chose Abraham, an idolater (Josh. 24:2), to be His friend (Isa. 41:8) and the father physically of Israel (Isa. 51:2; Luke 1:73; John 8:56) and spiritually of believing Gentiles (Rom. 4:16; Gal. 3:7). Joseph entered Egypt as a slave, rose in God's providence to be the prime minister (Gen. 41:39–44; 45:9, 26), and was used by God to preserve His people (Gen. 45:7; 50:20). After spending forty years in exile in the land of Midian (Acts 7:23, 30), Moses, the murderer, was used by God to deliver Israel from bondage in Egypt. A harlot named Rahab from the destroyed Canaanite city of Jericho became an ancestor of the Lord Jesus Christ (Matt. 1:5) and an example of a faithful believer (Heb. 11:31). David went from being a lowly shepherd to delivering Israel from the Philistines by killing Goliath, and eventually became Israel's greatest king. And despite living in the wilderness (Luke 1:80), wearing rough clothing, and eating a wild diet (Matt. 3:4), John the Baptist was declared by our Lord the greatest man who ever lived (Matt. 11:11).

Consistent with that pattern, when Jesus chose twelve men to be His official representatives, He chose common, ordinary men. The Twelve were not from the established religious elite; none were Pharisees, Sadducees, priests, Levites, rabbis, or scribes. None were exceptionally wealthy (with the possible exception of Matthew, who gained what he had by extorting his fellow Israelites). Nor were the apostles chosen from the intellectual elite—the Old Testament scholars; the literate; highly educated; the theologically astute. Instead, they were "uneducated and untrained men," noteworthy only for "having been with Jesus" (Acts 4:13). Several were fishermen, one was a tax collector and hence a traitor to his people, another was a political revolutionary. All except for Judas Iscariot were Galileans, scorned as unsophisticated and uncouth by the more cultured Judeans. Yet the lives and ministries of these men (minus Judas Iscariot and including Paul) would change the course of history.

Before examining each of these men in detail in the next few chapters, some general background information is in order. This introductory chapter will therefore discuss the setting for the Lord's choosing of the Twelve, His selecting them, His sending of them as His official representatives, and conclude by looking at their significance.

THE SETTING

It was at this time that He went off to the mountain to pray, and He spent the whole night in prayer to God. (6:12)

    The word **time** does not refer to calendar time, such as a specific day, week, or month, but is a general term for season, era, or period. It describes here the time of Christ's intensifying conflict with the scribes and Pharisees. They first appeared in Luke's account in 5:17, and their hostility toward Jesus quickly manifested itself (v. 21). Since that first incident, their opposition to Him had been steadily escalating (v. 30; 6:2, 7, 11). In view of that mounting hostility, which would culminate in His execution less than two years later, the time had come for Jesus to choose the men who would carry on His earthly ministry after His death. He knew that they needed intensive preparation and training in the time remaining before the cross for their roles as His official representatives.

    Recognizing the critical importance of His choice of these men, Jesus **went off to the mountain** alone **to pray** (cf. 5:16). The specific mountain on which the Lord prayed is not known, but there were many in the vicinity of the Sea of Galilee. In His humanity, having set aside the independent use of His divine attributes (Phil. 2:5–8), Jesus sought the Father's will in choosing the Twelve. So important was this decision to the future course of redemptive history that Jesus **spent the whole night in prayer to God.** _Dianuktereuōn_ (meaning, "to spend the whole night") appears only here in the New Testament. It denotes an activity that continues throughout an entire night. The Greek phrase translated **in prayer to God** is an unusual construction, and could be translated "in the prayer of God." Jesus spent the long hours of darkness in unceasing, fervent, persevering, inter-Trinitarian prayer to the Father before selecting the twelve apostles.

THE SELECTING

And when day came, He called His disciples to Him and chose twelve of them, (6:13_a_)

    In answer to our Lord's fervent, night-long intercession, God revealed His will as to which of the disciples were to be selected for special training and apostolic commissioning. Therefore **when day came,** Jesus **called His disciples to Him. Disciples** translates the plural form of _mathētēs_, which means, "student," "follower," or "learner." In Greek and Jewish culture prominent rabbis, orators, philosophers, or teachers would attract followers, who would travel with them from place to place. Because of His powerful, unparalleled teaching (John 7:46; Matt. 7:28–29), ability to heal any disease, cast out demons, raise the dead, and perform other miracles (e.g., 5:4–9; Matt. 14:14–21, 25–32; 15:32–38; John 21:5–11), the Lord Jesus Christ attracted a large number of disciples. Those with Him in the grain fields (6:1), for example, would have included more than merely the Twelve, who had not yet been chosen. The miraculous feedings of the five thousand and four thousand men (which would also have included thousands of women and children) indicate the vast size of the crowds that followed Jesus (cf. 12:1). Not all, of course, were genuine followers. Unwilling to accept the demands of following Christ (John 6:53–65), "many of His disciples withdrew and were not walking with Him anymore" (v. 66).

Out of the large group of disciples, some of whom came to Him on their own and others that He specifically called to follow Him (5:8–11, 27–28), Jesus **chose twelve of them.** As He would later remind them, "You did not choose Me but I chose you" (John 15:16; cf. 6:70; 13:18). Although Jesus chose the Twelve at this time, He did not officially commission them and grant them authority to heal and cast out demons until later (Luke 9:1).

That the Lord chose twelve men is not random, because that number was symbolic of the twelve tribes of Israel. The importance of the number was underscored by the addition of Matthias to take Judas's place (Acts 1:23–26). Since Israel and its leaders were apostate, the Twelve were to serve as the leaders of the new, true Israel of God—the redeemed, believing remnant. Jesus made that connection clear in Luke 22:29–30 when He told the Twelve that they would reign over Israel in the millennial kingdom: "Just as My Father has granted Me a kingdom, I grant you that you may eat and drink at My table in My kingdom, and you will sit on thrones judging the twelve tribes of Israel."

There are four lists of the twelve apostles in the New Testament (cf. Matt. 10:2–4; Mark 3:16–19; Acts 1:13). The names on all the lists appear in three groups of four, always in the same order, though the names in each group may be shuffled (except for the list in Acts, which omits Judas Iscariot, who had by that time committed suicide). These groups are arranged in order of decreasing intimacy with Christ. The first group consists of two pairs of brothers: Peter and James, and John and Andrew; the second of Philip, Bartholomew (Nathanael), Matthew, and Thomas; the last of James the son of Alphaeus, Simon the Zealot, Judas the son of James, and Judas Iscariot. Peter's name is always first in all four lists, and Judas Iscariot's last (except in Acts). The order of the names within each group sometimes varies, but Peter's name, as noted, is always first in group one, Philip's is always first in group two, and James the son of Alphaeus's always heads group three. Those in group one, Peter, James, John, and Andrew, were the first four called by Jesus to be His disciples (John 1:35–42), the most intimate with Him, and those about whom the most is known. While there is some information about those in group two, very little is known about group three.

The Twelve were a diverse group, not only in their occupations, as noted above, but also in their political views. Matthew and Simon, for instance, could not have been further apart. Matthew was a tax collector, a traitor who served the Roman occupiers by exploiting his own people. Simon, on the other hand, was a member of the Zealots, a faction radically opposed to Rome. Some of them, known as the Sicarii for the concealed daggers they carried, were terrorists. They resorted to kidnapping or even murdering Romans and Jews they suspected of being loyal to Rome. Were it not for their common devotion to Jesus Christ, Simon may well have murdered Matthew. It was that same devotion that molded all twelve men, different as they were in occupation, temperament, and political views, into a cohesive unit.

THE SENDING

whom He also named as apostles (6:13*b*)

Having chosen the Twelve, Jesus **named** or designated them **apostles.** *Apostolos* ("apostle") refers to a messenger, ambassador, or representative invested with the full authority of the one who sent him. The concept of an apostle can be traced to the Jewish concept of the *shaliach*, which also referred to a messenger sent with full authority to act on behalf of another. Some rabbis, for example, were sent to the Diaspora (Jews living outside of Palestine) with authority to act on behalf of the Sanhedrin on various matters. A *shaliach* could also act on behalf of an individual, similar to the modern-day legal concept of power of attorney. Thus in Jewish practice, the *shaliach* was the same as the one who sent him (cf. John 13:20; Gal. 4:14). David, for example, proposed marriage to Abigail through messengers, and she signified her acceptance of his proposal by washing their feet (1 Sam. 25:40–42). Jesus' designating the Twelve to act on His behalf would thus have been understood by everyone in that culture.

But before being sent out by Jesus, the Twelve needed to be personally mentored by Him. Mark 3:14 notes that the Lord chose them "so that they would be with Him." Only after that time of preparation did He "send them out to preach." Their call to be apostles was not an end in itself, but merely the next step in the sequential process of preparing them to carry on Christ's gospel ministry after His death. First, they believed in Him (cf. John 1:35–51). Second, He called them to leave their occupations and follow Him full time (Luke 5:6–11, 27–28). Third, He chose them to be apostles. Fourth, He sent them to preach the gospel to Israel (Matt. 10:1–6). Finally, He sent them out to evangelize the world (Acts 1:8). Because of their central role in the ministry of the gospel to Israel, Luke mentions them six times in his gospel. But emphasizing their foundational role in the church, he mentions them almost thirty times in Acts.

Their Significance

Despite their crucial role in the church and their proclamation of the saving message of the New Covenant, the apostles are often not given their due honor. Peter, James, and John, the three closest to the Lord, are the most familiar. Matthew (because of his gospel), Andrew, and Philip are less well known. Thomas, regrettably, is remembered chiefly for doubting Christ's resurrection (though there was far more to his story than that, as will be seen in chapter 7 of this volume), while Judas Iscariot, of course, is infamous for betraying Christ. The rest of the apostles are largely unknown; in fact, many Christians could not even name Bartholomew (Nathanael), James the son of Alphaeus, Simon the Zealot, and Judas the son of James. Yet all the apostles deserve respect for the vital ministry they performed—and they will be honored throughout eternity by having their names inscribed on the gates of the glorious city of New Jerusalem (Rev. 21:14).

The apostles were important for at least six reasons. First, as noted above, they were the foundation of the church. In Ephesians 2:20 Paul wrote that the church was "built on the foundation of the apostles and prophets, Christ Jesus Himself being the corner stone."

Second, the apostles received revelation "which in other generations was not made known to the sons of men, as it has now been revealed to His holy apostles and prophets in the Spirit" (Eph. 3:5). The entire New Testament was written by the apostles or their close associates. And before the New Testament was written, the believers "were continually devoting themselves to the apostles' teaching" (Acts 2:42). That teaching, as recorded in the New Testament, is still the only authoritative source of doctrine.

Third, the apostles were given to edify the church. According to Ephesians 4:11–12 God "gave some as apostles, and some as prophets, and some as evangelists, and some as pastors and teachers, for the equipping of the saints for the work of service, to the building up of the body of Christ."

Fourth, not only was their doctrine authoritative, but also their lives were exemplary. Ephesians 3:5 calls them the "holy apostles," leading Paul to exhort believers to be imitators of him (1 Cor. 4:16; 11:1; 1 Thess. 1:6).

Fifth, the apostles were given miraculous power to confirm their message. The marks of a true apostle, as Paul wrote to the Corinthians, were "signs and wonders and miracles" (2 Cor. 12:12). He reminded the Romans that he had carried out his ministry "in the power of signs and wonders" (Rom. 15:19). The writer of Hebrews noted that the message of salvation "was confirmed to us by those who heard [the apostles], God also testifying with them, both by signs and wonders and by various miracles and by gifts of the Holy Spirit according to His own will" (Heb. 2:3-4).

Finally, the apostles were greatly blessed (Luke 18:28-30) as they will be in eternity (Rev. 21:12-14).

But despite their privileges and importance, the apostles were by no means perfect; they were ordinary men, not stained-glass saints. They had several major weaknesses which the Lord had to correct.

First, they were obtuse and lacking in spiritual understanding, for which Jesus repeatedly rebuked them:

> Are you still lacking in understanding also? (Matt. 15:16)

> Do you not yet understand or remember the five loaves of the five thousand, and how many baskets full you picked up? Or the seven loaves of the four thousand, and how many large baskets full you picked up? How is it that you do not understand that I did not speak to you concerning bread? But beware of the leaven of the Pharisees and Sadducees. (Matt. 16:9-11)

> Why do you discuss the fact that you have no bread? Do you not yet see or understand? Do you have a hardened heart? (Mark 8:17)

> Do you not understand this parable? How will you understand all the parables? (Mark 4:13. See also Mark 9:32; Luke 9:45; 18:34; John 12:16; 20:9.)

The Lord remedied the apostles' ignorance by continually teaching them the truth (cf. Luke 24:45). Even after His resurrection, Jesus spent forty days with them "speaking of the things concerning the kingdom of God" (Acts 1:3).

Second, the apostles lacked humility. They were, frankly, egotistical, self-centered, and proud, focused on who among them was the greatest. On one occasion Jesus "began to question them, 'What were you discussing on the way?' But they kept silent, for on the way they had discussed with one another which of them was the greatest" (Mark 9:33–34). On another occasion

> an argument started among them as to which of them might be the greatest. But Jesus, knowing what they were thinking in their heart, took a child and stood him by His side, and said to them, "Whoever receives this child in My name receives Me, and whoever receives Me receives Him who sent Me; for the one who is least among all of you, this is the one who is great." (Luke 9:46–48)

Even the Lord's dramatic announcement at the Last Supper that He would be betrayed was followed by "a dispute among [the apostles] as to which one of them was regarded to be greatest" (Luke 22:24). James and John angled for the most prominent places in the kingdom by having their mother approach Jesus on their behalf (Matt. 20:20–21). Jesus responded to the apostles' self-seeking pride by setting an example of humility for them to follow (John 13:1–15).

Third, the apostles were weak in faith. Fearing that their boat would be swamped, they cried out, "Save us, Lord; we are perishing!" (Matt. 8:25). Jesus' response was a rebuke for their inability to trust: "Why are you afraid, you men of little faith?" (v. 26). When Peter began to sink after joining Jesus in walking on the Sea of Galilee, "Immediately Jesus stretched out His hand and took hold of him, and said to him, 'You of little faith, why did you doubt?'" (Matt. 14:31). The Lord also rebuked the apostles' lack of faith in Matthew 16:8, demanding of them, "You men of little faith, why do you discuss among yourselves that you have no bread?" Jesus responded to the apostles' doubt by performing miracles to strengthen their faith (cf. John 20:30–31).

Fourth, the apostles' (especially Peter [Matt. 26:69–75]) deserting of Jesus when He was arrested (Mark 14:50) demonstrates their lack of commitment. The Lord's answer for that sinful weakness was to pray for the apostles to remain faithful (Luke 22:31–32; John 17:11–26).

Finally, the apostles lacked power. Puzzled by their inability to cast out a demon they asked Jesus, "Why could we not drive it out?" (Matt. 17:19). Jesus remedied their lack of spiritual power by sending them the Holy Spirit (Acts 1:8).

Humanly speaking, then, the Twelve hardly seemed qualified for the momentous task to which Jesus had called them. But God uses less than adequate people, because that is all He has to work with. After being delivered from the unprecedented catastrophe of the worldwide flood, Noah got drunk and disgraced himself (Gen. 9:20–21). Abraham, the father of the nation of Israel and spiritual father of believing Gentiles, lied about Sarah. Fearing that the Egyptians would kill him and seize her if they knew she was his wife, he pretended she was his sister (Gen.

12:12–13). Later, his son Isaac did the same thing with his wife Rebekah (Gen. 26:7). Jacob extorted his brother Esau's birthright from him (Gen. 25:30–33). Moses' prideful disobedience of God's command kept him from entering the Promised Land (Num. 20:10–12). Aaron, Israel's first high priest, led the people into idolatry and immorality (Ex. 32:1–24). Joshua made a treaty with some of the inhabitants of Canaan, which the Lord had forbidden Israel to do (Josh. 9:3–27). David, Israel's greatest king, the "man after [God's] own heart" (1 Sam. 13:14), and the "sweet psalmist of Israel" (2 Sam. 23:1), committed adultery with Bathsheba (2 Sam. 11:1–4) and then murdered her husband in an attempt to cover up her resulting pregnancy (vv. 14–15). After his triumph over the prophets of Baal on Mount Carmel, Elijah fled in abject fear from one woman (1 Kings 19:1–3). Isaiah confessed himself to be "a man of unclean lips" (Isa. 6:5). Jonah disobeyed God's command to go to Nineveh and proclaim judgment (Jonah 1:1–2), and instead fled in the opposite direction. After being cast overboard in a raging storm and spending three days in the stomach of a huge sea creature (vv. 15–17), the reluctant prophet obeyed God's original mandate (3:1–3). But when the people of Nineveh repented, instead of rejoicing, Jonah became angry and wanted to die (4:1–3). Even the apostle Paul proclaimed himself to be the foremost of sinners (1 Tim. 1:15) and "the least of the apostles, and not fit to be called an apostle, because [he] persecuted the church of God" (1 Cor. 15:9).

Jesus knew the apostles' weaknesses, faults, and shortcomings. But He also saw in them the potential under His power to change the world. These twelve common men received the most noble of all callings, the ministry of the New Covenant, proclaiming the glorious truth of salvation in the Lord Jesus Christ. But like all ministers of the New Covenant, they had "this treasure in earthen vessels, so that the surpassing greatness of the power [would] be of God and not from [themselves]" (2 Cor. 4:7).

Common Men, Uncommon Calling— Part 2: Peter (Luke 6:14*a*)

3

Simon, whom He also named Peter, (6:14*a*)

Our society and its laws set standards and requirements for almost every enterprise. People have to demonstrate their qualifications for everything from jobs to driver's licenses to credit cards to loans. Doctors must be licensed, teachers credentialed, and lawyers admitted to the bar. Students must meet certain standards to be admitted to a college or university, and meet still other standards to receive their degrees. Many positions also require intangible qualifications, such as character, experience, self-motivation, and social skills.

As the Bible makes clear, God's standards for those who lead His people are extremely high. An elder must be

> above reproach, the husband of one wife, temperate, prudent, respectable, hospitable, able to teach, not addicted to wine or pugnacious, but gentle, peaceable, free from the love of money. He must be one who manages his own household well, keeping his children under control with all dignity (but if a man does not know how to manage his own household, how will he take care of the church of God?), and not a new convert, so that he will not become conceited and fall into the condemnation incurred by the devil. And he must have a good reputation with

those outside the church, so that he will not fall into reproach and the snare of the devil. (1 Tim. 3:2–7)

Leaders must be exemplary, since the standards their lives are measured against are the same ones all believers are to meet; God doesn't lower the standards for everyone else. Thus the writer of Hebrews exhorts believers to "remember those who led you, who spoke the word of God to you; and considering the result of their conduct, imitate their faith" (Heb. 13:7). The ultimate standard Christians are called to meet is "to be perfect, as [their] heavenly Father is perfect" (Matt. 5:48).

Such a lofty standard is, humanly speaking, impossible to meet. No one qualifies on his or her own merit to enter God's kingdom or to serve Him. Since there are no qualified people, God, in His grace, had to choose unworthy and unqualified people to minister for Him. Saving and sanctifying grace transforms them into useful servants. The Twelve, like all believers, were unqualified sinners saved by God's redeeming grace and sovereignly chosen by Him for service (John 15:16). They were not stained-glass saints, to be put on a pedestal, or worse, worshiped; they were like Elijah, who "was a man with a nature like ours" (James 5:17). In spite of all their human limitations, God used the apostles to turn the world upside down (cf. Acts 17:6) because they surrendered completely to Him whose power is perfected in weakness (2 Cor. 12:9). The gospel, not those who proclaim it, "is the power of God for salvation to everyone who believes" (Rom. 1:16; cf. 1 Cor. 1:18; 2:4–5; 2 Cor. 4:7).

Spiritual leadership differs markedly from natural leadership. Natural leaders trust their judgment and make their own decisions; spiritual leaders humbly seek God's will. Natural leaders are ambitious and driven; spiritual leaders seek God's will and glory. Natural leaders enjoy exercising authority over others; spiritual leaders seek to serve others (Matt. 23:11). Natural leaders are motivated by success; spiritual leaders by love for God. Natural leaders are independent; spiritual leaders are totally dependent on God.

There is no clearer example in Scripture of how God builds a spiritual leader than Peter. He was chosen and equipped by the Lord to be the spokesman for the Twelve, and as such is the most prominent of the apostles. Peter is mentioned more often in the gospels than anyone else except Jesus. None of the Twelve spoke as often as Peter did, nor did the Lord address anyone else as often as Peter. None of the disciples was so often rebuked by Jesus as Peter was, and no disciple had the temerity to rebuke the Lord except Peter. No one confessed Christ's true identity more boldly and explicitly than Peter, yet paradoxically, no one denied Him as vehemently and publicly as did Peter. No one received higher praise from Jesus than Peter, but neither did He address anyone else as

Satan. Yet God took this common man with an ambivalent, vacillating, impulsive, unsubmissive personality and molded him into the unquestioned leader of the Twelve and the boldest, most powerful preacher in the early years of the church.

Peter's birth name was **Simon** Barjona ("son of Jonas," or "John"; Matt. 16:17). Simon was a very common name in Israel; the New Testament lists several other men by that name, including another one of the apostles, Simon the Zealot, (Luke 6:15), one of Jesus' brothers (Matt. 13:55), a leper (presumably healed by Jesus) in Bethany (Mark 14:3), at whose house Mary (the sister of Martha) anointed Jesus with costly perfume (John 12:1–3), a Pharisee who invited Jesus to eat with him, and at whose house another woman anointed Jesus (Luke 7:36–50), a man from Cyrene, pressed by the Romans into carrying Jesus' cross (Mark 15:21), the father of Judas Iscariot (John 6:71), the false prophet Simon the magician (Acts 8:9–24), and Simon the tanner, at whose house in Joppa Peter stayed (Acts 9:43).

As noted in the previous chapter of this volume, Peter's name heads all four New Testament lists of the apostles. Emphasizing his primary position among the Twelve, Matthew 10:2 calls Peter the "first" of the apostles. *Prōtos* ("first") does not refer in this context to being first in sequence, but rather first in importance; it has the sense of "chief," or "most important." He was by trade a fisherman, along with his brother Andrew (Matt. 4:18). They were originally from the small village of Bethsaida (John 1:44), but had moved to Capernaum, the most significant town on the northern tip of the Sea of Galilee (Luke 4:31, 38), where Jesus had settled after leaving Nazareth (Matt. 4:13). Though it is impossible to be certain, a church building found in the ruins of Capernaum may have been built on the site of Peter's home. Peter was married, since Jesus healed his mother-in-law (Luke 4:38–39), and Paul noted that his wife accompanied him on his missionary journeys (1 Cor. 9:5).

That Jesus **named** Simon **Peter** is significant, as I explain in my book *Twelve Ordinary Men*:

> Luke's choice of words here is important. Jesus didn't merely give him a new name to replace the old one. He "also" named him Peter. This disciple was known sometimes as Simon, sometimes as Peter, and sometimes as Simon Peter.
>
> "Peter" was a sort of nickname. It means "Rock." (*Petros* is the Greek word for "a piece of rock, a stone.") The Aramaic equivalent was *Cephas* (cf. 1 Corinthians 1:12; 3:22; 9:5; 15:5; Galatians 2:9). John 1:42 describes Jesus' first face-to-face meeting with Simon Peter: "Now when Jesus looked at him, He said, 'You are Simon the son of Jonah. You shall be called Cephas' (which is translated, A Stone)." Those were apparently

the first words Jesus ever said to Peter. And from then on, "Rock" was his nickname.

Sometimes, however, the Lord continued to refer to him as Simon anyway. When you see that in Scripture, it is often a signal that Peter has done something that needs rebuke or correction.

The nickname was significant, and the Lord had a specific reason for choosing it. By nature Simon was brash, vacillating, and undependable. He tended to make great promises he couldn't follow through with. He was one of those people who appears to lunge wholeheartedly into something but then bails out before finishing. He was usually the first one in; and too often, he was the first one out. When Jesus met him, he fit James's description of a double-minded man, unstable in all his ways (James 1:8). Jesus changed Simon's name, it appears, because He wanted the nickname to be a perpetual reminder to him about who he *should* be. And from that point on, whatever Jesus called him sent a subtle message. If He called him Simon, He was signaling him that he was acting like his old self. If He called him Rock, He was commending him for acting the way he ought to be acting....

This young man named Simon, who would become Peter, was impetuous, impulsive, and overeager. He needed to become like a rock, so that is what Jesus named him. From then on, the Lord could gently chide or commend him just by using one name or the other.

After Christ's first encounter with Simon Peter, we find two distinct contexts in which the name Simon is regularly applied to him. One is a *secular* context. When Scripture refers to his house, for example, it's usually "Simon's house" (Mark 1:29; Luke 4:38). When it speaks of his mother-in-law, it does so in similar terms: "Simon's wife's mother" (Mark 1:30; Luke 4:38). Luke 5, describing the fishing business, mentions "one of the boats, which was Simon's" (v. 3)—and Luke says James and John were "partners with Simon" (v. 10). All of those expressions refer to Simon by his given name in purely secular contexts. When he is called Simon in such a context, the use of his old name usually has nothing to do with his spirituality or his character. That is just the normal way of signifying what pertained to him as a natural man—his work, his home, or his family life. These are called "Simon's" things.

The second category of references where he is called Simon is seen whenever Peter was displaying the characteristics of his unregenerate self—when he was sinning in word, attitude, or action. Whenever he begins to act like his old self, Jesus and the Gospel writers revert to calling him Simon. In Luke 5:5, for example, Luke writes, "Simon answered and said to Him, 'Master, we have toiled all night and caught nothing; nevertheless at Your word I will let down the net.'" That is young Simon the fisherman speaking. He is skeptical and reluctant. But as he obeys and his eyes are opened to who Jesus really is, Luke begins to refer to him by his new name. Verse 8 says, "When Simon Peter saw it, he fell down at Jesus' knees, saying, 'Depart from me, for I am a sinful man, O Lord!'"

We see Jesus calling him Simon in reference to the key failures in his career. In Luke 22:31, foretelling Peter's betrayal, Jesus said, "Simon, Simon! Indeed, Satan has asked for you, that he may sift you as wheat." Later, in the Garden of Gethsemane, when Peter should have been watching and praying with Christ, he fell asleep. Mark writes, "[Jesus] came and found them sleeping, and said to Peter, 'Simon, are you sleeping? Could you not watch one hour? Watch and pray, lest you enter into temptation. The spirit indeed is willing, but the flesh is weak'" (Mark 14:37–38). Thus usually when Peter needed rebuke or admonishment, Jesus referred to him as Simon. It must have reached the point where whenever the Lord said "Simon," Peter cringed. He must have been thinking, *Please call me Rock!* And the Lord might have replied, "I'll call you Rock when you act like a rock."

It is obvious from the Gospel narratives that the apostle John knew Peter very, very well. They were lifelong friends, business associates, and neighbors. Interestingly, in the Gospel of John, John refers to his friend fifteen times as "Simon Peter." Apparently John couldn't make up his mind which name to use, because he saw both sides of Peter constantly. So he simply put both names together. In fact, "Simon Peter" is what Peter calls himself in the address of his second epistle: "Simon Peter, a bondservant and apostle of Jesus Christ" (2 Peter 1:1). In effect, he took Jesus' nickname for him and made it his surname (cf. Acts 10:32).

After the resurrection, Jesus instructed His disciples to return to Galilee, where He planned to appear to them (Matthew 28:7). Impatient Simon apparently got tired of waiting, so he announced that he was going back to fishing (John 21:3). As usual, the other disciples dutifully followed their leader. They got into the boat, fished all night, and caught nothing.

But Jesus met them on the shore the following morning, where He had prepared breakfast for them. The main purpose of the breakfast meeting seemed to be the restoration of Peter (who, of course, had sinned egregiously by denying Christ with curses on the night the Lord was betrayed). Three times Jesus addressed him as Simon and asked, "Simon, son of Jonah, do you love Me?" (John 21:15–17). Three times, Peter affirmed his love.

That was the last time Jesus ever had to call him Simon. A few weeks later, on Pentecost, Peter and the rest of the apostles were filled with the Holy Spirit. It was Peter, the Rock, who stood up and preached that day.

Peter was exactly like most Christians—both carnal and spiritual. He succumbed to the habits of the flesh sometimes; he functioned in the Spirit other times. He was sinful sometimes, but other times he acted the way a righteous man ought to act. This vacillating man—sometimes Simon, sometimes Peter—was the leader of the Twelve. ([Nashville: W Publishing Group, 2002], 33–37. Emphasis in original.)

As noted earlier, how God dealt with Peter is a prime example of how He builds a leader. An examination of Peter's life reveals three key elements that combine to make up a true spiritual leader: the right raw material, the right life experiences, and the right virtues.

The Right Raw Material

The best answer to the question of whether leaders are born or made is that they possess certain innate abilities, which must then be shaped by their life experiences. Apparently, Peter possessed at least three such leadership traits.

First, he was inquisitive. Leaders understand that knowledge is power; hence people who do not ask questions do not make good leaders. Unlike those who are willing to remain ignorant about what they do not understand, do not care to listen to others' insights, are unconcerned about what they have not analyzed, and are content to leave problems unsolved, leaders have an insatiable curiosity.

Peter manifested his curiosity by asking more questions in the gospels than the rest of the Twelve combined. It was Peter who asked the Lord to explain a puzzling statement He had just made (Matt. 15:15), to whom another of Christ's teachings applied (Luke 12:41), how many times he was expected to forgive someone who offended him (Matt. 18:21), what reward the apostles would receive (Matt. 19:27), and (along with James, John, and Andrew) about the end times and the signs of Christ's return (Mark 13:3–4). Even after His resurrection Peter continued to pepper the Lord with questions (John 21:20–22). His constant desire for more knowledge and better understanding marks effective leaders.

Peter also possessed a second crucial trait of a leader—initiative. According to the humorous saying, there are three kinds of people: those who make things happen, those who watch things happen, and those who ask, "What happened?" Leaders are definitely those who make things happen, and Peter was no exception. Not only did he ask the most questions, he also was usually the first one to answer any question posed by the Lord—most notably when he made the great confession that Jesus is "the Christ, the Son of the living God" (see the discussion of this passage below). When a woman with a hemorrhage touched Jesus and was healed, He asked, "Who is the one who touched Me?" It was Peter who replied, "Master, the people are crowding and pressing in on You" (Luke 8:45).

But nowhere is Peter's initiative more clearly seen than in Gethsemane. When a large detachment of Roman soldiers and Jewish officials arrived to arrest Jesus, Peter immediately sprang into action. Without waiting for an answer from Jesus to the disciples' question, "Lord, shall we strike with the sword?" (Luke 22:49), Peter drew his, bravely but foolishly intending to hack his way through the entire detachment. He attacked first Malchus, the slave of the high priest, and cut off his ear (John 18:10). (Peter, of course, was after his head, not his ear, but Malchus's quick reflexes saved him.) In this case Peter's initiative was misguided, and earned him the Lord's rebuke (Luke 22:51; John 18:11).

Peter's initiative could at times cause him to act rashly without sensibly evaluating the situation. Yet it is easier to rein in someone who is overly aggressive than to attempt to motivate a passive, timid, hesitant person. When molded by his life experiences, and controlled by the Holy Spirit, Peter's courageous willingness to take the initiative would make him a bold and fearless preacher of the gospel (cf. Acts 2:14–40; 3:12–26; 4:8–12, 19–20; 5:29–32).

Finally, Peter was willing to get involved. Like all true leaders, he had to be where the action was. The classic illustration of that comes from the story of Jesus' walking on the water (Matt. 14:25–34). Terrified when the Lord appeared in the middle of the Sea of Galilee, the disciples assumed that what they saw was a ghost (v. 26). When Jesus reassured them that it was He (v. 27), Peter impulsively exclaimed, "Lord, if it is You, command me to come to You on the water" (v. 28). After the Lord told him to come, "Peter got out of the boat, and walked on the water and came toward Jesus" (v. 29). Leaving the other disciples behind in the boat mulling over whether the apparition was really Jesus or a ghost, Peter went to where the action was, where the Lord was. Once out of the boat Peter's faith abruptly failed (v. 30), and Jesus had to save him from drowning. People remember that Christ rightly rebuked him for his lack of faith (v. 31), but forget about the other disciples, who never even left the boat.

Similarly, while Peter denied the Lord, only he (and John) were in a position where that could happen; the rest of the apostles had fled for their lives (Matt. 26:56). Peter, however, was too involved to abandon Jesus completely. After the resurrection, that deep commitment to the Savior prompted Peter to go right past John, who had arrived at the empty tomb first but remained outside, and enter the tomb (John 20:4–6).

Those who refuse to get involved cannot effectively lead. People will not follow someone who remains out of the fray, issuing instructions from a position of safety and comfort. True leaders lead from the front, not the rear.

THE RIGHT LIFE EXPERIENCES

Peter's natural abilities needed to be shaped and molded by the experiences of his life before he could be the leader God meant him to be. Experience can be a hard teacher, and the lessons Peter learned were dramatic and often painful. He sometimes soared to the dizzying heights of theological insight, and other times plunged into the abyss of woeful ignorance—sometimes in the same incident (Matt. 16:16, 23). The gospels record five experiences that helped mold Peter into the man God could use.

The first experience was Peter's great revelation, described in John 6:66–69. After feeding a large crowd of five thousand men and thousands more women and children, Jesus presented Himself to them as the Bread of Life. When He challenged His hearers to commit themselves totally to Him, using the graphic metaphor of eating His flesh and drinking His blood (v. 53), "many of His disciples withdrew and were not walking with Him anymore" (v. 66). Turning to the Twelve Jesus asked, "You do not want to go away also, do you?" (v. 67). Based on the private miracle they had just seen during the night—Jesus walking on the lake—which ramped up their faith in Him beyond what even the miracle feeding did (Mark 6:52), Peter acted as the spokesman for the rest as he usually did (cf., John 13:36–37; Matt. 15:15; 16:16; 17:4; 18:21; 19:27; 26:33, 35; Mark 11:21; Luke 5:8; 8:45; 12:41) with the answer: "Lord, to whom shall we go? You have words of eternal life. We have believed and have come to know that You are the Holy One of God" (John 6:68–69). While it is true to Peter's conviction, along with the Twelve, that statement was nonetheless a revelation from God, like Peter's later, more explicit confession that Jesus was the Messiah and Son of God (Matt. 16:16–17).

This experience taught Peter that God would give him the message he was to proclaim through divine means (cf. John 14:26; 16:13–14). Though he was merely a fisherman, not educated in the rabbinic schools (Acts 4:13), he did not need to be concerned about what he would say, for God would reveal it to him. That confidence allowed Peter to boldly and fearlessly proclaim the gospel, as recorded in the early chapters of Acts.

Another life-shaping experience for Peter was the great promise given to him. In response to his confession of Jesus as the Messiah (Matt. 16:16), the Lord

> said to him, "Blessed are you, Simon Barjona, because flesh and blood did not reveal this to you, but My Father who is in heaven. I also say to

you that you are Peter, and upon this rock I will build My church; and the gates of Hades will not overpower it. I will give you the keys of the kingdom of heaven; and whatever you bind on earth shall have been bound in heaven, and whatever you loose on earth shall have been loosed in heaven." (vv. 17–19)

The foundation on which the church is built is the truth that the Lord Jesus Christ is the Messiah, the Son of God. It was Peter's privilege not only to articulate that reality, but also to preach it until his death. By so doing, he would shut the gates of hell so that its forces would not prevail against the church, and open the gates of heaven for all who believed, including both Jews (Acts 2:14–40) and Gentiles (Acts 10:1–48).

God even used Peter's great transgression to further mold and shape him. Perhaps no incident more clearly reveals Peter's mercurial temperament than his confession of Jesus as Messiah and its aftermath. After affirming Jesus' true identity through a revelation from God (Matt. 16:16–17) and receiving the promise and privilege described above, Peter was riding high. Yet amazingly, he immediately plunged into the depths of sinful folly by daring to rebuke the Lord. After Jesus solemnly warned the apostles of His coming rejection and death (v. 21), Peter brashly "took Him aside and began to rebuke Him, saying, 'God forbid it, Lord! This shall never happen to You'" (v. 22). There was no place in Peter's theology for a dying Messiah; like the rest of his fellow Israelites, he expected the Messiah to drive out the Roman oppressors and bring Israel to the place of covenant promise, prominence and glory. Christ's response was swift and devastating. The very man whom He had just pronounced blessed by God (v. 17) He now shockingly addressed as Satan (v. 23).

The lesson Peter learned from this incident was that he was not to overestimate his role, but to understand its firm limits within the divine plan (cf. Rom. 12:3). As Jesus' rebuke indicated, Peter could be just as available to Satan as he was to God. Because of their influence and the respect leaders command, they have the potential to be used by God, but also to be used by the devil. Leaders must learn, as Peter did, to operate within God's plan, as revealed in Scripture, and not alter it in order to pursue their own agenda.

Without question the most painful experience of Peter's life was his great rejection of Jesus Christ. On the night before His death, Jesus, quoting Zechariah's prophecy, warned the disciples that they would all temporarily abandon Him that very night (Matt. 26:31–32). Peter, however, confidently asserted that whatever the others might do, he was going to stick with Jesus (v. 33). When Jesus replied that Peter would deny Him three times, Peter forcefully insisted that he would never abandon the Lord (v. 35). But as always, Jesus was right and Peter was wrong. Not long after boldly proclaiming his undying loyalty to Jesus, Peter repeatedly and emphatically denied Him (vv. 69–74). After his final denial, "the Lord turned and looked at Peter. And Peter remembered the word of the Lord, how He had told him, 'Before a rooster crows today, you will deny Me three times'" (Luke 22:61). The realization of what he had done devastated Peter, "and he went out and wept bitterly" (v. 62). His proud self-confidence had been put to the test and found to be wanting.

This experience crushed Peter's self-confident reliance on his own strength and abilities. Leaders have to learn to rely on the Lord for strength; they must acknowledge that, as Martin Luther put it in his hymn "A Mighty Fortress Is Our God,"

> Did we in our own strength confide,
> Our striving would be losing.

Paul, the proud, self-righteous, self-confident Pharisee, came to recognize himself as the foremost of sinners (1 Tim. 1:16) and acknowledged, "But by the grace of God I am what I am, and His grace toward me did not prove vain; but I labored even more than all of them, yet not I, but the grace of God with me" (1 Cor. 15:10).

But having shattered Peter's self-confidence, the Lord did not leave him in that state. He brought a final experience into Peter's life, one that would prepare him for the important role he would play in the spread of the gospel. After Christ's death Peter and the rest of the apostles went to Galilee in obedience to His command (Matt. 28:10). But Peter announced to those who were with him, "I am going fishing" (John 21:3). Peter was not suggesting a little recreational fishing to pass the time until Jesus arrived, but intended to return to his former occupation (cf. *John 12–21*, The MacArthur New Testament Commentary [Chicago: Moody, 2008], 390). In light of his shameful denials of Christ, Peter no doubt felt inadequate to serve Him. The rest of the apostles agreed with Peter, and told him, "We will also come with you." Even when his course of action was wrong, they still followed Peter's lead. But the Lord had other plans for these men, and though "they went out and got into the boat . . . that night they caught nothing."

The following morning Jesus appeared, and revealed Himself to them by directing them to a large haul of fish (vv. 4–7). After breakfast (v. 9), Jesus addressed Peter. He knew that before he could play a leading role in building the church and preaching the gospel, Peter needed to be restored and recommissioned. He needed to be reassured that though he had forsaken Christ, Christ had not forsaken him. Therefore Jesus challenged Peter three times—once for each of his denials—to reaffirm his love for Him (vv. 15–17). Then He said something that must have thrilled

Peter."Truly, truly, I say to you," Jesus told him, "when you were younger, you used to gird yourself and walk wherever you wished; but when you grow old, you will stretch out your hands and someone else will gird you, and bring you where you do not wish to go" (v. 18). As the apostle John's footnote indicates, by saying that Jesus was "signifying by what kind of death [Peter] would glorify God" (v. 19).

Normally, such a prediction would bring alarm, not comfort. But the Lord's words reassured Peter that he would remain faithful to Him until death. There would be no more vacillating; Peter would not again forsake Jesus, but would faithfully carry out the ministry to which he had been called. Nearing the end of his life Peter wrote,

> Therefore, I will always be ready to remind you of these things, even though you already know them, and have been established in the truth which is present with you. I consider it right, as long as I am in this earthly dwelling, to stir you up by way of reminder, knowing that the laying aside of my earthly dwelling is imminent, as also our Lord Jesus Christ has made clear to me. And I will also be diligent that at any time after my departure you will be able to call these things to mind. (2 Peter 1:12–15)

He had become the man the Lord needed him to be.

THE RIGHT VIRTUES

The Lord's molding of the raw material of Peter's nature through his life experiences produced in him the virtues and character essential to a true spiritual leader.

The fundamental, foundational principle of spiritual leadership is submission to God and His Word. As noted above, Peter was aggressive, bold, and self-confident. He illustrated those traits when approached by those collecting the two-drachma temple tax. When they asked whether Jesus was going to pay that tax, Peter replied that He was. That reality apparently did not sit well with Peter. When he came into the house where Jesus was staying, the Lord knew what Peter was thinking. Before he could say a word, Jesus asked him, "What do you think, Simon? From whom do the kings of the earth collect customs or poll-tax, from their sons or from strangers?" (Matt. 17:25). When Peter replied, "from strangers," Jesus drew the logical conclusion that "the sons are exempt" (v. 26). Even earthly kings do not tax their children; therefore as the Son of God, Jesus was not obligated to pay the temple tax. But then came the lesson on submission. To avoid giving offense, Jesus directed Peter to "go to the sea and throw in a hook, and take the first fish that comes up; and when you open its mouth, you will find a shekel. Take that and give it to them for you and Me" (v. 27).

Peter got the point. Years later he exhorted Christians, "Keep your behavior excellent among the Gentiles, so that in the thing in which they slander you as evildoers, they may because of your good deeds, as they observe them, glorify God in the day of visitation" (1 Peter 2:12). Believers are to live their lives in such a way as to deny opponents any legitimate grounds for criticizing the gospel. Then in verses 13 to 18 Peter spelled out how to do that:

> Submit yourselves for the Lord's sake to every human institution, whether to a king as the one in authority, or to governors as sent by him for the punishment of evildoers and the praise of those who do right. For such is the will of God that by doing right you may silence the ignorance of foolish men. Act as free men, and do not use your freedom as a covering for evil, but use it as bondslaves of God. Honor all people, love the brotherhood, fear God, honor the king. Servants, be submissive to your masters with all respect, not only to those who are good and gentle, but also to those who are unreasonable.

Peter had come a long way from the man who had balked at paying the temple tax. But he had learned the lesson that although he was a subject of God's kingdom and merely a sojourner on earth, he nevertheless needed to submit to human authority for the Lord's sake.

Second, Peter learned restraint, or self-control. The danger facing decisive, action-oriented leaders is becoming angry when their goals are thwarted by those who do not share their vision, or who underperform. Peter's lack of restraint was clearly seen in his singlehandedly taking on those who came to Gethsemane to arrest Jesus (see the discussion above), which earned him the Lord's rebuke (John 18:11).

Once again, Peter learned his lesson. In his first epistle he wrote,

> For you have been called for this purpose, since Christ also suffered for you, leaving you an example for you to follow in His steps, who committed no sin, nor was any deceit found in His mouth; and while being reviled, He did not revile in return; while suffering, He uttered no threats, but kept entrusting Himself to Him who judges righteously. (1 Peter 2:21–23)

He understood the importance of following the Lord's example.

Third, Peter learned humility. Pride is an ever-present danger for leaders, because of their influence, and because people praise, respect, and admire them. It was Peter's proud self-confidence that lay behind his boast, noted above, that he would not abandon the Lord, and the hard fall that he subsequently took shattered that pride. As he closed his first epistle, he warned elders not to exalt themselves over those they lead

(1 Peter 5:3), then exhorted all believers,"Clothe yourselves with humility toward one another, for God is opposed to the proud, but gives grace to the humble.Therefore humble yourselves under the mighty hand of God, that He may exalt you at the proper time" (vv. 5–6). Peter's life, message, and leadership reflected the humility he had so painfully learned.

Fourth, Peter learned love. Leaders, even those in the church, can come to view people as a means to an end; to be task oriented rather than people oriented. But the essence of true spiritual leadership is humble, loving service to others. "If anyone wants to be first," Jesus told the Twelve, "he shall be last of all and servant of all" (Mark 9:35). On the night before His death, Jesus graphically illustrated that principle by humbly washing the disciples' dirty feet. That degrading task was usually assigned to the lowliest servant. But on that evening in the upper room, there was no servant. And none of the disciples, who as usual were arguing among themselves as to who was the greatest (Luke 22:24; cf. 9:46; Matt. 20:20–28), were going to eliminate themselves from contention by washing the others' feet.

Peter did not understand the significance of the Lord's action, and protested vehemently when the Lord came to wash his feet (John 13:6–10). But when Jesus told him, "If I do not wash you, you have no part with Me" (v. 8), Peter, in typical fashion, veered from one extreme to the other. "Lord," he said, "then wash not only my feet, but also my hands and my head" (v. 9).

In the context of His own example, Jesus' exhortation to the Twelve that believers are to love each other (vv. 34–35; cf. 15:12–13, 17) took on a heightened significance. Peter got the message, as his exhortation, "Above all, keep fervent in your love for one another, because love covers a multitude of sins" (1 Peter 4:8; cf. 1:22; 2:17; 2 Peter 1:7) indicates.

Fifth, Peter learned compassion in a most amazing way through the assault of Satan that led to his denials (Luke 22:31). But it was Peter's tearful, remorseful recovery from that most terrible failure that enabled him to strengthen others in their temptations (v. 32). Compassion is a virtue that leaders often lack. Focused on their goals and objectives, they often do not stop to care for the wounded. Not so Peter. Having experienced the Lord's restoration of him (in John 21, as noted above), he modeled the compassionate comforting of those struggling with sorrow or sin that should mark all leaders. In his first epistle, he wrote these words of comfort, expressing his compassion to those facing Satan's onslaughts:

> Be of sober spirit, be on the alert. Your adversary, the devil, prowls around like a roaring lion, seeking someone to devour. But resist him, firm in your faith, knowing that the same experiences of suffering are being accomplished by your brethren who are in the world. After you have suffered for a little while, the God of all grace, who called you to

His eternal glory in Christ, will Himself perfect, confirm, strengthen and establish you. (1 Peter 5:8–10)

That was no ivory tower exhortation; Peter had lived what he preached.

Finally, Peter learned courage—not the reckless impulsiveness that prompted him to slash off Malchus's ear, but rather a mature, settled determination to suffer for the cause of Christ. He would need that courage, since he would face trouble, opposition, persecution, and, ultimately martyrdom. As noted above, Jesus predicted Peter's martyrdom in John 21 when He told him, "Truly, truly, I say to you, when you were younger, you used to gird yourself and walk wherever you wished; but when you grow old, you will stretch out your hands and someone else will gird you, and bring you where you do not wish to go" (v. 18). "Now this He said," John noted, "signifying by what kind of death he would glorify God" (v. 19).

Peter showed his courage by boldly proclaiming Jesus as Savior and Lord to the very people who had crucified Him. Nor did he stop preaching, not even when ordered to do so by the Sanhedrin (Acts 4:18–20; 5:27–29). He exhorted all Christians to follow his courageous example when he wrote,

> But even if you should suffer for the sake of righteousness, you are blessed. And do not fear their intimidation, and do not be troubled, but sanctify Christ as Lord in your hearts, always being ready to make a defense to everyone who asks you to give an account for the hope that is in you, yet with gentleness and reverence." (1 Peter 3:14–15)

Peter eventually became the leader Jesus needed him to be. He was the primary figure in the first twelve chapters of Acts. He was the one who initiated the replacement of Judas with Matthias, who preached the first sermon in the church's history on the Day of Pentecost and who kept on preaching in defiance of the Sanhedrin, who, along with John, healed a lame man at the temple, who dealt with the hypocrisy of Ananias and Sapphira, who confronted the false teacher Simon Magus, who healed Aeneas and raised Dorcas from the dead, and who took the gospel to the Gentiles.

Along the way, Peter suffered persecution and imprisonment. Eventually, as the Lord had predicted, he was martyred for his unswerving faith in Jesus Christ. According to tradition Peter, after being forced to watch his wife's crucifixion, was himself crucified—head downward at his own request, since he felt himself unworthy of dying as his Lord had died. His life and ministry can be summed up in the closing words of the last epistle he wrote: "Grow in the grace and knowledge of our Lord and Savior Jesus Christ. To Him be the glory, both now and to the day of eternity. Amen" (2 Peter 3:18).

Common Men, Uncommon Calling— Part 3: Andrew, James (Luke 6:14*b*, *c*)

4

Andrew his brother; and James (6:14 *b, c*)

Chronicles of the past record numerous instances in which a small group of men facing overwhelming odds changed the course of history. Such events, often memorialized in books and movies, have become the stuff of legends. One of the earliest took place at the battle of Thermopylae in 480 B.C. during the Persian invasion of Greece. A small rearguard led by King Leonidas I of Sparta, consisting of 300 Spartans and several hundred men from other Greek city-states, faced hundreds of thousands of Persians led by Xerxes (the Ahasuerus of the book of Esther). Despite being hopelessly outnumbered, Leonidas and his men refused to retreat or surrender. In fact, when a Persian emissary demanded that they lay down their weapons Leonidas replied defiantly, "Come and get them." Though Leonidas and most of his men died defending the narrow pass, their courageous stand allowed the bulk of the Greek army to escape and survive.

In the waning days of World War II, Adolf Hitler launched a last, desperate offensive against the Western Allies. He hoped to seize the key Belgian port of Antwerp and split the British and American forces. Hitler believed the Western Allies would then sue for peace, allowing him to concentrate all his forces against the advancing Soviet armies in the east.

Squarely in the path of the German offensive through the Ardennes region was the Belgian town of Bastogne. All the major roads in the area converged on Bastogne, making its capture essential to the Germans. The American 101st Airborne Division (with a few other smaller units) withstood the onslaught of vastly superior German forces for a week, until relieved by elements of General George Patton's Third Army. Despite the odds, they refused to give up. When the Germans demanded that he surrender his forces, the American commander, General Anthony McAuliffe, made a contemptuous, one-word reply that Leonidas would have appreciated: "Nuts!" The 101st's stubborn, courageous defense delayed the German drive, which ultimately failed to reach its objectives.

Perhaps the most famous heroic stand in American history was that of the Texans at the Alamo. Less than 200 men, led by William Travis, James Bowie, and Davy Crockett, held out for nearly two weeks against thousands of Mexican troops under President Antonio Lopez de Santa Anna, who was seeking to crush the Texas Revolution. That delay allowed the Texans time to declare their independence, form a government, and draft a constitution. Further, the heroism of the Alamo's defenders, all of whom perished, and William Travis's eloquent letter addressed "To the People of Texas & All Americans in the World," inspired many men to join the Texas army. That army later routed Santa Anna's forces at the Battle of San Jacinto, securing Texas's independence.

The Bible illustrates the principle that God has often turned history using a few people, or even an individual, to accomplish His purposes. He chose Gideon to deliver the people of Israel from their Midianite oppressors (Judg. 6:1–6). At God's command, Gideon's initial force of thirty-two thousand was reduced to ten thousand (Judg. 7:3). But lest the people boast that the deliverance was from their own strength (v. 2), God directed Gideon to further reduce his force to three hundred men (vv. 6–8). The Lord used Gideon and that small force to rout the vast (v. 12) forces arrayed against them (vv. 16–25). Later in Judges, God used Samson to singlehandedly deliver the people of Israel from their perennial enemies the Philistines (Judg. 15:15–20). Still later in Israel's history, Elijah alone was enabled to triumph over 450 prophets of Baal on Mt. Carmel (1 Kings 18:17–40).

Less familiar, but no less significant, is the account of God's deliverance of Israel through Jonathan and his armor bearer. As in Samson's day, the Israelites were being oppressed by the Philistines. Jonathan's father, Saul, had already been disqualified as king because of his disobedience (1 Sam. 13:7–14). The Philistine invasion force was huge (v. 5), and the Israelites (except for Saul and Jonathan) had no weapons (vv. 19–22). Defeat seemed certain, leading many of "the people [to hide] themselves in caves, in thickets, in cliffs, in cellars, and in pits" (v. 6). Others fled and "crossed the Jordan into the land of Gad and Gilead" (v. 7). Israel seemed on the verge of being annihilated as a nation.

But Jonathan did not share the people's defeatism. Putting his trust in the Lord, he and his faithful armor bearer approached the Philistine camp and hailed it. Taking them for deserters seeking to surrender (1 Sam. 14:11), the Philistines called to the two men to come up to their camp. Jonathan, followed by his armor bearer, promptly attacked the Philistines, killing twenty of them (vv. 13–14). The result was panic in the Philistine camp, a panic heightened by an earthquake sent by God (v. 15). The Philistines fled in disarray (v. 16), and their flight quickly turned into a rout (vv. 20–23). The courage and faith of Jonathan and his armor bearer saved the nation (vv. 45–46). Jonathan's words in verse 6, "the Lord is not restrained to save by many or by few," summarize not only his own exploits, but also those of Gideon, Samson, and Elijah.

Just as God used individuals such as Gideon, Samson, Elijah, and Jonathan, to change the course of Israel's history, so also in the New Testament He used twelve men to change the course of the world's history. Those common, ordinary men, chosen, trained, and commissioned by the Lord Jesus Christ, are the subject of this section of Luke's gospel. Having introduced Peter (see the previous chapter of this volume), Luke turned to the next two members of the Twelve: Peter's brother Andrew, and James, the brother of John.

ANDREW

Andrew his brother (6:14*b*)

The designation of **Andrew** as **his** (Peter's) **brother** is indicative of his situation. Consistently overshadowed by his more famous sibling (he is usually referred to in the gospels in connection with Peter; cf. Matt. 4:18; 10:2; Mark 1:16, 29; John 1:40, 44; 6:8), Andrew is the least known of the inner circle of the apostles. He did not enjoy the same intimacy with Jesus as did Peter, James and John. For example, Andrew was not present with the other three at the transfiguration (Matt. 17:1), the healing of a synagogue official's daughter (Mark 5:37), or with the other three in Gethsemane (Mark 14:33). The picture the gospels paint of him is of a person content to serve quietly in the background.

Like Peter, Andrew was originally from the village of Bethsaida (John 1:44). The brothers later moved to the larger city of Capernaum, where they shared a house (Mark 1:21, 29) and operated a fishing business (Matt. 4:18). Peter and Andrew were devout Jews, committed to the worship of the true God. They were among the first of the Twelve to encounter the Lord Jesus Christ. Having taken a sabbatical from their fishing business, they traveled to the region around the Jordan and become followers of John the Baptist. They were among those "looking for the consolation of Israel" (Luke 2:25) by the coming of the Messiah promised in the Old Testament.

John's gospel relates the story of Andrew's first encounter with Jesus. Along with the apostle John, Andrew was with John the Baptist when he pointed out Jesus to them and said, "Behold, the Lamb of God!" (John 1:36). After hearing that, the two followed Jesus and stayed with Him for the rest of that day (vv. 37–39). That experience forever changed Andrew's life. Convinced that Jesus was exactly who John the Baptist had said He was, Andrew "found first his own brother Simon and said to him, 'We have found the Messiah'" (v. 41). Then, in what would become the pattern of Andrew's life and ministry, "he brought [Simon] to Jesus" (v. 42). It was then that the Lord gave Simon the name Peter and began training him to be the leader of the Twelve, as noted in the previous chapter of this volume.

After their initial encounter with Jesus, Andrew and Peter returned to Capernaum and resumed their fishing business. Months later, Jesus came to Galilee after initially ministering in Judea and Jerusalem. Walking along the shore of the Sea of Galilee, He found Peter and Andrew (Matt. 4:18), along with John and his brother James (v. 21). This time they did not seek the Lord; rather, He sought them. They became part-time disciples (vv. 19, 22), while still maintaining their fishing enterprise. Luke 5:1–11 records their final call to full-time discipleship, when they "left everything and followed Him" (v. 11).

Two other incidents in John's gospel provide further insight into Andrew's character. In the sixth chapter, John records the feeding of the five thousand men (with women and children nearer twenty-five thousand), which began when "Jesus, lifting up His eyes and seeing that a large crowd was coming to Him, said to Philip, 'Where are we to buy bread, so that these may eat?'" (v. 5). Overwhelmed by the scope of the problem, "Philip answered Him, 'Two hundred denarii worth of bread is not sufficient for them, for everyone to receive a little'" (v. 7). As far as Philip was concerned, feeding such an enormous crowd with their meager resources was out of the question. Andrew, however, had been mingling with the people and had found "a lad ... who [had] five barley loaves and two fish" (v. 9). Despite his own doubts, expressed in his rhetorical and perhaps cynical question, "What are these for so many people?" Andrew was always eager to bring people to Jesus. The Lord obliterated all cynicism and doubt when He used the small lunch to feed the vast crowd.

In his final appearance in the Gospels, Andrew, true to form, brought still more people to Jesus. In the tumultuous aftermath of the triumphal entry "some Greeks [most likely Gentile proselytes to Judaism] were going up [to Jerusalem] to worship at the feast [Passover]" (John 12:20). Seeking an audience with Jesus, they first approached Philip. They may have singled him out because he was from Bethsaida (v. 21), located near the largely Gentile region known as the Decapolis (Matt. 4:25; Mark 5:20; 7:31). Uncertain of how to handle the situation, "Philip came and told Andrew" about it, then "Andrew and Philip came and told Jesus" (John 12:22). There was no doubt or hesitation in Andrew's mind; when people wanted to see Jesus, he brought them to Him.

The three scenes, in which Andrew plays a prominent role, reveal that he was first and foremost a missionary. The passionate commitment of his heart was to bring people to Jesus. He was without prejudice, willingly ushering Gentiles as well as Jews to the Savior. Andrew was also a man whose faith overcame doubt, as in trusting that the Lord could possibly use the seemingly inadequate lunch of a young boy to accomplish His purposes. Andrew also exhibited humility, being content to remain in the shadow of his famous brother and serve in the background. There are people who will not play in the band unless they can bang the big drum, but Andrew was not one of them. He was more concerned about bringing people to Jesus than about who got the credit. He was not a man pleaser, but a servant of Christ, committed to "doing the will of God from the heart" (Eph. 6:6).

Andrew eventually paid the ultimate price for his devotion to the Lord Jesus Christ. According to tradition a provincial governor, angered that Andrew had led his wife to Christ, had him crucified on an X shaped cross. Despite the suffering he endured, Andrew continued to preach the gospel to the passersby for as long as he could speak. He died as he had lived—bringing people to the Savior.

JAMES

James (6:14c)

Like his brother John, **James** was the son of Zebedee, a prosperous fisherman (well off enough to have hired servants working for him [Mark 1:20]) on the Sea of Galilee. James and John were partners in a fishing business with the other pair of brothers that comprised the inner group of the Twelve, Peter and Andrew (Luke 5:10). James, like Andrew, is overshadowed by the other two apostles in the inner group, Peter and John. Scripture presents full-color portraits of them, but mere silhouettes of Andrew and James.

But the gospels' relative silence about James does not mean he was insignificant. His name appears second in the list of the Twelve after Peter's in Mark's gospel (Mark 3:16–17). And except for two occasions, James is listed first when he and John appear together. The two are inseparable in the gospels; James is never mentioned apart from John. And James was present at several key events with Peter and John, as noted above, that Andrew was not.

A key to understanding James's personality is the nickname Jesus gave both brothers. "Boanerges," as Mark notes, means, "Sons of Thunder" (Mark 3:17). That colorful term vividly describes their forceful personalities. James was zealous, passionate, and fervent. He may well have been the New Testament counterpart of Jehu, who declared, "Come with me and see my zeal for the Lord" (2 Kings 10:16). Jehu's zeal, however, was nothing but selfish, worldly ambition, since he "was not careful to walk in the law of the Lord, the God of Israel, with all his heart; he did not depart from the sins of Jeroboam, which he made Israel sin" (2 Kings 10:31).

James's zeal too was sometimes misguided, and expressed in ways that were less than gracious or righteous. On His way to Jerusalem for the final Passover of His ministry (Luke 9:51), Jesus "sent messengers on ahead of Him, and they went and entered a village of the Samaritans to make arrangements for Him" (v. 52). The Samaritans were the descendants of Jews who had intermarried with Gentiles after the fall of the northern kingdom to Assyria. The Jews regarded them as a polluted, unclean race, and avoided contact with them whenever possible (John 4:9). Centuries of mutual animosity made the Samaritans unwilling to "receive [Jesus]," all the more so "because He was traveling toward Jerusalem" (v. 53). They had their own worship centered on Mt. Gerizim, where the Jews had destroyed the Samaritan temple during the intertestamental period. The people in this Samaritan village wanted nothing to do with Jews traveling to Jerusalem to worship there.

Outraged at this egregious insult to Jesus, James, along with John, exclaimed angrily, "Lord, do You want us to command fire to come down from heaven and consume them?" (v. 54; cf. 2 Kings 1:9–12). Andrew wanted to bring the unsaved to Jesus; James wanted to incinerate them. The brothers' misguided zeal earned them a rebuke from the Lord, who said to them, "You do not know what kind of spirit you are of; for the Son of Man did not come to destroy men's lives, but to save them" (vv. 55–56; cf. 19:10). Their zeal not to allow Christ to be insulted was commendable; however in this case it was not according to knowledge (cf. Rom. 10:2).

A second incident reveals another side of James's personality. On this occasion James and John added a new twist to the apostles' ongoing debate over which of them was the greatest (cf. Mark 9:33–34; Luke

22:24). Seeking the prominent places of honor beside Jesus in His glorious kingdom, the two audaciously requested that the Lord grant them the privilege of sitting on His right and left hand (Mark 10:37). Moreover, they brought their mother with them to make the initial request to Jesus. She was evidently the sister of Jesus' mother Mary (as a comparison of Matt. 27:55–56, Mark 15:40, and John 19:25 suggests), making James and John Jesus' cousins. They were thus shamelessly exploiting their family ties to Jesus for their own self-aggrandizement—which understandably outraged the other ten apostles (Matt. 20:24).

Like the scribes and Pharisees, who "love[d] the place of honor at banquets and the chief seats in the synagogues" (Matt. 23:6) and Diotrephes, "who love[d] to be first" (3 John 9), James and John sought prestige, preeminence, and to be exalted above the rest of the apostles. Needless to say, the Lord rejected their self-serving request (Matt. 20:23) and then gave all the disciples a much-needed lesson on the importance of humility (vv. 25–28).

James sought power and prestige; Jesus gave him servanthood. He sought a crown of glory; Jesus gave him a cup of suffering. James was the first of the Twelve to die, and the only one whose death is recorded in the New Testament. According to Acts 12:1–2, "Herod the king laid hands on some who belonged to the church in order to mistreat them. And he had James the brother of John put to death with a sword." That Herod, seeking to halt the growth of the church, seized and executed James instead of Peter or John reveals that James had become a force for God. The erstwhile "Son of Thunder" had been mentored by Christ and molded by the Holy Spirit into a man whose zeal and ambition were redirected toward God and His kingdom.

Like Andrew, James led someone to Christ in his death. According to tradition, recorded by the early church historian Eusebius,

> the man who led [James] to the judgment seat, seeing him bearing his testimony to the faith, and moved by the fact, confessed himself a Christian. Both therefore ... were led away to die. On their way, he entreated James to be forgiven of him, and James considering a little, replied, "Peace be to thee," and kissed him; and then both were beheaded at the same time. (*Ecclesiastical History*, II. 9)

The life of James offers convincing testimony that a passionate individual, controlled by love, can be a powerful instrument in the hands of God.

Common Men, Uncommon Calling— Part 4: John (Luke 6:14*d*)

5

John (6:14*d*)

When God chooses people for His salvation purposes, He does not do so based on human standards. "The Lord did not set His love on you nor choose you because you were more in number than any of the peoples," Moses reminded the children of Israel, "for you were the fewest of all peoples, but because the Lord loved you and kept the oath which He swore to your forefathers, the Lord brought you out by a mighty hand and redeemed you from the house of slavery, from the hand of Pharaoh king of Egypt" (Deut. 7:7–8). Moses also downplayed his own qualifications for leadership, saying "to the Lord, 'Please, Lord, I have never been eloquent, neither recently nor in time past, nor since You have spoken to Your servant; for I am slow of speech and slow of tongue'" (Ex. 4:10; cf. 6:12). Jeremiah reacted in dismay to his call to be a prophet (Jer. 1:5), exclaiming, "Alas, Lord God! Behold, I do not know how to speak, because I am a youth" (v. 6).

No one was more greatly used by God in the spread of the gospel than the apostle Paul (cf. Rom. 15:19; 1 Cor. 15:10). Yet even he was not chosen because of any human qualifications he possessed. He regarded himself as "the very least of all saints" (Eph. 3:8), and "the least of the apostles, and not fit to be called an apostle, because [he had] persecuted the church of God" (1 Cor. 15:9). By his own admission Paul had been "a blasphemer and a persecutor and a violent aggressor" (1 Tim. 1:13; cf. Acts 8:3; 22:4–5; 26:9–11; Gal. 1:13; Phil. 3:6), and viewed himself as the foremost of sinners (1 Tim. 1:15). His opponents contemptuously said of him, "His letters are weighty and strong, but his personal presence is unimpressive and his speech contemptible" (2 Cor. 10:10), since Paul lacked the public persona and polished skills of a Greek orator (cf. 11:6).

Paul did have impressive religious qualifications from a human perspective (Acts 26:24; 2 Cor. 11:5, 22–33; Gal. 1:13–14; Phil. 3:4–6). But the trials he endured taught him the lesson that God's "grace is sufficient … for power is perfected in weakness" (2 Cor. 12:9). In 2 Corinthians 2:16 he asked the rhetorical question, "Who is adequate for these things?" and gave the answer in 3:5: "Not that we are adequate in ourselves to consider anything as coming from ourselves, but our adequacy is from God." No one is able in his own strength to properly serve almighty God. As Paul reminded the Corinthians, those whom God calls to salvation and service include "not many wise according to the flesh, not many mighty, not many noble; but God has chosen the foolish things of the world to shame the wise, and God has chosen the weak things of the world to shame the things which are strong" (1 Cor. 1:26–27).

The Twelve, like all believers, were not chosen by the Lord because of any superior spirituality they possessed. As has been noted in earlier chapters of this volume, they were common men—fishermen, tax collectors, political revolutionaries. Paul described himself and his fellow apostles as "men condemned to death … a spectacle to the world … fools for Christ's sake … weak … without honor. … hungry and thirsty … poorly clothed … roughly treated … homeless … working with [their] own hands … reviled … persecuted … slandered … the scum of the world, the dregs of all things" (1 Cor. 4:9–13). The Twelve were also scorned as uneducated and untrained Galileans (Acts 2:7; 4:13).

The only explanation for the gospel's impact is the power of God. He chooses to put the priceless truth of the glorious gospel in simple, ordinary, clay pots (2 Cor. 4:7) so that all the glory is His. The world is filled with people too consumed with their own interests, importance, and abilities to be used by God. But when He chose the men who would be the foundation of the church (Eph. 2:20), God did not choose learned scholars, eloquent orators, or self-righteous religious leaders. He chose twelve ordinary men, whose lives and ministries would forever change the course of history.

Having introduced Peter, Andrew, and James, Luke identified the fourth on his list of the twelve apostles, John. After examining his background, we will consider the two things that were the consuming passion of John's life: truth and love.

JOHN'S BACKGROUND

As noted in the previous chapter of this volume, John and his brother James were sons of Zebedee, the owner of a prosperous fishing business on the Sea of Galilee. The two brothers were partners in the enterprise with Peter and Andrew (Luke 5:10). John was likely the younger of the two, since James is usually listed first when they are mentioned together. His mother was Salome (see the discussion of Matt. 20:20–24 in chapter 4 of this volume), one of the women who ministered to Jesus (Matt. 27:55–56), possibly financially (cf. Luke 8:2–3). As was also noted in the previous chapter of this volume, Salome was likely the sister of Jesus' mother, Mary. In that case John would have been Jesus' cousin.

With the exception of Peter, John is the apostle about whom most is known. He was a member of the innermost group of the Twelve, those closest to Jesus, along with Peter, James, and Andrew. Only Peter, James, and John were present at the healing of the synagogue official's daughter (Mark 5:37), the transfiguration (Matt. 17:1), and went inside Gethsemane with Jesus (the other disciples apparently waited at the gate; cf. Matt. 26:36–37). In fact, the designation of John as the disciple whom Jesus loved (John 13:23; 19:26; 20:2; 21:7, 20) suggests that he may have been the closest of all the apostles to the Savior.

John had been a follower of John the Baptist (John 1:35) and, along with Andrew, was the first of the Twelve to encounter Jesus (vv. 36–40). He eventually returned to fishing on the Sea of Galilee, became a part-time follower of Jesus (Matt. 4:21), then a full-time disciple (Luke 5:10–11), and finally was chosen by the Lord to be a life-long apostle.

Like his brother James, John had a tempestuous, forceful personality, prompting the Lord to name them "Sons of Thunder" (Mark 3:17). John's volatile temperament expressed itself in his desire, along with James, to call down fire from heaven on the Samaritans who rejected Jesus (Luke 9:54). His aggressiveness and ambition are also seen in his and his brother's attempt to exploit their family ties to Jesus to obtain positions of honor and privilege in the kingdom (Matt. 20:20–23).

As He did with the rest of the Twelve, Jesus molded and shaped John into the man He wanted him to be. That involved learning that his zeal for the truth needed to be balanced with love, and indeed, those two things eventually came to characterize him.

That balance is hard to come by. Many Christians do not seem to understand its importance, and camp on one or the other. The result is either a cold, lifeless orthodoxy leading to prideful indifference, or a shallow, superficial sentimentality leading to tolerance of error. But both truth and love are essential to the kingdom of God and therefore inseparable. Paul made that clear in Ephesians 4:11–15. God gives gifted men

(v. 11) to equip believers for the mutual edifying of the body of Christ (v. 12), which results in spiritual maturity and Christlikeness (vv. 13–14). Then the apostle succinctly summarized spiritual maturity as "speaking the truth in love" (v. 15; cf. 1 Cor. 13:6; 1 Peter 1:22). Mature believers not only are firmly grounded in sound doctrine (1 Tim. 4:6; Titus 1:9; 2:1), but also manifest the fruit of the Spirit, love (Gal. 5:22; cf. v. 13; Rom. 5:5; 12:9).

John's Commitment to Truth

John's passionate concern for the truth permeates his writings; he uses the word "truth" forty-six times. For John, divine truth was supremely embodied in the Lord Jesus Christ; He was full of truth (John 1:14) and in Him God's salvation truth was fully revealed (v. 17). Those who profess to know Christ but do not obey Him are devoid of the truth (1 John 2:4; cf. 1:6, 8). Nothing brought John greater joy than to hear of Christians walking in the truth (3 John 4; cf. v. 3; 2 John 4).

His deep concern for the truth caused John to be black and white; to see things in stark contrast; to express himself in absolutes and opposites. He set light against darkness (John 1:5; 1 John 2:8–9), life against death (John 5:24; 1 John 3:14), the kingdom of God against the kingdom of the devil (John 3:3, 5; 8:44), the children of God against the children of Satan (1 John 3:10), the judgment of the righteous against the judgment of the wicked (John 5:24; Rev. 20:11–15), the resurrection of life against the resurrection of judgment (John 5:29), receiving Christ against rejecting Him (John 1:11–12), fruit against fruitlessness (John 15:2), obedience against disobedience (John 3:36). People either walk in the light, or in the darkness (John 12:35; 1 John 1:7), and are either of God, or of the world (1 John 2:15). Those born of God cannot sin (1 John 3:9), and those who reject Christ do not have God (John 5:23; 1 John 2:23), those who do good are of God, but those who do evil have not seen God (3 John 11).

John's passionate devotion to the truth also prompted him to warn against the danger of false teachers, who twist and pervert the truth. In his first epistle John listed three characteristics of such teachers (whom he labels "antichrists" [1 John 2:18] because they distorted and denied the truth about Jesus Christ). First, they arose within the church, but then left, taking their followers with them. As John noted, "They went out from us, but they were not really of us; for if they had been of us, they would have remained with us; but they went out, so that it would be shown that they all are not of us" (1 John 2:19). Second, they "denie[d] that Jesus is the Christ," thereby "[denying] the Father and the Son" (v. 22). Those who deny Jesus Christ's true nature as God incarnate also deny the Father, who testified to the Son (5:9–10; John 5:32–38; 8:19). Finally, false teachers try to deceive the faithful (1 John 2:26; cf. 3:7; Rom. 16:18; 1 Tim. 4:1; 2 Tim. 3:13; Titus 1:10; 2 John 7), as does their father (John 8:44), the devil (2 Cor. 11:3; Rev. 12:9).

John instructed his readers to avoid being deceived by those religious charlatans:

> Beloved, do not believe every spirit, but test the spirits to see whether they are from God, because many false prophets have gone out into the world. By this you know the Spirit of God: every spirit that confesses that Jesus Christ has come in the flesh is from God; and every spirit that does not confess Jesus is not from God; this is the spirit of the antichrist, of which you have heard that it is coming, and now it is already in the world. You are from God, little children, and have overcome them; because greater is He who is in you than he who is in the world. They are from the world; therefore they speak as from the world, and the world listens to them. We are from God; he who knows God listens to us; he who is not from God does not listen to us. By this we know the spirit of truth and the spirit of error. (1 John 4:1–6)

Christians must carefully compare any teaching purporting to come from God with the Bible. They must be like the Bereans, who were "examining the Scriptures daily to see whether these things were so" (Acts 17:11). At the core of every false system of belief is a denial of the truth regarding Jesus Christ. Therefore John cautioned that "every spirit that confesses that Jesus Christ has come in the flesh is from God; and every spirit that does not confess Jesus is not from God" (1 John 4:2–3). The mark of false teachers is that they reject the doctrine of the apostles as revealed in Scripture. But the apostles, as John wrote, "are from God; he who knows God listens to us; he who is not from God does not listen to us. By this we know the spirit of truth and the spirit of error" (v. 6).

In his second epistle, John again warned that "many deceivers have gone out into the world, those who do not acknowledge Jesus Christ as coming in the flesh" (v. 7). He reminded his readers that such false teachers "[go] too far and [do] not abide in the teaching of Christ." As a result, they "[do] not have God," because only "the one who abides in the teaching [about Christ] has both the Father and the Son" (v. 9). Apostate false teachers are not to be given Christian hospitality, since doing so aids the spread of their heretical teaching (vv. 10–11).

John's frequent use of the word "testify" (Gk., *martureō*) also reveals how important truth was to him. He wrote of the witness of John the Baptist (John 1:6–8), of the Father (John 5:37; 8:18), of the Scriptures (John 5:39); of the works Jesus did (John 10:25), of the Holy Spirit (John 15:26), of the disciples (John 15:27), and of Jesus (John 18:37).

JOHN'S COMMITMENT TO LOVE

No one was more committed to the truth than the apostle Paul. Yet he understood that devotion to the truth is of little value apart from love, as he wrote in his first inspired letter to the Corinthians:

> If I speak with the tongues of men and of angels, but do not have love, I have become a noisy gong or a clanging cymbal. If I have the gift of prophecy, and know all mysteries and all knowledge; and if I have all faith, so as to remove mountains, but do not have love, I am nothing. And if I give all my possessions to feed the poor, and if I surrender my body to be burned, but do not have love, it profits me nothing. (1 Cor. 13:1–3)

The pivotal turning point in which John, the Son of Thunder, began to see the importance of love came in the only incident in the Gospels in which he alone speaks. After the overwhelming experience of the transfiguration (Mark 9:1–10), the disciples got involved in another episode of their long-running debate over which of them was the greatest (vv. 33–34). Jesus gently rebuked the disciples, reminding them, "If anyone wants to be first, he shall be last of all and servant of all" (v. 35). He then took a child in His arms and used him to illustrate the point that the disciples needed to receive each other as they would Him (v. 37).

Convicted by the Lord's rebuke, John confessed to another instance of the disciples' misguided zeal: "Teacher, we saw someone casting out demons in Your name, and we tried to prevent him because he was not following us" (v. 38). This was sectarianism, an expression of intolerance toward those outside of their group. John's confession elicited another rebuke from Jesus, who told the disciples, "Do not hinder him, for there is no one who will perform a miracle in My name, and be able soon afterward to speak evil of Me. For he who is not against us is for us" (vv. 39–40).

John was characterized by courage, ambition, drive, passion, boldness, and a strong devotion to the truth, and people with those qualities are vital to the kingdom of God. But John's zeal for the truth had been deficient in love and compassion for people. If love without truth is characterless hypocrisy, truth without love is indecent brutality. This confession and the Lord's rebuke began moving him toward a proper balance of truth and love. Although never wavering in his fierce devotion to the truth, John learned the importance of love and emphasized it in his writings—so much so that he became known as the "apostle of love."

John used the word "love" more than one hundred times in his writings. He taught that God is love (1 John 4:8), that the Father loves the Son (John 3:35; 5:20) and the Son loves the Father (John 14:31), that God loves all people in general (John 3:16) and Christ's disciples in particular (John 14:21, 23; 16:27; 17:23), that Jesus loves those who believe in Him (John 13:1; 15:9) and that the supreme example of that love was His sacrificial death on their behalf (John 15:13; 1 John 3:16), that Jesus commanded believers to love one another (John 13:35; 15:12; cf. 1 John 3:11, 23; 2 John 5), that God's true spiritual children will love Jesus Christ (John 8:42) and that that love will manifest itself in obedience (John 14:15, 21, 23–24; 15:10; 1 John 2:5; 5:3; 2 John 6), that God's love motivated His adoption of believers as His children (1 John 3:1), that true love will manifest itself in actions (1 John 3:18), that love for other believers is a mark of genuine salvation (1 John 4:7–8, 20), that the supreme manifestation of God's love for His people was His sending Christ to be the propitiation for their sins (1 John 4:9–10), that love removes fear of punishment (1 John 4:18), and that God's love motivates Him to discipline believers (Rev. 3:19).

John's life after the close of the gospel accounts reflects his continuing commitment to both truth and love. As was the case in the Gospels, he was closely connected with Peter in the book of Acts (Acts 3:1–11; 4:13–20; 8:14–25) in proclaiming the truth—so much so that Paul referred to him as one of the pillars of the Jerusalem church (Gal. 2:9). John's unwavering, unceasing preaching of the truth eventually led to his exile to the rocky, barren island of Patmos, off the coast of Asia Minor. It was there that he received the amazing, incomparable series of visions that comprise the book of Revelation (Rev. 1:1, 4, 9; 22:8).

According to early Christian writers, John spent the last decades of his life in Ephesus, overseeing the churches in that region (Clement of Alexandria, *Who Is the Rich Man that Shall Be Saved?*, 42). According to Irenaeus (*Against Heresies*, 3.3.4), John lived until the time of the emperor Trajan (A.D. 98–117). He was the last of the apostles to die. Two vignettes from his years at Ephesus reveal that the apostle of love had lost none of his zeal for the truth. According to Polycarp, the second-century bishop of Smyrna who had been a disciple of the apostle John, "John, the disciple of the Lord, going to bathe at Ephesus, and perceiving [the heretic] Cerinthus within, rushed out of the bath-house without bathing, exclaiming, 'Let us fly, lest even the bath-house fall down, because Cerinthus, the enemy of the truth, is within'" (Irenaeus, *Against Heresies*, 3.3.4). Clement of Alexandria relates how at the risk of his own life John fearlessly entered the camp of a band of robbers and led its captain, who had once professed faith in Christ, to true repentance (*Who Is the Rich Man that Shall Be Saved?*, 42).

But John also never ceased to emphasize the importance of love. Nearing the end of his life, the apostle became so weak that he could no longer preach and had to be carried to church. According to the fourth-century church father Jerome, he constantly exhorted the congregation to love one another. When they finally asked him why he kept repeating that John replied, "It is the Lord's command, and if only this be done, it is enough" (Alfred Plummer, *The Epistles of St. John* [Reprint; Grand Rapids: Baker, 1980], xxxv).

Common Men, Uncommon Calling— Part 5: Philip, Bartholomew (Luke 6:14e, f)

Philip and Bartholomew (6:14e, f)

All those whom God calls to lead His people must meet the standards set forth in Scripture (cf. 1 Tim. 3:1–12; Titus 1:6–9). But beyond those required standards, the Lord uses men of widely divergent temperaments and personalities to lead His church.

Some are bold, assertive men of action. When Moses "saw an Egyptian beating a Hebrew, one of his brethren. . . . he struck down the Egyptian and hid him in the sand" (Ex. 2:11–12). Despite his doubts about his speaking ability (Ex. 4:10–13), Moses repeatedly confronted Pharaoh with God's demand that he let Israel go. He also did not hesitate to confront his own people when they complained (Ex. 17:2), sinned (Ex. 32:19–28), or challenged his leadership (Num. 16:1–50). His aggressive, forceful personality ultimately cost Moses the privilege of entering the Promised Land after he disobeyed God. Faced with yet another round of grumbling and complaining by the Israelites (Num. 20:2–5), Moses sought God's counsel (v. 6). The Lord instructed him to take his rod and speak to a rock, which would then produce the water the people were crying for (vv. 7–8). But instead of speaking to the rock, Moses spoke to the people, angrily denouncing them as rebels (vv. 9–10). He then struck the rock with his rod (v. 11), thereby, ironically, also rebelling against God (Num.27:14).As a result,Moses forfeited the right to lead the people into Canaan (Num.20:12).

Elijah was another bold leader.In the third year (1 Kings 18:1) of a devastating drought God had proclaimed through him (1 Kings 17:1), Elijah was confronted by Israel's wicked king Ahab.The king angrily said to him,"Is this you,you troubler of Israel?" (1 Kings 18:17).Not intimidated in the least, Elijah replied,"I have not troubled Israel, but you and your father's house have, because you have forsaken the commandments of the Lord and you have followed the Baals" (v. 18). Elijah then fearlessly challenged hundreds of false prophets to a public contest to see who was the true God,the Lord or Baal,and ordered the false prophets to be killed afterwards (vv. 19–40).

Later,after Ahab had murdered a man so he could seize his vine-yard (1 Kings 21:1–16), Elijah once again boldly confronted him.Ahab said to him sarcastically,"Have you found me,O my enemy?" Refusing to back down Elijah replied,"I have found you,because you have sold your-self to do evil in the sight of the Lord" (v. 20).He then pronounced God's judgment on Ahab and his evil wife Jezebel (vv.21–26).Shocked and ter-rified, Ahab "tore his clothes and put on sackcloth and fasted,and he lay in sackcloth and went about despondently" (v. 27). Because the king humbled himself, the Lord postponed the judgment (v. 29).Toward the end of his ministry,Elijah also rebuked Ahab's son and successor as king, Ahaziah (2 Kings 1:3–4).That confrontation included Elijah dramatically calling down fire from heaven to consume two detachments of soldiers sent to bring him to the king (vv.9–12).

The apostle Paul is the New Testament model of a bold, coura-geous leader. He fearlessly preached the gospel, in the face of threats, hostility, and persecution everywhere he went. That opposition began immediately after his conversion in Damascus, where his proclamation of Jesus as the Messiah so enraged the Jews that they sought to kill him (Acts 9:22–24). Paul faced similar opposition from his countrymen in Antioch (13:46), Iconium (14:1–2), Corinth (18:4–6, 12–16), Jerusalem (21:27–22:23; cf. 21:10–13), before the Sanhedrin (22:30–23:10), and in Rome (28:16–31).

Paul's preaching of the gospel also aroused hostility from the Gentiles.In Philippi he was beaten and imprisoned (16:16–40);in Athens he was mocked by the skeptical Greek philosophers (17:16–34); in Eph-esus his success in preaching the gospel sparked a riot by the devotees of the pagan goddess Artemis (19:23–41). Paul also courageously testi-fied to the Lord Jesus Christ before Gentile authorities, including Felix (24:1–26), Festus (25:1–12), Agrippa (26:1–32), and the emperor (25:12, 21–27; cf. 28:17–19).When the ship taking him to Rome encountered a severe storm, Paul, though only a prisoner, took charge of the situation (27:9–10, 21–26, 30–36).

Unlike many pastors today, Paul did not hesitate to denounce false teachers. He confronted the "Jewish false prophet whose name was Bar-Jesus" on the island of Cyprus (Acts 13:6), the Judaizers at Antioch (15:1–2), and Hymenaeus and Alexander at Ephesus (1 Tim. 1:20). He also repeatedly warned Christians to beware of such "savage wolves" (Acts 20:29; cf. 2 Cor. 11:2–4; Gal. 1:6–7; 6:12–13; Phil 3:2, 18–19; Col. 2:8, 18–23; 1 Thess. 2:14–16; 1 Tim. 1:3–7; 4:1–3; 6:3–5, 20–21; 2 Tim. 2:14, 16–18, 23; 3:1–9, 13; 4:14–15; Titus 1:9–16; 3:9–10).

Paul also confronted sinning believers, something that many pastors today are also reluctant to do. He rebuked the Corinthians (2 Cor. 10–13), the Galatians (Gal. 3–5), a man guilty of incest (1 Cor. 5:1–5), and undisciplined people who refused to work at Thessalonica (2 Thess. 3:6–12).

But not every leader is a Moses, Elijah, or Paul. The Lord also uses quiet, contemplative, analytical, cautious men. One such man was Paul's dear son in the faith, Timothy. Timothy was unquestionably a man of conviction, in whom Paul had the utmost confidence (Phil. 2:19–20). The apostle sent him to deal with the troubled situation at Corinth (1 Cor. 4:17), to Thessalonica (1 Thess. 3:2, 6), and possibly to Philippi (Phil. 2:19). Paul also installed Timothy as the pastor of the important church at Ephesus (1 Tim. 1:1–3). Timothy endured imprisonment for the cause of Christ (Heb. 13:23), possibly because of his loyal service to Paul (cf. 2 Tim. 4:9, 11, 13, 21).

Yet Timothy could also be fearful, hesitant, and lacking in self-confidence. Paul had to encourage and exhort him not to allow others to intimidate him because of his youth and lack of experience (1 Tim. 4:12–16). Timothy also needed to be more faithful in the exercise of his spiritual gift (2 Tim. 1:6), to stop being timid (v. 7; cf. 1 Cor. 16:10), and not to be ashamed to be identified with either the Lord or Paul, but be willing to suffer for the gospel (v. 8). Later in that same epistle, the apostle repeated his exhortation to Timothy to renew his commitment to his ministry and to be willing to suffer for the cause of Christ (2:1, 3).

Like all spiritual leaders, the apostles also were men of diverse temperaments. As noted in earlier chapters of this volume, Peter, James, and John were dynamic, upfront, take-charge individuals. Andrew, consistently overshadowed by his more prominent brother Peter, operated more in the background. The next two individuals on Luke's list of the Twelve, Philip and Nathanael (Bartholomew), were also quiet, analytical, reflective men content to work behind the scenes.

PHILIP

Philip (6:14*e*)

In all four of the New Testament lists of the Twelve, Philip's name appears fifth overall and first in the second group of four, which likely means that he was the leader of that group. **Philip** is a Greek name, which means "lover of horses." Like the rest of the Twelve, Philip was Jewish, but his Jewish name is not recorded. Since he had a Greek name, Philip may have come from a family of Hellenistic Jews (cf. Acts 6:1), who had adopted the Greek language and some aspects of Greek customs and culture. Like Andrew and Peter (John 1:44), Philip was originally from Bethsaida (John 12:21). As its name implies (Bethsaida means "house of fishing"), Bethsaida was primarily a fishing village, although Philip the Tetrarch, son of Herod the Great (Luke 3:1), enlarged and beautified it. Growing up in the same small village, Philip, Peter, and Andrew undoubtedly knew each other well. Like Peter and Andrew, Philip was probably also a fisherman (he was most likely one of the two unnamed disciples who went fishing with Peter in John 21:2–3). Philip is not mentioned in the Synoptic Gospels except in the lists of the apostles; all that is known about him comes from four incidents recorded in the gospel of John.

Philip first appears in John 1:43. The day after He called Andrew, John, and Peter (vv. 35–42), Jesus "purposed to go into Galilee, and He found Philip. And Jesus said to him, 'Follow Me'" (v. 43). Like the other three apostles, Philip apparently had also gone to the Jordan to hear John the Baptist. But while they had sought out Jesus at the direction of the Baptist, the Lord found Philip. This is the first time Jesus initiated contact with one whom He called to be an apostle. That is not to say, of course, that Jesus did not sovereignly choose and call the rest of them. "You did not choose Me," He told the Twelve, "but I chose you, and appointed you" (John 15:16; cf. 6:70). The unregenerate, being "dead in [their] trespasses and sins" (Eph. 2:1), alienated from God and hostile to Him (Col. 1:21), blinded (2 Cor. 4:4) and held captive (2 Tim. 2:26) by Satan, enslaved to sin (John 8:34), and unable to understand spiritual truth (1 Cor. 2:14), cannot seek God on their own initiative. Therefore as Jesus declared, "No one can come to Me unless the Father who sent Me draws him; and I will raise him up on the last day" (John 6:44), and, "No one can come to Me unless it has been granted him from the Father" (v. 65). That God was drawing Philip to seek Jesus is evident from his reaction: he immediately went and told Nathanael that he had found the Messiah (see the discussion of John 1:45 below).

Such a bold, impulsive reaction makes it clear that God was

working in Philip's heart. To instantly, unhesitatingly commit himself to Christ, with no hint of doubt or disbelief, was completely out of character for Philip, as his role in the feeding of the five thousand demonstrates. Seeing the huge crowd, which would have included thousands of women and children in addition to the five thousand men (Matt. 14:21), Jesus "said to Philip, 'Where are we to buy bread, so that these may eat?'" (John 6:5). That the Lord asked Philip that question suggests that he may have been the apostolic administrator, the one in charge of logistics such as arranging meals and lodging. Jesus, of course, was not trying to come up with a plan, "for He Himself knew what He was intending to do" (v. 6). Instead, "He was saying [this] to test" Philip, to reveal to him the weakness of his faith. True to form, he responded in unbelief. In typical bean counter fashion Philip, anticipating the difficulty of finding food for such a large crowd, had apparently been mentally estimating its size. By the time the Lord spoke to him, he had crunched the numbers and conclud-ed that the situation was hopeless; hence his reply, "Two hundred denarii [about eight months' wages for a common laborer] worth of bread is not sufficient for them, for everyone to receive a little" (v. 7). Too bogged down in arithmetic to be adventurous, Philip failed one of the key tests of leadership. Instead of having a sense of the possible, he had a sense of the impossible. His focus on facts and figures stifled his faith. Andrew, on the other hand, brought a boy with a small lunch to Jesus, and his faith was honored when Jesus miraculously used that meager resource to feed the crowd (see the discussion of this incident in chapter 4 of this volume).

An incident recorded in John 12 provides another example of Philip's analytical and overly cautious personality. Verse 20 introduces "some Greeks among those who were going up to worship at the feast." These were God-fearing Gentiles (cf. Acts 10:22; 17:4, 17), maybe even full-fledged converts to Judaism, who had come to Jerusalem for Passover. In the aftermath of the triumphal entry, they sought an audience with Jesus. Why they approached Philip (v. 21) is not clear, but John's note that Philip "was from Bethsaida of Galilee" suggests that may have been the reason. Bethsaida was near the Gentile region known as the Decapo-lis (Matt. 4:25; Mark 5:20; 7:31), and they may have been from that region. Further, since he was a Galilean Philip likely spoke Greek.

Their simple request to Philip, "Sir, we wish to see Jesus" (v. 21) caught him completely off guard. He was a "by the book" person, and there was no precedent for introducing Gentiles to Jesus; it was not in the manual. In fact, two of Jesus' previous statements argued against it, at least in Philip's mind. When He sent the Twelve out to preach the gospel Jesus had instructed them, "Do not go in the way of the Gentiles, and do not enter any city of the Samaritans; but rather go to the lost sheep of the house of Israel" (Matt. 10:5–6). And Philip had also heard the Lord say to a Canaanite woman, "I was sent only to the lost sheep of the house of Israel" (Matt. 15:24). That was enough to make him hesitant to bring these Gentiles to Jesus.

But in his narrow focus on methods and procedures, Philip missed the point. The Lord's statements were not intended to prohibit Gentiles from coming to Him, but merely emphasized that the priority of His ministry was Israel (cf. Rom. 1:16). Philip forgot that Jesus had also said that "the one who comes to Me I will certainly not cast out" (John 6:37) and, "I have other sheep [Gentiles], which are not of this fold [Israel]; I must bring them also, and they will hear My voice; and they will become one flock with one shepherd" (John 10:16). And He had commended the "great faith" of the Syrophoenician woman (Matt. 15:21–28).

Uncertain about how to proceed, "Philip came and told Andrew" (v. 22). Unlike Philip, Andrew had no doubt about how to handle the situation. If people wanted to come to Jesus, he was going to bring them (see the discussion of Andrew in chapter 4 of this volume). Andrew's reaction was swift and decisive; he "and Philip came and told Jesus" about the request (v. 22).

The last glimpse of Philip in the New Testament (the Philip in Acts is Philip the evangelist, not the apostle Philip) comes in the upper room on the night of Christ's betrayal and arrest. The Lord had just made the monumental statement, "I am the way, and the truth, and the life; no one comes to the Father but through Me" (John 14:6). He alone is the source of salvation (cf. Acts 4:12) and no one will go to heaven who does not by faith alone embrace Him alone as the Savior. Jesus followed that statement with an explicit declaration of His absolute deity and equality with the Father: "If you had known Me, you would have known My Father also; from now on you know Him, and have seen Him" (v. 7). To know Jesus is to know the Father (cf. John 1:18), since the Persons of the Trinity are one in their very essence. Having known Jesus through the years of His earthly ministry, the disciples in effect already knew the Father as well.

At this point Philip made one of the most distressingly foolish and ignorant statements any of the apostles ever made. He said to Jesus, "Lord, show us the Father, and it is enough for us" (v. 8). Unbelievably Philip, who had so eagerly embraced Christ at the beginning, missed the point. He failed to grasp not only what Jesus had just said, but also all the teaching he had heard and the miracles he had observed over the years of Christ's ministry. His skepticism, lack of faith, and inability to understand the significance of what he had seen and heard was heartbreaking.

Jesus rebuked Philip for his disappointing statement by demanding, "Have I been so long with you, and yet you have not come to know Me, Philip?" The Lord then reiterated plainly the truth that He had taught the apostles in verse 7: "He who has seen Me has seen the Father; how can you say, 'Show us the Father'?" (v. 9). He then reprimanded Philip for failing to grasp that reality, despite what he had seen and heard (v. 10), and challenged him to believe; to take his faith in Jesus as the Messiah to its logical conclusion (v. 11). The evidence Philip had seen pointed conclusively to one inescapable conclusion—Jesus was God incarnate, one in essence with the Father.

There is little reliable information about Philip's later life and ministry. The early Christian writers had a tendency to confuse him with Philip the evangelist (Acts 6:5; 8:26–40; 21:8). The fourth-century church historian Eusebius, for example, wrote of a Philip who lived in the city of Hierapolis in Asia Minor with his virgin daughters. But whether this was the apostle Philip or Philip the evangelist is unclear. According to the apocryphal *Acts of Philip*, the apostle Philip preached in Phrygia, Greece, and Syria before being martyred in Hierapolis in Asia Minor. *The Acts of Philip*, however, is not considered a reliable historical source.

It is perhaps to be expected that such a quiet, unassuming, behind the scenes person's history would be so obscure. That in no way, however, diminishes Philip's importance. This skeptical, analytical, pessimistic man of limited ability, weak faith, and imperfect understanding was nonetheless one of the twelve most important people in the history of the world.

BARTHOLOMEW (NATHANAEL)

Bartholomew (6:14f)

Philip's close companion **Bartholomew** appears by that name in all four New Testament lists of the Twelve, but the apostle John calls him Nathanael. Both names refer to the same individual. Bartholomew means "son of Tolmai" in Hebrew; thus, his full name was Nathanael, son of Tolmai. In the lists in the Synoptic Gospels, his name immediately follows Philip's, indicating the close relationship between the two. In fact, it was Philip who introduced Nathanael to the Savior.

The New Testament records even less information about Bartholomew than Philip. His only recorded appearance, apart from the lists of the apostles, is in John's account of his call by Christ (John 1:45–51). That encounter reveals both the strengths and weaknesses of Nathanael's personality.

After the Lord called Philip (v. 43), he immediately "found Nathanael and said to him, 'We have found Him of whom Moses in the Law and also the Prophets wrote—Jesus of Nazareth, the son of Joseph'"

(v. 45). His use of the plural pronoun "we" indicates that Philip already considered himself one of Jesus' followers. His description of Him as the one of whom Moses and the Prophets wrote (i.e., the Messiah) indicates that Philip knew that Nathanael was a student of the Old Testament; a seeker after divine truth. It may be that Philip and Nathanael had spent hours together poring over the Scriptures. Perhaps they had even come to the Jordan together to hear John the Baptist.

But Nathanael's reaction to his friend's excited claim reveals a different aspect of his personality. Responding with skepticism, if not outright scorn, he asked rhetorically, "Can any good thing come out of Nazareth?" (v. 46). This was not a question based on the Old Testament's prediction that the Messiah would be born in Bethlehem (Micah 5:2); it was an expression of prejudice. The Galileans were despised by the Judeans as uncouth and unsophisticated. Nathanael was himself a Galilean, from the village of Cana where Jesus turned the water into wine (John 21:2). His remark indicates that Nazareth was despised even by other Galileans—hardly the place one would expect the Messiah to hail from. So insignificant was Nazareth that it is not even mentioned in the Old Testament, the Talmud, or the writings of Josephus. It was inconceivable to Nathanael that the Messiah would come from such an obscure town.

Prejudice often blinds people to the truth. It was in one sense prejudice that kept the nation of Israel from accepting Jesus as the Messiah. Most of them shared Nathanael's disdain for Nazareth, and rejected Jesus out of hand. Had they taken the time to investigate, they would have discovered that He was born in Bethlehem, just as the Old Testament predicted the Messiah would be. That most of the men in His inner circle were Galileans and that He Himself had not been trained in the rabbinic schools (John 7:15) also did not endear Jesus to the elitist religious establishment. Nathanael's reaction reveals that he had not escaped the prejudice that was rampant in Jewish society.

Unfazed by Nathanael's cynical comment, Philip issued a simple challenge: "Come and see" (v. 46). To his credit, Nathanael's seeking heart overcame his prejudice, and he went with Philip to meet Jesus. To his utter amazement, the Lord greeted him as "an Israelite indeed, in whom there is no deceit!" (v. 47). Jesus' words were a powerful commendation of Nathanael's character. His characterization of him as "an Israelite indeed (*alēthōs*; 'truly,' 'actually,' 'in reality')" means far more than that Nathanael was a physical descendant of Abraham. Abrahamic descent alone does not make one a true Jew. As the apostle Paul wrote, "They are not all Israel who are descended from Israel" (Rom. 9:6), since "he is not a Jew who is one outwardly, nor is circumcision that which is outward in the flesh. But he is a Jew who is one inwardly; and circumcision is that which is of the heart, by the Spirit, not by the letter" (Rom. 2:28–29). Jesus identified Nathanael as one of the believing remnant, who worshiped the true and living God. Simeon and Anna were also examples of such (Luke 2:25–38).

Surprised that this man whom he had never met would greet him that way, Nathanael asked incredulously, "How do You know me?" (v. 48). How could Jesus know what was in his heart? The Lord's answer, which revealed His omniscience, shocked Nathanael. "Before Philip called you," He replied, "when you were under the fig tree, I saw you." But there is more to Jesus' response than merely His supernatural knowledge of Nathanael's location; He also knew the state of Nathanael's heart (cf. John 2:24–25). To escape the noise and, in hot weather, the stuffy heat of their houses, people often sought solitude under the shade of a fig tree. That was where Nathanael went to study, pray, and think.

The Lord's knowledge of Nathanael's heart removed all his doubts about Him and he exclaimed, "Rabbi, You are the Son of God; You are the King of Israel" (v. 49). Nathanael affirmed his belief in Christ's deity as the "Son of God" (cf. Ps. 2:12) and that he was the Messiah, the "King of Israel" (cf. Zech. 9:9). Jesus in turn affirmed Nathanael's faith "and said to him, 'Because I said to you that I saw you under the fig tree, do you believe?'" (v. 50). The Lord's reply should probably be taken as a statement, not a question. His omniscient knowledge of Nathanael's heart had convinced Nathanael of Jesus' identity, but far more was to follow. "You will see greater things than these," Jesus promised, "You will see the heavens opened and the angels of God ascending and descending on the Son of Man" (v. 51). The reference here is to Jacob's dream in which he saw a ladder descending from heaven (Gen. 28:12). Jesus is in reality what that ladder symbolized, the link between heaven and earth and thus the revealer of divine truth to mankind (cf. John 1:14, 17; 3:13; 6:33; 1 Tim. 2:5).

As is the case with his close companion Philip, little is known about Nathanael's life and ministry after Christ's resurrection and ascension. According to some accounts, he ministered in India. Other traditions place his ministry in Persia, Egypt, Armenia, and Asia Minor. Nor is there any agreement about how he died. Some accounts claim that Nathanael was martyred in Armenia, but those accounts differ over the manner of his death. Some say he was beheaded, others that he was skinned alive and then crucified (thus some works of art portray him holding his skin in his hands).

What is clear is that Nathanael remained faithful to the Lord Jesus Christ to the end, as he had been in the beginning. His life and ministry are a testimony to God's ability to use common, insignificant people to His glory.

Common Men, Uncommon Calling— Part 6: Matthew, Thomas, James the son of Alphaeus, Simon the Zealot Judas the son of James (Luke 6:15–16*a*)

7

Matthew and Thomas; James the son of Alphaeus, and Simon who was called the Zealot; Judas the son of James (Luke 6:15–16*a*)

A seemingly paradoxical biblical truth, one that appears counter-intuitive to human wisdom, is that God exalts the humble but humbles the proud. As the psalmist noted, "God is the Judge; He puts down one and exalts another" (Ps. 75:7). Moses was perhaps Israel's most honored leader. Yet according to Numbers 12:3, "Moses was very humble, more than any man who was on the face of the earth." "A man's pride will bring him low," Solomon warned, "but a humble spirit will obtain honor" (Prov. 29:23; cf. v. 25). Ezekiel 17:24 expressed that truth in picturesque language: "All the trees of the field will know that I am the Lord; I bring down the high tree, exalt the low tree, dry up the green tree and make the dry tree flourish. I am the Lord; I have spoken, and I will perform it" (cf. 21:26).

The New Testament also reveals God's sovereign humbling of the proud and exalting of the humble. In her Magnificat, Mary praised God because "He has brought down rulers from their thrones, and has exalted those who were humble" (Luke 1:52). So significant is this principle that the Lord Jesus Christ repeated it on three different occasions (Matt. 23:12; Luke 14:11; 18:14). James exhorted his readers, "Humble yourselves in the presence of the Lord, and He will exalt you" (James 4:10).

Jesus' choice of the Twelve was consistent with God's use of humble people (cf. 1 Cor. 1:26–29). None of them were members of Israel's religious establishment; they included no scribes, Pharisees, Sadducees, or priests. Nor were they taken from the social elite, the literate, the educated, or the theologically astute. None were from Jerusalem, the center of Jewish culture; except for the traitor Judas Iscariot, they were from Galilee, whose inhabitants were despised by the rest of the Jewish people. The Gospels portray the Twelve as plain, common, and ordinary men.

In spite of the fact that they were empowered to do miracles, the apostles were by no means the stars of the gospel accounts; they were at best the supporting cast. There are no records of the miracles they did (until the book of Acts) and very few instances of any significant act by any of them. While Peter made a profound statement acknowledging Jesus as the Messiah and Son of God (Matt. 16:16), he then brashly rebuked the Lord and was in turn sternly rebuked by Him (vv. 22–23). Peter's one impressive act, walking on the water, was spoiled when his faith failed (Matt. 14:28–31). When the apostles do appear in the narrative, it is usually to express their lack of faith (Matt. 8:26; 17:19–20), lack of understanding (Matt. 15:15–17; 16:5–12), or lack of humility (Mark 9:33–34; Luke 9:46–48).

But despite their shortcomings, the Twelve willingly gave up everything to follow Jesus Christ (Matt. 19:27; Luke 5:11), and made a permanent break with their past. That set them apart from many who temporarily followed Jesus, as an examination of John chapter 6 reveals. A large crowd was attracted to Jesus because He healed the sick (v. 2) and fed them (vv. 5–14). The next day many of them crossed the Sea of Galilee in search of Jesus (vv. 22–25). Knowing their hearts (cf. v. 64), the Lord rebuked them for following Him with improper motives (vv. 26–27). He then taught them profound truths about Himself that many were not prepared to accept (vv. 28–65), and "as a result of this many of His disciples withdrew and were not walking with Him anymore" (v. 66). Turning to the Twelve, Jesus asked them, "You do not want to go away also, do you?" (v. 67). Speaking for all of them, "Simon Peter answered Him, 'Lord, to whom shall we go? You have words of eternal life. We have believed and have come to know that You are the Holy One of God'" (vv. 68–69). Unlike the fickle crowds, the Twelve (with the exception of Judas; vv. 70–71) were convinced that Jesus was the Messiah as well as the Son of God.

MATTHEW

Matthew (6:15a)

Luke's introduction of **Matthew** marks the halfway point both in the second group of four apostles (Philip, Bartholomew, Matthew, and Thomas) and in the list of the Twelve. Although he was the author of one of the four Gospels, little is revealed in the New Testament about him. Matthew himself in his own gospel (9:9–10) and Luke (5:27–29) briefly describes his call by the Lord, and the reception for sinners he gave afterwards. Those two incidents mark Matthew's only appearances in the Gospels, apart from the lists of the apostles. Matthew's silence about himself in his gospel in particular reveals him to have been humble, self-effacing, and content to remain in the background.

Like several of the other apostles, he had two names: Matthew (Matt. 9:9) and Levi (Luke 5:27). He was a tax collector by profession, which makes his selection as an apostle all the more remarkable. Tax collectors were despised outcasts in Jewish society. They were traitors, who opportunistically collaborated with the Romans for their own financial gain. Tax collectors purchased tax franchises from the Romans, and anything they collected beyond what was required of them (cf. Luke 3:12–13) went into their own pockets. They practiced larceny, extortion, exploitation, and even loan sharking, loaning out money at exorbitant interest to those who were unable to pay their taxes. Tax collectors also employed thugs to physically intimidate people into paying whatever they demanded, and to beat up those who refused.

All of that infuriated the Jewish people, who believed that God was the only one to whom they should pay taxes. They scorned tax collectors, classified them as unclean, and banned them from the synagogues. Since the Jews considered tax collectors to be habitual liars, they were not permitted to give testimony in a Jewish court. Tax collectors came to symbolize the epitome of evil (cf. Matt. 18:17; 21:31; Luke 5:30; 7:34; 18:11).

There were two types of tax collectors, the _gabbai_, who collected the general taxes such as the land, poll, and income taxes, and the _mokhes_, who collected the more specific taxes, such as those on the transport of goods, letters, produce, using roads, crossing bridges, and almost anything else the greedy traitors could think of (cf. Alfred Edersheim, _The Life and Times of Jesus the Messiah_ [Grand Rapids: Eerdmans, 1974], 1:515–18). There were in turn two kinds of _mokhes_, the great _mokhes_, and the little _mokhes_. The great _mokhes_ did not actually collect taxes, but hired others to do so for him. The little _mokhes_ would be employed by a great _mokhes_ to actually collect taxes. Because they were the ones who interacted with the people on a regular basis, they were the ones who bore the brunt of their anger and hatred. Matthew was one such little _mokhes_ (Luke 5:27), one of the most despised and reviled men in Capernaum.

Yet when Jesus called him, Matthew unhesitatingly "left every-thing behind, and got up and began to follow Him" (Luke 5:28). Unlike some of the other apostles who had been fishermen (cf. John 21:1–3), Matthew could never go back to his profession. The great *mokhes* for whom he had worked would have immediately replaced him. Why was Matthew willing to walk away from his lucrative business and follow Jesus, not knowing what the future held? Despite being an outcast from Judaism, Matthew was nonetheless very familiar with the Old Testament. That is evident from his extensive quotations of the Old Testament, more than any other gospel writer. Matthew believed in the true God, and understood the Scriptures. Like most of his countrymen, he was expect-ing the Messiah to come. Apparently, through his interaction with those from whom he collected taxes, he had heard all about Jesus' miraculous works and powerful preaching. His heart was ready when the Lord called him, and his faith was strong enough for him to drop everything and obey that call.

The genuineness of Matthew's repentance and faith revealed itself in the banquet he gave in his home after Jesus called him (Matt. 9:10; Luke 5:29; with characteristic humility, Matthew did not mention that the reception was in his own house.). He invited his fellow tax col-lectors and other associated sinners—the riffraff of Jewish society.

After this reception, Matthew fades from the gospel record. Nei-ther is anything known for certain about his life and ministry after Pente-cost. Most accounts agree that he preached the gospel to the Jewish people before ministering to the Gentiles, possibly in the vicinity of the Caspian Sea, or in Persia, Macedonia, or Syria. Nor do the traditions agree on the place or manner of his death. According to some accounts, he was burned at the stake, while others state that he was beheaded or stoned to death. But in any case this man, who freely abandoned a lucra-tive, if criminal, career to follow the Lord Jesus Christ, never looked back. Matthew willingly gave his all for Him to the very end.

THOMAS

Thomas (6:15*b*)

His skeptical reply to the other apostles' claim to have seen the risen Lord Jesus Christ, "Unless I see in His hands the imprint of the nails, and put my finger into the place of the nails, and put my hand into His side, I will not believe" (John 20:25), has earned **Thomas** the nickname, "Doubting Thomas." In fact, that phrase has come to label a skeptical, habitually doubting person. While it is fair to say that Thomas tended to be a negative person, he was too good a man for such a one-dimensional appraisal of his character.

According to John 11:16, 20:24, and 21:2, Thomas was also called Didymus, which means, "twin." Whether he actually had a twin brother or sister, however, is not recorded in Scripture. His name is given in the Synoptic Gospels only in the lists of the apostles. But as he did with Philip and Bartholomew (Nathanael), the apostle John fleshes out some aspects of his character.

The first incident in which Thomas appears is recorded in John chapter 11. After His unambiguous claim to deity and equality with the Father (10:30), the enraged Jewish leaders sought to kill Jesus (vv. 31, 39). Because His time had not yet come (cf. John 7:30; 8:20), Jesus "went away again beyond the Jordan to the place where John was first baptizing, and He was staying there" (John 10:40), along with the Twelve.

While they were there, Jesus received the news that His close friend Lazarus, the brother of Mary and Martha, was seriously ill. He may even have died by the time the messenger they sent reached Jesus and the disciples. When He received the message, Jesus said, "This sickness is not to end in death, but for the glory of God, so that the Son of God may be glorified by it" (11:4). He did not mean that Lazarus was not going to die, but that death would not be the final outcome of his illness. The apostles, who assumed that Lazarus was therefore going to recover, were no doubt relieved to hear Jesus' words. That the Lord remained where He was for two more days (11:6) must have further reassured them that Lazarus would recover.

But then the Lord dropped a bombshell on them: "Then after this He said to the disciples, 'Let us go to Judea again'" (v. 7). Shocked and appalled, the disciples protested incredulously, "Rabbi, the Jews were just now seeking to stone You, and are You going there again?" (v. 8). Why leave a fruitful ministry (10:41–42), they reasoned, and travel to Bethany in the vicinity of Jerusalem (the town was only two miles from Jerusalem [John 11:18]) where they risked being arrested and executed? Jesus replied (vv. 9–10) that He and they were perfectly safe during the divinely-appointed duration of His earthly ministry (see the exposition of those verses in _John 1–11_, The MacArthur New Testament Commentary [Chicago: Moody, 2006], 455–56).

The Lord then explained why they had to return to Bethany: "Our friend Lazarus has fallen asleep; but I go, so that I may awaken him out of sleep" (v. 11). Still not grasping the situation, "the disciples then said to Him, 'Lord, if he has fallen asleep, he will recover'" (v. 12). Since Lazarus was apparently on the road to recovery, there seemed to be no logical reason to risk everything by returning to Judea. Finally, Jesus told them plainly, "Lazarus is dead, and I am glad for your sakes that I was not there, so that you may believe; but let us go to him" (vv. 14–15). At last, the disciples realized what had really happened and understood that it was futile to try to talk Jesus out of returning to Judea. But they were still very hesitant and fearful about going.

At this point Thomas took the lead. Rallying his fellow disciples, he said to them, "Let us also go, so that we may die with Him" (v. 16). His courageous statement was made all the more so by his pessimism—he fully expected that both they and Jesus would be killed. Yet his love and devotion were so strong that he preferred to die rather than to face life without the Lord.

That aspect of his nature is reinforced in Thomas's next appearance in John's gospel. In the upper room on the night before His death, Jesus told the apostles that He was going away to the Father's house to prepare a place for them, and would return to take them there (John 14:1–3). Because He had already told the disciples that He was returning to the Father (e.g., John 7:33; 13:1,3), Jesus expected them to know where He was going (v. 4). Dismayed at the thought of the Lord's leaving, Thomas exclaimed, "Lord, we do not know where You are going, how do we know the way?" (v. 5). His statement reflects both his intense love for Christ, and his extreme pessimism.

By now the disciples realized that Jesus was going to die, but they had no firsthand knowledge of what happens after death. Further, Jesus had just told them that they could not at that time go where He was going (John 13:33, 36). Thomas's plaintive question reflected their confusion and despair. If they did not know where the Lord was going, how could they follow Him there? The thought of losing Jesus was unbearable to Thomas, and he was engulfed in heartbroken despair.

By the time Thomas appears again in John's narrative, his worst fear had been realized: Jesus had died, and he had not. When the Lord appeared to the disciples for the first time after He rose from the dead, Thomas was not there (John 20:24). Where he was is not stated, but perhaps, devastated by the death of the Lord whom he supremely loved, he preferred to be alone with his sorrow and despair. In any case, when he returned, the other ten apostles greeted him excitedly with the news that Jesus had risen from the dead and appeared to them.

It was then that Thomas uttered the statement for which he is famous: "Unless I see in His hands the imprint of the nails, and put my finger into the place of the nails, and put my hand into His side, I will not believe" (v. 25). Thomas was not about to get his hopes up, only to have them dashed again. Although Thomas's skepticism earned him the nickname "Doubting Thomas," the other apostles had fared no better. They, too, had scoffed at the initial reports of Christ's resurrection (Luke 24:10–11), and only believed after He appeared to them (John 20:20).

Eight days later, Jesus once again appeared to the apostles. This time Thomas's grief had eased enough for him to be present with his companions. The Lord immediately confronted his lack of faith. "Reach here with your finger," He commanded Thomas, "and see My hands; and reach here your hand and put it into My side; and do not be unbelieving, but believing" (John 20:27). Thomas's simple, yet profound reply, "My Lord and my God!" (v. 28) is perhaps the greatest statement ever made by any of the apostles, equaled only by Peter's confession, "You are the Christ, the Son of the living God" (Matt. 16:16). His melancholy pessimism vanished in the glorious light of the risen Savior, and Thomas was transformed into a powerful evangelist. There is a strong tradition from the early centuries of the church that Thomas carried the gospel to India, where he was martyred. Some accounts say that he was thrust through with a spear—a fitting form of martyrdom for the one whose doubts were forever banished when he saw the mark of the spear in the Savior's side.

JAMES THE SON OF ALPHAEUS

James the son of Alphaeus (6:15c)

Despite his supreme privilege as one of the twelve men chosen by the Lord Jesus Christ to be His personal representatives, virtually nothing is known about **James**. All that the New Testament reveals about him is that his father's name was **Alphaeus**, his mother's name was Mary (Matt. 27:56; Mark 15:40), and that he had a brother named Joseph (Matt. 27:56) or Joses (Mark 15:40). Since Matthew's father was also named Alphaeus (Mark 2:14), it is possible that the two were brothers.

In Mark 15:40, James is referred to by his nickname "James the Less." *Mikros* ("Less") means, "little." The nickname may mean that James was small in stature. It may also mean that he was young in age. Most likely, however, it refers to his relative lack of importance and influence in comparison to the more famous James, the brother of John and member of the inner circle of the Twelve.

Where James ministered after Pentecost is not known. He may have preached the gospel in Persia, or Egypt, or both. According to some traditions, he was martyred by crucifixion in Egypt. This humble servant's only distinguishing mark is his obscurity. He sought no recognition, displayed no great leadership skills, asked no critical questions, and demonstrated no unusual insights. Only his name remains, and the honor due him as an apostle of the Lord Jesus Christ. There is a far greater record of his life and ministry in heaven.

SIMON THE ZEALOT

Simon who was called the Zealot (6:15*d*)

Matthew (10:4) and Mark (3:18) refer to **Simon** using the Aramaic word *cananaean*. That term is not a geographical reference either to the land of Canaan, or the village of Cana, but comes from a root word meaning "zealous," or "passionate" (hence the NASB translates it **Zealot** in those verses). Luke used the corresponding Greek word *Zēlōtēs*, which also means **Zealot**. Both terms mark Simon as a member of the radical Jewish faction known as the Zealots.

The Zealots were one of the four primary parties in first-century Israel, along with the Pharisees, Sadducees, and Essenes. They were passionately devoted to the law of God, and violently opposed any intrusion upon it by pagans, such as the Romans. They were political radicals, the terrorists and assassins of their day, perfectly willing to murder the Romans and their Jewish collaborators. By doing so, they believed they were doing God's work. The first-century Jewish historian Josephus wrote concerning the Zealots' fanaticism,

> But of the fourth sect of Jewish philosophy, Judas the Galilean was the author. These men agree in all other things with the Pharisaic notions; but they have an inviolable attachment to liberty, and say that God is to be their only Ruler and Lord. They also do not value dying any kinds of death, nor indeed do they heed the deaths of their relations and friends, nor can any such fear make them call any man Lord. And since this immovable resolution of theirs is well known to a great many, I shall speak no further about that matter; nor am I afraid that any thing I have said of them should be disbelieved, but rather fear, that what I have said is beneath the resolution they show when they undergo pain. (*Antiquities*, 18.1.6)

While precursors to the Zealots can be found in the Maccabean era of the intertestamental period, the movement itself began shortly after the death of Herod the Great. The Zealots, under Judas (cf. Acts 5:37), rose in rebellion against the census conducted by Quirinius (the second one in A.D. 6, not the first one a decade earlier that brought Mary and Joseph to Bethlehem). The Zealots also played a major role in the Jewish revolt against Rome (A.D. 66–73). After the fall of Jerusalem in A.D. 70, a band of Zealots fled to the fortress of Masada. There they held out until A.D. 73, then committed mass suicide rather than surrender to the Romans.

As a Zealot, Simon was a man devoted to the law of God, fiercely patriotic, passionate, and courageous. He hated the Romans and desperately wanted them out of Israel. He was the antithesis of Matthew, whose collaboration with the Romans had made him rich. Had they not both been followers of the Lord Jesus Christ, Simon would have had nothing to do with Matthew, and might even have murdered him. Like Judas Iscariot, Simon was looking for a messiah who would drive out the Romans. But unlike Judas, who betrayed Jesus when he saw that was not Jesus' plan, Simon embraced Him as Savior, Lord, and God incarnate.

Like many of the apostles, Simon's later ministry is shrouded in mystery and legend. According to some traditions, he preached the gospel in Persia and Armenia, others place his ministry in the Middle East and Africa, while some even have him ministering in Britain. Nor is there any agreement on the manner or place of his death, which some claim was by crucifixion, others by being sawn in two. Simon the Zealot, who had willingly faced death because of his passionate commitment to God's law, suffered it in the end because of his love for Jesus, the fulfillment of the law (Matt. 5:17; Luke 24:44).

JUDAS THE SON OF JAMES

Judas the son of James (6:16*a*)

While several of the apostles had two names, this **Judas** may have had three. Luke gave his formal name, **Judas the son of James**, while Matthew called him Thaddeus (Matt. 10:3) and, according to some less reliable Greek manuscripts, also gave him the name Lebbaeus. Both Thaddeus and Lebbaeus are nicknames; Thaddeus literally means, "breast child," while Lebbaeus means "heart child." Both could be rendered by the contemporary term "momma's boy." Those nicknames may indicate that Judas was the youngest child in his family.

Like the other apostles in this final group, little is known about Judas. Apart from the lists of the apostles, he made only one appearance in the New Testament. The scene was the upper room on the night of the Lord's betrayal, during His farewell discourse to the apostles. In John 14:21 Jesus told them that He would reveal Himself to those whose obedience proved the genuineness of their love for Him.

The disciples were puzzled by that statement. They expected Jesus to establish His earthly kingdom, a belief they still clung to even after His death and resurrection (Acts 1:6). After all, Jesus was the Savior of the world (John 4:42), the rightful heir of all things (Heb. 1:2), and the King of kings and Lord of lords (Rev. 19:16). The good news of forgiveness and salvation through His death and resurrection was to be proclaimed to the ends of the earth (Matt. 28:19–20).

Judas asked the question that was undoubtedly on the minds of the rest of the apostles:"Lord, what then has happened that You are going to disclose Yourself to us and not to the world? (John 14:22). The Lord's answer emphasized that His kingdom was not an external, political one (though He will one day reign over His earthly, millennial kingdom), but a spiritual one in the hearts of those who love and obey Him:"If anyone loves Me, he will keep My word; and My Father will love him, and We will come to him and make Our abode with him" (v. 23).

Judas spent the rest of his life extending the kingdom by preaching the truth of the gospel. According to tradition, he may have preached in such places as Samaria, Syria, Mesopotamia, and Libya. By some accounts Judas, the gentle, compassionate "momma's boy," suffered martyrdom with the fiery, passionate, former Zealot Simon.

Common Men, Uncommon Calling— Part 7: Judas Iscariot (Luke 6:16*b*)

8

Judas Iscariot, who became a traitor. (6:16*b*)

There are few people more despised than a **traitor**, a person who betrays the cause and trust of friends, groups, or country. Such heinous acts have historically resulted in the most severe punishment— often the death penalty.

There have been many notorious traitors throughout history. In the ancient world, the Athenian general Alcibiades revealed Athens's plans to the city's enemy, Sparta. As a result, the Athenians were defeated in battle by the Spartans during the Peloponnesian War. The Athenian soldier and noted historian Xenophon also turned traitor and fought for Sparta against his native city. As noted in chapter 4 of this volume, King Leonidas of Sparta and his vastly outnumbered force threw back repeated assaults by overwhelmingly superior Persian forces at Thermopylae. It was not until a traitor showed the Persians a way to outflank the Greek forces and attack them from the rear that Leonidas and his brave men were defeated.

During the American Revolution Simon Girty, a deserter from the Continental Army, led Native Americans in raids against the colonists. Girty was much feared for his brutality, so much so that he was dubbed the "Great Renegade." But the most infamous traitor of the Revolutionary War (and indeed in all of American history) was Benedict Arnold. Angered at being passed over for promotion and seeking money to support his extravagant lifestyle, Arnold offered to surrender the important fort at West Point to the British. When Arnold's plot was uncovered, he deserted to the British, and fought against his own countrymen.

The French general Henri Pétain had been a national hero in World War I. But after France was defeated by the Germans in World War II, he became the head of the Vichy government, which collaborated with the Nazis. Vidkun Quisling, whose name has become a synonym for "traitor," headed the puppet regime established by the Nazis in Norway. The English traitor William Joyce ("Lord Haw Haw"), and the American traitors Iva Ikuko Toguri D'Aquino ("Tokyo Rose") and Mildred Elizabeth Gillars ("Axis Sally") made propaganda broadcasts for the Japanese and Nazis respectively.

The Bible also records numerous traitors, including Absalom, who tried to usurp the throne of his father, David (2 Sam. 15:10–13); Ahithophel, David's counselor who joined Absalom's rebellion (2 Sam. 15:31); Sheba, who led a revolt of the northern tribes soon after Absalom's rebellion was defeated (2 Sam. 20:1–2); Jeroboam, whose revolt against Solomon resulted in the nation being split into two kingdoms, Israel and Judah (1 Kings 11:26ff.); Baasha, who murdered Jeroboam's son Nadab and seized his throne (1 Kings 15:25–28); Zimri, who killed Baasha's son Elah and took his place (1 Kings 16:8–20); Athaliah, Israel's only queen, who seized power after the death of her son, King Ahaziah (2 Kings 11:1–16); the servants of Joash, who conspired against him and killed him (2 Kings 12:20–21); the unnamed conspirators who assassinated King Amaziah (2 Kings 14:18–20); Shallum, whose conspiracy ended the brief reign of King Zechariah (2 Kings 15:8–10); Menahem, who murdered and replaced Shallum (2 Kings 15:14); Pekah, who overthrew and murdered Menahem's son Pekahiah (2 Kings 15:23–25); Hoshea, who killed Pekah and became the last king of the northern kingdom (2 Kings 15:30); Amon's servants, who conspired against him and murdered him (2 Kings 21:23); and the Persian officials Bigthan and Teresh, whose plot against King Ahasuerus was uncovered by Mordecai (Est. 2:21–23).

But the most notorious traitor of all time was Judas Iscariot. Judas had the unmatched privilege of being one of the twelve intimate followers of the Lord Jesus Christ during His earthly ministry. Yet inconceivably, after more than three years of living constantly with the incomparably perfect Son of God, observing the miracles He performed, and hearing His unparalleled teaching, Judas betrayed Him to His death by selling Him to His enemies. The dark, tragic story of Judas reveals him to have been the most profoundly wicked man in all of human history. It graphically illustrates the depths of evil of which the human heart is capable, even in the very best of circumstances.

Because of his heinous treachery, the early church universally detested and scorned Judas. His name appears last in every New Testament list of the apostles, except for the one in Acts 1—where it does not appear at all, since Judas had already committed suicide. In addition, whenever the gospel writers mention Judas they always identify him as the traitor who betrayed Jesus (Matt. 10:4; 26:25, 48; 27:3; Mark 3:19; 14:44; John 6:71; 12:4; 18:2), as Luke does here.

The story of Judas also demonstrates that Satan uses people to accomplish his evil purposes. He moved David to take a census of Israel that displeased God and resulted in His chastening of His people (1 Chron. 21:1–7). Satan also used demon-possessed false prophets to deceive King Ahab of Israel (1 Kings 22:19–23). He even used Peter to tempt Jesus to avoid the cross (Matt. 16:22–23). The future Antichrist will be "the one whose coming is in accord with the activity of Satan" (2 Thess. 2:9). With full complicity on the part of the apostate disciple, Satan entered Judas to manipulate him (John 13:2).

The melodrama that was Judas's life may be discussed under four headings: his name, call, disillusionment, and betrayal.

His Name

Judas was a common Jewish name (the New Testament records at least eight men with that name), and had no evil connotation before Judas Iscariot's betrayal of the Lord. It is the Greek translation of the Hebrew name "Judah," ("praised"). His father was Simon **Iscariot** (John 6:71; 13:2, 26); their surname is most likely the Greek translation of a Hebrew phrase that means "man of Kerioth." The Old Testament lists two villages named Kerioth, one in Moab (Jer. 48:24, 41; Amos 2:2), and another in the extreme southern part of Judah, about fifteen miles south of Hebron (Josh. 15:25). Judas Iscariot was almost certainly from the latter village, making him the only one of the Twelve who was not a Galilean. While there is no evidence that the other eleven ostracized him, Judas may have viewed himself as an outsider, which might have helped him to rationalize his detachment and treachery. That the other eleven knew little of Judas's background helps explain how he managed to become the group's treasurer (John 13:29)—a position he took advantage of to embezzle money (John 12:6).

By all outward appearances, Judas looked no different from the rest of the apostles. He did not appear sinister. The evil that would eventually manifest itself in his betrayal of the Savior lay hidden in the dark recesses of his heart. Thus when Jesus, on the very night that Judas betrayed Him, told the disciples, "Truly, truly, I say to you, that one of you will betray Me" (John 13:21), no one pointed an accusing finger at Judas. On the contrary, "the disciples began looking at one another, at a loss to know of which one He was speaking" (v. 22). Only Jesus knew Judas's evil heart from the beginning (John 6:64, 70).

HIS CALL

The Bible does not record when and where Judas first encountered Jesus. He may have been among those who went to the Judean wilderness to hear John the Baptist (Matt. 3:1–5), or he may have met the Lord at the outset of His ministry when "Jesus and His disciples came into the land of Judea, and there He was spending time with them and baptizing" (John 3:22). When the Lord first called Judas to follow Him is also not recorded in Scripture. With the other eleven, he was chosen to be an apostle (Luke 6:12–13). At that point (if he had not already done so), Judas left his former occupation and became a full-time follower of Christ. He even stayed with Him when many other false disciples abandoned Him (John 6:66–71). But though Judas was skilled as a hypocrite, appearing outwardly loyal to Jesus, he never gave Him his trust as Messiah and Lord. He was crass to the core, indifferent toward godly, spiritual matters.

Judas was probably young (perhaps in his early twenties), zealous, and patriotic. Like most of his fellow countrymen, he hated the Roman occupation of Israel, and longed for the Messiah (whom he thought of in political and military terms) to drive out the Romans and restore Israel's sovereignty. In that regard, he was no different from the rest of the apostles, who also hoped Jesus would establish an earthly kingdom (Acts 1:6). But unlike Judas, they also believed that Jesus was the Son of God (Matt. 16:16), who alone was the source of eternal life (John 6:68).

It was precisely that spiritual dimension that was absent in Judas. He saw Christ's miraculous power and fervently hoped that He would use it to throw off the yoke of Rome and establish His kingdom. Judas's motives, however, were not merely patriotic; he was also driven by greed and personal ambition. He hoped to reap the benefits—power, prestige, and wealth—that would be his in the kingdom as a member of Christ's inner circle. It was materialism, not spiritual realities, that fueled Judas's ambition.

It must be clearly understood that although Jesus chose Judas, Judas chose to follow Him of his own volition. He was not forced to become an apostle, nor was he compelled against his will to betray

Jesus. The biblical tension between divine sovereignty and human responsibility is evident in the calling of Judas, as it is with the rest of the Twelve. They chose to leave everything and follow Jesus (Matt. 19:27), but He chose them first (John 15:16).

That the Lord Jesus Christ would be betrayed and die for the sins of the world was foreordained in the eternal counsel of God. Centuries before it happened, the Old Testament prophesied Judas's role in the betrayal of Jesus. Psalm 41:9 says, "Even my close friend in whom I trusted, who ate my bread, has lifted up his heel against me." Jesus told the apostles in the upper room that that prophecy would be fulfilled in His own betrayal (John 13:18). Psalm 55:12–14 also refers to Judas's betrayal:

> For it is not an enemy who reproaches me, then I could bear it; nor is it one who hates me who has exalted himself against me, then I could hide myself from him. But it is you, a man my equal, my companion and my familiar friend; we who had sweet fellowship together walked in the house of God in the throng.

Zechariah 11:12–13 predicted the exact amount Judas would receive for betraying Jesus:

> I said to them, "If it is good in your sight, give me my wages; but if not, never mind!" So they weighed out thirty shekels of silver as my wages. Then the Lord said to me, "Throw it to the potter, that magnificent price at which I was valued by them." So I took the thirty shekels of silver and threw them to the potter in the house of the Lord.

Matthew's gospel cites that passage as a prophecy of Judas's betrayal of Christ (27:9–10). Thus long before Judas was born, his treachery was foreseen and designed into God's eternal plan. Jesus knew exactly the kind of man Judas was from the outset. But He chose him so that the divine plan revealed in the Old Testament prophecies would be fulfilled.

But on the other hand Judas freely chose to do what he did, and was fully accountable for his actions. That his betrayal was predetermined in no way contradicts the truth that he acted of his own volition. Jesus affirmed both realities when he said in Luke 22:22, "For indeed, the Son of Man is going as it has been determined [God's sovereignty]; but woe to that man by whom He is betrayed [Judas's responsibility]!" Peter expressed the tension between God's plan and human choice as they relate to Christ's death in his sermon on the Day of Pentecost: "This Man [Jesus], delivered over by the predetermined plan and foreknowledge of God, you nailed to a cross by the hands of godless men and put Him to death" (Acts 2:23). As He did with the others involved in Christ's death, the sovereign God, "who works all things after the counsel of His will" (Eph. 1:11), used the evil plans of Judas's wicked heart to bring about the good of redemption (cf. Gen. 50:20).

Judas had every opportunity to turn from his sin. Much of Christ's teaching applied directly to him, such as the parables of the unjust steward (Luke 16:1–13) and the wedding garment (Matt. 22:11–14), and Jesus' warnings against the love of money (Matt. 6:19–34), greed (Luke 12:13–21), and pride (Matt. 23:1–12). Judas was present when the Lord said to the Twelve, "Did I Myself not choose you, the twelve, and yet one of you is a devil?" (John 6:70). Just hours before his betrayal, Judas heard Jesus declare that not all the disciples were spiritually cleansed (John 13:18). But all of that left Judas unmoved. He determinedly hardened his heart and refused to repent, and went to that eternal hell where he belonged. Acts 1:25 calls it "his own place." There is an instructive parallel to this combination of divine decree and human will in Isaiah 10:5ff., where God prophecies that He will use Assyria as His rod of judgment on Israel, though Assyria has no intention of serving Jehovah. When Assyria has worked that decreed judgment, He will turn on her and destroy her for the very pride that motivated her to assault Israel.

His Disillusionment

Judas's initial excitement over being chosen as one of Christ's twelve most intimate followers did not last. At first, as noted above, all of the Twelve had shared the common Jewish belief and hope that the Messiah would be a political and military deliverer. The other eleven apostles eventually learned that Jesus had not come as the Lion of the tribe of Judah (Rev. 5:5), but as the suffering servant of Isaiah 53. But as that became evident, Judas grew disillusioned; his disillusionment turned to hatred; and that hatred motivated Judas's treachery. John's gospel records Judas's downward spiral to ultimate disaster.

John 12 opens with Jesus and the Twelve in Bethany on the Saturday before Passover (v. 1). While they were at a supper in the home of Simon the leper (Matt. 26:6), "Mary [the sister of Martha] then took a pound of very costly perfume of pure nard, and anointed the feet of Jesus and wiped His feet with her hair; and the house was filled with the fragrance of the perfume" (v. 3). This was an extravagant act of unrestrained love on the part of Mary, since the perfume was extremely expensive, and must have shocked those present.

Sputtering in outrage over what he considered to be a colossal waste of money, Judas demanded, "Why was this perfume not sold for three hundred denarii [a year's wages for an average laborer] and given to poor people?" (v. 5). But Judas's philanthropic concerns were merely a mask for his greed. "Now he said this," John explained, "not because he was concerned about the poor, but because he was a thief, and as he had the money box, he used to pilfer what was put into it" (v. 6). To see such a large sum of money elude his grasp after years of disappointed hope infuriated Judas, and he lashed out at Mary. So convincing was his pious display of concern for the needy that others present echoed his protest (Matt. 26:8–9; Mark 14:4–5). But the Lord came to Mary's defense. "Let her alone," He commanded Judas (the verb translated "let alone" is in the second person singular) "so that she may keep it for the day of My burial" (v. 7). In verse 8 the Lord reminded them all (the verbs and pronouns in this verse are plurals) that if they wanted to help the poor they would not lack opportunity since, He told them, "You always have the poor with you, but you do not always have Me." But Mary had chosen to save the perfume for this special occasion instead of selling it and giving the proceeds to the poor.

Judas was now at a crossroads. His avarice and greed had been unmasked by Jesus, and he could have humbly repented, confessed his sin, and sought forgiveness. But the pride, greed, and disillusionment that controlled his heart won out. Desperate to salvage something financially for the wasted years he had spent following Jesus, "Judas Iscariot, who was one of the twelve, went off to the chief priests in order to betray Him to them. They were glad when they heard this, and promised to give him money. And he began seeking how to betray Him at an opportune time" (Mark 14:10–11).

That "opportune time" came on the following Thursday evening. Jesus and the Twelve had gathered in the upper room for their final Passover meal together. After giving the disciples a remarkable example of humility by washing their feet, the Lord affirmed to them that by faith in Him they had been made spiritually clean—except for the one who would betray Him (John 13:10–11, 18). The prophecy of Psalm 41:9 would be fulfilled that very evening. "Truly, truly, I say to you," Jesus solemnly told them, "that one of you will betray Me" (v. 21). Appalled, "the disciples began looking at one another, at a loss to know of which one He was speaking" (v. 22). As noted earlier Judas, the consummate hypocrite, had so completely fooled the other apostles that no one suspected him. Jesus designated Judas as the betrayer by dipping the morsel (a piece of unleavened bread) into the common mixture of bitter herbs, water, salt, crushed dates, figs, and raisins, and handing it to him (v. 26). To be given the morsel by the host was a special honor; thus, the Lord showed kindness and compassion toward Judas to the very end.

But Judas spurned this final gesture of love from Jesus, as he had all the previous ones over the previous three years. With this ultimate rejection, the day of salvation closed for him (cf. 2 Cor. 6:2) and divine mercy faded and was replaced with divine judgment. Judas was in essence handed over to Satan (cf. 1 Tim. 1:20), who entered into him (v. 27). Having irrevocably crossed the line and sealed his eternal doom, Judas was dismissed by the Lord to carry out his wicked plot (v. 27).

His Betrayal

After leaving the upper room, Judas evidently went straight to the Sanhedrin to set his evil plans in motion. He informed them of the final, irreparable breach between himself and Jesus. More significantly, he told them that Jesus would be in Gethsemane later that evening (cf. Luke 22:39; John 18:2)—a secluded place where they could seize Jesus without fear of provoking a riot (cf. Matt. 26:3–5; Luke 22:6).

Judas did not betray Jesus in a moment of passion; he could not have pleaded temporary insanity. How long he had plotted in his wretched heart to betray the Savior is not revealed. But he had made his bargain with the Jewish leaders almost a week earlier, and had been looking for an opportunity to deliver Him into their hands ever since (Luke 22:6). His evil act was thus fully premeditated.

Judas next appears in John's narrative at the head of the large contingent of Roman soldiers and Jewish officials that arrived at Gethsemane to arrest Jesus. The Lord did not attempt to hide or escape, nor did He wait for Judas to single Him out. Completely in control of the situation, He went to meet the arresting party and calmly asked them who they were seeking (John 18:4). After they replied, "Jesus the Nazarene" (v. 5), Jesus identified Himself using the divine name "I am" (cf. Ex. 3:14). In response the entire detachment—including Judas—was slammed to the ground (vv. 5–6). Incredibly, despite that stunning display of Christ's divine power, Judas proceeded with his diabolical plan. Using the prearranged signal (Matt. 26:48), Judas brazenly "went to Jesus and said, 'Hail, Rabbi!' and kissed Him" (v. 49). To betray the Son of Man with a kiss of affection was the last act of Judas's devious hypocrisy; it was a cynical attempt to feign innocence and conceal his treachery. Judas used the symbol of love, respect, and homage to attempt to mask the evil in his heart. He profaned the Passover, Gethsemane, where Jesus had poured out His heart to the Father and been ministered to by an angel (Luke 22:41–44), and most of all the sinless Son of God.

The monumental sin of betraying Jesus produced unbearable guilt. Judas's conscience immediately came alive and began tormenting him. He was overwhelmed with remorse (but not genuine repentance). In a desperate but faithless and futile bid to gain relief from his tormenting conscience, he attempted to return to the Jewish leaders the paltry sum (thirty pieces of silver; the price of a slave [Ex. 21:32]) he had received from them (Matt. 27:3). Judas had been a useful tool to them, but now that they had Jesus in custody, the Jewish authorities had no further use for him. They contemptuously dismissed him, callously responding to his plaintive cry, "I have sinned by betraying innocent blood" by telling him, "What is that to us? See to that yourself!" (v. 4).

This was the end of the line for Judas. After throwing the thirty pieces of silver into the temple sanctuary, he went out and hanged himself (v. 5). In a fitting end to the tragic story of his life, he could not even do that successfully. Either the knot came undone, or the rope or the branch to which it was tied broke, and Judas plunged to his death in a gory fashion (Acts 1:18). Acts 1:25 records the chilling epitaph to the life of Judas, noting that that son of perdition (John 17:12), went to his own place—hell (Acts 1:25). In that place of unspeakable torment, his guilt-ridden conscience will refuse to be silenced for all eternity. Truly, as Jesus declared of him, "It would have been good for that man if he had not been born" (Mark 14:21).

Several compelling lessons may be drawn from the life of Judas:

First, Judas is history's greatest example of lost opportunity and wasted privilege. He heard Jesus teach day in and day out, and he personally interacted with Him. He saw firsthand the miracles Jesus performed, which proved that He was God in human flesh. But Judas refused Christ's invitation to exchange the oppressive burden of sin for the easy yoke of submission to Him (Matt. 11:28–30).

Second, Judas is the foremost illustration of the danger of loving money (1 Tim. 6:10). Riches meant more to him than the salvation of his soul (cf. Mark 8:36).

Third, Judas exemplifies the vileness and danger of spiritual betrayal. In every age there have been Judases, who professed to follow Christ but turned against Him. Judas's life is also a sobering reminder of the need for self-examination (2 Cor. 13:5).

Fourth, Judas was living proof of Christ's patience, mercy, and loving-kindness. Even when he arrived with the detachment to arrest Him, Jesus still courteously addressed Judas as "friend" (Matt. 26:50).

Fifth, the example of Judas is a sobering reminder that the devil will always be at work in the midst of God's people. Jesus illustrated that truth in the parable of the wheat and the tares (Matt. 13:24–30, 36–43).

Sixth, Judas proves the deadliness of hypocrisy. He was a fruitless branch, cut off and cast into the eternal fire of hell (John 15:6).

Finally, Judas demonstrated that there is nothing sinful men can do to thwart the sovereign will of God. Out of the seeming tragedy of the cross came the triumph of redemption; Satan's apparent victory was in reality his ultimate defeat (Heb. 2:14; 1 John 3:8; cf. Gen. 3:15). God used Judas's treachery for His own glory (cf. Gen. 50:20).

When Judas sold Jesus to His enemies, he was in effect selling his own soul to the devil. In the words of the nineteenth-century poet Hester H. Cholmondeley,

> Still as of old
> Men by themselves are priced—
> For thirty pieces Judas sold
> Himself, not Christ.

The Popularity and Power of Jesus
(Luke 6:17–19)

Jesus came down with them and stood on a level place; and there was a large crowd of His disciples, and a great throng of people from all Judea and Jerusalem and the coastal region of Tyre and Sidon, who had come to hear Him and to be healed of their diseases; and those who were troubled with unclean spirits were being cured. And all the people were trying to touch Him, for power was coming from Him and healing them all. (6:17–19)

The Bible is a priceless gem with many facets. Scripture is the law of the Lord, which is perfect, the testimony of the Lord, which is sure, the precepts of the Lord, which are right, the commandments of the Lord, which are pure, and the judgments of the Lord, which are true. The Word of God restores the soul, gives wisdom, produces joy, is the source of spiritual truth, instructs in worship, and warns against sin (Ps. 19:7–11).

The Bible's many-faceted divine truth reflects one unifying theme —the plan of redemption. God has chosen for His own glory to elect and redeem a people to be the objects of His love, subjects of His eternal kingdom, and the everlasting worshipers who offer perfect praise, honor, and service to Him forever. The Bible details that plan of redemption from its inception in eternity past to its consummation in eternity future. From predestination to justification through sanctification to glorification the Bible is the story of the outworking of God's gracious plan of salvation.

As that saving purpose unfolds through redemptive history, several recurring themes are revealed throughout both the Old and New Testaments.

First and foremost, Scripture is God's self-revelation of His character and deeds. He is the sovereign, creator, and ruler of the universe, who chose to make the human race and to reveal Himself to mankind. The Old Testament records that God unveiled Himself through the created universe (Ps. 19:1; especially man, who was created in His image [Gen. 1:26–27; cf. Ps. 139:13–14]), the work of angels (Heb. 2:2), signs, supernatural wonders (Deut. 6:22; Neh. 9:10), and visions (Gen. 15:1; 46:2; Isa. 1:1; Ezek. 1:1; Hos. 12:10), as well as through the prophets (2 Kings 17:13; Jer. 7:25; Dan. 9:6; cf. Heb. 1:1).

In the New Testament God also spoke through angels (Matt. 1:20; 28:5; Luke 1:11–20, 26–38; 2:9–12; Acts 5:19–20; 8:26; 10:3–7; 27:23–24; Rev. 1:1), signs, wonders, and miracles (Heb. 2:3–4), visions (Acts 9:10–16; 18:9; 26:12–19), the words of apostles (Acts 2:42; Eph. 3:4–5) and prophets (Acts 11:27–28; 21:10–11. But supremely, God has spoken in His Son, the Lord Jesus Christ (Heb. 1:2).

Scripture reveals secondly that God judges sin and disobedience. Only four of the Bible's 1,189 chapters—the first two, which take place before the fall (Gen. 1, 2) and the last two, which take place after the creation of the new heaven and the new earth (Rev. 21, 22)—do not occur in the context of a fallen, sin-cursed world. The disastrous consequences of sin began with Adam and Eve's expulsion from the Garden of Eden after the fall, and continued through Cain's murder of Abel, to the universal wickedness of the human race that brought the worldwide flood of Noah's day, the dark days of the judges, and the rebellion and idolatry of God's people that resulted in the destruction and deportation first of Israel, and then of Judah.

The New Testament also continues the saga of sin and its tragic results. The preaching of John the Baptist, the Lord Jesus Christ, and the apostles featured a call for repentance (Matt. 4:17; Mark 6:12; Luke 5:32; 13:1–5; 24:47; Acts 2:38; 3:19; 5:31; 17:30; 20:21; 26:20; 2 Peter 3:9). But the Jewish people and the Gentiles rejected the call and murdered the messengers. Their disobedience was even more flagrant than that in the Old Testament, because it was committed in the clearer light of New Testament truth.

A third feature in Scripture is the divine blessing for faith and obedience. Those who recognize their inability to keep God's holy law, acknowledge and repent of their sin, and ask God for forgiveness through the work of Christ, based solely on His grace and mercy, receive redemption and blessing, both for time and eternity. The heroes of faith in the Old Testament, from Abel through the patriarchs, to the believing remnant of Israel, and even Gentiles (such as those in Nineveh who repented under the preaching of Jonah) were the recipients of God's grace, mercy, and forgiveness because they repented of sin and entrusted themselves to God who gives mercy and grace to those who turn to Him in faith. The New Testament proclaims the saving gospel of the Lord Jesus Christ, which is "the power of God for salvation to everyone who believes, to the Jew first and also to the Greek" (Rom. 1:16).

Above all those wondrous realities is the overarching glory of both the Old and New Testaments—the Lord Jesus Christ. He is the one of whom "all the prophets bear witness that through His name everyone who believes in Him receives forgiveness of sins" (Acts 10:43). Therefore "the testimony of Jesus is the spirit of prophecy" (Rev. 19:10), and as the Lord declared, the Scriptures testify about Him (John 5:39; cf. Luke 24:27, 44).

In the Old Testament Jesus is the promised seed of the woman, who would crush the head of Satan (Gen. 3:15); the true sacrifice for sin to which the Old Testament sacrifices pointed (Heb. 9:11–28); the final Passover Lamb whom all the others foreshadowed (1 Cor. 5:7; cf. Ex. 12:3–11); the ark of safety, a refuge from the storms of judgment for all who are His (1 Peter 3:20–21; cf. Gen. 7:13–24); the Lion of the tribe of Judah (Rev. 5:5), who will destroy His enemies (Ps. 2:8–9) and reign forever (Luke 1:31–33); David's greater Son, who will sit on his throne (Luke 1:32), and yet David's Lord (Luke 20:41–44). His rule will encompass both an earthly millennial kingdom and an eternal kingdom of righteousness and salvation, and embrace Israel (Isa. 65:17–19; Zeph. 3:11–20), as well as the rest of humanity (cf. Dan. 7:14, 27; Zech. 14:16–21).

In the New Testament the Gospels record Jesus' virgin birth, perfectly righteous life, sacrificial and substitutionary death, bodily resurrection, and ascension to the Father's right hand. Acts records the spread of the good news of salvation in Christ and its impact on the world. The New Testament epistles explain the meaning and significance of the Savior's life, death, and resurrection. Revelation, the consummation of history, describes His return to judge the ungodly, reward the righteous, rule the earth for a thousand years, and then create the eternal new heaven and new earth.

In keeping with the centrality of the Lord Jesus Christ in Scripture, Luke carefully, systematically presents the story of His life and ministry, providing irrefutable proof that He is God the Son, the Lord, Messiah, and Savior. So far he has given the testimonies of angels (1:11–17, 26–33; 2:9–14), Zacharias (1:76–79), Elizabeth (1:41–45), Mary (1:46–55), the shepherds (2:15–20), Simeon (2:25–35), Anna (2:36–38), Jesus Himself at the age of twelve (2:49), the Father and the Spirit at His baptism (3:21–22), John the Baptist—the last and greatest of the Old Testament prophets (3:15–17), Jesus' genealogy (3:23–38), the fulfillment of Old Testament prophecy concerning Him (4:16–21), the singular and divine character of His authoritative preaching (4:32), His power over Satan (4:1–13), demons (4:33–36, 41), disease (4:38–40; 5:12–15, 17–25; 6:10), and the natural world (5:4–9), His authority to forgive sin (5:20–25), and His divine sovereignty over the Sabbath, the core of Israel's works system (6:1–11). Luke's inspired account has built a masterful case that Jesus was indeed God in human flesh, the Messiah and Lord.

Occasionally in his careful account of the Lord's life and ministry, Luke freezes the action into a still photo. This passage is the fourth such summary so far in his gospel (along with 4:14–15, 31–32, 40–41), and provides a rich recap of the Lord's ministry up to this point. As the video temporarily pauses, the ensuing snapshot reveals two important aspects of Christ's ministry: His popularity, and His power.

THE POPULARITY OF JESUS

Jesus came down with them and stood on a level place; and there was a large crowd of His disciples, and a great throng of people from all Judea and Jerusalem and the coastal region of Tyre and Sidon, (6:17)

By this point in His ministry, Jesus had become enormously popular, far more than anyone else in Israel had ever been. Huge crowds followed Him wherever He went (cf. 4:42; 5:15); a later crowd would number five thousand men (9:14). Including the women and children, there were likely more than twenty thousand people present on that occasion. Matthew and Mark record another crowd of similar size (Matt. 15:38; Mark 8:9), while Luke describes another incident where "so many thousands of people had gathered together that they were stepping on one another" (12:1).

Luke sorts the people present on this occasion into three groups. First were the newly appointed twelve apostles. After spending the night in prayer and choosing them (6:12–16), **Jesus came down with the** Twelve **and stood on a level place.** As will be discussed in chapter 10 of this volume, the sermon Jesus was about to preach in verses 20 to 49 is Luke's condensed version of the Sermon on the Mount (cf. Matt. 5–7). The **level place** was therefore not a plain, but rather a plateau on the side of the mountain mentioned in Matthew 5:1. Some identify the location with a plateau near Capernaum. Jesus, like the rabbis, customarily sat down when He taught (4:20; 5:3; Matt. 5:1; 13:2; John 8:2); He **stood** at this time because He was not yet teaching, but was healing those who were sick and casting out demons (v. 18).

The second group consisted of **a large crowd of His disciples.** The apostles were the messengers chosen by the Lord to preach the gospel. They were just beginning their formal training as the first genera-tion of gospel heralds. The **disciples**, on the other hand, were an assort-ment of people who were regular followers of Jesus. They were at various levels of understanding and commitment, but all considered Jesus to be their teacher. Some, as time would prove, were genuine followers; most, it seems, were not and would eventually desert Him (cf. John 6:66). A con-sistent pattern of obedience to Christ's word (John 8:31) distinguishes the wheat (true disciples) from the tares (false disciples), as the Lord's parable indicates (Matt. 13:24–30). Jesus in His divine omniscience knew who were the real disciples, and who were not (John 2:23–25; 6:64). The genuine were few (cf. Matt. 7:14).

The final group were the ever-present curious, whom Luke described as **a great throng of people.** Luke sometimes used *laos* (**peo-ple**) to refer to God's people (e.g., 1:68, 77; 2:32). But more often the term refers to those who were inquisitive, but uncommitted (e.g., 7:1, 29; 8:47; 9:13; 18:43; 19:48; 20:1; 21:38; 23:35). Luke distinguished them from Jesus' disciples, who had at least a nominal commitment to following Him. The large crowd was **from all Judea** (used here in a non-technical sense to refer to all of Israel, not just the southern region), including **Jerusalem**, the religious and cultural center of the nation. Some of those from Jerusalem were members of the religious establishment spying on Him (cf. 5:17).

In addition to those from Israel, this last group also included peo-ple from the **coastal region of Tyre and Sidon.** Those two cities were the most important ones in Phoenicia (cf. Jer. 47:4; Joel 3:4; Matt. 11:21–22; Acts 12:20), the region north and west of Galilee on the Mediterranean Sea, in modern day Lebanon. Phoenicia was a predomi-nantly Gentile area, but some Jews also lived there. **Tyre** and **Sidon** had been significant seaports in Old Testament times, until they were destroyed by the devastating judgment prophesied in Ezekiel 26–28. Their sordid immorality made the two cities emblematic of pagan reli-gion. Jesus' appeal knew no bounds; pagans, common people, and the religiously literate were all drawn to Him. And later He made a visit to the region of Tyre and Sidon (Mark 7:24–31).

THE POWER OF JESUS

who had come to hear Him and to be healed of their diseases; and those who were troubled with unclean spirits were being

cured. And all the people were trying to touch Him, for power was coming from Him and healing them all. (6:18–19)

The popularity of Jesus was largely the result of His power, displayed in three dimensions.

In the mental realm, Jesus' power found expression in His unprecedented teaching, which the people **had come to hear.** At the end of the sermon He was about to preach, "the crowds were amazed at His teaching; for He was teaching them as one having authority, and not as their scribes" (Matt. 7:28–29). When the chief priests and Pharisees demanded to know why the officers they had sent to arrest Jesus (John 7:32) had returned empty-handed, they replied, "Never has a man spoken the way this man speaks" (v. 46).

Unparalleled teaching, bringing the good news of salvation, eternal life, hope, peace, and joy to the minds of His hearers, was the preeminent aspect of the Lord's ministry. Miracles corroborated His claim to be the Son of God and verified that He taught the truth, but they could not save anyone (cf. John 12:37). Everywhere He went the Lord preached the good news that God would forgive those who are spiritually destitute, blind, oppressed, and held captive in sin's grip (cf. Luke 4:18) if they repented (Matt. 4:17). His mental agility, clarity, force, and depth were without parallel, and salvation came to those who heard His message and embraced the truth.

Jesus' words remain equally authoritative today. As Paul wrote to Timothy, "If anyone advocates a different doctrine and does not agree with sound words, those of our Lord Jesus Christ, and with the doctrine conforming to godliness, he is conceited and understands nothing" (1 Tim. 6:3–4). Pastors and teachers merely pass on the truths that He taught.

Jesus also demonstrated power over the physical realm; He not only had power over the mind, but also over the body. To verify that He spoke the truth, and to show His compassion, the Lord **healed** those who were sick **of their diseases** (cf. 4:38–39; 5:17–25; 6:6–10). Unlike modern perverse and selective phony faith healers, He cured **all the people** who **were trying to touch Him, for power was coming from Him and healing them all.** Further, His healings were miracles that required creative power; He created functioning eyes and ears in giving sight to the blind, hearing to the deaf, and the ability to speak to the mute, full function to crippled limbs, healing of incurable illnesses, such as leprosy, and raising the dead required creative power (Luke 7:22).

Finally Luke, in saying that **those who were troubled with unclean spirits were being cured,** shows Jesus' power over the world of spiritual beings. By casting out demons, Jesus demonstrated His absolute authority over the domain of Satan (cf. 4:33–35, 41). The Lord answered those who strangely and blasphemously accused Him of cast-ing out demons by the power of Satan by pointing out His obvious supremacy over him:

> If I cast out demons by the finger of God, then the kingdom of God has come upon you. When a strong man, fully armed, guards his own house, his possessions are undisturbed. But when someone stronger than he attacks him and overpowers him, he takes away from him all his armor on which he had relied and distributes his plunder. (11:20–22)

Jesus' power was comprehensive. He was able to minister to the mind by teaching the truth, the body by healing diseases, and the soul by casting out demons.

Several significant truths emerge from this brief, but important passage. First and foremost, Jesus' unparalleled teaching, miraculous power to heal, and absolute control of the realm of Satan and his demon hosts prove conclusively that He is God.

Second, the Lord of heaven's earthly ministry provides a preview of heaven. In that place of supreme joy and bliss, the redeemed will see God face-to-face and know Him to the fullest extent to which finite beings are capable (1 Cor. 13:12). All disease, disabilities, death, suffering, sorrow, and pain will be forever banished (Isa. 25:8; Rev. 21:4). Satan and the demons will be permanently incarcerated in hell (Matt. 25:41; Rev. 20:10), and no longer able to afflict or tempt God's people.

Third, the way Jesus manifested His power revealed His compas-sion. He could have demonstrated His divine power by performing any kind of miraculous act. But Jesus chose to do things beneficial to suffer-ing, oppressed sinners. His compassion was a constant theme of His min-istry. Matthew 9:36 notes that Jesus "felt compassion for [the people], because they were distressed and dispirited like sheep without a shep-herd." On another occasion, "He saw a large crowd, and felt compassion for them and healed their sick" (Matt. 14:14). When He encountered two blind men, Jesus was "moved with compassion [and] touched their eyes; and immediately they regained their sight and followed Him" (Matt. 20:34). When "a leper came to Jesus, beseeching Him and falling on his knees before Him, and saying, 'If You are willing, You can make me clean'" (Mark 1:40), Jesus once again was "moved with compassion [and] stretched out His hand and touched him, and said to him, 'I am willing; be cleansed'" (v. 41). Jesus halted a funeral procession for a widow's only son and raised him from the dead because "He felt compassion for her" (Luke 7:13).

This passage presents the Lord Jesus Christ as the compassionate and triumphant teacher, healer, and deliverer. Clearly divine, He deserves honor, worship, and obedience. And it is the responsibility of all who are His to go beyond mere curiosity, or even discipleship, and be messengers, taking the truth about Him to the lost world that so desperately needs to hear it (Matt. 28:18–20; Acts 1:8).

The Character of a True Christian
(Luke 6:20–26)

10

And turning His gaze toward His disciples, He began to say, "Blessed are you who are poor, for yours is the kingdom of God. Blessed are you who hunger now, for you shall be satisfied. Blessed are you who weep now, for you shall laugh. Blessed are you when men hate you, and ostracize you, and insult you, and scorn your name as evil, for the sake of the Son of Man. Be glad in that day and leap for joy, for behold, your reward is great in heaven. For in the same way their fathers used to treat the prophets. But woe to you who are rich, for you are receiving your comfort in full. Woe to you who are well-fed now, for you shall be hungry. Woe to you who laugh now, for you shall mourn and weep. Woe to you when all men speak well of you, for their fathers used to treat the false prophets in the same way." (6:20–26)

In his recounting of the magnificent story of the life and ministry of the Lord Jesus Christ, Luke amasses irrefutable evidence that He is the Messiah, God in human flesh, the Savior of the world. Of the many proofs Luke has presented so far (see the list in the previous chapter of this volume), none is more compelling than Christ's teaching. He was the most truthful, wise, and powerful preacher ever and His teaching consequently

91

drew massive crowds who were amazed and astonished by what they heard (cf.Matt.7:28–29;John 7:31–32,45–46).

Jesus spoke the truth with absolute divine authority on a wide spectrum of doctrinal and practical topics.He taught that God is creator (Matt. 19:4; Mark 10:6; 13:19), king (Matt. 5:35), father (Matt. 5:16; 23:9), and sovereign ruler of heaven and earth (Matt. 11:25; cf. 6:9–10). He is holy (John 17:11),merciful (Luke 6:36),gracious (Ps.103:8,even to unbelievers [Matt. 5:45]), perfectly righteous (Matt. 5:48; John 17:25), omniscient (Matt.6:8),and loving (John 14:21,23;16:27).

In His teaching concerning Himself,Jesus clearly,unequivocally, and emphatically declared His deity and absolute equality with the Father.The apostle John wrote that"the Jews were seeking all the more to kill Him,because He not only was breaking the Sabbath, but also was calling God His own Father,making Himself equal with God"(John 5:18). Jesus declared to the hostile Jewish leaders, "Truly, truly, I say to you, before Abraham was born,I am"(John 8:58),taking for Himself the name "I AM"by which God revealed Himself in the Old Testament (Ex.3:14). He again affirmed His deity in John 10:30 when He said to the Jews,"I and the Father are one." Unlike modern cultists, the unbelieving Jews understood clearly that Jesus was claiming to be God;that was why they sought to kill Him (John 5:18; 8:59; 10:31–33). If, as some skeptics say, they had misunderstood Him,Jesus' failure to clarify what He really meant is inexplicable—particularly when failing to do so cost Him His life (John 19:7).

Reinforcing His claim to deity, Jesus taught that He had come from heaven (John 3:13;6:38,51,62; 13:3; 16:28),sent by the Father (John 5:36–37) to do His will (John 6:38).He also claimed authority to forgive sins,a prerogative that belongs to God alone (Luke 5:20–24),and that He in fact possessed"all authority…in heaven and on earth"(Matt.28:18).

Jesus predicted His death and resurrection (Matt. 17:22–23; 20:18–19;Mark 8:31; John 2:19–21),and taught that His death would be the atoning sacrifice for sin (Matt.26:28;John 10:11,15) that would provide salvation (Luke 19:10; cf.5:31–32;Matt.20:28) for all who believe in Him (John 3:14–18). Jesus also taught that He will one day return in glory (Matt.24:27) to judge the wicked and establish His kingdom (Matt. 16:27;25:31–46).

The Holy Spirit,according to Jesus' teaching,is the third member of the Trinity,and hence God (Matt.28:19).Blaspheming Him by rejecting His testimony to Christ is the unforgivable sin (Matt. 12:32). The Spirit brings people to salvation through the new birth (John 3:5–8),indwells and empowers believers (Luke 24:49; John 7:38–39; 14:16–17; 16:7), inspired the writers of Scripture (Mark 12:36;John 14:26;16:13),and convicts the unbelieving world (John 16:7–11).

Jesus taught that mankind was created by God (Matt. 19:4). He spoke of God's providential care for humanity in general (Matt. 5:45) and His children in particular (Matt. 6:24–34; 10:28–31). But mankind is in a state of rebellion against God. The unregenerate are hard-hearted rebels (Matt. 19:8), who refuse to obey the Son of God (John 3:36). They will not come to the light of God's truth because they are evil and love the darkness of sin (John 3:19), thus proving themselves to be children of the devil (John 8:44). Because of their rejection of the Lord and only Savior Jesus Christ, unrepentant sinners will be judged (John 5:29; 12:48) and sentenced to eternal hell (Matt. 25:41; Mark 9:43–48).

The Lord presented Himself as the only way to God (John 14:6; cf. 10:7–9). He claimed to be the bread of life (John 6:35, 51), the good shepherd, who lays down His life for the sheep (John 10:11), the light of the world (John 8:12; 12:46), and the resurrection and the life (John 11:25). The Father sovereignly draws to Christ (John 6:37, 39, 44) those who will be saved through repentance (Mark 1:15; Luke 5:32; 13:3, 5; 24:47) and faith in the Son (John 1:12; 3:14–18, 36; 5:24; 6:40). They will receive eternal life (John 3:15–16) and spend eternity in heaven (John 14:2–3).

Foundational to all of Jesus' teaching was His commitment to the absolute authority of Scripture. As the inspired word of God (Matt. 15:3–6), the Scripture cannot be broken (John 10:35). In fact, it would be easier for heaven and earth to pass away than for any part of God's law to be altered (Matt. 5:18). Scripture is the rule of life (Matt. 4:4), and those who obey it are blessed (Luke 11:28).

The teaching of the Lord Jesus Christ is diametrically opposed to human thinking. Most of the Jewish people, particularly the religious leaders, found it repugnant, offensive, and threatening. In their minds it was so wrong that it had to have been satanic (cf. Mark 3:22). Then and now, the Lord's teaching shatters popular worldviews. It challenges men's motives, turns their world upside down, and stands their thinking on its head. It makes no attempt at political correctness and ignores conventional wisdom.

The Beatitudes recorded in this passage are a prime example. From the human perspective, it seems foolish to say that poverty, hunger, sorrow, and rejection are the producers of blessings, and riches, satisfaction, happiness, and honor. But as God incarnate, Jesus authoritatively defines who is blessed and who is cursed. What He said on this occasion and throughout His ministry demanded a paradigm shift of monumental proportions. Sadly the Jewish people, especially the religious leaders, refused to think outside the narrow box of first-century Judaism. To this day the world, like them, continues to reject Christ's message.

As noted in the previous chapter of this volume, the crowd that gathered to hear the Lord preach this sermon consisted of three groups: the apostles, the uncommitted, curious crowd, and the disciples. Luke's note that as He began to preach Jesus turned **His gaze toward His disciples** indicates that the Sermon on the Mount is directed primarily at them (although the woes were addressed to the crowd in general). The disciples were at various levels of commitment and understanding, but they followed Jesus and considered Him their teacher.

Despite the claims of some, the Sermon on the Mount is not a statement of ethics, but a sermon on salvation. Trying to apply the principles in this sermon apart from regeneration is futile. Since He came "to seek and to save that which was lost" (Luke 19:10), salvation was central to the Lord's teaching. At the outset of His public ministry "Jesus began to preach and say, 'Repent, for the kingdom of heaven is at hand'" (Matt. 4:17). He taught that people are sinners, lacking the power and resources to deliver themselves, and thus are slaves to sin (John 8:34). The only way to escape divine judgment (cf. Luke 13:1–5) is through repentant faith in the Son of God (John 3:16–18, 36; 5:24; cf. Luke 18:13–14). It is not outwardly religious, superficially moral people who are saved, but rather people overwhelmed with their sinfulness, who cry out to God for forgiveness and mercy.

Jesus' message shocked and outraged the self-righteous religious people of Israel. This was not what they expected from their Messiah. They imagined that He would be pleased with their righteousness and religious ritual, and welcome them into the kingdom. Instead, Jesus scathingly denounced them as hypocrites (Matt. 23:1–33), and compared them unfavorably to the despised outcasts of Jewish society (Matt. 21:31–32). His message was unacceptable and intolerable, leading His nation to reject and murder Him.

Luke presents a condensed account of the Sermon on the Mount, which Matthew 5–7 recorded in more detail. However, neither gospel writer recorded everything Jesus said on this occasion. (Although the Lord undoubtedly repeated the themes of this sermon throughout His ministry, the Sermon on the Mount is one continuous message, preached on one occasion, and not a collection of Jesus' sayings.) Even Matthew's longer account can be read in about ten minutes, and the Lord surely preached much longer than that. There are minor variations in Matthew's and Luke's accounts, but those are to be expected in the process of translating (the Lord spoke in Aramaic and Matthew and Luke wrote in Greek) and condensing Jesus' message. (For a defense of the view that Matthew and Luke recorded the same sermon, see William Hendriksen, *Exposition of the Gospel According to Luke*, New Testament Commentary [Grand Rapids: Baker, 1978], 334–35; D. A. Carson, *Matthew*, in Frank E. Gaebelein, ed. *The Expositor's Bible Commentary* (Grand Rapids: Zondervan, 1984), 8:125–26.)

Jesus closed this sermon by dividing those who hear (or read) it into two groups (see the exposition of vv. 47–49 in chapter 12 of this volume). He likened those who hear and obey His teaching to a man who builds a house on a solid foundation of rock. Such people are untouched by the storm of divine judgment (John 5:24). On the other hand, those who reject His teaching are like a man who built his house on sand. They will be swept away to damnation by the flood of divine judgment (John 3:36).

Jesus had the same two groups in view as He opened His message, describing them with the terms "blessed" and "woe." *Makarios* ("blessed") refers to those in the most beneficial, favored position, who experience the true well-being that comes from a right relationship with God. *Ouai* ("woe") refers to those in the worst, most unfavorable condition, who experience the calamity, disaster, and damnation reserved for the wicked. Everyone falls into one of those two categories; there is no middle ground.

The Lord's use of these terms was not a wish, nor was He merely praying for God's blessing or cursing on people. On the contrary, they are absolute statements of fact; divine verdicts rendered by God's authoritative judgment. The concept of divine blessing and cursing was well-known to Jesus' audience from the Old Testament (cf. Deut. 27, 28).

Luke's account of the Beatitudes reveals four blessings bestowed on the righteous, and four woes pronounced on the wicked. Each blessing has a promised benefit connected to it, while each woe has a corresponding promised threat. As noted above, the blessings and woes seem backwards from the perspective of self-righteous sinners. But the Lord's words paint His composite portrait of the blessed and the cursed.

THE BLESSED

"Blessed are you who are poor, for yours is the kingdom of God. Blessed are you who hunger now, for you shall be satisfied. Blessed are you who weep now, for you shall laugh. Blessed are you when men hate you, and ostracize you, and insult you, and scorn your name as evil, for the sake of the Son of Man. Be glad in that day and leap for joy, for behold, your reward is great in heaven. For in the same way their fathers used to treat the prophets." (6:20b–23)

The first characteristic of those who are **blessed** is that they are **poor.** *Ptōchos* (**poor**) derives from the verb *ptōssō*, which means, "to cringe and cower in fear." It describes those who are utterly destitute and entirely dependent on others for support. They are at the bottom rung of the social scale. Reduced to begging, they cower and cringe in begging humiliation. While the Bible commends helping those in need (e.g., Lev. 25:35; Deut. 15:7–8; Prov. 19:17; Isa. 58:6–7; Gal. 2:10), poverty itself is not a blessing. In fact, in Proverbs 30:8–9, a righteous man asked the Lord to preserve him from poverty so that he would not be tempted to steal and thus profane the name of the Lord.

But Jesus was not teaching that those who are materially and economically poor are thereby blessed. As Matthew's parallel account of this sermon indicates, the Lord was speaking of those who are "poor in spirit" (Matt. 5:3). The blessed are those who understand their spiritual poverty and the bankrupt condition of their soul, no matter how much or how little wealth they possess. They acknowledge that they are bankrupt in righteousness and have absolutely no spiritual resources with which to obtain God's favor, and that salvation cannot be by good works, morality, or religious rituals. They are like the repentant tax collector in Luke 18:13, who "was even unwilling to lift up his eyes to heaven, but was beating his breast, saying, 'God, be merciful to me, the sinner!'" (cf. Pss. 34:18; 51:17; Isa. 57:15; 66:2). Jesus described such people in Luke 4:18 as poor, captives, blind, and oppressed, and proclaimed the gospel of God's forgiveness, grace, and mercy to them.

Such an acknowledgment of spiritual deficiency was unthinkable to the proud, self-righteous people of Israel. They saw themselves as the spiritual elite, whose good works, religious observances, and Abrahamic ancestry had earned them entrance to God's kingdom. The Lord completely overturned that self-serving assessment. In reality, they were like the people in the Laodicean church, who said, "'I am rich, and have become wealthy, and have need of nothing,' and [did] not know that [they were] wretched and miserable and poor and blind and naked" (Rev. 3:17).

The promise to the spiritually destitute is that theirs **is the kingdom of God.** The present tense verb **is** indicates that more than just the future blessings of the earthly millennial kingdom are in view. Believers enjoy now the kingdom blessings of "righteousness and peace and joy in the Holy Spirit" (Rom. 14:17). They are "heirs of God and fellow heirs with Christ" (Rom. 8:17), and possessors of the the kingdom blessings of eternal life, grace, mercy, forgiveness, joy, hope, security, comfort, peace, love, and righteousness.

A second mark of the blessed is **hunger.** As Matthew 5:6 indicates, this hunger does not result from lack of food, but from lack of righteousness. It is an intense, deep, all-consuming longing for acceptance with God. The picture is of impoverished, starving spiritual beggars, longing for the righteousness that they cannot obtain on their own. The psalmist described this yearning for God when he wrote, "As the deer pants for the water brooks, so my soul pants for You, O God. My soul thirsts for God, for the living God; when shall I come and appear before God?" (Ps. 42:1–2). In a similar vein David wrote, "O God, You are my God; I shall seek You earnestly; my soul thirsts for You, my flesh yearns for You, in a dry and weary land where there is no water" (Ps. 63:1).

The blessing pronounced on the spiritually hungry is that they **shall be satisfied.** *Chortazō* (**satisfied**) literally refers to fattening animals, which will eat until they cannot eat any more. When used of humans, it means to eat one's fill, or to be completely satiated. Those who truly hunger for righteousness will be fully satisfied. Psalm 34:10 promises that "they who seek the Lord shall not be in want of any good thing." The most beloved of all Psalms opens, "The Lord is my shepherd, I shall not want" (Ps. 23:1). In Jeremiah 31:14 God declares, "My people will be satisfied with My goodness" (cf. Ps. 107:1–9; Isa. 25:6; Luke 12:37; 13:29).

The third Beatitude pictures the blessed as those **who weep now.** This is the emotional breakdown that follows recognition of spiritual bankruptcy and lack of righteousness. These mourners view themselves as the poor, prisoners, blind, and oppressed (cf. 4:18), and are burdened, disappointed, fearful, and hurting. Theirs is the sorrow of repentance, of which James wrote: "Be miserable and mourn and weep; let your laughter be turned into mourning and your joy to gloom. Humble yourselves in the presence of the Lord, and He will exalt you" (James 4:9–10). It is the "sorrow that is according to the will of God [which] produces a repentance without regret, leading to salvation" (2 Cor. 7:10).

Those who mourn will not only be comforted (Matt. 5:4), but will even **laugh,** expressing the joy, relief, and freedom of the forgiven. Psalm 30:5 promises, "Weeping may last for the night, but a shout of joy comes in the morning." In Jeremiah 31:13 God promises, "I will turn their mourning into joy and will comfort them and give them joy for their sorrow." At His second coming the Lord Jesus Christ will "comfort all who mourn ... in Zion, giving them a garland instead of ashes, the oil of gladness instead of mourning, the mantle of praise instead of a spirit of fainting" (Isa. 61:2–3; cf. 35:10; 51:3, 11).

The final Beatitude is perhaps the most paradoxical and, from the human perspective, most incomprehensible of all. The first three describe how the repentant sinner views himself; the fourth describes how the world sees him. The Lord used four verbs, **hate, ostracize, insult, and scorn** to sum up the vitriol, hostility, and animosity poured out on His disciples by the unbelieving world. This fourth Beatitude indicates that the work of the first three has been accomplished. Genuine salvation has occurred, and the disciples' changed lives are an evident rebuke to all. The world's hostile reaction to Christ's followers is evidence that they are among the blessed, since the world does not reject its own.

The underlying reason for sinners' hatred, ostracism, insults, and scornful denunciation of the **name** (Christian) that believers bear **as evil** is because of their association with **the Son of Man.** The Lord elaborated on that truth in His charge to the Twelve before sending them out to preach (Matt. 10:16–33). In verse 16 Jesus likened the opponents they would face to vicious wolves (cf. Matt. 7:15; Acts 20:29). He further cautioned the apostles that they would be severely punished in the courts and synagogues (cf. 2 Cor. 11:24), including being put out of the synagogue (John 9:22, 34; 16:2), and by rulers (Matt. 10:17–18). Families will be divided when some members identify with Christ (v. 21; cf. Luke 12:51–53). All of this hatred will be directed at believers because they name the name of the Lord Jesus Christ (vv. 22, 24–25), whom the unbelieving world hates (John 15:18–19; 16:33).

Jesus' prediction came to pass. The apostles faced persecution from the Jewish authorities (Acts 4:1–22; 5:17–40), as did the church as a whole (Acts 8:1, 3); Herod murdered James, the brother of John (Acts 12:1–2); Stephen was martyred (Acts 7:58–60); Paul's life amply fulfilled the Lord's words about him to Ananias, "I will show him how much he must suffer for My name's sake" (Acts 9:16; cf. 2 Cor. 11:22–33); and eventually, as noted in previous chapters of this volume, most of the apostles were martyred for their bold preaching of the gospel.

But instead of being fearful and despondent when persecution comes, Jesus commanded believers to **be glad in that day and leap for joy.** The phrase **in that day** indicates that persecution will not be the constant lot of believers, but will happen occasionally. Acts 2:47 describes a time when the church had "favor with all the people" (cf. 5:13), while 9:31 records another time when "the church throughout all Judea and Galilee and Samaria enjoyed peace, being built up; and going on in the fear of the Lord and in the comfort of the Holy Spirit, it continued to increase." Peter informed his readers that trials last "a little while," and only happen "if necessary" (1 Peter 1:6).

When they do face the world's hostility, believers are to regard it as a time to be **glad,** to be completely carried away to the point that they even **leap for joy.** The reason for such exuberance on the part of persecuted believers is twofold. First, they rejoice because they know that their **reward is great in heaven.** To properly handle trials and opposition, Christians must have an otherworldly perspective. They must keep in mind, as Paul wrote to the Corinthians, that "momentary, light affliction is producing for us an eternal weight of glory far beyond all comparison, while we look not at the things which are seen, but at the things which are not seen; for the things which are seen are temporal, but the things which are not seen are eternal" (2 Cor. 4:17–18; cf. Rom. 8:18). It was that heavenly focus that allowed the apostles, after having been beaten by the Sanhedrin, to leave "the presence of the Council, rejoicing that they had been considered worthy to suffer shame for His name" (Acts 5:41). Paul and Silas, having been beaten and put in the stocks at Philippi, nevertheless were "praying and singing hymns of praise to God" (Acts 16:25). Paul told the Colossians, "I rejoice in my sufferings for your sake, and in my flesh I do my share on behalf of His body, which is the church, in filling up what is lacking in Christ's afflictions" (Col. 1:24). Enduring suffering and hostility is a mark of genuine saving faith (cf. Matt. 10:22; 24:13).

Not only their future reward in heaven, but second their association with the heroes of faith of the past should motivate believers to joyously endure hostility. They are in the noblest of company, **for in the same way,** Jesus declared, **their fathers used to treat the prophets** (cf. Luke 11:47–51; 13:34; Acts 7:52; Rom. 11:3; 1 Thess. 2:15; James 5:10).

THE CURSED

"But woe to you who are rich, for you are receiving your comfort in full. Woe to you who are well-fed now, for you shall be hungry. Woe to you who laugh now, for you shall mourn and weep. Woe to you when all men speak well of you, for their fathers used to treat the false prophets in the same way." (6:24–26)

The use of the strong adversative conjunction *plēn* (**but**) indicates that the woes pronounced on those who reject Jesus Christ are in direct contrast to the blessings granted to His true believers. The first **woe** was not pronounced on the materially **rich.** Being wealthy in and of itself is not sinful; Abraham, Job, Nicodemus, and Joseph of Arimathea were rich, and according to Deuteronomy 8:18 God grants the power to obtain wealth. The rich in view here are those who imagine themselves to be rich in the spiritual realm, who think that their righteous deeds are sufficient to obtain salvation. A prime example is the Pharisee in the Lord's story, who "was praying this to himself: 'God, I thank You that I am not like other people: swindlers, unjust, adulterers, or even like this tax collector. I fast twice a week; I pay tithes of all that I get'" (Luke 18:11–12). The curse pronounced on them is that they **are receiving** their **comfort in full** in this life. What awaits them in eternity is the comfortless, ceaseless torment of hell (cf. Luke 16:25).

The second curse is on those **who are well-fed now.** These are the people who are totally satiated with their hypocritical self-righteousness. Unlike those who hunger for a righteousness they know they do not have and cannot earn, they imagine that they have everything they need, and lack nothing. The curse pronounced on them is that they **shall be** eternally **hungry**, experiencing the gnawing, never-ending hunger of a lost soul in hell.

A third mark of the cursed is that they **laugh now.** Smugly content with their religious achievements and superficial morality, they happily contemplate the eternal bliss that they foolishly imagine awaits them in the eternal kingdom. The sobering reality, however, is that while "many will come from east and west, and recline at the table with Abraham, Isaac and Jacob in the kingdom of heaven," many who think that they are "sons of the kingdom will be cast out into the outer darkness" (Matt. 8:11–12). In sharp contrast to the everlasting joy promised to the true disciples, "in that place [hell] there will be weeping and gnashing of teeth" (v. 12; cf. 13:42, 50; 22:13; 24:51; 25:30; Luke 13:28).

The final contrasting woe pronounced on the cursed is that of popularity. **"Woe to you when all men speak well of you,"** Jesus warned, **"for their fathers used to treat the false prophets in the same way."** The Lord had earlier linked the unpopular true disciples to the true prophets; here He linked the false disciples to the false prophets. Refusing to acknowledge their spiritual poverty, arrogant self-righteousness, and baseless contentedness, the cursed enjoy the company of others, having their ears tickled by the deceitful lies of the false prophets (2 Tim. 4:3). "An appalling and horrible thing has happened in the land," God declared. "The prophets prophesy falsely ... and My people love it so!" (Jer. 5:30–31). Those who embrace their teaching will share the false prophets' doom (cf. Jer. 14:14–15; 23:14–15, 25–34; Ezek. 13:9).

There are only two kinds of people in the world. Christ's true followers, the spiritually poor, hungry, sorrowful, and rejected, cry out to God for pardon and mercy through the sacrifice of Jesus Christ. They are blessed with eternal riches, satisfaction, joy, acceptance, and reward. In contrast, those who see themselves as spiritually full, rich, happy, and accepted will be cursed with eternal poverty, emptiness, sorrow, and judgment.

Kingdom Love
(Luke 6:27–38)

11

"But I say to you who hear, love your enemies, do good to those who hate you, bless those who curse you, pray for those who mistreat you. Whoever hits you on the cheek, offer him the other also; and whoever takes away your coat, do not withhold your shirt from him either. Give to everyone who asks of you, and whoever takes away what is yours, do not demand it back. Treat others the same way you want them to treat you. If you love those who love you, what credit is that to you? For even sinners love those who love them. If you do good to those who do good to you, what credit is that to you? For even sinners do the same. If you lend to those from whom you expect to receive, what credit is that to you? Even sinners lend to sinners in order to receive back the same amount. But love your enemies, and do good, and lend, expecting nothing in return; and your reward will be great, and you will be sons of the Most High; for He Himself is kind to ungrateful and evil men. Be merciful, just as your Father is merciful. Do not judge, and you will not be judged; and do not condemn, and you will not be condemned; pardon, and you will be pardoned. Give, and it will be given to you. They will pour into your lap a good measure—pressed down, shaken together, and

running over. For by your standard of measure it will be measured to you in return." (6:27–38)

There are many things that mark a true Christian, including repentance (2 Cor. 7:10; 1 John 1:8–10), humility (James 1:21; 4:6, 10; 1 Peter 5:5), living for the glory of God (1 Cor. 10:31), prayer (Luke 18:1; Eph. 6:18; Phil. 4:6), separation from the world (James 4:4; 1 John 2:15–17), spiritual growth (Eph. 4:11–15; 1 Peter 2:2; 2 Peter 3:18), bearing spiritual fruit (Matt. 13:23; John 15:5, 8), obedience (Matt. 7:21; John 15:14; 1 Peter 1:1–2; 1 John 2:3–5), hunger for God's Word (1 Peter 2:1–2), and a transformed life (2 Cor. 5:17).

But the most foundational mark of a genuine believer in Jesus Christ is love. First, Christians love God, which Jesus declared to be the greatest and most important principle in Scripture (Matt. 22:37–38; cf. Deut. 6:5; 11:1; Josh. 22:5; Rom. 8:28; 1 Cor. 2:9; 1 John 5:2). Love for fellow believers also marks Christ's true disciples (John 13:34–35; cf. 15:12; 1 Thess. 4:9; Heb. 13:1; 1 Peter 1:22; 4:8; 1 John 3:11, 14; 4:7, 21; 2 John 5).

Along with loving God and fellow believers, Christians are also to love unbelievers. While they are forbidden to love the evil, satanic world system (1 John 2:15–17), believers are nevertheless to love the lost sinners trapped within it. By doing so they follow the example of their heavenly Father, who "causes His sun to rise on the evil and the good, and sends rain on the righteous and the unrighteous" (Matt. 5:45), and the Lord Jesus Christ, who loved even those who rejected Him (Mark 10:21; cf. Luke 23:34).

Jesus opened the Sermon on the Mount by describing how the righteous view themselves (6:20–26). He declared blessed those who are spiritually poor, acknowledging their utter lack of any resources by which they might obtain salvation; who are hungry, longing desperately for the righteousness that only God can give; who mourn, consumed with grief and sorrow over their sin; and who are persecuted, yet consider it cause for rejoicing when they are hated, ostracized, and insulted for their loyalty to Jesus Christ.

In this next section of His message, the Lord addressed His genuine disciples (those **who hear,** understand, and obey God's word, in contrast to unbelievers, who have no such capacity [1 Cor. 2:14]), instructing them on how they are to view others. They are to be marked not only by hatred of their own sin, but also by love for their enemies.

The command to love one's enemies provides an important balance against any tendency toward isolation. Some believers, overwhelmed by a sense of sinful inadequacy, might seek to withdraw themselves. Others might want to avoid the influence of and persecution by evil people. Some Christians caught up in politics even view non-believers as the enemy, rather than the mission field. But for Christ's true followers to isolate themselves, hate or resent the lost and their agenda, violates the church's mandate to preach the gospel to the lost world (Matt. 28:19–20; cf. Rom. 10:14–15). Besides, as Paul reminded the Corinthians, to avoid all contact with unbelievers is impossible (1 Cor. 5:9–10).

This important portion of our Lord's kingdom teaching reveals that His true disciples are to be marked by a supernatural love that does good to others—even their enemies. The passage unfolds six aspects of kingdom love: its commands, the reactions to it, the principle behind it, its essence, its benefits, and its goal.

THE COMMANDS OF KINGDOM LOVE

But I say to you who hear, love your enemies, do good to those who hate you, bless those who curse you, pray for those who mistreat you. (6:27–28)

As noted above, the Lord addressed these four simple yet profound commands to His genuine disciples, those **who hear** and obey His word. They describe a supernatural love that is vastly different from the world's love. Vengeance is a virtue to unbelievers, who make heroes out of those who take nothing from anyone, who lash out at those who wrong them and make them pay. Joseph Stalin, perhaps the most brutal and vindictive dictator of the twentieth century, captured the essence of the world's lust for revenge when he said, "To choose one's victim, to prepare one's plan minutely, to slake an implacable vengeance, and then to go to bed—there is nothing sweeter in the world" ("Death in the Kremlin: Killer of the Masses" [*Time* magazine, March 16, 1953; http://www.time.com/time/magazine/article/0,9171,935828-7,00.html; accessed 12 January 2010]). Millions of people tasted the bitterness of Stalin's "implacable vengeance," suffering torture, exile, and death.

Attitudes were little different in Jesus' day, not even in Israel. First-century Judaism was narrow, exclusive, intolerant, and hence largely loveless and condemning. Hatred of their enemies, especially Gentiles (and above all their Roman occupiers), was elevated to the status of a spiritual virtue (cf. Matt. 5:43). The medieval Jewish scholar Maimonides recorded the Talmud's maxim that a Jew should not rescue a Gentile who fell into the sea. Some Zealot extremists took that contemptuous disregard for Gentile life one step further by actually murdering Romans. Many Jews thus found Jesus' command **love your enemies** to be incomprehensible, shocking, and unacceptable.

But such vengeful hatred of one's enemies was contrary to the

Old Testament law. It is true that the imprecatory Psalms call for God's promised judgment on His foes. But to arrogate that right to themselves, as some Jews did, contradicted God's declaration in Deuteronomy 32:35 that vengeance belongs to Him (cf. Rom. 12:19; Heb. 10:30). Instead of seeking revenge, Proverbs 25:21 commands, "If your enemy is hungry, give him food to eat; and if he is thirsty, give him water to drink" (cf. Ex. 23:4–5). Leviticus 19:18 summarizes the Old Testament teaching on how to view one's enemies: "You shall not take vengeance, nor bear any grudge against the sons of your people, but you shall love your neighbor as yourself." The term "neighbor" refers to anyone in need (Luke 10:29–37), not merely to fellow Jews.

Instead of seeking revenge, Christ's disciples are to **do good to those who hate** them. *Kalōs* (**good**) describes what is inherently, not superficially, good. It refers here to doing things that will benefit one's enemies. When they love like that, believers will "overcome evil with good" (Rom. 12:21; cf. 1 Peter 3:9).

Paradoxically, love and hate are linked in connection with the gospel. The Lord's command to the apostles in John 15:17, "This I command you, that you love one another" was followed immediately by a warning that the world would hate them (vv. 18, 19). Since sinners love darkness rather than light (John 3:19), and believers are children of light (Eph. 5:8), who present Jesus Christ as the light of the world (John 8:12), they can expect to be hated by the world.

Surprisingly, the most intense hatred always comes from religious people. Nothing is more precious to religious sinners than the illusion of their virtue and lofty position before God. They in effect erect their own personal tower of Babel, a monument to their own supposed piosity. But the gospel strips away sinners' religious veneer of self-righteousness and reveals them to be wretched, helpless, blind rebels, facing eternal judgment. In response to being unmasked, they lash out in hatred at those who proclaim the truth to them.

When believers face hatred, they are to respond by seeking the welfare of those who hate them, thereby reinforcing their supernatural message with supernatural love. The credibility of the gospel is at stake and believers must love the lost evangelistically.

Christ's disciples must not only manifest love for their enemies by what they do, but also by what they say. Instead of reviling them, they are to **bless those who curse** them; to say good things in response to their evil words. Many of Christ's followers were vilified, cursed, and ostracized in an unofficial way, just as Jesus had warned would happen (Matt. 10:35–37; Luke 12:51–53). Others were cursed in an official way by being excommunicated from the synagogue, which Jesus had also predicted would be the case (John 16:2; cf. 9:22, 34; 12:42).

This command does not preclude warning unbelievers of the consequences of their sin, as the Lord Himself did (cf. 6:24–26; Matt. 23:13–36). Apart from such warnings, there could be no conviction of sin (cf. John 16:7–11). Unbelievers must be confronted with the reality that apart from repentance from sin and faith in the Lord Jesus Christ they are cursed (1 Cor. 16:22). But when Christ's followers confront sinners they must, like Paul, have an attitude of deep concern and love for them (cf. Rom. 9:1–3; 10:1). And, like Paul, they must be willing to pay whatever price is necessary to take the gospel to the lost (cf. 1 Cor. 9:22; 2 Cor. 11:22–33).

Finally, Jesus commanded His followers to **pray for those who mistreat** them. Specifically in this context, they are to pray for their salvation, as Jesus (Luke 23:34) and Stephen (Acts 7:59–60) did.

THE REACTIONS OF KINGDOM LOVE

Whoever hits you on the cheek, offer him the other also; and whoever takes away your coat, do not withhold your shirt from him either. Give to everyone who asks of you, and whoever takes away what is yours, do not demand it back. (6:29–30)

Kingdom love is marked not only by how it acts toward others, but also by how it reacts to what others do. Jesus gave four illustrations of how to respond properly to ill treatment from the children of Satan.

The command, **whoever hits you on the cheek, offer him the other also** does not preclude the self-defense mechanisms God has provided for self-preservation. Jesus was not forbidding His followers to defend themselves if they were dangerously attacked. In Luke 22:36 He instructed the apostles to buy a sword for protection if they did not have one. Governments are in place to protect their citizens with swords, and prevent evil action and anarchy (cf. Rom. 13:3–4, and Luke 3:14, where John the Baptist did not forbid men to be soldiers, but told them not to abuse their authority). When the disciples were put out of the synagogues, as Jesus warned would happen (John 16:2), they would often be beaten (as Paul was five times [2 Cor. 11:24]) or slapped across the face. When dishonored with such insults and unable to defend themselves, they were not to retaliate, but to accept that mistreatment and continue to love their oppressors.

Jesus demonstrated the proper response to being unjustly humiliated during His trial before the high priest. When one of the officers struck Him (John 18:22), He did not turn His head and ask to be struck again. But neither did He lash out in anger and revenge at His mistreatment. Instead, He calmly pointed out the injustice of the act (v. 23). To turn the other cheek is, like Jesus did, to accept hostility and ill treatment without hatred or retaliation, but to show love in return.

The second illustration is similar to the first one. **Whoever takes away your coat** (whether by theft or legal action [cf. Matt. 5:40]), Jesus said, **do not withhold your shirt from him either.** Many people owned only one **coat,** or cloak, which also served as a blanket when they slept. Because of that, the Mosaic law required that any coat taken as a pledge had to be returned before sunset (Ex. 22:26; Deut. 24:13). To keep a person's cloak would constitute serious abuse. But when that happens, Christ's disciples are not to retaliate, but rather to continue to lovingly minister to those who persecute them—even if that results in losing their **shirt** (inner garment) as well.

The third illustration, being willing to **give to everyone who asks of you,** takes place in the context of borrowing and lending (cf. v. 34; Matt. 5:42). The assumption is that the person asking has a legitimate need, since Scripture condemns laziness and indolence (cf. Prov. 6:6–12; 20:4; 24:30–34; 2 Thess. 3:10). That a person may take advantage of a Christian's generosity and not repay the loan should not keep the believer from graciously, lovingly meeting the need.

The final illustration, when someone **takes away what is yours,** envisions a situation where someone actually robs a believer. Even in a case of outright theft, Christians are not to descend to retaliation, but to continue showing love and **not demand** the stolen item **back.** As R. C. H. Lenski notes, "The disciple loses less by letting his things be taken wrongfully then he would by with a selfish heart clamoring to have them returned" (*The Interpretation of St. Luke's Gospel* [Minneapolis: Augsburg, 1946], 364).

No matter what the circumstances, kingdom love does not seek revenge (Prov. 24:29; Rom. 12:17, 19) when wronged. Christ's true disciples will follow His example, who "while being reviled, He did not revile in return; while suffering, He uttered no threats, but kept entrusting Himself to Him who judges righteously" (1 Peter 2:23).

THE PRINCIPLE OF KINGDOM LOVE

Treat others the same way you want them to treat you. (6:31)

Versions of this, the so-called Golden Rule, existed in the rabbinic writings, Greek philosophy, and in Hinduism and Buddhism. Those formulations, however, cast the rule in a negative sense; they advocate not doing to others what you would not want them to do to you. The Greek philosopher Isocrates wrote, "Do not do to others that which angers you

when they do it to you" (*Nicocles*, 3.60). In his *Analects,* Confucius coun-
seled, "Never impose on others what you would not choose for yourself"
(XV.24). The apocryphal book of Tobit commands, "Do that to no man
which thou hatest" (4:15). The famous Jewish rabbi Hillel summed up the
Torah in the statement, "What is hateful to you, do not to your neighbor"
(Talmud; Shabbat 31a).

There is a subtle but significant difference in the way the Lord
phrased this principle. The negative versions of the Golden Rule are the
epitome of human ethics. Yet they are little more than self-serving expressions of self-love, concerned primarily with obtaining good treatment for
oneself in return. Jesus, however, calls for selfless love, love that focuses
solely on the well-being of its object. The love He commands seeks to
treat others the way it would want to be treated by them—even if they do
not love that way in return. That is how God loves, and that supernatural
love is impossible on the human level. Only Christians are capable of it,
"because the love of God has been poured out within our hearts through
the Holy Spirit who was given to us" (Rom. 5:5).

THE ESSENCE OF KINGDOM LOVE

**If you love those who love you, what credit is that to you? For
even sinners love those who love them. If you do good to those
who do good to you, what credit is that to you? For even sinners
do the same. If you lend to those from whom you expect to
receive, what credit is that to you? Even sinners lend to sinners
in order to receive back the same amount.** (6:32–34)

The transcendent, supernatural quality of kingdom love
becomes most evident when contrasted with the love of the unregenerate. *Hamartōloi* (**sinners**) refers to unbelievers, those outside of the
kingdom of God (cf. Matt. 26:45; Mark 2:16; Luke 15:7; 18:13; Rom. 5:8; 1 Tim.
1:15). Their love is reciprocal; they love those who love them.

But the love Jesus' disciples are to exhibit is very different from
that of the lost world. **If you love those who love you,** Jesus told them,
what credit is that to you? Such love is indistinguishable from that of
the unregenerate. **Even sinners**—including tax collectors, the dregs of
Jewish society (Matt. 5:46)—**love those who love them.** Similarly, to **do
good to those who do good to you** brings no **credit,** for again, **even
sinners do the same.** Such a self-serving attitude allows others' goodness to limit one's own. It also opens the door for people to justify seeking vengeance on those who fail to do good to them. Finally, Jesus asked,
If you lend to those from whom you expect to receive, what credit

is that to you? Even sinners lend to sinners in order to receive back the same amount. The Lord is not speaking here of lending to someone who will never repay the loan (the word **amount** is not in the Greek text), since Scripture teaches that everyone should pay his debts (cf. Rom. 13:8). His point is that lending to people to create an obligation, such as expecting that they will in turn lend to you, is another example of the reciprocal, self-serving love of the unregenerate.

Merely to love like sinners do is no gospel witness; that kind of love will not convince anyone that the person manifesting it belongs to God's kingdom. It gives no evidence of a regenerated, transformed life. But the supernatural love of God demonstrated in the lives of believers is a powerful apologetic for the truth of the gospel.

THE BENEFITS OF KINGDOM LOVE

But love your enemies, and do good, and lend, expecting nothing in return; and your reward will be great, and you will be sons of the Most High; for He Himself is kind to ungrateful and evil men. Be merciful, just as your Father is merciful. (6:35–36)

In a point-by-point contrast to the selfish, *quid pro quo* love of unbelievers described above, Jesus commanded His disciples to **love** their **enemies,** not merely those who love them, **do good** to all, not only those who do good to them, **and lend** with no strings attached, **expecting nothing in return.** Such love is neither natural nor normal by human standards, but the benefit of loving that way, Jesus promised, is that their **reward will be great.**

The **reward** in view here is not the eternal, heavenly reward mentioned in 6:23, but one in the world of men. When Christians love with the unconditional, supernatural love God puts in their hearts (Rom. 5:5), sinners will be astounded. This is a love that is foreign to their experience, and shows that those who manifest it are **sons of the Most High** (a name used fifty times of God that emphasizes His sovereignty). It validates the gospel's claim to have the power to supernaturally transform those who believe it.

Believers can "adorn the doctrine of God" (Titus 2:10) and be imitators of Him (Eph. 5:1) by showing kindness to others, **for He Himself is kind to ungrateful** (2 Tim. 3:2) **and evil men** (Rom. 3:10; 2 Tim. 3:13). In common grace God gives sinners what they do not deserve; He "causes His sun to rise on the evil and the good, and sends rain on the righteous and the unrighteous" (Matt. 5:45; cf. Ps. 145:15–17). Christ's disciples also demonstrate kingdom love when they are **merciful, just as** their **Father is merciful.** Mercy is the flip side of kindness. God's mercy causes Him to withhold the judgment that sinners deserve. He is "patient …not wishing for any to perish but for all to come to repentance" (2 Peter 3:9). But those who spurn His mercy and ignore His kindness (Rom. 2:4) by refusing to repent of their sins and turn to Jesus Christ in humble faith will face eternal damnation (John 3:36). When believers love like God does, demonstrating kindness and mercy, they give evidence to the watching world that He is their Father.

THE GOAL OF KINGDOM LOVE

Do not judge, and you will not be judged; and do not condemn, and you will not be condemned; pardon, and you will be pardoned. Give, and it will be given to you. They will pour into your lap a good measure—pressed down, shaken together, and running over. For by your standard of measure it will be measured to you in return. (6:37–38)

Christ closed this section of His sermon by giving four commands, two negative and two positive that, if obeyed, will lead to the ultimate purpose of loving others with kingdom love.

The first command, **do not judge, and you will not be judged,** does not preclude assessing a person's spiritual condition and confronting their sin (cf. 6:42–45; 17:3; Matt. 7:6; 1 Cor. 5:5, 11–13; 1 Tim. 5:20; 2 Tim. 4:2; James 5:20; 2 John 10). In fact, Christians are commanded to be discerning, to be "shrewd as serpents and innocent as doves" (Matt. 10:16; cf. Col. 4:5). (I discuss the importance of discernment in the church in my book *Reckless Faith: When the Church Loses Its Will to Discern* [Wheaton, Ill.: Crossway, 1994].) What this command does forbid is harsh, critical, compassionless, vengeful condemnation of one's enemies as if one was vested with final judgment power (see the discussion of v. 28 above).

The second command, **do not condemn, and you will not be condemned,** is similar to the first. It adds a sense of finality to the idea of judging, of setting oneself up as executioner. Christians need to keep in mind that apart from God's grace they would be no better than the unregenerate. As Paul reminded Titus,

> For we also once were foolish ourselves, disobedient, deceived, enslaved to various lusts and pleasures, spending our life in malice and envy, hateful, hating one another. But when the kindness of God our Savior and His love for mankind appeared, He saved us, not on the basis of deeds which we have done in righteousness, but according to His mercy, by the washing of regeneration and renewing by the Holy

Spirit, whom He poured out upon us richly through Jesus Christ our Savior, so that being justified by His grace we would be made heirs according to the hope of eternal life. (Titus 3:3–7)

Instead of judging and condemning others, Christians are called to **pardon, and** they **will be pardoned.** They are never more like their heavenly Father than when they forgive others. There is no room in kingdom love for holding grudges or being bitter. Like Jesus (Luke 23:34) and Stephen (Acts 7:59–60), believers are to forgive their enemies no matter how hostile they may be (cf. 17:3–4; Matt. 18:21–22; Mark 11:25).

The final command, **give, and it will be given to you,** calls for generosity. In return **they** (i.e., unbelievers) **will pour into your lap a good measure—pressed down, shaken together, and running over.** The Lord's illustration, taken from a scene His hearers would be very familiar with, vividly pictures the blessing the disciples will receive. J. Jeremias writes,

> The measuring of the corn is a process which is carried out according to an established pattern. The seller crouches on the ground with the measure between his legs. First of all he fills the measure three-quarters full and gives it a good shake with a rotary motion to make the grains settle down. Then he fills the measure to the top and gives it another shake. Next he presses the corn together strongly with both hands. Finally he heaps it into a cone, tapping it carefully to press the grains together; from time to time he bores a hole into the corn and pours a few more grains into it, until there is literally no more room for a single grain. In this way, the purchaser is guaranteed an absolutely full measure; it cannot hold more (cited in Darrell L. Bock, *Luke 1:1–9:50,* The Baker Exegetical Commentary on the New Testament [Grand Rapids: Baker, 1994], 607–8).

The goal of all four commands is to have sinners not judge or condemn believers, but be forgiving and generous. If that is happening, it indicates that unbelievers have accepted them, and they have an opportunity to proclaim the gospel. When believers love non-believers like God does—compassionately, kindly, mercifully, and forgivingly—they demonstrate the transforming power of salvation.

The Danger of Following the Wrong Spiritual Teacher (Luke 6:39–49)

12

And He also spoke a parable to them: "A blind man cannot guide a blind man, can he? Will they not both fall into a pit? A pupil is not above his teacher; but everyone, after he has been fully trained, will be like his teacher. Why do you look at the speck that is in your brother's eye, but do not notice the log that is in your own eye? Or how can you say to your brother, 'Brother, let me take out the speck that is in your eye,' when you yourself do not see the log that is in your own eye? You hypocrite, first take the log out of your own eye, and then you will see clearly to take out the speck that is in your brother's eye. For there is no good tree which produces bad fruit, nor, on the other hand, a bad tree which produces good fruit. For each tree is known by its own fruit. For men do not gather figs from thorns, nor do they pick grapes from a briar bush. The good man out of the good treasure of his heart brings forth what is good; and the evil man out of the evil treasure brings forth what is evil; for his mouth speaks from that which fills his heart. Why do you call Me, 'Lord, Lord,' and do not do what I say? Everyone who comes to Me and hears My words and acts on them, I will show you whom he is like: he is like a man building a house, who dug deep and laid a foundation

on the rock; and when a flood occurred, the torrent burst against that house and could not shake it, because it had been well built. But the one who has heard and has not acted accordingly, is like a man who built a house on the ground without any foundation; and the torrent burst against it and immediately it collapsed, and the ruin of that house was great." (6:39–49)

In Matthew's account of the Sermon on the Mount, Jesus closed this powerful sermon by exhorting His hearers to "enter through the narrow gate; for the gate is wide and the way is broad that leads to destruction, and there are many who enter through it. For the gate is small and the way is narrow that leads to life, and there are few who find it" (Matt. 7:13–14). As the references to two gates, two ways, two destinations, and two groups illustrate, the choice every person faces is between heaven and hell; between salvation and damnation; between the only true religion and the false one in a myriad of forms.

Making that all-important choice more confusing and complicated are false teachers "who," Jesus warned, "come to you in sheep's clothing, but inwardly are ravenous wolves" (v. 15). Motivated by greed (Isa. 56:11; Jer. 6:13; 8:10; Mic. 3:5; Phil. 3:18–19; 2 Peter 2:1–3, 14), these emissaries of Satan, wearing the wool robe of the prophets, try to prevent people from entering the narrow path to heaven and to steer them instead onto the broad path to hell.

God's attitude toward false teachers stands in sharp contrast to the inclusiveness and tolerance of error that pervades contemporary evangelicalism. Scripture denounces them as blind men, mute dogs unable to bark; dreamers lying down who love to slumber; ignorant (Isa. 56:10); demented fools (Hos. 9:7); reckless, treacherous men (Zeph. 3:4); ravenous wolves (Matt. 7:15); blind guides of the blind (Matt. 15:14; cf. 23:16); hypocrites (Matt. 23:13); fools (v. 17); whitewashed tombs full of bones (v. 27); serpents; a brood of vipers (v. 33); thieves and robbers (John 10:8); savage wolves (Acts 20:29); slaves of their own appetites (Rom. 16:18); hucksters peddling the word of God (2 Cor. 2:17); false apostles; deceitful workers (2 Cor. 11:13); servants of Satan (v. 15); purveyors of a different gospel (Gal. 1:6–8); dogs; evil workers (Phil. 3:2); enemies of the cross of Christ (Phil. 3:18); conceited and understanding nothing (1 Tim. 6:4); men of depraved minds deprived of the truth (v. 5); men who have gone astray from the truth (2 Tim. 2:18); captives of the devil (v. 26); deceivers (2 John 7); ungodly persons (Jude 4); and unreasoning animals (v. 10). As a result, the Bible also pronounces severe judgment on them (Deut. 13:5; 18:20; Jer. 14:15; Gal. 1:8–9; Rev. 2:20–23).

The reason for such seemingly harsh language is the deadly danger false teachers pose because they engage in Satan's most distinctive wickedness and the most devastating sin; they lead people astray from the truth of God's Word (Isa. 3:12; 9:16; Jer. 14:13; 23:26–27, 32; 50:6; Matt. 23:13, 15; 24:4–5, 24; Luke 11:46, 52; Rom. 16:17–18; Col. 2:4, 8, 18; 1 Thess. 2:14–16; 2 Tim. 3:13; Titus 1:10; 2 John 7)—including the need for repentance from sin (Jer. 6:14; 8:11; 23:21–22; Lam. 2:14; Ezek. 13:10, 16, 22). Left unchecked, the demon doctrines they peddle (1 Tim. 4:1) will ravage souls and corrupt the church (Acts 20:29–30; 2 Tim. 2:17–18), lulling many into a false sense of security regarding their salvation.

The subject of Jesus' sermon is true discipleship. In verses 20–26 He defined disciples as repenters, overwhelmed with their sin and desperate for the righteousness only God can give. True disciples are also marked by love (vv. 27–38), even for those who hate and persecute them. True discipleship is synonymous with submission to the lordship of Christ. This section makes that important point in a negative way, since following Jesus Christ as Lord means avoiding false spiritual leaders. The Lord first described the character of those deceivers. He then challenged His hearers to make the most important decision of their lives—between the saving truth of God and the damning lies of Satan; between submitting to Him, or following false teachers.

THE DECEIVERS

And He also spoke a parable to them: "A blind man cannot guide a blind man, can he? Will they not both fall into a pit? A pupil is not above his teacher; but everyone, after he has been fully trained, will be like his teacher. Why do you look at the speck that is in your brother's eye, but do not notice the log that is in your own eye? Or how can you say to your brother, 'Brother, let me take out the speck that is in your eye,' when you yourself do not see the log that is in your own eye? You hypocrite, first take the log out of your own eye, and then you will see clearly to take out the speck that is in your brother's eye. For there is no good tree which produces bad fruit, nor, on the other hand, a bad tree which produces good fruit. For each tree is known by its own fruit. For men do not gather figs from thorns, nor do they pick grapes from a briar bush. The good man out of the good treasure of his heart brings forth what is good; and the evil man out of the evil treasure brings forth what is evil; for his mouth speaks from that which fills his heart." (6:39–45)

Four characteristics of false teachers mark them as dangerous and unreliable spiritual guides: they are blind, earthly, hypocrites, and evil.

FALSE TEACHERS ARE BLIND

And He also spoke a parable to them: "A blind man cannot guide a blind man, can he? Will they not both fall into a pit? (6:39)

Parabolē (**parable**) can refer to an extended analogy (cf. 12:16; 15:3; 18:9; 19:11), but also to a simple proverb (cf. 4:23; 5:36), as it does here. This parable reflects a problem that was all too familiar to the people of Jesus' day. Blindness was common in the ancient world, as it still is today in various parts of the world. Dangers were everywhere for the blind, including unfenced quarries, crevices and precipices, and dry wells that had not been covered or filled in with dirt. The truth that **a blind man cannot guide a blind man** is self-evident; since a blind man cannot see where he himself is going he cannot safely or reliably lead another blind person. The likely result is that they will **both fall into a pit** and be severely injured or killed.

Blindness is used metaphorically in both the Old and New Testaments to describe being void of truth and lacking spiritual insight (e.g., Isa. 42:7; 43:8; 44:18; Jer. 5:21; Ps. 82:5; Acts 26:18; 2 Cor. 4:4; 1 John 2:11; Rev. 3:17). The spiritual principle is obvious: those who follow leaders who do not know the way to God's kingdom will never get there. Instead, they will all fall into the pit of hell. Jesus was referring in particular to Israel's blind religious guides, the scribes and Pharisees. On another occasion, He used this same parable of the blind leading the blind to refer specifically to them (Matt. 15:14), while in His diatribe against the Pharisees Jesus repeatedly excoriated them for their spiritual blindness (Matt. 23:16, 17, 19, 24, 26). The inevitable outcome was that they led their followers to the same hell to which they were headed (Matt. 23:15).

On the other hand Jesus is the "way, and the truth, and the life; no one comes to the Father but through [Him]" (John 14:6; cf. Acts 4:12). Because He is the "Light of the world" those who follow Him "will not walk in the darkness, but will have the Light of life" (John 8:12; cf. 9:5; 12:46; Eph. 5:8; 1 Thess. 5:5; 1 Peter 2:9). Christ alone opens the eyes of the spiritually blind (Luke 4:18).

FALSE TEACHERS ARE EARTHLY

A pupil is not above his teacher; but everyone, after he has been fully trained, will be like his teacher. (6:40)

Like the first description of false teachers above, this pithy statement is also self-evident (see the similar statements in Matt. 10:24; John

13:16; 15:20). **A pupil is not** able to rise **above his teacher,** since a teacher cannot impart knowledge that he or she does not possess. Teachers' limitations and errors will inevitably be mirrored in their students.

Since false teachers neither come from God nor know the way to God, they cannot bring people to Him. In ancient days students often followed their teachers regularly, and received instruction in the context of daily life experiences. That allowed teachers to reproduce themselves in their students in practical, not just theoretical ways, but even those **fully trained** in that manner could at best only **be like** their **teacher.** If he did not understand the truth of God, neither would they. As Hosea said, "Like people, like priest" (Hos. 4:9).

On the other hand, those who follow Jesus will become like Him. "We know that when He appears we will be like Him," John wrote, "because we will see Him just as He is" (1 John 3:2).

FALSE TEACHERS ARE HYPOCRITES

Why do you look at the speck that is in your brother's eye, but do not notice the log that is in your own eye? Or how can you say to your brother, 'Brother, let me take out the speck that is in your eye,' when you yourself do not see the log that is in your own eye? You hypocrite, first take the log out of your own eye, and then you will see clearly to take out the speck that is in your brother's eye. (6:41–42)

This humorous anecdote illustrates a very serious issue. In addition to being spiritually blind and ignorant of divine truth, false teachers also lack integrity; they are hypocrites. They presume to be able to provide others with the answers to their spiritual questions, but are void of the truth, even for themselves. In a cartoon-like illustration, Jesus pictures a hypocrite looking **at the speck that is in** his **brother's eye, but** failing to **notice the log that is in** his **own eye.** The words used for the objects make the false teachers' deceptive pretense even more ludicrous. *Kaphos* (**speck**) refers to a small piece of wood, chaff, or straw, while *dokos* (**log**) describes a large beam, such as those used in the floor or roof of a building.

The Lord's illustration graphically depicts the absurdity of false teachers saying to someone, **"Brother, let me take out the speck that is in your eye,"** while failing to **see the log that is in** their **own eye.** Blinded by the massive sin of self-righteousness, false teachers are in no position to deal with the lesser sins of others. They cannot overcome their own sin, since false religion cannot restrain the flesh. Yet they still presumptuously view themselves as "a guide to the blind, a light to those who are in darkness, a corrector of the foolish, [and] a teacher of the immature" (Rom. 2:19–20). **You hypocrite,** Jesus scathingly said to them, **first take the log out of your own eye, and then you will see clearly to take out the speck that is in your brother's eye.** The Lord repeatedly denounced the Jewish religious leaders as hypocrites, who "outwardly appear righteous to men, but inwardly … are full of hypocrisy and lawlessness" (Matt. 23:28; cf. vv. 13–15, 23, 25, 27, 29; 6:2, 5, 16; 15:7; 22:18; Luke 12:1, 56; 13:15). Only by confessing and repenting of their own sin of self-righteousness would they be able to see clearly the sins of others.

Unlike false teachers, Jesus is the sinless (Heb. 4:15), spotless (1 Peter 1:19), undefiled (Heb. 7:26) one in whom the Father is well-pleased (Matt. 3:17). Consequently, His penetrating vision is crystal clear, allowing Him to see every trace of sin (cf. Rev. 1:14). And it is through His sacrificial death alone that sin can be atoned for (Heb. 9:26; 10:12).

FALSE TEACHERS ARE EVIL

For there is no good tree which produces bad fruit, nor, on the other hand, a bad tree which produces good fruit. For each tree is known by its own fruit. For men do not gather figs from thorns, nor do they pick grapes from a briar bush. The good man out of the good treasure of his heart brings forth what is good; and the evil man out of the evil treasure brings forth what is evil; for his mouth speaks from that which fills his heart. (6:43–45)

Beneath the self-righteous façade of false teachers lies deadly evil. Jesus used another self-evident illustration, this one from the realm of agriculture, to make this point. The fruit a tree produces is an unfailing indicator of that tree's health. Thus **there is no good tree which produces bad fruit, nor, on the other hand, a bad tree which produces good fruit.** Good trees do not produce bad, inedible fruit, nor do bad trees produce good, edible fruit. Taking the image one step further, the Lord added the equally self-evident fact that **each tree is known by its own fruit.** Plants produce fruit according to their nature, therefore **men do not gather figs from thorns, nor do they pick grapes from a briar bush.**

In this parable, the bad trees are false teachers, as Matthew's parallel account makes clear. In Matthew 7:15 the Lord warned, "Beware of the false prophets, who come to you in sheep's clothing, but inwardly are ravenous wolves." Then in verse 16 He used the same illustration recorded by Luke: "You will know them by their fruits. Grapes are not gathered from thorn bushes nor figs from thistles, are they?" thus connecting it to the false teachers of verse 15. Similarly, in Matthew 12:33 Jesus said to the Pharisees, "Either make the tree good and its fruit good, or make the tree bad and its fruit bad; for the tree is known by its fruit." Then in the next verse He applied that statement to them: "You brood of vipers, how can you, being evil, speak what is good? For the mouth speaks out of that which fills the heart" (v. 34).

The application of the parable is clear. **The good man out of the good treasure of his heart brings forth what is good; and the evil man out of the evil treasure brings forth what is evil.** Just as trees produce fruit in keeping with their nature, so also do people. The hearts of the righteous, having been transformed by the regenerating work of salvation (Jer. 31:33; Ezek. 36:25–27; John 3:5; Titus 3:5), hold **good treasure;** the hearts of the unregenerate hold **evil treasure.** Just as what the fruit trees bear reveals their nature, so also what people say reveals the nature of their heart, since the **mouth speaks from that which fills** the **heart** (cf. Prov. 10:32; Matt. 15:18). How people speak most clearly reveals what is in their heart.

Those who follow false spiritual teachers will manifest the same corruption that they do. Only those who follow the Lord Jesus Christ can produce the fruit of repentance (Luke 3:8) that marks a transformed life (2 Cor. 5:17).

THE DECISION

"Why do you call Me, 'Lord, Lord,' and do not do what I say? Everyone who comes to Me and hears My words and acts on them, I will show you whom he is like: he is like a man building a house, who dug deep and laid a foundation on the rock; and when a flood occurred, the torrent burst against that house and could not shake it, because it had been well built. But the one who has heard and has not acted accordingly, is like a man who built a house on the ground without any foundation; and the torrent burst against it and immediately it collapsed, and the ruin of that house was great." (6:46–49)

Jesus closed His sermon by challenging His hearers to make a choice. People face decisions throughout their lives, choices about diet, medical care, lifestyle, career, relationships, and education, to name a few. But the one that far overshadows all the rest is the choice that fixes a person's eternal destiny. The concluding parable of the Sermon on the Mount reveals two aspects of that decision: its nature and its consequences.

THE NATURE OF THE DECISION

"Why do you call Me, 'Lord, Lord,' and do not do what I say? (6:46)

Religion thrives in the world because people want to live after death in heaven, however they define it. Whether conceived of as the nirvana of Buddhism, the paradise of Islam, the eternal progression to godhood of Mormonism, or the freedom from the cycle of reincarnation and union with Brahman of Hinduism, religions offer some form of bliss, happiness, fulfillment, or reward on a higher plane after this life.

In this age of tolerance and rejection of absolute truth (especially religious truth), there is a widespread belief that anyone who is sincere in their faith will go to heaven. Even many professing evangelicals hold to an inclusive view of the gospel. God, they maintain, will accept those who are sincere in their religious commitment, even if they never leave their false religions, or profess faith in Jesus Christ. In fact, some even argue that they may actually be aided in coming to God by those false religions.

But the gospel is uncompromisingly exclusive. Jesus declared, "I am the way, and the truth, and the life; no one comes to the Father but through Me" (John 14:6). The early Christians proclaimed the truth that "there is salvation in no one else [other than Jesus Christ]; for there is no other name under heaven that has been given among men by which we must be saved" (Acts 4:12).

If there were any religion apart from biblical Christianity close enough to the truth that its followers might get to heaven, it would be Judaism. After all, Christians and Jews have much in common. Both believe in the God of Abraham, Isaac, and Jacob. Both believe that God is holy, sovereign, omniscient, omnipresent, immutable, creator, sustainer, and judge. Both believe in the reality of sin and the need for righteousness. Both believe in virtues such as humility, honesty, kindness, and forgiveness. And Jews believe in the Old Testament Scriptures.

But it was to people who held those very beliefs that Jesus addressed this sermon. Many were fascinated by Him, as evidenced by the huge crowds that followed Him wherever He went. Some even identified themselves as His disciples and affirmed Him to be in some sense their master or teacher. Yet despite all of that, many fell short of salvation because, as the Lord's pointed question **"Why do you call Me, 'Lord, Lord,' and do not do what I say?"** makes clear, they failed to obey Him.

   Submission to Jesus Christ as Lord is a non-negotiable element of true salvation. Romans 10:9 says plainly, "If you confess with your mouth Jesus as Lord, and believe in your heart that God raised Him from the dead, you will be saved" (cf. 1 Cor. 12:3). Saving faith is obedient faith. Acts 6:7 relates that "a great many of the priests were becoming obedient to the faith." Three times in Romans the apostle Paul spoke of obedience in connection with saving faith (1:5; 15:18; 16:26). Jesus is "to all those who obey Him the source of eternal salvation" (Heb. 5:9), and Peter wrote that the goal of salvation is "to obey Jesus Christ" (1 Peter 1:2). Those who love Jesus will keep His commandments (John 14:15, 23; 15:10; cf. 1 John 5:3). On the other hand, "He who does not obey the Son will not see life, but the wrath of God abides on him" (John 3:36), because "not everyone who says to Me, 'Lord, Lord,' will enter the kingdom of heaven, but he who does the will of My Father who is in heaven will enter" (Matt. 7:21), Paul pronounced a curse on those who reject Jesus Christ (1 Cor. 16:22). "But prove yourselves doers of the word, and not merely hearers who delude themselves," warned James (James 1:22). To have God on one's lips but not in one's heart is profane blasphemy.

   The non-negotiable requirements of confessing sin, repenting of it, and trusting in the Lord Jesus Christ as the only Savior are necessary for salvation. Those who fail in those respects but trust in good works and religious ritual will not see heaven, no matter how sincere their religious beliefs.

THE CONSEQUENCES OF THE DECISION

Everyone who comes to Me and hears My words and acts on them, I will show you whom he is like: he is like a man building a house, who dug deep and laid a foundation on the rock; and when a flood occurred, the torrent burst against that house and could not shake it, because it had been well built. But the one who has heard and has not acted accordingly, is like a man who built a house on the ground without any foundation; and the torrent burst against it and immediately it collapsed, and the ruin of that house was great." (6:47–49)

   This unforgettable illustration reveals the inescapable consequences of the decision one makes about Jesus Christ. The one **who comes to** Him **and hears** His **words and acts on them . . . is like a man building a house, who dug deep and laid a foundation on the rock.** The phrase **dug deep** alludes to the deep heart searching that marks true repentance. The only **foundation** for salvation is Jesus Christ

(1 Cor. 3:11), while **rock** refers to God in the Old Testament (e.g., Deut. 32:4, 15, 18; 2 Sam. 22:2–3; 23:3; Pss. 18:2; 28:1; 78:35; 95:1; Isa. 26:4; 30:29) and Christ in the New (1 Cor. 10:4; 1 Peter 2:5–8).

On the other hand, **the one who has heard and has not acted accordingly, is like a man who built a house on the ground without any foundation.** This religious edifice appeared superficially to be identical to the first house, and was located in the same region, since the same storm affected both. As was illustrated in the parable of the wheat and the tares (Matt. 13:24–30), false believers are often indistinguishable from true believers until judgment comes and sweeps their self-righteous religious edifice away. But when the **flood** and **torrent** of divine judgment and fury **burst** against each **house** the results were dramatically different. When the storm of judgment hit the house built on the solid foundation of salvation in Christ it **could not shake it, because it had been well built.** Those who build their lives on the foundation of the gospel have nothing to fear from the storm of judgment, since Jesus promised, "Truly, truly, I say to you, he who hears My word, and believes Him who sent Me, has eternal life, and does not come into judgment, but has passed out of death into life" (John 5:24; cf. 3:16, 18; Rom. 8:1; 1 John 4:17). The other religious house, having no grounding in Christ and the gospel, could not stand. When **the torrent** of divine judgment **burst against it . . . immediately it collapsed, and the ruin of that house was great.**

The choice every person faces is clear. Those who follow the blueprint provided by false teachers and foolishly build their spiritual houses on the sand of human achievement will be swept into hell by the flood of divine judgment. But those who build on the solid foundation of faith in the Lord Jesus Christ will not be shaken (cf. Rom. 9:33; 10:11; 1 Peter 2:6). The hymn "The Solid Rock" expresses their joyous confidence:

> My hope is built on nothing less
> Than Jesus' blood and righteousness;
> I dare not trust the sweetest frame,
> But wholly lean on Jesus' name.
>
> On Christ the solid rock I stand;
> All other ground is sinking sand.
> All other ground is sinking sand.

The Man Who Amazed Jesus
(Luke 7:1–10)

13

When He had completed all His discourse in the hearing of the people, He went to Capernaum. And a centurion's slave, who was highly regarded by him, was sick and about to die. When he heard about Jesus, he sent some Jewish elders asking Him to come and save the life of his slave. When they came to Jesus, they earnestly implored Him, saying, "He is worthy for You to grant this to him; for he loves our nation and it was he who built us our synagogue." Now Jesus started on His way with them; and when He was not far from the house, the centurion sent friends, saying to Him, "Lord, do not trouble Yourself further, for I am not worthy for You to come under my roof; for this reason I did not even consider myself worthy to come to You, but just say the word, and my servant will be healed. For I also am a man placed under authority, with soldiers under me; and I say to this one, 'Go!' and he goes, and to another, 'Come!' and he comes, and to my slave, 'Do this!' and he does it." Now when Jesus heard this, He marveled at him, and turned and said to the crowd that was following Him, "I say to you, not even in Israel have I found such great faith." When those who had been sent returned to the house, they found the slave in good health. (7:1–10)

There is no doubt that Jesus Christ is the most amazing person who ever lived. The gospels repeatedly record that people were astounded, astonished, even traumatized by the words He spoke and the miracles He performed. His divine knowledge and supernatural power exceed all comprehension.

After hearing the Sermon on the Mount, "the crowds were amazed at His teaching" (Matt. 7:28). In the next chapter of Matthew's gospel, Jesus calmed a raging storm on the Sea of Galilee that was so intense that the disciples feared for their lives (Matt. 8:25). But afterward the realization that God incarnate was in the boat with them terrified them even more than the storm outside the boat had. Verse 27 records that they "were amazed, and said, 'What kind of a man is this, that even the winds and the sea obey Him?'" After He cast a demon out of a mute man "the crowds were amazed, and were saying, 'Nothing like this has ever been seen in Israel'" (Matt. 9:33; cf. Mark 7:37). When Jesus taught in the synagogue in His hometown of Nazareth, "they were astonished, and said, 'Where did this man get this wisdom and these miraculous powers?'" (Matt. 13:54; cf. Luke 4:22). Those who heard Him teach in the synagogue in Capernaum (Mark 1:22) and in the temple (John 7:14–15) had similar reactions.

The huge crowds that flocked to Jesus along the shore of the Sea of Galilee "marveled as they saw the mute speaking, the crippled restored, and the lame walking, and the blind seeing; and they glorified the God of Israel" (Matt. 15:31). After the rich young ruler rejected Him, the Lord told His disciples, "Truly I say to you, it is hard for a rich man to enter the kingdom of heaven" (Matt. 19:23). Since in Jewish culture the wealthy were thought to have the inside track to heaven, "when the disciples heard this, they were very astonished and said, 'Then who can be saved?'" (v. 25). "Seeing a lone fig tree by the road, [Jesus] came to it and found nothing on it except leaves only; and He said to it, 'No longer shall there ever be any fruit from you.' And at once the fig tree withered" (Matt. 21:19). Despite all the miracles they had witnessed during their time with Jesus, "the disciples were amazed and asked, 'How did the fig tree wither all at once?'" (v. 20).

The Jewish religious leaders' futile attempts to trap Jesus failed, leaving both them (Matt. 22:22) and the crowds (v. 33; cf. Mark 11:18) stunned by His answers. Unlike those who were astonished by what Jesus said, Pilate was astonished by what He did not say. The governor was accustomed to hearing the accused prisoners brought before him either vehemently protest their innocence or desperately plead for clemency. Therefore he was "quite amazed" when Jesus maintained a majestic calm and remained silent (Matt. 27:14). The disciples understandably were amazed when they saw the resurrected Christ (Luke 24:12, 41).

But while Jesus frequently amazed people, there are only two times in the gospels when He is said to have been amazed. As noted above, the people in Jesus' hometown of Nazareth were first astonished, then angered by Jesus' teaching. In response, as Mark records, Jesus "wondered at their unbelief" (Mark 6:6). The other time Jesus was amazed was because of the faith of a Roman soldier. This passage is the story of Jesus' encounter with that man, who was not a Jew, but a Gentile centurion. Luke's account presents first the context, and then the content of his faith that amazed Jesus.

The Context of the Centurion's Amazing Faith

When He had completed all His discourse in the hearing of the people, He went to Capernaum. And a centurion's slave (7:1–2*a*)

Luke's chronological note that this incident took place **when** Jesus **had completed all His discourse** (the Sermon on the Mount in 6:20–49) **in the hearing of the people** is of great significance. The theme of the Lord's sermon was true discipleship, and this Roman soldier was a living model of the genuine faith of a disciple of Jesus Christ. Everything that Jesus said was characteristic of a true disciple marked this man.

After preaching the Sermon on the Mount, Jesus **went to Capernaum,** and that city provides the geographical setting for this story. **Capernaum,** Jesus' adopted hometown (Matt. 4:13) and headquarters for His Galilean ministry, was located on the northwest shore of the Sea of Galilee within walking distance of the hillside where the Lord delivered the Sermon on the Mount. Its name means, "city of Nahum," but whether it was named for the Old Testament prophet Nahum is not known. Capernaum was the main city on the northern shore of the Sea of Galilee, and was a significant enough town to have had this centurion with his detachment of soldiers stationed there. A royal official (most likely in the service of Herod Antipas) also lived there (John 4:46). In Luke 10:15 Jesus rebuked its people for their exalted view of their city's importance: "And you, Capernaum, will not be exalted to heaven, will you? You will be brought down to Hades!" In fulfillment of the Lord's words, Capernaum was eventually destroyed so completely that its precise location is unknown.

Luke's reference to the **centurion** provides the biographical setting for this story. Centurions, so named because they were in charge of approximately one hundred soldiers, were the backbone of the Roman army. A Roman legion at full strength consisted of 6,000 men, and was divided into ten cohorts of 600 men each. A centurion commanded 100 of these men, and a legion therefore had 60 centurions, each of whom reported to one of the legion's six tribunes (cf. Acts 22:25–26). The Roman historian Polybius described centurions as "not so much venturesome daredevils as natural leaders of a steady and sedate spirit, not so much men who will initiate attacks and open the battle as men who will hold their ground when worsted and hard pressed and be ready to die at their posts" (*Histories* vi. xix-xlii, cited in Naphtali Lewis and Meyer Reinhold, eds. *Roman Civilization: Sourcebook 1: The Republic* [New York: Harper & Row, 1966], 435).

Since Galilee was under the rule of Herod Antipas during the life of Christ, Roman troops were not normally stationed there. This centurion may have been overseeing some of Herod's soldiers, or a small detachment of Roman troops may have been assigned to Capernaum (Leon Morris, *The Gospel According to St. Luke*, The Tyndale New Testament Commentaries [Grand Rapids: Eerdmans, 1975], 136). He most likely was not an Italian, but a native of one of the nearby territories, such as Syria. That he was a Gentile is clear from verses 4 and 5. He was a career soldier, having risen from the ranks by proving to be a strong, responsible, reliable man and a brave, loyal, and skilled fighter. His responsibilities included keeping order, enforcing the law, and overseeing the collection of taxes.

Like all the other centurions mentioned in the New Testament (Mark 15:39; Acts 10:1–2; 22:25–26; 23:17–18; 27:1, 42–43), this one is portrayed favorably. Along with the centurion in charge of Jesus' crucifixion, and Cornelius (Acts 10:44–48), he became a believer in Jesus Christ.

THE CONTENT OF THE CENTURION'S AMAZING FAITH

a centurion's slave, who was highly regarded by him, was sick and about to die. When he heard about Jesus, he sent some Jewish elders asking Him to come and save the life of his slave. When they came to Jesus, they earnestly implored Him, saying, "He is worthy for You to grant this to him; for he loves our nation and it was he who built us our synagogue." Now Jesus started on His way with them; and when He was not far from the house, the centurion sent friends, saying to Him, "Lord, do not trouble Yourself further, for I am not worthy for You to come under my roof; for this reason I did not even consider myself worthy to come to You, but just say the word, and my servant will be healed. For I also am a man placed under authority, with soldiers under me; and I say to this one, 'Go!' and he goes, and to another, 'Come!' and he

comes, and to my slave, 'Do this!' and he does it." Now when Jesus heard this, He marveled at him, and turned and said to the crowd that was following Him, "I say to you, not even in Israel have I found such great faith." When those who had been sent returned to the house, they found the slave in good health. (7:2a–10)

Four aspects of the centurion's exemplary faith stand out in the narrative: his great love, his great generosity, his great humility, and his great trust.

HIS GREAT LOVE

a centurion's slave, who was highly regarded by him, was sick and about to die. When he heard about Jesus, he sent some Jewish elders asking Him to come and save the life of his slave. When they came to Jesus, they earnestly implored Him, saying, "He is worthy for You to grant this to him; for he loves our nation (7:2a–5a)

The centurion's love can be seen first in his attitude toward his **slave.** *Doulos* (**slave**) is a specific term describing a person purchased, owned, and completely subject to the will and control of his master. The centurion also referred to his slave using the term *pais* (v. 7) which, though often used of slaves (cf. 1:54, 69; 15:26; Matt. 14:2), literally means, "child," or "son." In the context of this story, the term suggests the great affection the centurion had for his slave. The use of *pais* may also mean that the slave was a young boy. *Entimos* (**highly regarded**), is also used to refer to a distinguished guest at a banquet (Luke 14:8). In Philippians 2:29 Paul used it to described Epaphroditus and other men who were to be honored in the church, while Peter used it to describe the Lord Jesus Christ (1 Peter 2:4, 6). It signifies that the centurion had an extraordinary level of affection for his slave.

The centurion's love for his slave was in marked contrast to the typical view of slaves in the Greco-Roman world. Aristotle described a slave as a living tool (*Ethics*, 1161b). The legal scholar Gaius noted that it was universally accepted that masters possessed the power of life and death over their slaves (*Institutes*, 1.52). The Roman writer Varro insisted that the only difference between a slave, an animal, and a cart was that the slave talked (*Agriculture*, 1.17). Slaves were often abused, young boys in particular, since pedophilia was not uncommon.

Because of his affection for his slave, the centurion was deeply concerned about him when he **was sick and about to die.** Luke did not describe his disease or symptoms, but Matthew noted that the young man was paralyzed and in severe pain (Matt. 8:6).

The centurion's compassion drove him in desperation to seek the Lord's help. He had **heard** much **about Jesus,** who had moved from Nazareth to Capernaum (Matt. 4:13) and was very well-known in that region (Luke 4:14, 37; Matt. 4:23–25). Somewhere along the way, he had heard more than the usual superficial talk about Jesus' miracles. As the story unfolds, it becomes clear that he knew enough about Jesus to recognize who He really was.

Believing that he was not worthy to go to Jesus personally (see the discussion of his humility below), the centurion **sent some Jewish elders asking Him to come and save the life of his slave.** That these leaders in the Jewish community would consent to do so for a Gentile soldier is amazing, and demonstrates the high regard they had for him. In contrast to the centurion's humble sense of unworthiness they, in keeping with their works-righteous religious system, touted his worthiness. **When they came to Jesus, they earnestly implored Him, saying, "He is worthy for You to grant this to him."** His personal merit, they argued, obligated Jesus to help him—just as in their religious system their self-righteousness obligated God to save them.

The reason the centurion was worthy, they told Jesus, was that **he loves our nation.** Though not meritorious in the sense of obligating God to do anything for him, the centurion's love for God's people was both surprising and commendable. Jews and Gentiles usually hated and despised each other. "Anti-semitism is not a new thing," writes William Barclay. "The Romans called the Jews a filthy race; they spoke of Judaism as a barbarous superstition; they spoke of the Jewish hatred of humankind; they accused the Jews of worshipping an ass's head and annually sacrificing a Gentile stranger to their God" (*The Gospel of Luke,* The New Daily Study Bible [Louisville: Westminster John Knox, 2001], 101). For their part, the Jews refused to associate with Gentiles (cf. Acts 10:25–28; 11:2–3; Gal. 2:11–13). But this centurion overcame those prejudices, recognized the Jews as God's chosen people, and loved them.

HIS GREAT GENEROSITY

and it was he who built us our synagogue. (7:5*b*)

The centurion's love was not mere abstract sentimentality; he expressed it practically by building the Jews of Capernaum a **synagogue.** The use of the pronoun *autos,* in addition to the third person singular verb translated **built,** emphasizes the centurion's personal role. The Jewish elders gave him sole credit for building their synagogue.

Centurions were well paid, earning between 3,750 and 7,500 denarii, in contrast to the lowest paid soldiers, who earned a mere 75 denarii (Darrell L. Bock, *Luke 1:1–9:50,* Baker Exegetical Commentary on the New Testament [Grand Rapids: Baker, 1994], 635), so he was able to finance the construction.

The primary function of the synagogue was to teach the word of God, and his building of the synagogue reflected the centurion's love for the truth. Like Cornelius (Acts 10:1–2), he was a true God-fearer. Somehow, despite the generally apostate condition of the Judaism of his day (cf. Matt. 23:13, 15; Rom. 2:24), the centurion had heard and believed the truth that Jesus Christ was the Messiah, Savior, and Lord.

HIS GREAT HUMILITY

Now Jesus started on His way with them; and when He was not far from the house, the centurion sent friends, saying to Him, "Lord, do not trouble Yourself further, for I am not worthy for You to come under my roof; for this reason I did not even consider myself worthy to come to You, (7:6–7a)

One of the marks of a genuine disciple of Jesus Christ is the acknowledgment of spiritual bankruptcy (6:20) and accompanying humility that the centurion displayed. His view of himself was radically different from that of the Jewish elders. After agreeing to heal the centurion's servant (Matt. 8:7), **Jesus started on His way with** the elders and a large crowd of curious onlookers, eager to see yet another miracle (Luke 7:9). **When** they were **not far from the house, the centurion** sent word for the Lord to come no nearer.

His desperation had prompted his emotional request for Jesus to come and heal his slave. But he had become increasingly convicted of his utter sinfulness and felt unworthy to have Jesus enter his house. Unlike the proud, self-righteous Jewish elders, he was too ashamed of himself and his sinfulness to be in Jesus' presence. His attitude is reminiscent of Peter, who exclaimed, "Go away from me Lord, for I am a sinful man, O Lord!" (Luke 5:8), and the tax collector, who "was even unwilling to lift up his eyes to heaven, but was beating his breast, saying, 'God, be merciful to me, the sinner!'" (Luke 18:13).

Accordingly, the centurion sent a second delegation to Jesus, this one consisting of his **friends, saying to Him** through them, **"Lord, do not trouble Yourself further.** *Skullō* **(trouble)** means, "to be bothered," "annoyed," or "agitated." He understood that his sin was an affront to Jesus' holiness, but did not yet fully understand His provision of grace and mercy. All he knew was that he was **not worthy for** the Lord **to come under** his **roof.** In fact, it was because of his sense of sinfulness and unworthiness that he did **not even consider** himself **worthy to come to** Jesus in the first place. He was a true penitent, with a broken and contrite heart that the Lord would not despise (Ps.51:17).

HIS GREAT TRUST

but just say the word, and my servant will be healed. For I also am a man placed under authority, with soldiers under me; and I say to this one, 'Go!' and he goes, and to another, 'Come!' and he comes, and to my slave, 'Do this!' and he does it." Now when Jesus heard this, He marveled at him, and turned and said to the crowd that was following Him, "I say to you, not even in Israel have I found such great faith." When those who had been sent returned to the house, they found the slave in good health. (7:7b–10)

Instead of having Jesus enter his house, the centurion proposed that He **just say the word, and** his **servant** would **be healed.** He was absolutely confident that the Lord spoke with divine power and authority, as the illustration he gave reveals: **For I also am a man placed under authority, with soldiers under me; and I say to this one, 'Go!' and he goes, and to another, 'Come!' and he comes, and to my slave, 'Do this!' and he does it.** " As a military commander, the centurion was **under** the **authority** of his superior officers and used to obeying their orders. He also knew what it meant to give orders to the **soldiers** serving **under** him, as well as his **slave,** and have them obeyed. He understood that Jesus had that same authority over life and death.

When Jesus heard this remarkable expression of the centurion's humble faith, **He marveled at him.** Here is a glimpse of Jesus' true humanity, since as God He is omniscient and cannot be surprised by anything. But just as in His humanity He became tired (John 4:6), hungry (Matt. 4:2), and thirsty (John 19:28; cf. 4:7), so also could He be astonished at the faith displayed by this Roman soldier.

Hearing the centurion's words, Jesus **turned and said to the crowd that was following Him, "I say to you, not even in Israel have I found such great faith."** On the one hand, the Lord's statement affirmed the centurion's **great faith.** But on the other hand, the sad reality that **not even in Israel** could the Messiah find that kind of faith was an indictment of God's chosen people. Matthew records that the Lord added the sobering warning, "I say to you that many will come from east and west, and recline at the table with Abraham, Isaac and Jacob in the kingdom of heaven; but the sons of the kingdom will be cast out into the outer darkness; in that place there will be weeping and gnashing of teeth" (Matt. 8:11–12). Trusting in their self-righteousness and external ceremonialism, the Jewish people lacked genuine, saving faith. Even Christ's disciples possessed only weak, "little" faith (Matt. 6:30; 8:26; 14:31; 16:8). That a Gentile set the example for genuine faith was a rebuke of the Jewish people, who had missed the truth in spite of all their privileges (Rom. 9:4–5). As the apostle Paul would later write, "For I testify about them that they have a zeal for God, but not in accordance with knowledge. For not knowing about God's righteousness and seeking to establish their own, they did not subject themselves to the righteousness of God" (Rom. 10:2–3).

The epilogue to the story provides a fitting tribute to the centurion's remarkable faith. Matthew noted that, compelled by his desperate, loving concern for his slave, he eventually could not stand to wait any longer. His great love overcame his sense of unworthiness, and he went out to meet Jesus. He reaffirmed in person the message he had sent through his friends that he was unworthy to have Jesus enter his house, and his belief that the Lord could heal his servant by merely speaking a word. Whether he returned with **those who had been sent** or remained with Jesus is not stated. But when his friends returned **to the house, they found the slave in good health.** The Lord had honored the unusual faith of the man by granting his request.

Jesus' Power over Death (Luke 7:11–17)

14

Soon afterwards He went to a city called Nain; and His disciples were going along with Him, accompanied by a large crowd. Now as He approached the gate of the city, a dead man was being carried out, the only son of his mother, and she was a widow; and a sizeable crowd from the city was with her. When the Lord saw her, He felt compassion for her, and said to her, "Do not weep." And He came up and touched the coffin; and the bearers came to a halt. And He said, "Young man, I say to you, arise!" The dead man sat up and began to speak. And Jesus gave him back to his mother. Fear gripped them all, and they began glorifying God, saying, "A great prophet has arisen among us!" and, "God has visited His people!" This report concerning Him went out all over Judea and in all the surrounding district. (7:11–17)

Without question, Jesus Christ is the most well-known person in human history. All the world's major civilizations know something of Him; only isolated people groups and individuals are unaware of Him. But paradoxically, while Jesus is history's most well-known figure, He is at the same time its least known. For while most are familiar with His name and some of the facts of His life and His influence through history, few understand who He truly is. Opinions concerning Jesus Christ are diverse, and wrong views about Him abound. Islam views Him as simply a prophet, who in fact did not die on the cross; in the Mormon pantheon Jesus is a created being, the spirit brother of Satan; to the Jehovah's Witnesses He is Michael the archangel incarnate; blasphemous rock musicals portray Him as a countercultural hero, but just a man; pseudo-scholars reinvent Him as a cynical philosopher, social critic, politically correct sage, liberator of the oppressed, and misguided martyr. The list of errant views goes on ad infinitum, ad nauseam.

But while there are a myriad of satanically-spawned false views of Jesus, there is only one correct one revealed in Scripture. Peter articulated it when he declared, "You are the Christ, the Son of the living God" (Matt. 16:16), and Thomas affirmed it when he exclaimed, "My Lord and my God!" (John 20:28). Jesus Christ is God the Son, the second person of the Trinity incarnate, and for those who reject that truth there can be no salvation. As Jesus solemnly warned the scoffing, unbelieving Jews, "Unless you believe that I am He [God; cf. Ex. 3:14], you will die in your sins" (John 8:24; cf. v. 58; 5:18; 10:30–33). Those who preach a false Christ (2 Cor. 11:4) are cursed; devoted to eternal destruction in hell (1 Cor. 16:22; Gal. 1:8–9). The deity of the Lord Jesus Christ is the foundational truth of the Christian faith.

While "no one has seen God at any time" Jesus Christ, "the only begotten God who is in the bosom of the Father, He has explained Him" (John 1:18). "Explained" translates a form of the verb *exēgeomai,* the source of the English word "exegesis" (the method and practice of interpreting Scripture). Only Jesus can interpret God to man, since "no one knows the Son except the Father; nor does anyone know the Father except the Son, and anyone to whom the Son wills to reveal Him" (Matt. 11:27). When even His disciples failed to grasp that truth, Jesus rebuked them for their obtuseness:

> "If you had known Me, you would have known My Father also; from now on you know Him, and have seen Him." Philip said to Him, "Lord, show us the Father, and it is enough for us." Jesus said to him, "Have I been so long with you, and yet you have not come to know Me, Philip? He who has seen Me has seen the Father; how can you say, 'Show us the Father'?" (John 14:7–9)

As noted in chapter 9 of this volume, as Luke unfolds the history of Jesus' life and ministry, he (like the other gospel writers) continually demonstrates His deity and absolute equality of nature with God. This passage is one of many occasions when Jesus manifested His deity—this time by raising a young man from the dead. The passage reveals three implicit evidences of Christ's deity, followed by one explicit and undeniable one, and concludes by reporting the response of those who witnessed the miracle.

DIVINE PURPOSE

Soon afterwards He went to a city called Nain; and His disciples were going along with Him, accompanied by a large crowd. (7:11)

The phrase **soon afterwards** points back to the healing of the centurion's servant recorded in the previous passage (7:1–10). It is an indefinite time designation, but suggests an interval of a few days at most. **Nain** was a tiny village about twenty miles southwest of Capernaum, and six miles southeast of Jesus' hometown of Nazareth. On the other side of the hill on which Nain stood was the village of Shunem, where Elisha raised a young boy from the dead (2 Kings 4:8–37). About three miles away was the village of Endor, where Saul visited a medium (1 Sam. 28:7–25). Jesus, along with **His disciples** and **accompanied by a large crowd,** made the full day's journey from Capernaum to this small, nondescript town.

God always acts with a fixed purpose, never whimsically, and there are no unexpected contingencies or coincidences for Him. The sovereign plan of God is settled, unchanging, and infallibly brought to fulfillment. In Isaiah 46:9–10 God declared, "I am God, and there is no other; I am God, and there is no one like Me, declaring the end from the beginning, and from ancient times things which have not been done, saying, 'My purpose will be established, and I will accomplish all My good pleasure.'" In Isaiah 55:11 He added, "My word ... which goes forth from My mouth ... will not return to Me empty, without accomplishing what I desire, and without succeeding in the matter for which I sent it."

As God incarnate, Jesus also acted with unalterable resolve to accomplish divine purposes. On His way from Judea to Galilee, Jesus "had to pass through Samaria" (John 4:4). He had a divinely predetermined appointment with a Samaritan woman, whose sinful lifestyle He would expose, to whom He would reveal His messiahship, and through whose testimony of faith in Him would lead many in her village to believe in Him (vv. 5–42). He knew the divine timetable for His death, resurrection, and ascension, so "when the days were approaching for His ascension, He was determined to go to Jerusalem" (Luke 9:51). In Luke 13:33 He reaffirmed His determination to follow the divine timetable when He said, "Nevertheless I must journey on today and tomorrow and the next day; for it cannot be that a prophet would perish outside of Jerusalem." Jesus knew precisely where and when His death was ordained in the plan of God to take place.

One of the blasphemous ideas espoused by some who falsely call themselves evangelicals is Open Theism. According to that view, God neither infallibly knows nor sovereignly plans the future. Jesus, however, not only knew the future, but acted to make certain that God's purposes unfolded exactly as planned.

Circumstances that perhaps had not yet happened when Jesus and His entourage began the day's journey from Capernaum to Nain would be in place to set up an amazing display of Jesus' divine power. When they set out neither the apostles, the rest of Jesus' disciples, nor the thrill seeking crowd knew why they were going to Nain, or what they would see when they got there. In fact, the young man may not yet have died, since Jewish custom dictated that the funeral and burial take place soon after death. But Jesus did know, and made this journey to an "off the beaten path" village because it was God's plan that He encounter a funeral procession there.

DIVINE PROVIDENCE

Now as He approached the gate of the city, a dead man was being carried out, the only son of his mother, and she was a widow; and a sizeable crowd from the city was with her. (7:12)

God's superintending control over all human choices, actions, and events to effect His predetermined purposes is known as His providence. Unlike a miracle, when God supernaturally interrupts or suspends the natural course of events, His providence involves perfectly controlling natural events to infallibly bring about His purposes. Given the staggering complexities involved in coordinating even relatively simple events, God's providence is in some ways even more awe inspiring than the miracles He performs.

God's providential control over events flows directly from His sovereign authority, omnipotence, and omniscience. "The mind of man plans his way," says Proverbs 16:9, "but the Lord directs his steps," while verse 33 adds another illustration: "The lot is cast into the lap, but its every decision is from the Lord." Proverbs 21:1 reveals that God's providential control over human events extends to rulers: "The king's heart is like channels of water in the hand of the Lord; He turns it wherever He wishes." One example is Cyrus, ruler of the Persian empire:

> Now in the first year of Cyrus king of Persia—in order to fulfill the word
> of the Lord by the mouth of Jeremiah—the Lord stirred up the spirit of

Cyrus king of Persia, so that he sent a proclamation throughout his kingdom, and also put it in writing, saying, "Thus says Cyrus king of Persia, 'The Lord, the God of heaven, has given me all the kingdoms of the earth, and He has appointed me to build Him a house in Jerusalem, which is in Judah. Whoever there is among you of all His people, may the Lord his God be with him, and let him go up!'" (2 Chron. 36:22–23)

Though God is not the author of evil (Hab. 1:13), even calamities are under His control, as the prophet Amos notes: "If a calamity occurs in a city has not the Lord done it?" (Amos 3:6). It was one such calamity, whose events God sovereignly ordained in keeping with His purposes, that is the subject of this passage.

Although a village the size of Nain probably would not have had a wall around it, Nain did have a **gate.** Located at the head of the main street, the gate served as a point of entrance for the city. It was also the place where people gathered to socialize, and where the elders met to adjudicate matters (cf. Deut. 25:7–10; Ruth 4:1–11; Isa. 29:21). In God's providential timing, Jesus and His entourage **approached the gate of the city** after their journey from Capernaum just as **a dead man was being carried out.** The funeral was over, and the people were removing the corpse on a bier or stretcher to the burial site outside of town.

Heightening the pathos of this funeral was the reality that the dead man was **the only son of his mother** (cf. 8:42; 9:38). Making the tragic loss even worse, **she was a widow.** Already bereft of her husband, she had with the death of her son lost her last means of support. His passing also marked the end of the family line. The death of an only son symbolized the epitome of grief in the Old Testament. Jeremiah 6:26 exhorted Israel to "mourn as for an only son, a lamentation most bitter." In Amos 8:10 God warned of a coming judgment on Israel that would be "like a time of mourning for an only son, and the end of it will be like a bitter day." Zechariah 12:10 likens Israel's future mourning over her rejection of Jesus Christ to that for the death of an only son:

> I will pour out on the house of David and on the inhabitants of Jerusalem, the Spirit of grace and of supplication, so that they will look on Me whom they have pierced; and they will mourn for Him, as one mourns for an only son, and they will weep bitterly over Him like the bitter weeping over a firstborn.

This woman and her son's bier were at the head of **a sizeable crowd from the city** that made up the funeral procession. It would have included the friends and loved ones of the bereaved family, others from the village, and the musicians and professional wailing women that were part of every Jewish burial. This saddest of all sad scenes in Jewish family life set the stage for the Lord of heaven to reveal Himself in divine power.

DIVINE COMPASSION

When the Lord saw her, He felt compassion for her, and said to her, "Do not weep." (7:13)

Surveying the sad, chaotic scene, the Lord's heart went out to the widow and **He felt compassion for her. Compassion** translates a form of the verb *splagchnizomai,* which is related to a noun that describes the inner parts of the body. Like the modern use of "heart" or "gut," the inward parts of the body were viewed figuratively as the seat of the emotions due to the physical effects such emotions have on the body.

One of the most perverse misinterpretations of Scripture is the idea that the God of the Old Testament is angry, wrathful, and vengeful, while the Lord Jesus Christ is meek, compassionate, and loving. But the Old Testament reveals God's compassion, grace, and mercy, while in the New Testament Christ cleansed the temple (Matt. 21:12–13; John 2:13–17), warned of eternal damnation in hell (Matt. 5:22, 29, 30; 18:9; 23:33; 25:41; John 8:24), was angry at sin (Mark 3:5), and warned His hearers,

> Do not think that I came to bring peace on the earth; I did not come to bring peace, but a sword. For I came to set a man against his father, and a daughter against her mother, and a daughter-in-law against her mother-in-law; and a man's enemies will be the members of his household. (Matt. 10:34–36)

In contrast to the false deities of other religions, it is the nature of the true and living God to feel compassion for suffering sinners. Even after giving His law and judging the idolaters who made the golden calf, He told Moses, "I will be gracious to whom I will be gracious, and will show compassion on whom I will show compassion" (Ex. 33:19), and later described Himself as

> The Lord, the Lord God, compassionate and gracious, slow to anger, and abounding in lovingkindness and truth; who keeps lovingkindness for thousands, who forgives iniquity, transgression and sin; yet He will by no means leave the guilty unpunished, visiting the iniquity of fathers on the children and on the grandchildren to the third and fourth generations. (Ex. 34:6–7)

According to Psalm 103:8, "The Lord is compassionate and gracious, slow to anger and abounding in lovingkindness," while Psalm 116:5 exults,

"Gracious is the Lord, and righteous; yes, our God is compassionate" (cf. Deut. 4:31; 2 Chron. 30:9; Neh. 9:17, 31; Ps. 111:4; Lam. 3:22; Joel 2:13; Jonah 4:2). God's compassion caused Him to deliver His people when "He could bear the misery of Israel no longer" (Judg. 10:16); "He, being compassionate, forgave their iniquity and did not destroy them; and often He restrained His anger and did not arouse all His wrath" (Ps. 78:38).

The New Testament portrays the Lord Jesus Christ as a "merciful and faithful high priest" (Heb. 2:17). He was not "a high priest who cannot sympathize with our weaknesses, but One who has been tempted in all things as we are, yet without sin" (Heb. 4:15). He repeatedly felt compassion for lost, suffering sinners (cf. Matt. 9:36; 14:14; 15:32; 20:34; Mark 1:41). It was His compassion that prompted the Lord, true to His nature as merciful, to comfort this devastated woman, and say to her reassuringly, **"Do not weep."**

DIVINE POWER

And He came up and touched the coffin; and the bearers came to a halt. And He said, "Young man, I say to you, arise!" The dead man sat up and began to speak. And Jesus gave him back to his mother. (7:14–15)

Christ's acting with divine purpose, providential arranging of contingencies to bring about God's plan, and compassion for those who suffer all lead to the conclusion that He is God. His stunning display of power, however, directly demonstrates His deity.

That Jesus **came up and touched the coffin** reveals His power over sin. According to Numbers 19:11–22, anyone who touched a dead person or anything associated with that person became ceremonially unclean. But Jesus, as holy God incarnate, was not defiled by touching the dead man's **coffin** (or stretcher); He remained "holy, innocent, undefiled, separated from sinners and exalted above the heavens" (Heb. 7:26).

This incident also reveals Jesus' power over people. Normally, attempting to halt a funeral procession and touching the corpse would have produced outrage, and the person who did so might even have been physically attacked by the angry mourners. But because of the Lord's commanding, authoritative presence, **the bearers came to a halt.**

But most significant, Jesus demonstrated His power over death. As the creator (John 1:3) whose spoken word called the universe into existence (Ps. 33:6, 9), **He** merely **said, "Young man, I say to you, arise!"** (cf. 8:54–55; John 11:43). At that moment life surged into the dead man's body—just as it will for all the dead on that day when "all who are in the tombs will hear His voice, and will come forth; those who did the good deeds to a resurrection of life, those who committed the evil deeds to a resurrection of judgment" (John 5:28–29).

It should be noted that since no one asked Jesus to raise the dead man, this miracle was not contingent on anyone's faith. Faith is not a prerequisite for God's power to operate; God sovereignly activates His power in accordance with His will. Some of Jesus' healings involved faith, others did not. But to view human faith as the operative principle instead of God's sovereign will is an egregious, even blasphemous error. Faith was always present in salvation, but not all miracles.

At Jesus' command **the dead man sat up and began to speak.** As was always the case, Jesus healed instantly and completely. There was no prolonged period of post-resurrection therapy for this man. He was immediately restored to full strength, **and Jesus gave him back to his mother.**

THE RESPONSE

Fear gripped them all, and they began glorifying God, saying, "A great prophet has arisen among us!" and, "God has visited His people!" This report concerning Him went out all over Judea and in all the surrounding district. (7:16–17)

Needless to say, the raising of the dead man brought an abrupt, unexpected, and shocking end to the funeral. **Fear** (*phobos;* the source of the English word "phobia") **gripped . . . all** who had witnessed it. They were traumatized, overwhelmed with terror at the manifestation of God's presence and power (cf. Ex. 3:6; Judg. 13:20–22; Isa. 6:5; Ezek. 1:28; Matt. 17:1–6; Mark 4:41; Rev. 1:17). In response, **they began glorifying God** (cf. 2:13–14, 20; 5:26; 13:13; 17:18; 18:43), and affirming that **God** had **visited His people.** In the Old Testament, that phrase refers to God's coming to help His people (Ruth 1:6; 1 Sam. 2:21; Ps. 106:4; Zech. 10:3; cf. Luke 1:68, 78). The people of Israel had been longing for such a visitation for four centuries, during which time God had been silent. Now they realized that God had indeed visited them, for only the creator can give life to the dead.

The point of the miracle was to comfort this brokenhearted woman, not to garner publicity for Jesus. Nevertheless **this report** (that God had visited His people) **concerning Him went out** far (**all over Judea;** representing here the entire land of Israel) **and** near (**all the surrounding district** around Nain).

But the sad reality is that they missed the point that God was actually present in the person of Jesus Christ. To them, He was nothing more than **a great prophet** who had **arisen among** them, like Elijah and Elisha, both of whom raised a dead person by the power of God (1 Kings 17:17–24; 2 Kings 4:18–36). Unlike the resurrections performed by Jesus, however, those resurrections were not a result of the prophets' own power, but came in answer to the prophets' prayers (1 Kings 17:20–22; 2 Kings 4:33). They failed to see the truth that Jesus was the ultimate prophet of whom Moses spoke in Deuteronomy 18:15–18—the Messiah, God in human flesh.

At the close of His earthly ministry, Jesus lamented the opportunity Israel had missed by failing to recognize who He truly is:

> When He approached Jerusalem, He saw the city and wept over it, saying, "If you had known in this day, even you, the things which make for peace! But now they have been hidden from your eyes. For the days will come upon you when your enemies will throw up a barricade against you, and surround you and hem you in on every side, and they will level you to the ground and your children within you, and they will not leave in you one stone upon another, because you did not recognize the time of your visitation." (Luke 19:41–44)

As a result of Israel's rejection, God took "from among the Gentiles a people for His name" (Acts 15:14), while Israel remains largely spiritually blind (Rom. 10:1–3; 2 Cor. 3:15).

In contrast to those who witnessed the resurrection at Nain that day, Martha, Lazarus's sister, understood the implication of her brother's imminent resurrection. After Jesus declared, "I am the resurrection and the life; he who believes in Me will live even if he dies, and everyone who lives and believes in Me will never die" He asked her, "Do you believe this?" (John 11:25–26). Martha affirmed her conviction that He was indeed the Messiah: "Yes, Lord; I have believed that You are the Christ, the Son of God, even He who comes into the world" (v. 27).

That alone is the correct view of Jesus Christ, that He is God the Son, the second person of the Trinity incarnate, who came to earth "to give His life a ransom for many" (Matt. 20:28) and "save His people from their sins" (Matt. 1:21), who "was delivered over because of our transgressions, and was raised because of our justification" (Rom. 4:25). Those who reject that truth will die in their sins (John 8:24), for "there is salvation in no one else; for there is no other name under heaven that has been given among men by which we must be saved" (Acts 4:12).

Are You the Coming One?
(Luke 7:18–23)

15

The disciples of John reported to him about all these things. Summoning two of his disciples, John sent them to the Lord, saying, "Are You the Expected One, or do we look for someone else?" When the men came to Him, they said, "John the Baptist has sent us to You, to ask, 'Are You the Expected One, or do we look for someone else?'" At that very time He cured many people of diseases and afflictions and evil spirits; and He gave sight to many who were blind. And He answered and said to them, "Go and report to John what you have seen and heard: the blind receive sight, the lame walk, the lepers are cleansed, and the deaf hear, the dead are raised up, the poor have the gospel preached to them. Blessed is he who does not take offense at Me." (7:18–23)

The noted eighteenth-century hymn writer Charles Wesley composed more than 7,000 hymns in his life, including the magnificent Christmas hymn "Come, Thou Long Expected Jesus." The lyrics express rich theological truth concerning the incarnation of the Lord Jesus Christ:

> Come, thou long expected Jesus,
> Born to set thy people free;

From our fears and sins release us;
Let us find our rest in Thee.
Israel's strength and consolation,
Hope of all the earth Thou art;
Dear Desire of every nation,
Joy of every longing heart.

Born Thy people to deliver,
Born a child and yet a King.
Born to reign in us forever,
Now thy gracious kingdom bring.
By Thine own eternal spirit
Rule in all our hearts alone;
By Thine all sufficient merit,
Raise us to thy Glorious throne.

Wesley's identification of Jesus as "the long expected one" reflects John the Baptist's question in this passage, **Are You the Expected One** (i.e., the Messiah; Pss. 40:7 [cf. Heb. 10:5–7]; 118:26; Mark 11:9; Luke 3:16; John 1:27)?

Jesus repeatedly claimed to be the Expected One promised in the Old Testament. He said that Abraham joyously hoped for Him (John 8:56), Moses wrote of Him (John 5:46), and David called Him Lord (Matt. 22:41–45). He upbraided two of His disciples on the day of His resurrection for being "foolish men and slow of heart to believe in all that the prophets have spoken!" concerning Him (Luke 24:25), and "then beginning with Moses and with all the prophets, He explained to them the things concerning Himself in all the Scriptures" (v. 27).

The Old Testament is filled with references to the Expected One that point unmistakably to Jesus Christ.

- The Expected One, along with the Father and the Spirit, created everything (Gen. 1:1, 26; cf. John 1:1–3).
- His coming was first promised to Adam and Eve immediately after the Fall. God reassured them that Satan, who had deceived and devastated them, would himself be destroyed by the Expected One (Gen. 3:15; cf. 1 John 3:8).
- God's killing of animals to provide clothes to cover Adam and Eve's shame pictured His sacrifice for sin (Gen. 3:21).
- The Expected One was to be a descendant of Abraham (Gen. 22:18; cf. Acts 3:25; Gal. 3:16), from the tribe of Judah (Gen. 49:10; cf. Heb. 7:14).
- The Old Testament priest Melchizedek ("king of righteousness";

Heb. 7:2) pictured the Expected One in that his lack of a recorded genealogy symbolized Christ's perpetual priesthood (cf.
Heb. 6:20).
· Abraham's offering of his son Isaac (Gen. 22:1–14) symbolizes
the sacrifice of the Expected One; just as God provided a ram as
a substitute for Isaac, so also is Jesus the sacrifice for sinners
(1 John 2:1–2).
· Joseph, scorned and rejected by his brothers, nevertheless
became their deliverer. In the same way Jesus "came to His own,
and those who were His own did not receive Him. But as many
as received Him, to them He gave the right to become children
of God, even to those who believe in His name" (John 1:11–12).
· Noah's ark, a place of refuge from God's wrath, pictures Jesus—
the true ark of safety in whom believers ride safely above the
waves of divine judgment.
· The angel of the Lord (Gen. 16:7–13; 22:11–18; 31:11–13; Ex.
3:2–6; Judg. 6:11–23; 13:2–22) was the pre-incarnate manifestation of the Expected One.
· Every spotless, innocent lamb offered as a sacrifice pictured the
final sacrifice of the "Lamb of God who takes away the sin of the
world" (John 1:29; cf. 1 Peter 1:18–19).
· The manna in the wilderness foreshadowed the coming of the
Expected One, the true bread of life (John 6:31–58).
· Aaron and all the high priests who succeeded him pictured the
Lord Jesus Christ, the great high priest (Heb. 2:17; 3:1; 4:14–15;
6:20) who was to come.
· The fiery serpent in the wilderness, to whom sinners bitten by
poisonous snakes looked and were healed, symbolizes Jesus,
who declared, "As Moses lifted up the serpent in the wilderness,
even so must the Son of Man be lifted up; so that whoever
believes will in Him have eternal life" (John 3:14–15).
· The Expected One was to be the ultimate prophet of whom
Moses spoke (Deut. 18:15–19; cf. Acts 3:22–23; 7:37).
· Boaz, Ruth's kinsman-redeemer (Ruth 4:1–12) was a type of
Christ, the redeemer of His people (Matt. 1:21).
· Like David, the shepherd king, the Messiah would come as a shep-
herd (John 10:11) and King (Matt. 27:11; John 1:49; Rev. 17:14).
· The filling of the temple with God's glory (1 Kings 8:10–11) pro-
vided a glimpse of the glory of Jesus (John 1:14).
· The Expected One is the Son of God and King of Psalm 2, the
resurrected one of Psalm 16, the crucified one of Psalm 22, the
shepherd of Psalm 23, and the betrayed one of Psalm 41.
· Isaiah predicted that the Messiah would be a light shining on

those who walk in darkness (9:2), be born of a virgin (7:14), bear exalted titles (9:6), be God with us (7:14; cf. Matt. 1:23), be a descendant of David (11:1), and sit on his throne (9:7). Isaiah also described the crucifixion of the Messiah and its profound theological implications in chapter 53.

• The rest of the prophets filled in other details concerning Jesus, the Expected One. Micah predicted His birth in Bethlehem (5:2); Jeremiah, Herod's slaughter of the innocent male babies (31:15; cf. Matt. 2:17–18); Hosea, the flight of Joseph, Mary, and Jesus into Egypt (11:1; cf. Matt. 2:15); Joel saw that through the coming of the Expected One the Spirit of God would be poured out (2:28–32; cf. Acts 2:16–18); Daniel predicted His death (9:26); Zechariah predicted the triumphal entry (9:9), the exact amount Judas would receive for betraying Jesus (11:12–13), the piercing of Jesus' side (12:10), and the disciples' forsaking of Him (13:7).

But despite the clear testimony of the Old Testament that Jesus was the Expected One—testimony confirmed by Zacharias, Elizabeth, the angel Gabriel, the angels who announced Christ's birth to the shepherds, John the Baptist, the Father and the Holy Spirit at Jesus' baptism, and Jesus' astonishing, unprecedented teaching and power over disease, demons, and death—most did not believe in Him. His widespread public teaching and visible, undeniable miracles were met with criticism, indifference, rejection, hatred, and finally murder.

Honest doubt, on the other hand, is not a bad starting point, but it is a bad finishing point. Even the noblest of saints, such as Abraham (Gen. 17:17), Sarah (Gen. 18:12), Moses (Ex. 3:10–15), Gideon (Judg. 6:13–23, 36–40), Elijah (1 Kings 19:1–14), and the apostles (Matt. 6:30; 8:26; 14:31; 16:8; 28:17; Luke 12:28; 24:38; John 20:24–25) had their moments of doubt. The capacity to doubt is an aspect of the rationality that is part of the image of God in man. A healthy skepticism, being able to discern truth from error, is critically important. For example, the Bible commends the noble-minded Bereans, who "received the word" preached by Paul and Silas "with great eagerness, examining the Scriptures daily to see whether these things were so" (Acts 17:11).

Even the greatest man who ever lived up to his time (Matt. 11:11), John the Baptist, struggled with doubt. He had believed that Jesus was the Messiah. He had witnessed the testimony to His identity by the Father and the Spirit when he baptized Jesus. John had declared that Jesus was "the Lamb of God who takes away the sin of the world!" (John 1:29), and testified concerning His identity to the Jewish leaders (vv. 26–27). But despite his powerful witness to Jesus as the Messiah, doubts had arisen in John's mind regarding His identity. This passage gives the reasons for John's doubt, and Jesus' response to that doubt.

JOHN'S DOUBT

The disciples of John reported to him about all these things. Summoning two of his disciples, John sent them to the Lord, saying, "Are You the Expected One, or do we look for someone else?" When the men came to Him, they said, "John the Baptist has sent us to You, to ask, 'Are You the Expected One, or do we look for someone else?'" (7:18–20)

John fulfilled his mission to prepare the people for the coming of Messiah and to point Him out when He arrived. He then faded from the scene, as he himself had foreseen would happen (John 3:30). Once Jesus was introduced, the inspired gospel writers put the spotlight on Him. As this passage begins, John had been in prison for many months, perhaps as long as a year. Matthew (14:1–12) and Mark (6:14–29) give the story of his imprisonment and eventual execution by Herod Antipas, the son of Herod the Great and ruler of Galilee and Perea (Luke 3:1). John had fearlessly rebuked Herod for his illegitimate marriage to Herodias, the wife of his brother Philip (Mark 6:17–18). Enraged, Herodias sought to have John put to death. Herod, however, awed by John's righteous and holy character (v. 20) and fearful of the crowds who revered him as a prophet (Matt. 14:5), refused. Instead, he kept him a prisoner at his summer palace at Machaerus, located east of the Dead Sea on a hill overlooking it.

While their teacher was in prison, some of **the disciples of John** followed Jesus (Matt. 9:14) and kept John informed with reports (Matt. 11:2). After some of them **reported to him about all the things** Jesus was doing, John's doubt became so acute that he took action. As all believers should, John took his doubts directly to the Lord and asked Him to resolve them. Since he was still in prison, John summoned **two of his disciples** and **sent them to the Lord** to ask Him on his behalf, **"Are You the Expected One, or do we look for someone else?"** So **when the men came to Him, they said, "John the Baptist has sent us to You, to ask, 'Are You the Expected One, or do we look for someone else?'"** Four reasons may be discerned for the doubt John's question expressed. By extension, they are also the causes for doubt in many believers.

First, John was experiencing a personal tragedy. His ministry had been the most significant of all the Old Testament prophets, since he was the forerunner and herald of the Messiah. John had faithfully, selflessly, and fearlessly carried out his prophetic duty. Yet despite that, he found himself locked in a prison cell. That seemed inconsistent both with his faithfulness, Messiah's power, and God's purpose. Surely the Messiah had the power to free him. And when Messiah came, bad things should have happened to evil people, not to His faithful forerunner.

After all, John had done exactly what God had called him to do. Though like all people he was a sinner, there is no hint of faithlessness in his ministry, or gross sin that could have caused him to view his imprisonment as God's chastening. Further, he had been filled with the Spirit from his mother's womb and was faithful to a Nazirite vow—the epitome of separation and dedication to God (Luke 1:15). John's doubt, like Job's, arose in part from his inability to understand why God had allowed his negative circumstances, since he rightly perceived himself as a loyal, sacrificial servant of the Lord. His situation was the opposite of that of the repentant thief on the cross, who freely acknowledged that his terrible circumstances were exactly what he deserved (Luke 23:41). Every situation that believers find themselves in is subject to the sovereign purpose of God whether it is perceived as deserved or undeserved.

A second cause of John's doubt was popular influence. He was in part a victim of current misconceptions about the Messiah. Contemporary Judaism ignored the prophecies of the suffering (Ps. 22) and sin-bearing work (Isa. 53) of the Messiah, focusing instead on His coming to crush Israel's enemies and establish His glorious kingdom. So deeply ingrained was that perception among the Jewish people that even after Jesus rose from the dead the apostles asked Him, "Lord, is it at this time You are restoring the kingdom to Israel?" (Acts 1:6).

Jesus, however, showed no sign of throwing off the yoke of Rome, or destroying the wicked, or establishing Israel's sovereignty, or creating prosperity for all. On the contrary, He deliberately defused an attempt to make Him king by force (John 6:15). Nor could the disciples understand the Lord's repeated prediction of His death (e.g., Matt. 16:21–23; 17:22–23; 20:18–19; Luke 24:6–7, 46). Such behavior was puzzling to many of Jesus' followers, including John. Illegitimate, unbiblical expectations can only lead to doubt and loss of joy when they are not met.

Jewish tradition also held—with no biblical warrant—that a series of prophets would reappear, culminating in the Messiah. That led to confusion and doubt about Jesus. Was He the Messiah, or one of those resurrected prophets (Luke 9:19)? That is why in reply to the Lord's question, "Who do people say that the Son of Man is?" (Matt. 16:13) the disciples replied, "Some say John the Baptist; and others, Elijah; but still others, Jeremiah, or one of the prophets" (v. 14). John's question to Jesus, **Are You the Expected One, or do we look for someone else?** reflects that popular misconception.

Third, John's doubt stemmed from incomplete revelation. Lack of information breeds doubt (cf. Matt. 22:29), and John was missing one crucial piece of information not clearly revealed in the Old Testament. It is true that the Old Testament implies two advents for Messiah, one as the suffering servant, and the other as the conquering king. But the Old Testament does not explicitly reveal the already 2,000-year gap between those two advents. During that time the Lord would turn from disobedient, rejecting Israel (Matt. 23:37–39) to the Gentiles and establish the church, which is made up of both Jews and Gentiles. Not until that period ends and all Israel is saved (Rom. 11:26) will Jesus return, establish His glorious kingdom, and fulfill all the promises of the Abrahamic and Davidic covenants. It was their failure to understand that truth that prompted the apostles' post-resurrection question to the Lord about establishing His kingdom noted above.

The cure for such doubt is to read, study, understand, and meditate on God's revelation in Scripture, as the opening words of the book of Psalms reveal:

> How blessed is the man who does not walk in the counsel of the wicked,
> Nor stand in the path of sinners,
> Nor sit in the seat of scoffers!
> But his delight is in the law of the Lord,
> And in His law he meditates day and night.
> He will be like a tree firmly planted by streams of water,
> Which yields its fruit in its season
> And its leaf does not wither;
> And in whatever he does, he prospers. (Ps. 1:1–3)

To keep Joshua from doubting his ability to lead Israel in the conquest of Canaan, God commanded him, "This book of the law shall not depart from your mouth, but you shall meditate on it day and night, so that you may be careful to do according to all that is written in it; for then you will make your way prosperous, and then you will have success" (Josh. 1:8). It was Nathanael's understanding of the Old Testament that removed any doubt in his mind that Jesus was the Messiah (John 1:49; cf. 5:39). As mentioned earlier, the Bereans turned to the Scriptures to verify the teaching they received. Since it contains the mind of Christ (1 Cor. 2:16) and reveals "everything pertaining to life and godliness" (2 Peter 1:3; cf. 3:18), Scripture provides the cure for doubt.

The final and perhaps most significant reason for John's doubt was his wrong expectation. John was a fiery preacher, warning of God's impending judgment and calling for repentance (cf. Luke 3:3–17). His warning of judgment picked up where the Old Testament ended (Mal.

4:1), and John expected the Messiah to execute that judgment on the wicked when He arrived.

But Jesus, instead of bringing destruction and judgment upon unbelievers, brought to them healing and compassion. The ax was not laid at the root of the trees, nor did the winnowing fork toss the chaff into the fire (Luke 3:9, 17). The Day of the Lord with all its fury and judgment of the wicked, had not arrived. That did not make sense to John, who had called for sinners to repent in order to avoid Messiah's soon and sudden judgment.

JESUS' RESPONSE

At that very time He cured many people of diseases and afflictions and evil spirits; and He gave sight to many who were blind. And He answered and said to them, "Go and report to John what you have seen and heard: the blind receive sight, the lame walk, the lepers are cleansed, and the deaf hear, the dead are raised up, the poor have the gospel preached to them. Blessed is he who does not take offense at Me." (7:21–23)

As the great high priest who sympathizes with the weaknesses of His people (Heb. 4:15), Jesus dealt gently with John's doubt. **At** the **very time** that the two messengers from John arrived, **He cured many people of diseases and afflictions and evil spirits; and He gave sight to many who were blind.** This was a special display of His miraculous power especially for their benefit and John's. Jesus had rejected the Pharisees' similar requests (cf. Matt. 12:38–42; 16:1–4), because they asked in unbelief. John, however, was seeking to have his faith strengthened and completed.

After the display Jesus **said to** the messengers, **"Go and report to John what you have seen and heard: the blind receive sight, the lame walk, the lepers are cleansed, and the deaf hear, the dead are raised up, the poor have the gospel preached to them."** The miraculous signs Jesus had performed were unmistakable evidence that the kingdom had been inaugurated (although it will not be present in its fullest sense until Christ returns and establishes His earthly millennial kingdom) and the King was present. John, steeped in the Old Testament, knew that such passages as Isaiah 26:19 and Daniel 12:2 point to a future resurrection of the **dead** associated with Messiah's kingdom. The resurrections Jesus performed were a preview of that resurrection. Similarly, Isaiah 35:5–6 associates healing the **blind, lame,** and **deaf** with the messianic kingdom, while Isaiah 61:1 describes the King's preaching of the **gospel** to humble, captive, oppressed, spiritually blind sinners (cf. Luke 4:17–21). Jesus then told the messengers to remind John, **"Blessed is he who does not take offense at Me."** He needed to rise above his personal tragedy, the popular views of the day, his lack of complete revelation, and his wrong expectations and put his complete faith and trust in the convincing evidence that Jesus was the Messiah.

How did John's story end? The resolution of his doubt can be inferred from Matthew's and Mark's gospels. As noted above, Herod's wife Herodias hated John and wanted him put to death. Eventually, at a gala birthday celebration for Herod, Herodias's daughter (Salome, according to Josephus) performed a lewd dance for Herod and his guests. Captivated by her performance and seeking to impress his guests, Herod impulsively promised the girl whatever she wanted. When she asked her mother what to ask for, Herodias promptly replied, "The head of John the Baptist" (Mark 6:24). Trapped by his foolish promise and unwilling to lose face before his guests, Herod granted her request and had John decapitated.

After John was beheaded, his disciples came and took away his body for burial. Then, significantly, "they went and reported to Jesus" (Matt. 14:12). Clearly, John had overcome his doubts and was satisfied that Jesus was the Messiah, or his disciples would not have sought out Jesus to tell Him of John's death.

Though not immune to it, true believers will, like John, be lifted by the truth above their doubt and reaffirm their faith in Jesus as Lord, Messiah, and Savior. They will be led to trust His wisdom above human wisdom, believe unreservedly all that the Bible teaches about Him, hear and obey His word with joy, entrust their lives to Him both now and for eternity, give their lives to proclaiming His gospel of salvation, desire always to do what pleases Him, revere, worship, and obey Him, trust His purpose for their lives, have confidence in His sovereign control of events, be grateful to Him as the source of all their good and thank Him for it, surrender body, mind, spirit, time, abilities, and possessions to His control, live their lives for Him no matter what is required of them, and, if asked, willingly die for Him.

Those who do so will find Jesus to be all they could ever need or want—Savior, Bread of life, Light of the world, Shepherd of their souls, the resurrection and the life, the way, the truth, and the life, the only way to God, and the one who will one day return for His own to usher them into the glorious presence of God, where faith will become sight and all doubts will forever vanish.

The Greatest Man Who Ever Lived (Luke 7:24–30)

16

When the messengers of John had left, He began to speak to the crowds about John, "What did you go out into the wilderness to see? A reed shaken by the wind? But what did you go out to see? A man dressed in soft clothing? Those who are splendidly clothed and live in luxury are found in royal palaces! But what did you go out to see? A prophet? Yes, I say to you, and one who is more than a prophet. This is the one about whom it is written, 'Behold, I send My messenger ahead of You, who will prepare Your way before You.' I say to you, among those born of women there is no one greater than John; yet he who is least in the kingdom of God is greater than he." When all the people and the tax collectors heard this, they acknowledged God's justice, having been baptized with the baptism of John. But the Pharisees and the lawyers rejected God's purpose for themselves, not having been baptized by John. (7:24–30)

The primary goal of Jesus' ministry was to demonstrate that He was the promised Messiah, King, and redeemer, who would fulfill the promises of the Abrahamic, Davidic, and New covenants. Therefore His goal in this passage was not merely to honor John the Baptist, although he was deserving of honor. Christ's main point in discussing John was to show how his ministry revealed and established Jesus to be the Expected One (cf. the discussion of that term in the previous chapter of this volume).

Most people in Israel initially accepted John as God's prophet who spoke for God as all true prophets did in the past. This was monumental since there had not been one for four centuries. All three of the Synoptic Gospels refer to the vast crowds that flocked to the Jordan River to hear him (Matt. 3:5–6; Mark 1:5; Luke 3:7, 10). Herod Antipas hesitated to execute John because the crowds viewed him as a prophet (Matt. 14:5), while the Jewish leaders feared that if they denied John's authenticity, "all the people [would] stone [them] to death, for they [were] convinced that John was a prophet" (Luke 20:6; cf. Matt. 21:26; Mark 11:32).

What makes the people's belief that John was a prophet all the more remarkable is the nature of his message. John the Baptist was no man-pleasing flatterer, but preached a fiery message of coming judgment and the need for repentance. He denounced both the crowds (Luke 3:7) and their leaders (Matt. 3:7) as venomous snakes scrambling to escape the furious wrath to come. Still more amazing, many of those who heard John preach were willing to be baptized by him—a proselyte baptism normally reserved for Gentiles converting to Judaism. By accepting baptism at his hands, the Jews were acknowledging themselves to be outside the covenants and the promises, and no better than uncircumcised Gentiles. But despite John's forceful condemnation of their sin and his call for them to repent, the people kept coming to hear the prophet announcing Messiah's arrival. They agreed with Jesus' assessment of John the Baptist, **I say to you, among those born of women there is no one greater than John.**

There was a glaring inconsistency in their acceptance of John, however. Their dilemma was that while they acknowledged John as a prophet, for the most part they did not accept John's message that Jesus was the Messiah. Beyond what John said, the Lord had clearly demonstrated by the truth of His declaration that He was the Expected One, God in human flesh. He had traveled all over Galilee healing the sick, casting out demons, and raising the dead (as He had just done at Nain [7:11–15]). In fact, Jesus had just finished putting on a display of His divine power for the messengers from John the Baptist (7:20–22). All that was done in fulfillment of Old Testament prophecy (cf. Isa. 61:1).

At this point, Jesus seized the opportunity to confirm His messiahship and put the crowds in an untenable position by pointing out the reality that because they accepted John as a prophet, they must therefore accept his testimony to Jesus being the Messiah. If John were a prophet, that testimony was true; on the other hand if his testimony was not true, then he was not a prophet. And John could hardly have deserved the honor of being called the greatest man who ever lived if he lied about Jesus being the Messiah.

Based on societal norms, John would not be considered great. He would be viewed as anti-social, abrasive, politically incorrect, and in general a bothersome, irritating nuisance. He had no wealth, social prominence, or formal education. He achieved nothing notable by the typical standard of measure; he held no position, built no organization, and left no literary works. But God's standards for greatness are the absolute antithesis of the world's, and by those standards John was greater than anyone before him, including all the exalted persons of the Old Testament record, like Adam, Noah, Abraham, Moses, Joshua, David, Solomon, and all of the prophets (cf. Luke 1:15). In this passage Jesus lists three features that mark John's greatness; his personal character, privileged calling, and powerful contribution.

JOHN'S PERSONAL CHARACTER

When the messengers of John had left, He began to speak to the crowds about John, "What did you go out into the wilderness to see? A reed shaken by the wind? But what did you go out to see? A man dressed in soft clothing? Those who are splendidly clothed and live in luxury are found in royal palaces! (7:24–25)

As noted in chapter 15 of this volume, John was imprisoned and unable to come to Jesus in person. Apparently experiencing some doubts, based on what was happening to him and not happening with Jesus, John sent two of his disciples to ask Him if He was really the Messiah. In response, the Lord put on a convincing display of His divine power for their benefit and sent them back to John (7:21–23). After **the messengers of John had left, He began to speak to the crowds about** him. Jesus drove home His point that it was inconsistent for the people to accept John as a prophet, but reject Him as Messiah. Three rhetorical questions form His response. The first two emphasize John's personal character.

The Lord's first question, **"What did you go out into the wilderness to see? A reed shaken by the wind?"** stresses that John the Baptist was not a vacillator, swaying here and there in the breezes of popular opinion, but a man of firm, unshakeable convictions. Those convictions led him to fearlessly confront Herod Antipas, which led to John's arrest and eventual execution. It was his uncompromising boldness and passionate commitment to the truth that caused thousands of people to travel up to forty or fifty miles or more into the **wilderness** where John spent his entire ministry (Matt. 3:1; cf. v. 3; Isa. 40:3) to hear him preach repentance in readiness for the Messiah.

Jesus then asked a second rhetorical question that further reveals John's character. **"What did you go out to see? A man dressed in soft clothing? Those who are splendidly clothed and live in luxury are found in royal palaces!"** *Malakos* (**soft**) is translated "effeminate" in 1 Corinthians 6:9. It calls to mind the frilly, lacy, embroidered clothing that has always been worn by the pampered nobility. John's wardrobe was just the opposite; it consisted simply of "a garment of camel's hair and a leather belt" (Matt. 3:4). Instead of the fancy delicacies of some royal court, his diet consisted of "locusts and wild honey" (v. 4).

But John was no effeminate flatterer of nobility; he was not a panderer living **in luxury** in Herod's palace, but a prisoner languishing in a dungeon. William Hendriksen writes,

> Those who wear "soft" garments are the people without backbone, sycophants who readily kowtow to those in authority and are rewarded with a high office in the king's palace, a position that enables them to be gorgeously appareled and to live luxuriously in harmony with the high station in life to which they have attained. (*Exposition of the Gospel According to Luke*, New Testament Commentary [Grand Rapids: Baker, 1978], 396)

John not only spoke like a prophet, but also lived like one. There was not a trace of self-aggrandizement in his life. He did not live a life of indulgent luxury, but of austerity and self-denial, of separation from the world and devotion to God. John's denial and devotion may be seen in his lifelong abstention from alcoholic beverages (Luke 1:15), which suggests that he had taken a Nazirite vow (cf. Num. 6:2–4). John's prophetic integrity rang true with the people because of his unimpeachable personal character.

JOHN'S PRIVILEGED CALLING

But what did you go out to see? A prophet? Yes, I say to you, and one who is more than a prophet. This is the one about whom it is written, 'Behold, I send My messenger ahead of You, who will prepare Your way before You.' (7:26–27)

As noble as John's character was, an even more significant element of his greatness was his privileged calling. When the people trekked into the wilderness to see John, they all knew that they were going **out to see a prophet.** As noted above, John was highly regarded by the people, so much so that they even wondered if he himself might be the Messiah (Luke 3:15). John had all the marks of a prophet; he powerfully proclaimed the word of God, confronted sin, warned of coming judgment, called for repentance, and lived a life of self-denial.

But Jesus went beyond merely identifying John as a prophet, declaring him to be **one who is more than a prophet.** John was not only a prophet himself, but also one who was prophesied to come. Paraphrasing Malachi 3:1 to give it its correct interpretation Jesus reminded the crowd, **"This is the one about whom it is written, 'Behold, I send My messenger ahead of You, who will prepare Your way before You.'"** John was the prophet whom Malachi predicted would prepare the way for the Messiah (cf. Isa. 40:3–5; Luke 3:4–6). It was his unique privilege of being Messiah's forerunner that set him apart for unparalleled greatness. While the other Old Testament prophets predicted that Messiah would come; John announced that He had arrived. For them it was a matter of faith; for John it was sight. He had the privilege of not only seeing the Messiah, but also of talking with Him, and hearing the Father's audible testimony concerning Him.

Malachi's identification of this coming prophet as Elijah (Mal. 4:5) raises the question of whether John the Baptist was Elijah returned, since John explicitly denied that he was (John 1:21). The true interpretation of Malachi's prediction was made clear before John was born. In his announcement of John's miraculous birth to his father Zacharias, the angel Gabriel said of him, "It is he who will go as a forerunner before Him [Messiah] in the spirit and power of Elijah" (Luke 1:17). Thus, when John denied that he was Elijah, he meant that he was not that very Old Testament prophet returned from heaven, and clarified what the Jews wrongly expected (see Luke 9:8 and the discussion of Luke 7:18–20 in chapter 15 of this volume).

The truth is that had the Jews believed in Jesus, John the Baptist would have become the fulfillment of the Elijah-like prophet of whom Malachi wrote. In Matthew's parallel account of this passage, Jesus noted, "If you are willing to accept it [the truth that He was the Messiah], John himself is Elijah who was to come" (Matt. 11:14). When the apostles asked Him, "Why is it that the scribes say that Elijah must come first?" (Mark 9:11) Jesus replied,

> Elijah does first come and restore all things. And yet how is it written of the Son of Man that He will suffer many things and be treated with contempt? But I say to you that Elijah [John the Baptist] has indeed come, and they did to him whatever they wished, just as it is written of him. (vv. 12–13)

Since Israel rejected Messiah and His kingdom, there must be another Elijah-like prophet who will come in fulfillment of Malachi's prophecy just before Christ's return to establish His glorious, earthly, millennial kingdom. Unrelated to that prophet to come, who will bear some resemblance to the ministry of Elijah, there will also appear two witnesses who will minister during the tribulation (Rev. 11:3–12), one of which may actually be Elijah.

But Israel's unbelief does not diminish John's stature. He was the forerunner of the Messiah, the fulfillment of Malachi's (Mal. 3:1) and Isaiah's (40:3–5) prophecies. His privileged calling made him the last and greatest of the Old Testament prophets, the last preacher of the age of promise, the bridge into the age of fulfillment, and the first preacher in the New Testament.

JOHN'S POWERFUL CONTRIBUTION

When all the people and the tax collectors heard this, they acknowledged God's justice, having been baptized with the baptism of John. But the Pharisees and the lawyers rejected God's purpose for themselves, not having been baptized by John. (7:29–30)

Whether these two verses record words spoken by Jesus or are Luke's editorial comment is not clear, but the latter is more likely. John's profound impact on the nation is evident from the response both of those who initially accepted his message, and those who rejected it. So great was John's influence that he literally divided the nation. **When all the** common **people,** including even the hated and reviled **tax collectors, heard** John's powerful preaching **they acknowledged God's justice,** or righteousness. They admitted that they were sinners and that God was holy, righteous, and just to condemn them for their sin and call them to repentance. They also agreed to be **baptized with the baptism of John,** thus publicly acknowledging themselves to be outside of God's kingdom and no better off than the pagan Gentiles.

On the other hand, the religious elite, **the Pharisees and the lawyers, rejected God's purpose for themselves,** and refused to repent and be **baptized by John.** The **lawyers,** or scribes, were the self-styled experts in the law. They gave advice and direction in religious, criminal, and governmental matters. Most of them were **Pharisees,** proud, aloof, self-righteous, and viewing themselves as spiritually superior to the common people (cf. John 7:49). Unlike the people, they were not at all willing to acknowledge that they were sinners.

The common people were thrilled for a while by John's ministry. They were excited to have a prophet among them again after four centuries without any word from God. The people eagerly anticipated the arrival of the long-desired Messiah, of whom John was the forerunner. But John's identification of Jesus as the Messiah put them in a quandary. Amazingly, instead of accepting the testimony of the one whom they had hailed as God's great prophet, the people refused to embrace Jesus. Some even chose to escape their dilemma by revising their view of John to accommodate their rejection of Jesus. Some said the worst according to Luke 7:33 where the Lord said, "For John the Baptist has come eating no bread and drinking no wine, and you say, 'He has a demon!'" Others, according to John 5:35, were temporarily impressed by John. In the words of Jesus, "He was the lamp that was burning and was shining and you were willing to rejoice *for a while* in his light" (emphasis added).

All the euphoria surrounding John and his ministry was short-lived. Awed and traumatized by John's powerful preaching and caught up in the crowd mentality, many people made superficial, emotional commitments. Later, under the influence of the religious leaders, they turned away from John and his teaching. They began to deny what they had once affirmed regarding John to justify their rejection of Jesus. So completely did they abandon John that there was no public outcry when corrupt Herod executed him. Many similarly were swept up in the excitement of Jesus' triumphal entry. But the same frenzied mob that shouted "Hosanna!" on that occasion would just a few days later scream, "Crucify Him!" Like the rocky and thorny soils (cf. Luke 8:6–7), their commitment was shallow, superficial, and fading fast.

But despite his exemplary personal character, uniquely privileged calling, and undeniably powerful contribution, the shocking truth is, Jesus told His hearers, that although **among those born of women there is no one greater than John; yet he who is least in the kingdom of God** (the sphere of salvation where God rules over His people) **is greater than he.** That surprising statement can be understood in two ways. First, the kingdom of God is an eternal, spiritual reality, while John's ministry was an earthly, temporal one (although John himself, of course, was also in the kingdom). Thus, although no one ever had a more significant earthly function than John, everyone in the kingdom has greater spiritual privileges. Eternal salvation far surpasses the highest earthly privilege.

But there is another sense in which the Lord's words can be understood. The kingdom of God takes on various distinct forms. It existed in the Old Testament where God ruled as king over Israel (cf. 1 Sam. 8:7; 12:12; Isa. 33:22). It was a kingdom based on the promise of the coming Messiah. But there was another form of the kingdom that both John the Baptist (Matt. 3:1–2) and Jesus (Matt. 4:17) said was imminent, inaugurated with the coming of Messiah. This was not a different sphere of salvation, but rather the fulfillment of the kingdom promised in the Old Testament. All believers in the era of fulfillment enjoy greater privileges than even John, the greatest man of the era of promise, enjoyed.

Having inaugurated the era of fulfillment with His coming, Jesus could say to His disciples, "Blessed are the eyes which see the things you see, for I say to you, that many prophets and kings wished to see the things which you see, and did not see them, and to hear the things which you hear, and did not hear them" (Luke 10:23–24). The writer of Hebrews notes that "all these [the heroes of faith from the era of promise], having gained approval through their faith, did not receive what was promised, because God had provided something better for us, so that apart from us they would not be made perfect" (Heb. 11:39–40).

In contrast to John and the others in the era of promise, believers in the era of fulfillment have the full record of the life of Christ in the gospels, the spread of the gospel by the Spirit's power in Acts, the explanation of Christ's person and work and the purpose of God in salvation in the epistles, and the details of Christ's glorious return to establish His earthly kingdom and the eternal state that follows it in the book of Revelation. Believers in the era of fulfillment also have the indwelling Holy Spirit to empower (Acts 1:8) and guide them (1 John 2:20, 27). As a result, we understand truths not understood by those in the era of promise, not even by its greatest prophet, John the Baptist. Paul identifies those truths as mysteries, hidden in the Old Testament, but revealed in the New. They include:

- The mystery of Christ's incarnation (Col. 2:2–3); that He would be both God and man, a truth hinted at in the Old Testament (e.g., Isa. 7:14; 9:6), but not made clear.
- The mystery of Israel's unbelief (Rom. 11:25–29).
- The mystery of Gentile salvation (Rom. 16:25–26).
- The mystery of Jews and Gentiles united in one body (Eph. 2:11–22).
- The mystery of the indwelling of Christ in believers (Col. 1:25–27).
- The mystery of lawlessness embodied in the future antichrist (2 Thess. 2:7–8).
- The mystery of the rapture of the church (1 Cor. 15:51).
- The mystery of the summing up of all things in Christ (Eph. 1:9–10).

Those in the era of fulfillment have full revelation concerning the depravity of man, Christ's substitutionary atonement, resurrection, ascension, and future return in glory, heaven and hell, the justification, sanctification, and glorification of believers; in short, we have in the word of God the revelation of the mind of Christ (1 Cor. 2:16) and the full purpose of God (Acts 20:17–20, 27).

The cross and empty tomb mark the point at which promise became fulfillment. Believers on this side of the resurrection are greater than John the Baptist, not in terms of personal character or influence, but because they have the privilege of proclaiming the fullness of the gospel. John preached that sinners needed to repent and be reconciled to God to prepare themselves for Messiah's coming. But to believers in the era of fulfillment, God "has committed . . . the word of reconciliation" (2 Cor. 5:19), sending us out as ambassadors for Christ, pleading with sinners to be reconciled to God through Him (v. 20; cf. Matt. 28:19–20). Our message is to proclaim the full truth of the Savior's death and resurrection.

The Parable of the Brats: Style Versus Substance (Luke 7:31–35)

17

"To what then shall I compare the men of this generation, and what are they like? They are like children who sit in the market place and call to one another, and they say, 'We played the flute for you, and you did not dance; we sang a dirge, and you did not weep.' For John the Baptist has come eating no bread and drinking no wine, and you say, 'He has a demon!' The Son of Man has come eating and drinking, and you say, 'Behold, a gluttonous man and a drunkard, a friend of tax collectors and sinners!' Yet wisdom is vindicated by all her children." (7:31–35)

The term "brat" is a coarse word, simple and yet loaded with vivid meaning. It is a pejorative term that calls to mind children who are unruly, disobedient, objectionable, obstreperous, refractory, recalcitrant, incorrigible, obstinate, and intractable. The Bible describes them as those who dishonor their parents (Deut. 27:16), fools who reject their father's discipline (Prov. 15:5), shameful and disgraceful children who reject their parents (Prov. 19:26), and selfish children who bring shame to their parents (Prov. 29:15). Being disobedient to parents appears among the list of serious sins that mark those who reject God (Rom. 1:30; 2 Tim. 3:2) and Scripture warns of stern punishment for rebellious children (cf. Deut. 27:16; Prov. 30:17)—including being executed (Ex. 21:15; Deut. 21:18–21).

Jesus directed this parable of the brats to the people of His society, in particular those present on that occasion. He likened their response to the gospel to that of bratty children—belligerent, ungrateful, and impossible to satisfy. Yet the principle is timeless. In every age there will be people who respond to the gospel message of repentance, faith, forgiveness, and salvation like the brats of that generation did.

It should be noted that in contrast to today's politically correct emphasis on tolerance, neither John the Baptist nor Jesus hesitated to confront and rebuke people with strong and offensive language. When the Jewish leaders came to see him, John abruptly greeted them with the decidedly non-seeker-friendly challenge, "You brood of vipers, who warned you to flee from the wrath to come?" (Matt. 3:7). According to Luke's account, he asked the shallow, superficial repenters in the crowds, who shared the religious leaders' prideful insincerity (Luke 3:7), the same question. Jesus labeled the scribes and Pharisees hypocrites (Matt. 6:2, 5, 16; 23:13, 15, 23, 25, 27, 29), blind guides (Matt. 15:14; 23:16, 24), sons of hell (Matt. 23:15), fools (Matt. 23:17), robbers (John 10:8), whitewashed tombs (Matt. 23:27), and serpents (Matt. 23:33).

The gospel message had up to this point in history been preached by only two men, John the Baptist and Jesus. The Twelve had not yet been sent out to preach (Luke 9:1–2), nor had the seventy (Luke 10:1). But although their styles of ministry differed markedly, many of the people who heard John and Jesus had the same offended, defiant, hostile, obstinate response to both of them.

At the outset of his ministry, this last prophet and first preacher of the gospel had been immensely popular. Huge crowds had journeyed into the wilderness near the Jordan River to hear him preach and to be baptized by him (Matt. 3:5–6). They had acknowledged John to be a true prophet of God, the forerunner to Messiah predicted by Malachi (Mal. 3:1).

The religious elite, on the other hand, haughtily refused to confess their sin, repent, or be baptized by John (Luke 7:30). Smugly secure in their self-righteous legalism, they viewed the common people who were interested in John with contempt (cf. John 7:49). They had no use for the wilderness preacher; rejecting his call for repentance, they were annoyed by his warning of coming judgment, and infuriated by his bold denunciation of them as a "brood of vipers" (Matt. 3:7). Their religious pride caused them to reject the gospel's call for humble repentance; their devotion to superficially, outwardly keeping the law caused them to reject the gospel's provision of grace, mercy, and forgiveness; their sense of spiritual superiority (cf. Mark 2:16; Luke 15:1–2; John 9:34) caused them to reject as ludicrous the gospel's promise of forgiveness for even the most wretched sinners.

Eventually the common people, under the influence of the apostate religionists, began to have doubts about Jesus. Though astonished by His unparalleled preaching (Matt. 7:28–29; cf. John 7:46) and the miracles He performed (John 2:23; 3:2; 6:2), they grew increasingly restive over the leaders' rejection of Him and His refusal to assume the role of the conquering military and political ruler that they wrongly expected Messiah to be (cf. John 6:14–15). As noted in the previous chapter of this volume, becoming uncomfortable with Jesus caused many to rethink their view of John the Baptist. John had unequivocally declared that Jesus was the Messiah. If they continued to believe that he was Messiah's forerunner, they faced the dilemma of how to reconcile that belief with their denial of Jesus' claims. In the end, the majority rejected both John (Luke 7:33; John 5:35) and Jesus (John 6:66). Since John was by this time a prisoner, the brunt of their opposition and hostility was directed at Jesus.

This parable may be divided into four sections: the introduction, the illustration, the application, and the conclusion.

THE INTRODUCTION

"To what then shall I compare the men of this generation, and what are they like? (7:31)

After the parenthetical comment (most likely by Luke) in verses 29 and 30, Jesus continued speaking, as He had been since 7:22. This phrase is a Hebraism, commonly used in the Midrash to introduce an analogy explaining a spiritual reality. The parable or analogy that follows will give the Lord's assessment of **the men of this generation.** The term **generation** refers to the people of Jesus' day, in particular the Pharisees and scribes and those who followed them in rejecting John the Baptist and Jesus (vv. 29–30). *Genea* (**generation**) is used frequently in Luke's gospel in a negative sense as a term of condemnation. In 9:41 Jesus spoke of this generation as an "unbelieving and perverted generation," and in 11:29 described it as a "wicked generation," guilty of all the blood of the murdered prophets (vv. 50–51) and above all of rejecting the Lord Jesus Christ (17:25). By extension, the term can refer to any perverse and faithless generation (cf. Deut. 32:5; Judg. 2:10; Jer. 7:29; Acts 2:40; Phil. 2:15). The Lord's timeless illustration that follows applies to anyone in any generation who rejects the gospel.

The Illustration

They are like children who sit in the market place and call to one another, and they say, 'We played the flute for you, and you did not dance; we sang a dirge, and you did not weep.' (7:32)

Though a scene such as the Lord described, children at play, is a familiar one throughout human history, this is the only reference in the Bible to children playing a game. Unlike modern cities, towns and villages in first-century Palestine had no designated parks or playgrounds. Most of them, however, had an *agora,* a large open area near the middle of the town used as a **market place.** It was also the place for public gatherings and became a convenient playground for children. Jesus pictures a time when the *agora* was not being used as a market place and children were playing in it.

When they play, children frequently imitate adult behaviors. Apparently children in Jesus' day often played two games that reflected the most significant events in Jewish social life: weddings and funerals. Historically, weddings and funerals have marked life's happiest and saddest occasions. Weddings in Israel were ornate, elaborate affairs, often lasting for a week and involving processions through the streets as well as feasting (cf. Matt. 25:1–12; John 2:1–10). Funerals featured elements of public mourning and a public procession to the burial, along with fasting (Luke 7:11–16), so children would have been familiar with both.

In Jesus' story, some children had been trying to organize a game. They sat **in the market place and** called to some of the other children who had refused to play, **"We played the flute for you, and you did not dance."** This suggests that these children had attempted to involve the others in a game of make-believe wedding, since music and dancing were integral parts of a wedding celebration. But those invited would not join in the game; they were stubborn, indifferent, and surly. Refusing to be happy and participate in the dancing and singing, they preferred instead to pout and sulk.

The first group of children then tried to involve the others in a mock funeral. But they refused to play that game either, prompting the children who invited them to complain, **"We sang a dirge, and you did not weep."** Their frustration is understandable, since no matter what game they designed, the others would not play. The nature of the game was not the issue, since the peevish brats would not play either the happy or the sad game. They serve as an apt illustration of the people of that generation—ill-tempered malcontents.

THE APPLICATION

"For John the Baptist has come eating no bread and drinking no wine, and you say, 'He has a demon!' The Son of Man has come eating and drinking, and you say, 'Behold, a gluttonous man and a drunkard, a friend of tax collectors and sinners!'" (7:33–34)

Having given His hearers a simple illustration, Jesus applied it to Himself and John. First, He likened John's ministry to the funeral game. **Eating bread** and **drinking wine** symbolized the normal pattern of social life. In the Olivet Discourse Jesus told His hearers that when He returns life will be continuing normally, just as in the "days before the flood [when] they were eating and drinking, marrying and giving in marriage, until the day that Noah entered the ark" (Matt. 24:38). John's radically ascetic lifestyle was a total disconnect from and condemnation of Jewish society. Instead of **eating bread,** John's "food was locusts and wild honey"; instead of stylish clothes, he wore "a garment of camel's hair and a leather belt around his waist" (Matt. 3:4); instead of living in luxurious surroundings, he "lived in the deserts until the day of his public appearance to Israel" (Luke 1:80). Even after he began his ministry, John remained in the desolate wilderness near the Jordan (Matt. 3:1). His Nazirite vow, forbidding the **drinking** of **wine** (Luke 1:15), and his diet, a kind of fasting, further isolated John from the normal course of life. Cultural trends and the fads of society had no influence on him.

John's ministry was a somber, serious dirge sounding a warning of coming judgment and proclaiming to sinners the need for repentance and mourning over sin. The tone of his preaching was fearful, frightening, and confrontational; John's message was a severe one, with little emphasis on grace and mercy. His focus was on God's wrath and vengeance, and he challenged his hearers to repent or be consumed by the fiery judgment that was coming (Luke 3:8, 9, 17). He had no use for shallow, superficial hypocrites, denouncing them as a "brood of vipers" (v. 7), desperately trying to escape the flames of judgment.

The reaction of the spiritual brats to John the Baptist's austere self-denial and message of judgment was shocking. At first they had hailed him as a true prophet of God, the forerunner of the Messiah prophesied by Isaiah and Malachi. But soon after they contemptuously dismissed him as having **a demon.** The present tense of the verb translated **you say** indicates that some of those hearing Jesus speak were among the very ones who had denounced John as being demon-possessed. The reason for that astounding conclusion was that bizarre behavior was frequently associated with demon possession. The Gerasene demoniac, for instance, lived in a cemetery, wore no clothes, was extremely violent, screamed constantly, and mutilated himself (Matt. 8:28; Mark 5:1–5; Luke 8:26–27). John's behavior was so different, unique, and anti-social that some concluded that it could only be explained as the madness associated with demon possession. Many would come to the same blasphemous conclusion regarding Jesus (cf. Luke 11:19; John 7:20; 8:48; 10:20).

The people's motive for so labeling John was their hatred of his message. Their hearts were hard and impenetrable, causing them to reject the divine diagnosis of their condition that he proclaimed. Being proud and self-righteous, they hated John's condemnation of them as sinners, desperately in need of repentance and forgiveness. They at - tacked John's person in order to justify their rejection of his message. They refused to join with him.

But the spiritual brats' rejection of the gospel did not stop with John. The term **Son of Man**, a messianic title taken from Daniel 7:13, was the Lord's favorite designation of Himself, which He used more than eighty times. Unlike John the Baptist, Jesus came **eating and drinking;** that is, He participated in the normal enjoyments and occasions of social life, including weddings (John 2:1–11) as well as funerals (Luke 7:11–16; John 11:1–44). John's ministry took place in the wilderness, but Jesus traveled extensively through the towns and villages of Israel (cf. Matt. 9:35; Mark 6:6, 56; 8:27; Luke 8:1; 13:22). If John's ministry was reminiscent of a funeral, Jesus' ministry more closely resembled a wedding. In fact, the Lord likened His ministry to a wedding, picturing Himself as the bride-groom and the disciples as the bridegroom's attendants (Matt. 9:15; cf. John 3:29).

Because John was aloof and did not associate with people, they denounced him as demon possessed. But because Jesus interacted with people, even the outcasts of society, His enemies scornfully denounced Him as **a gluttonous man and a drunkard, a friend of tax collectors and sinners.** That Jesus frequently associated with those whom they viewed as the dregs of society never ceased to infuriate the Jewish religious leaders. When the Lord attended a banquet given by the former tax collector Matthew after his call to follow Him, the Pharisees confronted His disciples and demanded, "Why is your Teacher eating with the tax collectors and sinners?" (Matt. 9:11). Luke records later in his gospel that "all the tax collectors and the sinners were coming near Him to listen to Him" (Luke 15:1). Predictably shocked and outraged, "both the Pharisees and the scribes began to grumble, saying, 'This man receives sinners and eats with them'" (v. 2). When Jesus did the unthinkable and invited Himself to the house of the hated tax collector Zaccheus, "they all began to grumble, saying, 'He has gone to be the guest of a man who is a sinner'" (Luke 19:7).

The Lord rebuked that evil generation for rejecting both divine messengers who proclaimed the truth, despite their different styles of ministry. John was sober, severe, stark, a preacher of judgment, calling for repentance, weeping in light of God's wrath, and keeping himself separate from sinners. Jesus, in contrast, was tender, merciful, gracious, compassionate, a preacher of blessing who mingled with sinners, whom He came to seek and save.

In the end, it is not the style of ministry that matters but its substance. The people ultimately rejected the ministries of both John and Jesus. Though their emphases may have differed, both John and Jesus called for repentance, promised forgiveness, warned of judgment, and proclaimed the coming of the kingdom. The outward form of ministry is never the issue, but rather the truth of the message. In every generation there will be spiritual brats who reject the truth, like those who refused to mourn with John or laugh with Jesus.

THE CONCLUSION

Yet wisdom is vindicated by all her children. (7:35)

Not all who hear the gospel message will reject it; **wisdom,** Jesus said, **is vindicated** (justified or proven true) **by all her children,** or as Matthew's parallel account phrases it, "deeds" (Matt. 11:19). Both terms refer to the product of true spiritual wisdom, which is salvation (2 Tim. 3:15). Despite the scoffing spiritual brats, the gospel will always produce results; there will always be some who accept it. Their lives will demonstrate the power of salvation **wisdom.**

The Lord's masterful illustration reveals that there are two kinds of spiritual children in every generation: folly's brats and wisdom's children. The brats are fools devoid of true wisdom and marked by a hatred of the truth and rejection of those who proclaim it. On the other hand, wisdom's children, the redeemed, are known by the righteous deeds their transformed lives produce (Eph. 2:10; cf. 2 Cor. 5:17). The preacher's style is not the determining factor; "the gospel," not the cleverness of the messenger, "is the power of God for salvation to everyone who believes" (Rom. 1:16). The same "word of the cross" that "is foolishness to those who are perishing" is to those "who are being saved . . . the power of God" (1 Cor. 1:18).

The Transformed Sinner
(Luke 7:36–50)

18

Now one of the Pharisees was requesting Him to dine with him, and He entered the Pharisee's house and reclined at the table. And there was a woman in the city who was a sinner; and when she learned that He was reclining at the table in the Pharisee's house, she brought an alabaster vial of perfume, and standing behind Him at His feet, weeping, she began to wet His feet with her tears, and kept wiping them with the hair of her head, and kissing His feet and anointing them with the perfume. Now when the Pharisee who had invited Him saw this, he said to himself, "If this man were a prophet He would know who and what sort of person this woman is who is touching Him, that she is a sinner." And Jesus answered him, "Simon, I have something to say to you." And he replied, "Say it, Teacher." "A moneylender had two debtors: one owed five hundred denarii, and the other fifty. When they were unable to repay, he graciously forgave them both. So which of them will love him more?" Simon answered and said, "I suppose the one whom he forgave more." And He said to him, "You have judged correctly." Turning toward the woman, He said to Simon, "Do you see this woman? I entered your house; you gave Me no water for My feet, but she has wet My

feet with her tears and wiped them with her hair. You gave Me no kiss; but she, since the time I came in, has not ceased to kiss My feet. You did not anoint My head with oil, but she anointed My feet with perfume. For this reason I say to you, her sins, which are many, have been forgiven, for she loved much; but he who is forgiven little, loves little." Then He said to her, "Your sins have been forgiven." Those who were reclining at the table with Him began to say to themselves, "Who is this man who even forgives sins?" And He said to the woman, "Your faith has saved you; go in peace." (7:36–50)

Much evidence for the truthfulness of the Christian faith can be amassed from such fields as science, history, philosophy, and fulfilled prophecy. Yet the truth of the gospel is also evidenced by the testimony of the transformed lives of the redeemed.

The profound account of the transformation of Saul—zealous, Christian-persecuting Pharisee—to Paul—apostolic missionary—has led, directly or indirectly, to the conversion of millions of people through the centuries. The transformed lives of the believers in Corinth (1 Cor. 6:9–11) provided a powerful witness in that debauched city. In 1 Peter 4:3–4 Peter described the impact of believers' lives on unbelievers:

> For the time already past is sufficient for you to have carried out the desire of the Gentiles, having pursued a course of sensuality, lusts, drunkenness, carousing, drinking parties and abominable idolatries. In all this, they are surprised that you do not run with them into the same excesses of dissipation, and they malign you.

The dramatic change in the life of the hated tax collector Levi (Matthew) was immediately evident to those who attended the reception he gave in Jesus' honor (Luke 5:27–29). Even more astonishing was the turnaround in Zaccheus's life. As a chief tax collector (Luke 19:2), he oversaw several tax collectors like Matthew, and was thus even more despised. Yet his life was forever changed the day Jesus passed through Jericho (v. 1) and brought salvation to him (v. 9)—a change noted by the others present (v. 7). The marked change in the life of the Samaritan woman of Sychar led many more people from her village to believe in Jesus (John 4:39–42). An equally miraculous and uniquely stunning transformation was wrought in the demon-possessed Gerasene man, who went from being a deadly, naked maniac to a sane missionary (Luke 8:26–39).

The main thrust of this passage appears on the surface to be the transformed life of the sinful woman. But she was merely one element of the story, which focuses primarily on the Lord evangelizing a Pharisee. Jesus used her as a testimony to him and the others present of the truth and power of the gospel. Ironically, Jesus demonstrated His power to forgive sins and transform lives by using the very type of person the Pharisees despised the most. In reality, the self-righteous, hypocritical religious leaders were the worst possible sinners; people who believe they are not lost and think they do not need redemption cannot be saved.

The Lord Jesus Christ came to seek and save the penitent and believing lost (Luke 19:10)—the self-righteous members of the religious establishment as well as the outcast riff raff of society. In keeping with that truth, Luke records two other occasions when Jesus had a meal at a Pharisee's house (11:37–54; 14:1–24). In both instances, the Pharisees had no genuine interest in Jesus. Having already rejected Him and His message, they were merely attempting to gather evidence they could use to condemn Him. In 14:1 Luke notes that the Pharisees present were "watching [Jesus] closely," while after the meal recorded in chapter 11, "the scribes and the Pharisees began to be very hostile and to question Him closely on many subjects, plotting against Him to catch Him in something He might say" (vv. 53–54).

This incident is not to be confused with the later anointing of Jesus by Mary, the sister of Martha and Lazarus (Matt. 26:6–13; Mark 14:3–9; John 12:1–8). The story recorded in this passage took place in Galilee, not Bethany; the unnamed woman was a sinner (most likely a prostitute, as noted below) not Mary; this anointing happened much earlier in the Lord's ministry, not during Passion Week, at the house of Simon the Pharisee, not Simon the leper. The only superficial similarity is that the owners of both houses were named Simon. However Simon was an extremely common name in Israel. The New Testament lists several other men by that name, including two of the apostles, Simon Peter and Simon the Zealot, (Luke 6:14–15), one of Jesus' brothers (Matt. 13:55), a man from Cyrene forced by the Romans to carry Jesus' cross (Mark 15:21), the father of Judas Iscariot (John 6:71), the false prophet Simon the magician (Acts 8:9–24), and Simon the tanner, at whose house in Joppa Peter stayed (Acts 9:43).

As the story opens, **one of the Pharisees was requesting** the Lord **to dine with him.** Where this incident took place is not known, except that it was in Galilee during Jesus' Galilean ministry, which Luke describes in 4:14–9:50. Like the other Pharisees who invited Jesus to a meal, this Pharisee had no personal interest in Him. He was not an open-minded inquirer, but had like the majority of the Pharisees, already decided that Jesus was a blasphemer, arrogating to Himself the right to forgive sins that belongs to God alone (Luke 5:21). These self-appointed guardians of legalistic, external, ritualistic religion hated Jesus' message of grace, repentance, and forgiveness, and His call for sincere love of God from the heart. They also hated Him for pointedly rebuking their hypocritical self-righteousness (Matt. 23), and for associating with the outcasts of society (Luke 7:34). Having already reached a conclusion regarding Jesus, they were busy accumulating evidence against Him. This Pharisee's invitation to Jesus was part of that evidence-gathering process. No self-respecting Pharisee would invite any association with a blasphemer, except to do him harm.

Jesus, of course, was well aware of this man's motive for inviting Him. Despite the fact that inviting someone to a banquet was normally a sign of friendship and honor, He understood that the Pharisee was a hypocrite and that his intentions toward Him were evil. Yet Jesus graciously reached out to this lost sinner, exposing him to the power that He has to transform lives. The Lord **entered the Pharisee's house and,** as was customary, **reclined at the table.** Since roads were either dusty or muddy, it was prudent to keep the guests' feet as far away from the table as possible. Lying down leaning on one's elbow was both a sanitary and a comfortable position for the prolonged conversation that accompanied such a meal.

It was not uncommon to invite a visiting rabbi to a Sabbath meal or a special banquet, giving those present the opportunity to discuss theological, cultural, and social issues with him. There is some evidence that on such occasions the doors were often left open so that those not invited to the meal could stand around the perimeter of the room and listen in on the dialogue. That is undoubtedly what happened on this occasion.

The story revolves around two main characters: the sinful woman, and the self-righteous man.

THE SINFUL WOMAN

And there was a woman in the city who was a sinner; and when she learned that He was reclining at the table in the Pharisee's house, she brought an alabaster vial of perfume, and standing behind Him at His feet, weeping, she began to wet His feet with her tears, and kept wiping them with the hair of her head, and kissing His feet and anointing them with the perfume. (7:37–38)

The Greek text of verse 37 literally reads, "and behold" (*kai idou*), emphasizing that a startling, shocking thing was about to happen. What was shocking was that this **woman** was well-known **in the city** as **a sinner,** a term for the most despised people in society (cf. Prov. 11:31; Matt. 9:10–13; Luke 19:7). In all likelihood, she was a prostitute, a professional adulteress; immoral, impure, and living a flagrantly sinful life at a public level. There is no reason to identify her, as some do, with Mary Magdalene. Mary is introduced just a few verses away (8:2) as if for the first time; if she were this sinful woman, Luke would have named her here, not later.

Having **learned that** Jesus **was reclining at the table in the Pharisee's house,** and knowing that the doors could be left open, the woman went there with a specific plan in mind. **She brought** with her **an alabaster vial of perfume.** Not only was **perfume** part of the trade of being a prostitute, it was also widely used by women in general. That the vial in which the **perfume** was stored was made from **alabaster,** an expensive kind of marble quarried in Egypt, indicates that the perfume was valuable. The woman intended to anoint Jesus' head with the **perfume,** instead of the more common and less expensive olive oil normally used for such purposes (cf. v. 46; Pss. 23:5; 133:2; 141:5; Eccl. 9:8). Waiting for her opportunity, she took up a position **standing behind** Jesus **at His feet.** She evidently was not immediately recognized by the other people there; certainly the Pharisee would have been outraged that she defiled the purity of his house and would have ordered her to leave. It may be that the banquet took place in the evening, and the dim light from the candles and lamps masked her identity.

As she stood silently wondering how she was going to get to where she could anoint Jesus' head, the woman was suddenly overcome with emotion and began **weeping.** Because of where she was standing, **she began to wet His feet with her tears.** *Brechō* (**wet**) literally means, "to rain" (Matt. 5:45; Luke 17:29; James 5:17; Rev. 11:6). The emotional dam had burst, and her tears flooded down on the feet of Jesus in a gentle rain.

Bent over as she wept, the woman noticed that the host had neglected to provide for Jesus' feet to be washed (v. 44), so she **kept wiping them with the hair of her head.** In that culture, washing the feet of another person was considered degrading, something done by only the lowliest slaves (cf. John 1:27). But what would have shocked the onlookers even more than the woman's washing of Jesus' feet was her letting down her hair. For a Jewish woman to do so in public was considered indecent, even immoral. But overwhelmed with emotion, she was not concerned with the shame she might face.

After finishing washing them, the woman began **kissing** Jesus' feet. *Kataphileō* (**kissing**) is an intense word. In Luke 15:20 it describes the father's kissing of the prodigal son on his return home. Luke used it in Acts 20:37 to describe how the elders of the church at Ephesus kissed Paul when he took his leave of them. The woman's kissing of Jesus' feet was a striking expression of affection. Then, unwilling or unable to wait any longer, she did what she had come to do and anointed the Lord's feet **with the perfume.** This was a staggering display of honor rendered to Jesus in the midst of those who sought only to dishonor Him.

THE SELF-RIGHTEOUS MAN

Now when the Pharisee who had invited Him saw this, he said to himself, "If this man were a prophet He would know who and what sort of person this woman is who is touching Him, that she is a sinner." And Jesus answered him, "Simon, I have something to say to you." And he replied, "Say it, Teacher." "A moneylender had two debtors: one owed five hundred denarii, and the other fifty. When they were unable to repay, he graciously forgave them both. So which of them will love him more?" Simon answered and said, "I suppose the one whom he forgave more." And He said to him, "You have judged correctly." Turning toward the woman, He said to Simon, "Do you see this woman? I entered your house; you gave Me no water for My feet, but she has wet My feet with her tears and wiped them with her hair. You gave Me no kiss; but she, since the time I came in, has not ceased to kiss My feet. You did not anoint My head with oil, but she anointed My feet with perfume. For this reason I say to you, her sins, which are many, have been forgiven, for she loved much; but he who is forgiven little, loves little." Then He said to her, "Your sins have been forgiven." Those who were reclining at the table with Him began to say to themselves, "Who is this man who even forgives sins?" And He said to the woman, "Your faith has saved you; go in peace." (7:39–50)

The woman's actions could have put Jesus in a very bad light. After all, she was a notorious sinner. Letting down her hair, washing, kissing, embracing, and anointing His feet was a serious breach of propriety. That may have led some to wonder why she felt the freedom to be so familiar with Him and reach an obvious, but wrong, conclusion. The Lord's sinless, unblemished character (John 8:46) precluded any thoughts of impropriety on His part, even on the part of His enemies.

The Pharisee drew an equally false conclusion: he chalked up the Lord's reaction not to evil, but to ignorance. That, however, was proof to him that Jesus could not be who He claimed to be because, the Pharisee reasoned, **"If this man were a prophet He would know who and what sort of person this woman is who is touching Him, that she is a sinner."** How could Jesus tell them things they did not know if

He did not even know what they themselves knew about this woman? After all no sensible religious teacher, let alone one claiming to be the Messiah, would ever allow such a woman to touch Him. The Pharisee was both disgusted by the scene he was witnessing, and at the same time satisfied, because it confirmed his belief that Jesus' ignorance of this woman's wickedness was proof that He was not a true prophet.

Our Lord's words to the Pharisee, now introduced as **Simon,** inject a touch of irony into the story. Simon had assumed that Jesus did not know the woman's true character and hence was not a true prophet. But although Simon had not verbalized his question, He **answered him.** His knowledge of Simon's thoughts proved that Jesus was in fact a true prophet (cf. Luke 5:22). Interrupting any conversation that may have been taking place, Jesus said to him, **"Simon, I have something to say to you."** Respectfully polite but cold, Simon **replied, "Say it, Teacher."** The Lord communicated the point He intended to make by means of a simple parable or analogy: **"A moneylender had two debtors: one owed five hundred denarii, and the other fifty.** Their debts differed dramatically (five hundred denarii was about a year and half's wages for a common laborer; fifty about two month's wages), but neither could repay their debt. Fortunately for both the moneylender had mercy on them, and **when they were unable to repay, he graciously forgave them both.** In addition to its use here in a business sense, (**graciously forgave**) *charizomai*, is used in a theological sense to describe the forgiveness that God grants believers in Christ (Rom. 8:32; Eph. 4:32; Col. 2:13; 3:13).

What made the moneylender's act so generous is that by forgiving the debts of the two individuals, he incurred those debts in full. Paul understood that principle when he magnanimously offered to take on the debt Philemon would otherwise have incurred when he forgave his runaway slave Onesimus: "But if he has wronged you in any way or owes you anything, charge that to my account; I, Paul, am writing this with my own hand, I will repay it" (Philem. 18–19). Similarly, when God forgives believers' sins He incurs their debt, and Jesus Christ died to pay it.

Then the Lord got to the point of His illustration by asking Simon, **"So which of them will love him more?"** Hesitating to give a straight-forward reply **Simon answered and said, "I suppose the one whom he forgave more."** He may have been being sarcastic, since the answer to the Lord's question was obvious, or cautious, suspecting that somehow Jesus intended to embarrass him if he gave the wrong answer. But he got it right, and Jesus **said to him, "You have judged correctly."** The principle was simple and obvious: whoever is forgiven the most will love the forgiver the most; great love comes from great forgiveness.

Turning toward the woman, Jesus then applied the principle illustrated in the parable to her and Simon. Addressing Simon, the Lord contrasted her obvious love for Him with his cold indifference. **"Do you see this woman? I entered your house; you gave Me no water for My feet, but she has wet My feet with her tears and wiped them with her hair. You gave Me no kiss; but she, since the time I came in, has not ceased to kiss My feet. You did not anoint My head with oil, but she anointed My feet with perfume."** Her demonstration of love for Jesus gave clear evidence of her transformed life; she loved much because she had been forgiven much. In contrast, Simon had insulted Jesus by failing to offer the normal courtesy of providing **water for** His **feet** (cf. Gen. 18:4; 19:2; 24:32; 43:24; Judg. 19:21; John 13:4–5) or greeting Him with the customary **kiss** (cf. Gen. 29:13; 45:15; Ex. 4:27; 18:7; Rom. 16:16). And while he had failed to **anoint** the Lord's **head with** inexpensive olive **oil, she** had anointed His **feet with** costly **perfume.**

Continuing to address Simon, the one He sought to reach, Jesus said, **"For this reason I say to you, her sins, which are many, have been forgiven, for she loved much; but he who is forgiven little, loves little."** The perfect tense verb (describing action completed in the past with continuing results in the present) translated **have been forgiven** indicates that the woman had already been forgiven before she came there that day. This was her opportunity to show her gratitude and love to the one who had graciously forgiven her. Then, addressing the woman, Jesus reaffirmed that she had already been forgiven (again the verb is in the perfect tense), saying **to her, "Your sins have been forgiven."** Her outpouring of love for the Savior was the mark of her transformed life.

That transformation was evident to **those who were reclining at the table with** Christ and they **began to say to themselves, "Who is this man who even forgives sins?"** That Jesus took it upon Himself to forgive her sins, instead of saying God had forgiven her, was not lost on them. Christ's parting words **to the woman, "Your faith has saved you; go in peace,"** made it clear that her love and the good deeds she had done to Him were the result of her salvation, not its cause (Eph. 2:10). Salvation is by **faith** alone (John 5:24; 6:40; Rom. 3:28; 5:1; Gal. 2:16; 3:24; Eph. 2:8–9; Phil. 3:9; 2 Tim. 3:15), and produces eternal **peace** (Acts 10:36; Rom. 15:13; Eph. 2:14; Col. 1:20).

It is their love for the Lord Jesus Christ that is the believers' most powerful witness to the lost world. An ungrateful, loveless Christian undercuts the testimony of the gospel and such attitudes are incompatible with God's gracious forgiveness.

The Scope of Jesus' Ministry (Luke 8:1–3)

19

Soon afterwards, He began going around from one city and village to another, proclaiming and preaching the kingdom of God. The twelve were with Him, and also some women who had been healed of evil spirits and sicknesses: Mary who was called Magdalene, from whom seven demons had gone out, and Joanna the wife of Chuza, Herod's steward, and Susanna, and many others who were contributing to their support out of their private means. (8:1–3)

The plan of God that unfolded in the life and ministry of the Lord Jesus Christ is counterintuitive to conventional human wisdom. Modern so-called experts on ministry methodology would not have devised such a narrow strategy to bring salvation to the world by limiting the exposure of the Son of God to the small, weak, embattled, and oft-conquered nation of Israel. Nor would their plan have called for Him to live the first thirty years of His life in obscurity in a tiny hamlet (Nazareth) in a backwater region (Galilee), and then spend the overwhelming majority of His three years of ministry within the borders of Israel. They would have been puzzled by His rejection of all religiously trained and influential leaders, and in their place His choice of twelve common, ordinary men to be His closest associates in ministry and preachers. And scorning the influential and powerful, He spent His time with common people, especially the poor and outcasts of society. Jesus' welcoming of sinners and withering criticism of the religious elite could only be viewed as counterproductive to the impact of His message. Modern marketers would hardly have been surprised that Jesus wound up being rejected by the nation and being executed as a result of the hatred of the leaders.

But worldly experts who think like that would be dead wrong in their evaluation of God's strategy. With a breathtaking economy of effort, the Lord Jesus Christ perfectly and precisely carried out the ministry given Him by the Father (John 17:4). Working within the limits set by the Father allowed Jesus' brief three years of ministry to set in motion the most powerful force for truth the world has ever known. Over the generations the gospel has spread to every corner of the globe and the church has continued to expand worldwide.

Jesus' simple, fixed, and precisely focused ministry stands in sharp contrast to modern concepts of the ministry. Mimicking worldly management theories, ministries today are often designed to have the widest possible impact, and with that goal in mind to be diverse, eclectic, synergistic, tolerant, and culturally connected. Enormous amounts of time, money, and manpower are poured into strategies, plans, and activities designed to influence as many people as possible. The goal is to create a matrix of perceptions, cultural expectations, and felt needs that can be met at the broadest level by the ministry. The divine model of ministry by the Lord Jesus Christ in the plan and power of heaven needed none of those devices.

This brief summary passage (cf. 4:14–15, 31–32, 40–41; 6:17–19) marks the transition into the final phase of the Lord's Galilean ministry. It provides a remarkable insight into the divinely-imposed limitations that made Jesus' ministry so effective. Six insights into the scope of His ministry may be discerned. Jesus' ministry was limited sovereignly, geographically, theologically, humanly, socially, and materially.

THE SCOPE OF JESUS' MINISTRY
WAS LIMITED SOVEREIGNLY

Soon afterwards, He began going around (8:1*a*)

The phrase **soon afterwards** refers back to the incident involving the sinful woman and the self-righteous Pharisee recorded in 7:36–50. Shortly after that incident, in keeping with the Father's design, Jesus began **going around** Galilee for the final phase of His ministry there (8:4–9:50). Though the statement is general, the divine design was specific.

The Lord always acted in accord with the Father's will. In John 5:30 He said, "I do not seek My own will, but the will of Him who sent Me." Earlier He had told His disciples, "My food is to do the will of Him who sent Me and to accomplish His work" (John 4:34). It was to do the Father's will that He came into the world, as He explained in John 6:38: "For I have come down from heaven, not to do My own will, but the will of Him who sent Me."

Jesus did the tasks the Father gave Him to do in the Father's timing. He made certain that the most important of those tasks, His sacrificial death, did not take place until the precise time determined by the Father. Before that time, "no man laid his hand on Him, because His hour had not yet come" (John 7:30; cf. v. 1; 8:20; Luke 13:33).

Finally, Jesus ministered to the people to whom the Father sent Him. He told a Syro-Phoenician woman, "I was sent only to the lost sheep of the house of Israel" (Matt. 15:24). "Do not go in the way of the Gentiles," He commanded the Twelve when He sent them out to preach, "and do not enter any city of the Samaritans; but rather go to the lost sheep of the house of Israel" (Matt. 10:5–6). Narrowing His focus even more, Jesus said that He did "not come to call the righteous but sinners to repentance" (Luke 5:32; cf. 4:18–19). He judicially abandoned the proud, self-righteous scribes and Pharisees, telling His disciples, "Let them alone; they are blind guides of the blind. And if a blind man guides a blind man, both will fall into a pit" (Matt. 15:14). When "some of the scribes and Pharisees said to Him, 'Teacher, we want to see a sign from You'" (Matt. 12:38) Jesus "answered and said to them, 'An evil and adulterous generation craves for a sign; and yet no sign will be given to it but the sign of Jonah the prophet'" (v. 39; cf. Luke 11:29). The Lord's example illustrates the principle that concentration is the key to multiplication. The way to multiply a ministry is by intensely teaching people the life-changing truths of Scripture, not by manipulation and clever marketing gimmicks.

THE SCOPE OF JESUS' MINISTRY
WAS LIMITED GEOGRAPHICALLY

from one city and village to another (8:1*b*)

That Jesus would restrict the scope of His ministry by spending so much of it traveling **from one city and village to another** in Galilee is inexplicable from the perspective of modern philosophy of ministry. Jerusalem, the cultural and intellectual center of Israel, should have been His target. Galilee, on the other hand, was a largely rural area, whose plebian residents were scorned by the sophisticated Judeans. When some said of Jesus, "This is the Christ" others scoffed at them, saying "Surely the Christ is not going to come from Galilee, is He?" (John 7:41). When Nicodemus protested the Pharisees' judging of Christ without investigating Him they mocked him. "You are not also from Galilee, are you?" they said scornfully. "Search, and see that no prophet arises out of Galilee" (v. 52). Later the Sanhedrin was astonished that simple Galileans like Peter and John could speak so confidently, boldly, and intelligently (Acts 4:13).

Everywhere Jesus went became His pulpit, the hillsides, valleys, and public squares of Galilee were filled with huge crowds that flocked to hear Him (cf. vv. 4, 19, 40, 45). Some argue that the rising animosity of the Jewish religious leaders had caused Jesus to be banned from preaching in the synagogues. As evidence, they point to the lack of any reference to synagogues in this summary statement. But a summary need not go into exhaustive detail, so the argument from silence is unconvincing. Further, Matthew 9:35, 13:54, and John 6:59 record Jesus preaching in Galilean synagogues after the events of this passage, while Luke 13:10 records His preaching in a Judean synagogue, which also came later chronologically. After His arrest, Jesus told the high priest Annas, "I have spoken openly to the world; I always taught in synagogues and in the temple, where all the Jews come together; and I spoke nothing in secret" (John 18:20), implying that He continued preaching in the synagogues throughout His ministry.

Despite the limited geographic extent of His ministry, Jesus has influenced the entire world through the Spirit-inspired record of His life and ministry recorded in the Gospels and the power of His church.

THE SCOPE OF JESUS' MINISTRY
WAS LIMITED THEOLOGICALLY

proclaiming and preaching the kingdom of God (8:1c)

Jesus did not cover a broad spectrum of subjects in His preaching. He did not emphasize social or political issues, engage in speculative philosophical discussions, or offer self-help lessons based on success and prosperity. The sole focus of the Lord's ministry was limited to **proclaiming and preaching the kingdom of God** (cf. 4:43; 9:11; 16:16; Matt. 4:17; Acts 1:3). The terms **proclaiming and preaching** define the methodology of Christ's ministry, while the **kingdom of God** defines its content. *Kērussō* (**proclaiming**) means to publicly and authoritatively herald an official message that must be listened to and obeyed. *Euangelizō* (**preach-**

ing), the source of the English words "evangelize" and "evangelism," refers to announcing the good news of the gospel.

Despite the claims of some, the terms **kingdom of God** and kingdom of heaven are synonymous. The latter term appears only in Matthew's gospel, which was addressed to the Jewish people, in deference to their prohibition against speaking the name of God. In Matthew 19:23–24, Jesus used the two terms interchangeably. Both refer to the sphere of salvation, where God reigns over the redeemed (Matt. 19:26; cf. 21:31; Mark 1:15; John 3:3–5; Acts 8:12).

To preach the kingdom of God is to proclaim the good news that sinners can be delivered from Satan's kingdom of darkness into the kingdom of God's beloved Son (Col. 1:13). Sinners respond to the call to enter the kingdom first of all by repentance. Both John the Baptist (Matt. 3:2–8) and Jesus (Matt. 4:17; Luke 5:32; 13:3, 5) called for sinners to repent and condemned those who refused to repent (Matt. 11:20–21; 12:41). Jesus also instructed His disciples to preach that same message (Mark 6:12; Luke 24:47). Entrance to God's kingdom also requires faith. Jesus not only called for repentance, but also taught that sinners need to believe the gospel in order to be saved (Mark 1:15; cf. Luke 7:50; John 6:29; 8:24; 12:36).

Those who enter the kingdom of God through repentance and faith will manifest love for God. Jesus declared that the greatest commandment is to love God with all one's heart, soul, mind, and strength (Mark 12:28–30). They are also marked by a complete and final commitment to obeying God. When one would-be follower said to Him "I will follow You, Lord; but first permit me to say good-bye to those at home" (Luke 9:61) Jesus replied, "No one, after putting his hand to the plow and looking back, is fit for the kingdom of God" (v. 62). The Lord illustrated that total commitment in the parables He told in Matthew 13:44–46:

> The kingdom of heaven is like a treasure hidden in the field, which a man found and hid again; and from joy over it he goes and sells all that he has and buys that field. Again, the kingdom of heaven is like a merchant seeking fine pearls, and upon finding one pearl of great value, he went and sold all that he had and bought it.

Reflecting the absolute commitment that marks those in the kingdom of God Paul wrote,

> Whatever things were gain to me, those things I have counted as loss for the sake of Christ. More than that, I count all things to be loss in view of the surpassing value of knowing Christ Jesus my Lord, for whom I have suffered the loss of all things, and count them but rubbish so that I may gain Christ. (Phil. 3:7–8)

The Lord also taught that those in the kingdom must live in obedience to the King; the Sermon on the Mount in particular describes in detail the characteristics of those who have entered the kingdom of God. Even after our Lord's resurrection this was the theme of His teaching for the forty days before His return to heaven, expanding His apostles' knowledge of the features of the kingdom (Acts 1:3).

THE SCOPE OF JESUS' MINISTRY
WAS LIMITED HUMANLY

The twelve were with Him, (8:1*d*)

As noted earlier in this chapter, concentration of effort is the key to multiplication of ministry. Jesus ministered constantly to the huge crowds that followed Him everywhere. Yet the Lord focused most of His attention on the Twelve who (apart from the betrayer Judas) would continue His ministry after His ascension. As noted in their biographies given in chapters 2 through 8 of this volume, they were remarkably ordinary men. None of the Twelve were among the elite or influential of Jewish society; their ranks included no scribes, Pharisees, Sadducees, priests, rabbis, or synagogue rulers. They did not come from wealthy or influential families, and had no friends in high places. The Twelve frequently disappointed Him with their weak faith (e.g., Matt. 8:26; 14:31) and lack of insight (Matt. 15:15–16; 16:8–11; Mark 4:10–13; 9:32; John 12:16; 20:9). All of them abandoned Him in His hour of need (Matt. 26:56). But He poured His life into them, and turned them into men who would turn the world upside down.

The apostle Paul also understood the importance of pouring his life into a limited group of people. Writing shortly before his execution to Timothy, one of those who would carry on his ministry after his death, Paul charged him, "The things which you have heard from me in the presence of many witnesses, entrust these to faithful men who will be able to teach others also" (2 Tim. 2:2). The four generations evident here—Paul, Timothy, the faithful men, and the others—mark the ongoing process of multiplication that has continued down through the centuries to this day.

At this stage of their training, the Twelve had not yet been empowered and sent out to preach, teach, heal, and cast out demons. They were observing, listening, and learning. Only later would Jesus send them out on a preaching tour by themselves (9:1–6).

THE SCOPE OF JESUS' MINISTRY
WAS LIMITED SOCIALLY

and also some women who had been healed of evil spirits and sicknesses: Mary who was called Magdalene, from whom seven demons had gone out, and Joanna the wife of Chuza, Herod's steward, and Susanna, (8:2–3*a*)

Not only were the twelve men traveling with Jesus, but, surprisingly, **also some women.** For a rabbi to have women accompanying Him was virtually unprecedented. Like many others in the ancient world, the rabbis had a low view of women and refused to teach them. Jesus' action was politically incorrect; it flew in the face of conventional wisdom. Given the lowly status of women in Jewish society, they had little influence they could use to help Him. But despite that these women traveled with Jesus, though not necessarily all the time, or all at once. They had **been healed** spiritually **of evil spirits and** physically of **sicknesses.** How many there were is not stated, but Luke names three of the many others who followed the Lord. This entourage made Jesus socially unacceptable when measured by rabbinic standards.

Mary who was called Magdalene (after her hometown of Magdala, on the western shore of the Sea of Galilee about three miles north of Tiberias) figures prominently in the accounts of the Lord's death, burial, and resurrection (Matt. 27:56; Mark 15:47; John 20:1–18). This is her only other appearance in the Gospels. (As noted in the previous chapter of this volume, she was not the sinful woman who anointed Jesus at the house of Simon the Pharisee [Luke 7:36–50]). Nor does the fact that **seven demons had gone out** of her prove that she had lived an immoral life, since there is no necessary connection between demon possession and immorality.

Joanna was **the wife of Chuza, Herod's steward** (a high ranking official, possibly the manager of Antipas' estate). Like Mary Magdalene, she was a witness to Jesus' burial and resurrection (Luke 23:55; 24:10), and probably the crucifixion as well. Christ's influence reached into Herod Antipas' household, as well as the tiny village of Magdala. Another person close to Herod Antipas, Manaen, would later become one of the leaders of the church at Antioch (Acts 13:1).

Nothing is known of **Susanna,** since Luke gives no information about her, and her name appears nowhere else in Scripture.

Jesus brought into the kingdom all whom the Father gave Him (John 6:37), men and women from every strata of life. There were no limits on the scope of His ministry in that regard. Women, including Elizabeth (Luke 1:5–25, 39–45, 57–60), Mary (Luke 1–2), Anna (Luke 2:36–38),

Peter's mother-in-law (Matt. 8:14–15), the widow at Nain (Luke 7:12–15), Mary and Martha (Luke 10:39–42; John 11:1–45; 12:1–8), the woman in the parable of the lost coin (Luke 15:8–10), the widow in the parable of the unjust judge (Luke 18:3–5), and the widow who offered her last two coins (Luke 21:1–4), played a role in the life and ministry of Jesus Christ that far exceeded their significance in contemporary Jewish society.

THE SCOPE OF JESUS' MINISTRY
WAS LIMITED MATERIALLY

and many others who were contributing to their support out of their private means. (8:3b)

In addition to the women mentioned above, **many others,** both men and women, supported Christ's ministry by **contributing to their** [Jesus and the Twelve] **support out of their private means.** Jesus' ministry depended on the small contributions of others whose lives He had changed. The disciples had left everything to follow Him (Matt. 19:27), including their professions (Mark 1:20; Luke 5:28) and their homes (Luke 18:28). Jesus Himself had "nowhere to lay His head" (Luke 9:58), and at the time of His death owned nothing but the clothes He wore (Luke 23:34). The meager contributions they received were generous enough that Jesus and the Twelve were able to contribute to the poor (John 13:29). None of them personally prospered, as the frustration of Judas evidences (John 12:1–6).

The Lord's ministry demonstrates the biblical principle that "those who proclaim the gospel [are] to get their living from the gospel" (1 Cor. 9:14; cf. Luke 10:7; 1 Tim. 5:17–18). Therefore "the one who is taught the word is to share all good things with the one who teaches him" (Gal. 6:6). That does not repay believers' debt to God. The debt of sin they could never pay has been paid in full by the death of the Lord Jesus Christ (Col. 2:13–14) and they no longer owe it. But transformed by God's grace Christians, out of love and gratitude, seek to imitate the sacrificial, loving grace He bestowed on them.

The Lord Jesus Christ carried out God's sovereign will, ministered where God placed Him, proclaimed God's message, poured Himself into discipling a few faithful men, embraced both men and women from all walks of life, and depended on the contributions of those who had benefited from His ministry. He is the perfect model for all those who serve Him in gratitude and love.

Receptivity to the Gospel: The Parable of the Soils (Luke 8:4–15)

20

When a large crowd was coming together, and those from the various cities were journeying to Him, He spoke by way of a parable: "The sower went out to sow his seed; and as he sowed, some fell beside the road, and it was trampled under foot and the birds of the air ate it up. Other seed fell on rocky soil, and as soon as it grew up, it withered away, because it had no moisture. Other seed fell among the thorns; and the thorns grew up with it and choked it out. Other seed fell into the good soil, and grew up, and produced a crop a hundred times as great." As He said these things, He would call out, "He who has ears to hear, let him hear." His disciples began questioning Him as to what this parable meant. And He said, "To you it has been granted to know the mysteries of the kingdom of God, but to the rest it is in parables, so that seeing they may not see, and hearing they may not understand. Now the parable is this: the seed is the word of God. Those beside the road are those who have heard; then the devil comes and takes away the word from their heart, so that they will not believe and be saved. Those on the rocky soil are those who, when they hear, receive the word with joy; and these have no firm root; they believe for a while, and in time of temptation fall

away. The seed which fell among the thorns, these are the ones who have heard, and as they go on their way they are choked with worries and riches and pleasures of this life, and bring no fruit to maturity. But the seed in the good soil, these are the ones who have heard the word in an honest and good heart, and hold it fast, and bear fruit with perseverance. (Luke 8:4–15)

The good news of salvation is so inexplicably wonderful and glorious that words cannot express its magnificence. Those who have experienced salvation's blessings—forgiveness of sin (Acts 10:43) and freedom from its tyranny (Rom. 6:1–7); justification (Rom. 3:20–28); eternal life (John 3:16); peace with God (Rom. 5:1); adoption into the family of God (Rom. 8:15); the indwelling (2 Tim. 1:14); filling (Eph. 5:18); and empowering (Acts 1:8) of the Holy Spirit; a clear conscience (Heb. 10:22); the hope of heaven (1 Peter 1:4); the mind of Christ (1 Cor. 2:16) revealed in the word of truth (John 17:17)—find it hard to understand how anyone could reject it. After all, who would turn down eternal life in favor of eternal punishment? Who would hold on to hell and reject heaven? Who would refuse everlasting joy and peace and in its place prefer instead misery and pain?

The parable the Lord related in this passage answers the question of why throughout redemptive history most people have rejected the gospel (Matt. 7:14; 22:14; Luke 13:23–24). It is crucial to a proper understanding of evangelism, and reveals what kind of responses believers can expect when they present the gospel. Jesus' simple illustration provides profound and unforgettable insight into the subject of receptivity to the gospel. He makes it clear that the issue is not the gospel message, nor is it the skill or methodology of those proclaiming it. The determining factor is the condition of the hearer's heart.

The importance of the heart cannot be overstated. "Watch over your heart with all diligence," counseled Solomon, "for from it flow the springs of life" (Prov. 4:23). Jesus noted that "the mouth speaks out of that which fills the heart" (Matt. 12:34), and warned that "the things that proceed out of the mouth come from the heart, and those defile the man. For out of the heart come evil thoughts, murders, adulteries, fornications, thefts, false witness, slanders" (Matt. 15:18–19; cf. Mark 7:21–23). Scripture describes such a heart as

- wicked (Prov. 26:23)
- desperately sick (Jer. 17:9)
- perverse (Prov. 11:20)
- evil (Gen. 8:21; Jer. 3:17)
- insane (Eccl. 9:3)

- unclean (Jer. 4:14)
- deceitful (Jer. 17:9)
- disloyal (1 Kings 15:3)
- errant (Ps. 95:10)
- unrepentant (Rom. 2:5)
- unbelieving (Heb. 3:12)
- blind (Rom. 1:21)
- deceived (Isa. 44:20)
- hardened (Eph. 4:18)
- proud (Prov. 16:5; 21:4)
- greedy (2 Peter 2:14)
- foolish (Rom. 1:21)
- idolatrous (Ezek. 14:3–4)
- rebellious (Jer. 5:23)
- perverse (Ps. 101:4; Prov. 11:20)
- stubborn (Jer. 5:23)
- dull (Acts 28:27)

All of those negative terms expose the depths of human depravity.

Matthew's account provides the setting for this parable. On the day He told it, Jesus left a house (probably the one where His mother and brothers found Him [Matt. 12:46–50]) and went to the shore of the Sea of Galilee (13:1). Because of the large crowds that pressed Him, Jesus got into a boat and sat down to teach the people (cf. Luke 5:3), who stood on the beach (Matt. 13:2). The **large crowd** consisted not only of people from the immediate vicinity, but also from **various** other **cities.** Drawn by the rapidly spreading news of Jesus' power over nature and the demonic realm, and His ability to heal any and all diseases and even raise the dead, they gathered to experience firsthand His powerful miracles and amazing teaching.

When the crowds arrived, the Lord **spoke** to them **by way of a parable.** *Parabolē* (**parable**) means to put one thing alongside another for comparison. Parables were a common rhetorical device employed by the rabbis. Here, as He often did, Jesus put a story alongside a spiritual truth to make that truth more clearly understood. While parables could be brief illustrations (e.g., 5:36–39; 6:39; Matt. 13:31–32, 33, 44, 45–46), they could also be extended analogies, as is this one. Parables placed profound theological truth in familiar settings, making it vivid, interesting, unforgettable, and easily recalled.

Though Jesus made up such analogies all through His ministry, this parable marked a major turning point. From this time on Jesus spoke to the crowds only in parables (Matt. 13:34). That was a deliberate act of judgment on His part. Those who would not believe now could not; the

fools who hated knowledge (Prov. 1:22) were deprived of it. By presenting His teaching in parables, Jesus hid the truth from rejecting unbelievers and revealed it only to His faithful followers. Without an explanation,
a parable can mean anything or nothing; it is little more than a riddle. The
Lord's veiling of the truth means that judgment had fallen on Israel so
that they could no longer understand the teaching of their own Messiah.
Those who had rejected Him were fixed in the darkness they loved
(John 3:19). Only the Lord's disciples understood the parables, because
only they received His explanation of them. Mark's account of this incident records that Jesus "was saying to [His disciples], 'To you has been
given the mystery of the kingdom of God, but those who are outside get
everything in parables, so that while seeing, they may see and not perceive, and while hearing, they may hear and not understand, otherwise
they might return and be forgiven'" (Mark 4:11–12).

In this passage the Lord told the parable to the crowds, and then
interpreted it in private to His disciples.

THE PARABLE

**"The sower went out to sow his seed; and as he sowed, some fell
beside the road, and it was trampled under foot and the birds of
the air ate it up. Other seed fell on rocky soil, and as soon as it
grew up, it withered away, because it had no moisture. Other
seed fell among the thorns; and the thorns grew up with it and
choked it out. Other seed fell into the good soil, and grew up, and
produced a crop a hundred times as great."** (8:5–8a)

This simple story described an activity that was very familiar to
Jesus' hearers, since Galilee was largely an agricultural region. In fact, as
they stood along the shore that day they may even have seen this taking
place in the distance. When a **sower went out to sow his seed** he used
a method known as broadcasting. That involved walking up and down
the furrows in the plowed field scattering the seed by hand. The seed
would fall on different types of soil, of which the Lord mentions four.

Some of the seed **fell beside the road.** Jesus was not referring to a thoroughfare or highway, but to the beaten paths that separated the narrow strips of cultivated land. Farmers used those paths to
access their plowed fields, and travelers used them to travel through
the countryside (cf. Matt. 12:1). The paths were not plowed, and in the
dry, semi-arid climate of Israel they would become virtually as hard as
concrete. The seed that fell on those paths had no chance of penetrating the hard-packed soil. What was not **trampled under foot** by people

walking along the paths the **birds of the air ate.**
Some of the **other seed fell on rocky soil.** Jesus was not referring
to soil strewn with rocks and boulders, since those would have been turned
up by the plowing and removed. In many places, however, there was an
underlying rock bed deep enough below the surface to avoid being struck
by the plow. The plants' roots could not penetrate that rock bed to reach the
water table beneath it. As a result they **withered away, because** the thin
layer of topsoil retained insufficient **moisture** for them to survive.
Still **other seed fell among the thorns.** *Akantha* (**thorns**) is a
general term for the category of thorny (it is the word used to describe
the crown of thorns placed on Jesus' head [Matt. 27:29; John 19:2]),
prickly weeds that are useless and particularly harmful in cultivated crop-
land. Even the most careful, diligent plowing could not always remove
all of the weed's roots. The result was a soil that looked good when the
farmer sowed the seed, but the tragic reality was that there was other life
in it. The noxious weeds grew faster than the good plants, blocking the
sunlight and consuming the water and nutrients from the soil. As a result
the thorns grew up with the good plants **and choked** them **out.**
But the situation was not entirely hopeless. Some **seed** managed
to fall **into the good soil, and grew up, and produced a crop a hundred times as great.** This soil had none of the drawbacks of the other
three; it was soft, deep, and free of weeds. As a result, it produced an
amazing crop. Matthew 13:8 and Mark 4:8 refer to a crop yield of thirty,
sixty, or one hundredfold; Luke mentions only the greatest yield (cf. Gen.
26:12). All were far above the average yield a farmer could expect.

THE INTERPRETATION

**As He said these things, He would call out, "He who has ears to
hear, let him hear." His disciples began questioning Him as to
what this parable meant. And He said, "To you it has been granted to know the mysteries of the kingdom of God, but to the rest it
is in parables, so that seeing they may not see, and hearing they
may not understand. Now the parable is this: the seed is the word
of God. Those beside the road are those who have heard; then
the devil comes and takes away the word from their heart, so that
they will not believe and be saved. Those on the rocky soil are
those who, when they hear, receive the word with joy; and these
have no firm root; they believe for a while, and in time of temptation fall away. The seed which fell among the thorns, these are
the ones who have heard, and as they go on their way they are
choked with worries and riches and pleasures of this life, and**

bring no fruit to maturity. But the seed in the good soil, these are the ones who have heard the word in an honest and good heart, and hold it fast, and bear fruit with perseverance. (8:8b–15)

As He told this story, Jesus **would call out, "He who has ears to hear, let him hear"** (cf. 14:35; Matt. 11:15; 13:43; Mark 4:23). That challenge distinguished between those who desired to understand what He was teaching, and those who did not. Unsurprisingly, only **His disciples** were interested, and they **began questioning Him as to what this parable meant.** Jesus' response revealed the incredible privilege that was theirs: **"To you it has been granted to know the mysteries of the kingdom of God."** The **mysteries** of which the Lord spoke are spiritual truths hidden through the Old Testament era and revealed in the New (see the discussion of New Testament mysteries in chapter 16 of this volume). The **kingdom of God,** as noted in chapter 19 of this volume, refers to the sphere of salvation where God reigns over His people. But as noted above, **to the rest** who reject the truth, **parables** are an act of judgment, **so that seeing they may not see, and hearing they may not understand** (cf. Matt. 13:12–13). Matthew records that Jesus elaborated on that statement of judgment by quoting from Isaiah's familiar prophecy:

> In their case the prophecy of Isaiah is being fulfilled, which says, "You will keep on hearing, but will not understand; you will keep on seeing, but will not perceive; for the heart of this people has become dull, with their ears they scarcely hear, and they have closed their eyes, otherwise they would see with their eyes, hear with their ears, and understand with their heart and return, and I would heal them." (Matt. 13:14–15; cf. Isa. 6:9–10)

Because they willfully hardened their hearts against the truth, God judicially hardened them, just as He did with Pharaoh (cf. Ex. 8:15; 14:8). While such people cannot understand spiritual truth (1 Cor. 2:14), believers can (v. 16; cf. Matt. 13:16–17, 51).

Having made it clear that the truth contained in the **parable** was for His disciples only, Jesus identified its key elements. Significantly, He did not name the sower (as He so identified Himself in His explanation of the parable of the wheat and the tares [Matt. 13:37]), since the sower is not the issue. Anyone who proclaims the gospel is a sower. Jesus identified **the seed** as **the word of God,** specifically in this context the gospel message of salvation. Peter used that same analogy when he wrote, "You have been born again not of seed which is perishable but imperishable, that is, through the living and enduring word of God" (1 Peter 1:23; cf. Rom. 10:17). No artificial, synthetic seed can replace the divine seed and produce better results; attempting to alter the gospel message to make it more palatable to unbelievers brings judgment (Gal. 1:8–9) and can only result in false conversions. The soil represents the heart (vv. 12, 15), and the four types of soil describe the various conditions of the souls of those who hear the gospel.

THE ROADSIDE SOIL

Those beside the road are those who have heard; then the devil comes and takes away the word from their heart, so that they will not believe and be saved. (8:12)

The hard-packed, impenetrable soil **beside the road** (pathway through the fields) symbolizes those **who have heard** the gospel but reject it outright. Like that soil, the hearts of such people are hardened against the truth. The Old Testament refers to them as hard-hearted (Ps. 95:8; Prov. 28:14) and stiff-necked (Deut. 10:16; 2 Kings 17:14; Neh. 9:29; Jer. 7:26). They are stubbornly resolute and rigid in their indifference and hostility to the gospel, motivated by their love of sin. The heart of such people is a thoroughfare, constantly trampled and packed down by the sins that traverse it. It is never plowed by conviction, self-examination, honest assessment of guilt, and repentance. It is as callous to the sweet reasonings of grace as it is to the fearful terrors of judgment.

Interestingly, such hard-hearted people are often not atheists, but highly and seriously religious. A prime example was the Jewish religious leaders of Christ's day. So firmly shut were their minds to the truth of God that they hated, opposed, and ultimately killed His Son, the very Messiah they had longed for (cf. Matt. 21:33–46).

Because the sin-hardened hearts of those who permanently reject the gospel are impervious to God's truth, their father (John 8:44) **the devil comes and takes away the word from their heart, so that they will not believe and be saved.** Satan does that through false teachers (Matt. 7:15–20), fear of man (John 12:42), embarrassment at identifying with Jesus Christ (Matt. 10:33), pride (James 4:6), doubt that causes them not to **believe and be saved,** and, most of all, through the love of sin (John 3:19).

THE ROCKY SOIL

Those on the rocky soil are those who, when they hear, receive the word with joy; and these have no firm root; they believe for a while, and in time of temptation fall away. (8:13)

The shallow **rocky soil** pictures those who make a superficial profession of faith. These people seem at first to be the opposite of the hard-hearted ones represented by the roadside soil. Far from rejecting the truth **when they hear** it proclaimed, they initially **receive the word with joy.** Their euphoria may convince many that their conversion is real. They are not only interested and receptive, but also exuberant and exhilarated—but not for long. The problem is that since **these have no firm root they** only **believe for a while.**

Perseverance marks genuine saving faith. "If you continue in My word," Jesus told some who professed faith in Him, "then you are truly disciples of Mine" (John 8:31). Paul wrote to the Colossians that those who have been reconciled to God will "continue in the faith firmly established and steadfast, and not moved away from the hope of the gospel" (Col. 1:23). The writer of Hebrews reminded his readers, "We have become partakers of Christ, if we hold fast the beginning of our assurance firm until the end" (Heb. 3:14; cf. v. 6; 4:14; Matt. 24:13).

Joy, on the other hand, is not the distinguishing mark of true salvation. In fact, a truer indication of genuine conversion is mourning (Matt. 5:4; cf. James 4:9). Joy is sometimes characteristic of genuine salvation, but sometimes of false salvation. People often respond to the gospel for the wrong reasons. They may have experienced a broken relationship, a divorce, the death of a loved one, the loss of a job, or been diagnosed with a serious disease. The expectation that Jesus will fix everything for them on their terms is exciting, and fills them with a false joy. But these people are like the man in the Lord's parable who crashed a wedding party without having the proper attire and was thrown out (Matt. 22:11–13). Since their faith is not genuine, they lack the robe of righteousness that clothes the redeemed (Isa. 61:10).

Nor is the absence of joy a distinguishing mark of a false conversion. Emotion is not a definitive indicator of spiritual reality. Salvation is a work of God, a divine transaction that may or may not produce an immediate emotional reaction. True saving faith will stand the test of time and assurance, peace, and joy are wrought by the Holy Spirit in the heart of the redeemed.

What makes it evident that the faith of those symbolized by the rocky soil is superficial and non-saving is that **in time of temptation** they **fall away.** The scorching heat of the sun reveals that plants in the rocky soil lack a deep root structure. Because of that they are unable to draw the nutrients and moisture from the soil that they need to survive. In the same way **temptation** (*peirasmos;* "temptation," "trial," "testing"), affliction, and persecution (Matt. 13:21) cause false believers to **fall away** from their profession of faith.

Right after experiencing the miracle that had the greatest impact numerically of any the Lord performed, the feeding of the 5,000 (John 6:1–13), many would-be disciples "withdrew and were not walking with Him anymore" (v. 66). They were fervently hoping that Jesus would be the conquering king who would oust the hated Romans and usher in a glorious kingdom for Israel. But they found Christ's teaching on the true nature of salvation and His call for total commitment to Him (vv. 26–65) unacceptable, and permanently abandoned Him. As the apostle John would later write, "They went out from us, but they were not really of us; for if they had been of us, they would have remained with us; but they went out, so that it would be shown that they all are not of us" (1 John 2:19).

The faith of true believers, in contrast, is not crushed by trials, but strengthened by them. James encouraged believers, "Consider it all joy, my brethren, when you encounter various trials, knowing that the testing of your faith produces endurance. And let endurance have its perfect result, so that you may be perfect and complete, lacking in nothing" (James 1:2–4). When faced with a painful trial that the Lord chose not to remove (2 Cor. 12:7–9) Paul responded, "Most gladly, therefore, I will rather boast about my weaknesses, so that the power of Christ may dwell in me. Therefore I am well content with weaknesses, with insults, with distresses, with persecutions, with difficulties, for Christ's sake; for when I am weak, then I am strong" (vv. 9–10). The writer of Hebrews exhorted believers undergoing trials to remember that "all discipline for the moment seems not to be joyful, but sorrowful; yet to those who have been trained by it, afterwards it yields the peaceful fruit of righteousness" (Heb. 12:11). Peter wrote, "After you have suffered for a little while, the God of all grace, who called you to His eternal glory in Christ, will Himself perfect, confirm, strengthen and establish you" (1 Peter 5:10).

When tests and trials come, they reveal whether faith is real or superficial. The same trials that perfect righteousness in believers harden unbelievers in their sin.

THE THORNY SOIL

The seed which fell among the thorns, these are the ones who have heard, and as they go on their way they are choked with worries and riches and pleasures of this life, and bring no fruit to maturity. (8:14)

The seed which fell among the thorns pictures another group of those **who have heard** the gospel and initially accepted it. But the truth is soon crowded out not by suffering, but by pleasure. This soil appears good; it is not hard-packed, it is deep and has no underlying rock bed. But there are impurities in it, other life that is native to it. On the other hand the seed, the word of God, is not natural in the hearts of sinners. As a result though the seeds sprout, **they are choked with worries and riches and pleasures of this life** (cf. Matt. 13:22) which, as they did with the rich young ruler (Luke 18:18–25), keep the people pictured by the thorny soil from receiving eternal life.

These double-minded people (James 1:8) illustrate the truth that a person "cannot serve God and wealth" (Matt. 6:24). They are consumed with temporal things—sinful pleasures, longings and desires, ambition, career, homes, cars, prestige, relationships, fame—all of which choke the seed of the gospel so that they **bring no fruit to maturity.** The seed of the gospel will not produce the fruit of righteousness unless the heart is purged.

This is the preoccupied worldly heart, swept away by the deceitfulness of riches. Paul wrote of such people, "Those who want to get rich fall into temptation and a snare and many foolish and harmful desires which plunge men into ruin and destruction" (1 Tim. 6:9). The apostle John warned his readers,

> Do not love the world nor the things in the world. If anyone loves the world, the love of the Father is not in him. For all that is in the world, the lust of the flesh and the lust of the eyes and the boastful pride of life, is not from the Father, but is from the world. The world is passing away, and also its lusts; but the one who does the will of God lives forever. (1 John 2:15–17)

There is nothing wrong in enjoying the things that God graciously provides (1 Tim. 6:17). The priority, however, is to "seek first His kingdom and His righteousness, and all these things will be added to you" (Matt. 6:33). Those who understand the true value of the gospel would willingly give up all to possess it if that was what the Lord asked (Matt. 13:44–46).

THE GOOD SOIL

But the seed in the good soil, these are the ones who have heard the word in an honest and good heart, and hold it fast, and bear fruit with perseverance. (8:15)

In contrast to the first three soils, **the seed in the good soil** produces genuine salvation. This last soil represents **the ones who have heard the word in an honest and good heart,** one that is genuinely and truly good without duplicity. They are those who understand **the word** (Matt. 13:23), accept it (Mark 4:20), and **hold it fast** in ongoing obedience (cf. Luke 11:28; John 14:15,21; 15:10). Unlike the roadside soil, where the seed never penetrates, the rocky soil where it sprouts briefly and withers, and the thorny soil where it is choked out, the good soil is properly prepared. The seed will grow into mature plants that **bear fruit with** the **perseverance** that marks genuine faith (see the discussion of perseverance above). As noted above, those who abandon their profession of faith prove that it was never real.

Fruit encompasses the good works that accompany salvation (Matt. 3:8; John 15:16), including both attitudes (Gal. 5:22–23) and actions (Col. 1:10; Phil. 1:11). Attitude fruit produces action fruit, and to attempt to generate action fruit apart from it results in legalism, such as that which the Lord condemned in the scribes and Pharisees. As both Matthew's (13:23) and Mark's (4:20) accounts reveal, there are varying degrees of fruitfulness. All believers, however, will bear some genuine fruit (Eph. 2:10); fruitlessness is a mark of false, non-saving faith (John 15:2; cf. Matt. 3:10).

A proper understanding of this masterful parable should have a profound influence on how the church does evangelism. Jesus taught that the variable is not the method or skill of the one presenting the gospel, or the message itself—the things that are frequently the focus of contemporary evangelistic methodology. The variable is the heart. More specifically, it is not the nature of the heart; in the Lord's analogy all four soils are made up of the same dirt. The determining factor in how people respond to the gospel is the influences that prevail upon and dominate their hearts.

Conviction, which prepares the heart to receive the gospel, is the work of the Holy Spirit (John 16:8), and salvation itself is the work of God. But the Spirit's work of conviction does not take place in a vacuum. He uses the proclamation of the gospel message of sin and the need for salvation to do His convicting work in the human heart. "How then will they call on Him in whom they have not believed?" Paul asked rhetorically. "How will they believe in Him whom they have not heard? And how will they hear without a preacher?" (Rom. 10:14), since "faith comes from hearing, and hearing by the word of Christ" (v. 17).

Believers must present the full message of salvation and not merely focus on its blessings. Before people can experience those blessings they must come to grips with the reality that they are sinners, facing God's wrath and eternal judgment. They must acknowledge that their only hope lies in the salvation He has provided through the sacrificial death of His Son. Therefore Christians must explain sin to the lost before presenting God's gracious offer of forgiveness. As the Puritan pastor and theologian John Owen noted, those who would have their souls justified by grace must have their sins judged by the law (*The Forgiveness of Sin* [Reprint; Grand Rapids: Baker 1977], 60). Only then will the hard soil be plowed, the rock bed broken up, and the weeds removed, preparing the good soil to produce the fruit of salvation.

Be Careful How You Listen
(Luke 8:16–21)

21

"Now no one after lighting a lamp covers it over with a container, or puts it under a bed; but he puts it on a lampstand, so that those who come in may see the light. For nothing is hidden that will not become evident, nor anything secret that will not be known and come to light. So take care how you listen; for whoever has, to him more shall be given; and whoever does not have, even what he thinks he has shall be taken away from him." And His mother and brothers came to Him, and they were unable to get to Him because of the crowd. And it was reported to Him, "Your mother and Your brothers are standing outside, wishing to see You." But He answered and said to them, "My mother and My brothers are these who hear the word of God and do it." (8:16–21)

Listening is an important and often neglected skill. Good listeners are good friends and make for good company. They make good teachers and counselors. Poor listeners, on the other hand, want only to hear themselves talk, and even when they appear to be listening they often are only planning what they are going to say next. Solomon described poor listeners as those who bring folly and shame to themselves by giving an answer without fully listening to the question (Prov.

18:13).They cheat themselves out of the best in life's relationships.

But while listening to other people has temporal value, listening to God has eternal significance. Christ's warning in verse 18, "Take care how you listen," is a constant theme in Scripture.The command, "Hear the word of the Lord" appears about thirty times in the Old Testament (e.g., 2 Kings 20:16; Ps. 50:7; Isa. 1:10; 28:14; 48:1; Jer. 2:4; Ezek 18:25). In such passages as Psalm 81:8; Isaiah 41:1; 44:1; 46:3, 12; 49:1, 51:1, 7; 55:2–3, and Jeremiah 11:4, 7; 17:20; 42:15 God exhorted His people to listen to Him.At the transfiguration God commanded, "This is My beloved Son, listen to Him!" (Mark 9:7).The repeated phrase, "Today if you hear His voice" (Ps. 95:7; Heb. 3:7, 15; 4:7) further emphasizes the importance of listening to God.

But all too often Israel failed to listen to God's word. In Psalm 81:11–13 God lamented, "My people did not listen to My voice, and Israel did not obey Me. So I gave them over to the stubbornness of their heart, to walk in their own devices. Oh that My people would listen to Me, that Israel would walk in My ways!" Isaiah 30:9 described the children of Israel as "a rebellious people, false sons, sons who refuse to listen to the instruction of the Lord," while in Jeremiah 13:10 God indicted them as a "wicked people, who refuse to listen to My words." "This has been your practice from your youth," God said in Jeremiah 22:21, "that you have not obeyed My voice" (cf. 7:26; 11:10; 17:23; 35:17; 36:31; 40:3; Ps. 106:25; Isa. 28:12; 66:4). Not only rebellious Israel, but also all those who reject the truth are guilty of failing to listen to the Lord speaking in Scripture. As Jesus pointed out in the parable of the soils, the people represented by all four soils hear the word (Luke 8:12, 13, 14, 15); what differentiates people is how they react to the truth they hear.

The kind of listeners people are reveals their spiritual condition. Many make a superficial response to the Lord Jesus Christ, but He will one day say to them, "I never knew you; depart from Me, you who practice lawlessness" (Matt. 7:23; 25:11–12).Jesus said that such are the ones who hear His words, but fail to act on them (Matt. 7:26). When the flood of divine judgment comes, their spiritual houses, lacking a solid spiritual foundation, will be swept away (v. 27).On the other hand, those who hear Christ's words and obey them are His true disciples (v. 24; cf. John 8:31–32, 47; 10:3–5, 16, 27; 1 Cor. 2:12–16).

Jesus challenged those who identified themselves as His disciples, who were gathered around Him to hear His explanation of the parable of the soils, to take care how they listen. He noted four ways in which true hearers listen to the word: evangelistically, authentically, fruitfully, and obediently.

A True Hearer Listens Evangelistically

"Now no one after lighting a lamp covers it over with a container, or puts it under a bed; but he puts it on a lampstand, so that those who come in may see the light. (8:16)

This simple parable or story, also used by Jesus in Luke 11:33 and Matthew 5:15, is self-evident and easily understood. The purpose of a lamp is to give light, thus **no one after lighting a lamp covers it over with a container, or puts it under a bed.** The terra cotta lamps used in Israel were shaped like a saucer, with a spout and a handle, and used oil and a wick to provide light. To light a lamp and then put it under a bed or container would be pointless, since doing so would extinguish the lamp. Instead, lamps needed to be placed **on a lampstand** or a wall shelf **so that those who come in may see the light.**

While light in Scripture is often a metaphor for holiness (Matt. 5:14–16; Rom. 13:12), for truth (Pss. 36:9; 119:105, 130; Prov. 6:23; Acts 26:23; Eph. 5:9; 1 Thess. 5:5), and also for spiritual life in Christ (John 1:4), the specific feature the Lord communicated through this analogy is that genuine disciples do not hide the truth of the gospel. Instead, they listen to the revelation of God's Word and then proclaim it to others. Peter described Christians as "a chosen race, a royal priesthood, a holy nation, a people for God's own possession, so that [they] may proclaim the excellencies of Him who has called [them] out of darkness into His marvelous light" (1 Peter 2:9). In his defense before Herod Agrippa, Paul said that Jesus had sent him both to the Jews and to the Gentiles "to open their eyes so that they may turn from darkness to light and from the dominion of Satan to God, that they may receive forgiveness of sins and an inheritance among those who have been sanctified by faith in [Jesus Christ]" (Acts 26:18). Paul was thankful for the Roman Christians because their "faith [was] being proclaimed throughout the whole world" (Rom. 1:8; cf. 16:19). The apostle commended the Thessalonians because "the word of the Lord [had] sounded forth from [them], not only in Macedonia and Achaia, but also in every place [their] faith toward God [had] gone forth" (1 Thess. 1:8). Jesus likened true hearers of the word to a brilliantly lit city on a hill whose light cannot be hidden (Matt. 5:14). True conversion results in a desire for telling the gospel story. Genuine disciples respond to the truth evangelistically; that is, they not only take it in, but they also give it out. Lack of zeal for sharing the truth may reveal that God's work of salvation has not been wrought in the heart.

Jesus may also have had another issue in mind when He gave this analogy. In Luke 8:10 He had told the disciples, "To you it has been granted to know the mysteries of the kingdom of God, but to the rest it is in parables, so that seeing they may not see, and hearing they may not understand." As noted in the discussion of that verse in the previous chapter of this volume, that was an act of judgment on Jesus' part. Those who rejected the truth would have it hidden from them. The disciples may have thought that they were to render the same judgments and decide for themselves who to present the truth to.

But it is not the believers' place to make such a determination; only God knows a person's true spiritual condition. Christians are responsible to obey the Great Commission and "make disciples of all the nations, baptizing them in the name of the Father and the Son and the Holy Spirit" (Matt. 28:19; cf. Acts 1:8). And when they were ready, Jesus would send the Twelve out to preach the gospel to all whom they encountered (Luke 9:1–6). What He had explained to them in secret, they were to proclaim publicly (cf. Matt. 10:27).

A TRUE HEARER LISTENS AUTHENTICALLY

For nothing is hidden that will not become evident, nor anything secret that will not be known and come to light. (8:17)

Although commentators offer various interpretations of this statement, it seems reasonable to understand it as talking about authenticity; what a person is on the inside. Because **nothing is hidden that will not become evident,** or to put it another way, there is nothing **secret that will not be known and come to light,** the true condition of the heart will eventually be revealed. Generally speaking, time and truth go hand in hand. Given enough time the truth comes out for men to see. It is, of course, never hidden from God.

That principle is repeated throughout Scripture. Jesus gave it again in Matthew 10:26. In the Old Testament David wrote that "the righteous God tries the hearts and minds" (Ps. 7:9). In Psalm 90:8 Moses said to God, "You have placed our iniquities before You, our secret sins in the light of Your presence." Solomon closed the book of Ecclesiastes with the sobering warning that "God will bring every act to judgment, everything which is hidden, whether it is good or evil" (Eccl. 12:14). In the New Testament Paul spoke of a "day when, according to my gospel, God will judge the secrets of men through Christ Jesus" (Rom. 2:16), and noted that when "the Lord comes [He] will both bring to light the things hidden in the darkness and disclose the motives of men's hearts" (1 Cor. 4:5). In His message to the church at Thyatira Jesus said, "I am He who searches the minds and hearts; and I will give to each one of you according to your deeds" (Rev. 2:23; cf. Ps. 44:21; Jer. 11:20; 17:10; John 2:24–25; Acts 1:24; Heb.4:13).

Jesus' words evidently are a warning against hypocrisy, as an examination of the parallel statement in Luke 12:1–2 suggests. In verse 1 the Lord "began saying to His disciples first of all, 'Beware of the leaven of the Pharisees, which is hypocrisy.' " I Ie cautioned His hearers to avoid imitating the Pharisees, who "say things and do not do them" (Matt. 23:3); who "outwardly appear righteous to men, but inwardly . . . are full of hypocrisy and lawlessness" (v. 28). He exhorted them not to be like the false disciples who call Him "Lord, Lord," but do not obey Him (Matt. 7:21–22; Luke 6:46); who build their spiritual houses on the sand (Matt. 7:26–27).

All such hypocrisy will eventually be unmasked, because "there is nothing covered up that will not be revealed, and hidden that will not be known" (12:2). Since that phrase in the context of chapter 12 clearly refers to exposing hypocrisy, it likely has that same meaning in the present passage. In light of the coming judgment, Jesus called for self-examination on the part of those who claim to be His disciples.

A True Hearer Listens Fruitfully

So take care how you listen; for whoever has, to him more shall be given; and whoever does not have, even what he thinks he has shall be taken away from him." (8:18)

As noted above, Jesus' exhortation to **take care how you listen** is the theme of this entire section. Specifically, He warned that people must be aware that the consequences are serious. Positively, **whoever** is a true disciple and **has** eternal life, **to him more shall be given.** The good soil is marked by varying levels of productivity, but it invariably produces the fruit of salvation; as Jesus told the apostles gathered in the upper room, "My Father is glorified by this, that you bear much fruit, and so prove to be My disciples" (John 15:8; cf. v. 16). Constant production of fruit watered by the ceaselessly flowing stream of divine grace (John 1:16; cf. Eph. 1:3–8; 2:7–10; Phil. 1:11) marks true disciples of the Lord Jesus Christ.

But Christ's promise of blessing for true disciples is balanced by His warning to false disciples that **whoever does not have, even what he thinks he has shall be taken away from him.** In the end, the false disciples lose everything. All of their self-righteous works that they had counted on to bring them salvation will turn out to be nothing but rubbish (Phil. 3:8), vain things that cannot save (Acts 14:15). Like the wicked, lazy, unfaithful slave in the parable of the talents (Matt. 25:14–30), they will be cast "into the outer darkness … [where] there will be weeping and gnashing of teeth" (v. 30).

A TRUE HEARER LISTENS OBEDIENTLY

And His mother and brothers came to Him, and they were unable to get to Him because of the crowd. And it was reported to Him, "Your mother and Your brothers are standing outside, wishing to see You." But He answered and said to them, "My mother and My brothers are these who hear the word of God and do it." (8:19–21)

Both Matthew (12:46–50) and Mark (3:31–35) place this event involving Jesus' **mother and brothers** earlier in His ministry, before the parable of the soils. Luke places it here because it fits the theme of this section of his gospel, the importance of properly hearing the word.

As they usually are in the New Testament, Jesus' **brothers** are associated with His **mother,** Mary (Matt. 13:55; John 2:12; Acts 1:14). Contrary to the Roman Catholic dogma of Mary's perpetual virginity, these are Jesus' half-brothers, the biological children of Joseph and Mary. The belief that Mary remained a virgin after giving birth to Jesus is foreign to the New Testament and the apostolic era, first appearing in the apocryphal literature of the second century. To avoid the obvious implication of the texts that speak of Jesus' brothers (and sisters; Matt. 13:56), Catholics have argued that these were Joseph's children from a prior marriage and hence Jesus' step brothers. There is no evidence, however, of such a marriage. Further, if that were the case one of those older brothers would have been Joseph's heir and hence the rightful king of Israel, not Jesus (Alfred Plummer, *A Critical and Exegetical Commentary on the Gospel According to St. Luke,* The International Critical Commentary [Edinburgh: T. & T. Clark, 1922], 224). All historical evidence points to both Joseph and Mary being young teenagers when they married, making a previous marriage and family nonsense.

Others have argued that these were Jesus' cousins, not His brothers. But *adelphos* ("brother") is never used in the New Testament in the sense of "cousin." In fact, the New Testament writers had a word available that specifically means "cousin" (*anepsios*), and when Paul referred to Barnabas's cousin Mark he used that word (Col. 4:10). Further evidence that these were Jesus' actual brothers comes from Psalm 69. In this messianic psalm Messiah says in verse 8, "I have become estranged from my brothers and an alien to my mother's sons." Here "brothers" cannot mean "cousins," or "step brothers," since the term refers to Messiah's mother's sons.

The clear implication of such passages as Matthew 1:18 ("before they came together"), 25 ("kept her a virgin until she gave birth to a Son") and Luke 2:7 ("she gave birth to her firstborn son") is that Mary and Joseph had normal sexual relations and produced children after Jesus' birth.

Having arrived at the place where Jesus was teaching, Mary and His brothers **were unable to get to Him because of the crowd.** They had to "[send] word to Him and [call] Him" (Mark 3:31). Their request to speak with Jesus (Matt. 12:46) was passed through the crowd (v. 47) **and it was reported to Him, "Your mother and Your brothers are standing outside, wishing to see You."** Mark 3:20–21 reveals that they were concerned about the massive crowds that followed Jesus everywhere, and fearful of the rising hostility of the Jewish religious leaders. Having erroneously concluded that Jesus had taken leave of His senses (Mark 3:21), Mary and His brothers had come to rescue Him. That Joseph does not appear here or anywhere in the New Testament after the incident in the temple (Luke 2:41–50) suggests that he was dead by this time. Jesus' assigning Mary into the care of the apostle John at the cross (John 19:27) further confirms that Joseph was dead.

The Lord's brothers did not believe in Him (John 7:5) until after the resurrection (Acts 1:14), but Mary understood who He was from the beginning. She knew that He had come to "save His people from their sins" (Matt. 1:21), and acknowledged her own need for a Savior (Luke 1:47). She confessed that she was neither sinless nor co-redemptrix with Jesus.

Jesus' care for Mary and willingness to redeem His brothers indicates that He was not indifferent toward them. However His reply, **"My mother and My brothers are these who hear the word of God and do it,"** seems at first glance to suggest otherwise. But that is not the case. Christ's point is that relationships to Him are not defined in human terms by physical or family ties. While Jesus was not indifferent to His family, neither was He subservient to them. Those who have a relationship with Him are the ones who **hear the word of God and do it.** The Lord made that point again later in Luke's gospel. Seeking to honor Mary "one of the women in the crowd raised her voice and said to Him, 'Blessed is the womb that bore You and the breasts at which You nursed'" (Luke 11:27). But human relationships are not the issue, as His reply, "On the contrary, blessed are those who hear the word of God and observe it" (v. 28) indicates. Only those who are "doers of the word, and not merely hearers who delude themselves" (James 1:22), who hear His words and act on them (Matt. 7:24), who continue in His word (John 8:31), and who demonstrate their love for Him by obeying Him (John 14:15, 21, 23; 15:10) have a spiritual relationship with the Lord Jesus Christ.

The picture of such people given in this passage is clear. They are true hearers of the word, who listen to it evangelistically, authentically, fruitfully, and obediently. The challenge Jesus issued that day on the shore of the Sea of Galilee is the same one He makes to everyone: "Take care how you listen."

Calm in the Storm (Luke 8:22–25)

22

Now on one of those days Jesus and His disciples got into a boat, and He said to them, "Let us go over to the other side of the lake." So they launched out. But as they were sailing along He fell asleep; and a fierce gale of wind descended on the lake, and they began to be swamped and to be in danger. They came to Jesus and woke Him up, saying, "Master, Master, we are perishing!" And He got up and rebuked the wind and the surging waves, and they stopped, and it became calm. And He said to them, "Where is your faith?" They were fearful and amazed, saying to one another, "Who then is this, that He commands even the winds and the water, and they obey Him?" (8:22–25)

God has a plan to redeem both His people and His planet. That plan began to unfold immediately after the fall, when God promised that a redeemer would come who would destroy Satan (Gen. 3:15; cf. 1 John 3:8). That redeemer, the Messiah, the Lord Jesus Christ, came to offer Himself as a sacrifice and "save His people from their sins" (Matt. 1:21). He will come again in glory and majesty to destroy the wicked (Rev. 19:11–16) and rule the earth (Rev. 11:15; 20:4, 6). He will restore peace, justice, truth, righteousness, and joy to the renewed planet.

Obviously, to reverse the curse on both fallen mankind and the earth will require immense, incomprehensible, inconceivable power. In the kingdom Satan and his demon hosts will be bound (Rev. 20:1–3) and the saints will reign with Christ (vv. 4–6; Dan. 7:18, 27; 1 Cor. 6:2). Sin will be instantaneously punished (Ps. 2:9; Isa. 11:3–4), and peace (Isa. 2:4; 9:6–7; Mic. 4:3), joy (Isa. 12:3–4), and the knowledge of God (Isa. 11:9) will dominate the earth. Health and healing will replace disease and death (Isa. 29:18; 33:24; 35:5–6).

Even nature will change. Natural enemies will live together in peace; "the wolf will dwell with the lamb, and the leopard will lie down with the young goat, and the calf and the young lion and the fatling together; and a little boy will lead them ....The nursing child will play by the hole of the cobra, and the weaned child will put his hand on the viper's den" (Isa. 11:6, 8). Carnivorous animals will eat straw like oxen (Isa. 11:7). Crops will flourish (Isa. 30:23–25; Joel 2:21–27), even in what is now barren desert (Isa. 35:1–2; 35:6–7). In short, paradise lost will become paradise regained.

The power required to redeem lost sinners and restore the cursed earth is beyond human ability or comprehension; it belongs only to God. In Psalm 62:11 David said, "Power belongs to God." Job expressed that same truth poetically when he exclaimed, "The thunder of His power who can understand?" (Job 26:14 NKJV; cf. 36:22). Psalm 79:11 and Nahum 1:3 speak of the greatness of God's power, while Psalms 29:1–10 and 68:32–35 describe it. So clear is the evidence of God's power that it leaves unrepentant sinners without excuse for their rejection of Him (Rom. 1:20). God's power is revealed in His sovereign rule over all things (Ps. 66:7), raising Christ (2 Cor. 13:4) and believers (1 Cor. 6:14) from the dead, saving lost sinners (Rom. 1:16; 1 Cor. 1:18), rescuing the righteous (Neh. 1:10; Ps. 106:8), and destroying the wicked (Rom. 9:22).

Creation itself reveals God's mighty power (Jer. 10:12). The earth is twenty-five thousand miles in circumference, eight thousand miles in diameter and weighs approximately six sextillion tons. It spins on its axis at about one thousand miles per hour, and travels in its approximately one hundred fifty million-mile orbit around the sun at about one thousand miles a minute. The sun itself makes a vast orbit around the center of the Milky Way galaxy.

At the other end of the size spectrum, a teaspoon full of water contains trillions of atoms, while the material in an atom accounts for only about one trillionth of its volume. If the empty space were to be squeezed out of a human body, it would be reduced in size to a tiny fraction of a cubic inch. From the vastness of space to the infinitesimally small realm of the atom, God upholds all things by the word of His power (Heb. 1:3).

In his inspired record of the life and ministry of the Lord Jesus Christ, Luke makes His identity unmistakably clear. He is the Messiah, God the Son, the second person of the Trinity incarnate. His genealogy reveals that Jesus was a descendant of David, and thus Israel's rightful king (3:23–38). He had a unique virgin birth (1:26–35; 2:1–7; cf. Isa. 7:14). At His baptism the Father affirmed that Jesus was His beloved Son (3:21–22). The account of His temptation revealed His absolute authority over Satan (4:1–13), and He also exercised that same authority over the demons (4:33–35, 41). Jesus also demonstrated power over disease (4:40; 5:15, 17; 6:17–19; 7:1–10) and death (7:11–15). His supernatural power over disease, death, Satan, demons, and the forces of nature shows that He alone has the power to reverse the curse and usher in the kingdom. That power awed and terrified those who witnessed it in action, as they realized that they were sinners in the presence of Holy God (5:8; 8:25, 37, 47, 56).

The Lord Jesus Christ had displayed His power over the natural realm in an earlier incident recorded by Luke (5:4–9). In this far more dramatic demonstration of that power, Jesus calmed a raging storm on the Sea of Galilee. The story may be divided into three parts: the calm before the storm, the calm during the storm, and the calm after the storm. The epilogue, relating the disciples' terror at the display of divine power they had witnessed, might be titled the storm after the calm.

THE CALM BEFORE THE STORM

Now on one of those days Jesus and His disciples got into a boat, and He said to them, "Let us go over to the other side of the lake." So they launched out. But as they were sailing along He fell asleep; (8:22–23a)

Luke's note that the event he was about to relate took place **on one of those days** indicates that his chronology is purposely vague and indefinite. As noted in the previous chapter of this volume, he was not following a strict time sequence in this section of his gospel, but was arranging his material thematically. Mark's account reveals that this incident took place on the evening of the same day that Jesus taught several parables, including that of the soils (Mark 4:35). Most likely after eating a meal in nearby Capernaum (cf. Matt. 8:5), **Jesus and His disciples got into a boat,** probably a fishing vessel owned by Peter, Andrew, James, or John. (Although they had already become full-time followers of Jesus [Luke 5:11], they apparently still had their boats [cf. John 21:3]). Mark's account records that there were other small boats accompanying the one the Lord was in (Mark 4:36).

Seeking to escape the ever-present crowds for a time of rest, Jesus **said to** the disciples, **"Let us go over to the other side of the lake."** Leaving the vicinity of Capernaum on the northwest tip of the Sea of Galilee, they headed for the region known as Gerasa, on the eastern shore. There Jesus had a divine appointment with a demon-possessed maniac, whom He would heal (8:26–39).

Known today as Yam Kinneret and variously called in Scripture the Lake of Gennesaret (Luke 5:1), the Sea of Chinnereth (Num. 34:11; Josh. 13:27) or Chinneroth (Josh. 12:3), and the Sea of Tiberias (John 6:1; 21:1), the Sea of Galilee is a large (approximately thirteen miles wide by seven miles long) freshwater lake that is the most significant geographical feature of Galilee. The Jordan River, which arises from several sources near Mt. Hermon and flows into the lake from the north, is its main source of water. At about 680 feet below sea level, the Sea of Galilee is the lowest freshwater lake on the planet. The Jordan exits the southern end of the lake, and flows south into the Dead Sea, which is 1,300 feet below sea level.

The lake is about thirty miles east of the Mediterranean Sea, situated in a bowl-shaped section of the Jordan Valley, which is part of the Great Rift Valley running from Syria in the north to Mozambique on the African continent in the south. The lake is surrounded by steep hills on all sides, which are a major factor in the development of the sudden, violent, sometimes life-threatening storms that the lake is known for. Cooler air from the higher elevations flows down the slopes and collides with the warmer air nearer the lake's surface. In addition, as the air flows through the ravines and canyons it is compressed, and its speed intensifies. Most powerful of all are the winds that flow from the eastern desert down off the large plateau region above the lake known as the Golan Heights. In 1992 the winds from one such storm generated waves ten feet high that crashed into the city of Tiberias on the western shore, inflicting considerable damage.

After dark (cf. Matt. 8:16) Jesus and the disciples **launched out** onto the lake. As they **were sailing along** Jesus, exhausted from a long day of crowds and preaching, **fell asleep.** Mark adds the detail that the Lord was asleep in the stern of the boat, His head pillowed on a cushion (Mark 4:38). Along with being fully God, Jesus was fully human, therefore subject to hunger (Matt. 4:2; 21:18), thirst (John 4:7; 19:28), and fatigue (cf. John 4:6). This incident is the only place in Scripture that pictures Jesus sleeping. He was calmly, peacefully resting, despite knowing that the storm was coming. Trusting in His Father's plan, He was secure in the knowledge of His sovereign power and ability to calm the wind and waves.

It should be noted that the reference to the Lord's disciples encompasses more than merely the twelve apostles. *Mathētēs* (disciple) refers to a learner, student, or follower, someone who attached himself to a teacher. It is used of people who had some interest in Jesus, but does not necessarily indicate a high level of commitment to Him. In fact, at this point some of the Lord's disciples were not saved; John 6:66 notes that "many of His disciples withdrew and were not walking with Him anymore." When a would-be disciple said to Him, "I will follow You, Lord; but first permit me to say good-bye to those at home" (Luke 9:61) Jesus replied, "No one, after putting his hand to the plow and looking back, is fit for the kingdom of God" (v. 62). Along with a man who professed willingness to follow Jesus wherever He went (v. 57) and one who when challenged to follow the Lord chose instead to wait for his inheritance (v. 59), this man chose earthly things over a full, saving commitment to the Lord Jesus Christ.

The people illustrated by the rocky and thorny soils in the parable of the soils were also professed disciples of Christ who received His word, yet were never truly redeemed (see the exposition of 8:4–15 in chapter 20 of this volume). Genuine disciples will manifest not only repentance, confession, and obedience, but also perseverance. Jesus was about to put on a display of His divine power designed to move those who witnessed it to genuine faith in Him. (For a further discussion of the meaning of the term "disciple," see chapter 21 of my book *The Gospel According to Jesus* [revised and expanded edition; Grand Rapids: Zondervan, 1994].)

The Calm During the Storm

and a fierce gale of wind descended on the lake, and they began to be swamped and to be in danger. They came to Jesus and woke Him up, saying, "Master, Master, we are perishing!" (8:23b–24a)

All of a sudden the lake's tranquility was shattered as **a fierce gale of wind descended on** it. *Lailaps* (**fierce gale**) describes a powerful storm, potentially one with hurricane force winds. *Katabainō* (**descended**) is the root of the meteorological term "katabatic," which refers to winds created by air flowing downhill. The term accurately describes the storm-producing winds that plunge down the surrounding heights to strike the low-lying Sea of Galilee, as noted above. Mark added the adjective *megas* ("great") to the noun *lailaps* (Mark 4:37 ESV), while Matthew described the storm as literally "a great shaking [*seismos*, from which the English word "seismology" derives] on the sea" (Matt. 8:24).

Clearly, this was no ordinary storm, but one so severe as to be life threatening. The massive waves churned up by the powerful winds were breaking over the boat (Mark 4:37) and covering it (Matt. 8:24). As a result, the boat was filling up with water (Mark 4:37) to the point that it **began to be swamped,** putting the disciples in grave **danger.** Despite the raging storm, with its howling winds and towering waves, Jesus was still peacefully sleeping the rest of complete exhaustion and confident sovereignty in the stern (Matt. 8:24; Mark 4:38). While chaos and pandemonium raged all about Him, He remained untroubled in the storm, calmly asleep.

The disciples, on the other hand, were panic stricken. Since many of them were fishermen, used to the lake and its treacherous weather, they understood how strong a storm their boats could endure and knew that their survival was threatened by this one. Desperate and terrified, fearing for their lives, **they came to Jesus and woke Him up, saying, "Master, Master, we are perishing!"** Matthew's account says they called Jesus "Lord" (Matt. 8:25), while Mark notes that they addressed Him as "Teacher" (Mark 4:38). Far from being contradictory, as some skeptics imagine, the gospel writers' accounts accurately reflect the chaos and confusion that reigned on that stormy night. This was no orderly, organized delegation calmly presenting their petition to Jesus, but rather a panicked mob facing imminent death. Thus, some cried out, "Lord," some "Teacher," and others **Master.** The disciples had witnessed the Lord's power over disease, demons, and death. Some of them had seen His power to control the fish in the Sea of Galilee (Luke 5:5–9). But could He control the enormous power of wind and water?

With no human solution available, they came to the One who had demonstrated divine power in the past. Perhaps some of the disciples remembered Psalm 65:5–7:

> O God of our salvation,
> You who are the trust of all the ends of the earth and of the farthest sea;
> Who establishes the mountains by His strength,
> Being girded with might;
> Who stills the roaring of the seas,
> The roaring of their waves.

or Psalm 89:9:

> You rule the swelling of the sea;
> When its waves rise, You still them.

Surely someone recalled Psalm 107:23–31:

Those who go down to the sea in ships,
Who do business on great waters;
They have seen the works of the Lord,
And His wonders in the deep.
For He spoke and raised up a stormy wind,
Which lifted up the waves of the sea.
They rose up to the heavens, they went down to the depths;
Their soul melted away in their misery.
They reeled and staggered like a drunken man,
And were at their wits' end.
Then they cried to the Lord in their trouble,
And He brought them out of their distresses.
He caused the storm to be still,
So that the waves of the sea were hushed.
Then they were glad because they were quiet,
So He guided them to their desired haven.
Let them give thanks to the Lord for His lovingkindness,
And for His wonders to the sons of men!

In their time of desperate need, the disciples appealed to the One who alone could save them.

THE CALM AFTER THE STORM

And He got up and rebuked the wind and the surging waves, and they stopped, and it became calm. And He said to them, "Where is your faith?" (8:24b–25a)

Awakened by the disciples' desperate pleas, Jesus **got up and rebuked the wind and the surging waves.** His exact words according to Mark 4:39 were "Hush, be still." Instantly obeying the voice of the Creator, the wind and waves **stopped, and it became calm.** Skeptics, determined to deny the miraculous at all costs, have pointed out that storms on the Sea of Galilee often stop as rapidly as they start. But while the wind might have died down almost at once, it would have taken much longer for the waves to subside. When Jesus commanded the wind and waves to stop, both did so instantly, and it became absolutely calm (both Matthew and Mark use the adjective *megas* ["great"] to describe the glassy calm).

Having calmed the storm, Jesus used the incident to teach His shocked and astonished disciples the lesson He wanted them to learn. As they sat in their boats on the now perfectly still surface of the lake, **He said to them, "Where is your faith?"** (cf. 12:28; Matt. 6:30; 14:31; 16:8; 17:20). They had seen Him perform countless miracles, so their lack of faith on this occasion was distressing and inexcusable. On the other hand, this was the first time that one of the Lord's miracles had directly involved them, and beyond that reality their lives were at stake. That made it far more difficult for them to remain detached and objectively analyze the situation. Paul, in contrast, was able to remain calm throughout the two-week-long storm that ended in shipwreck (Acts 27:14–44). But he had already faced persecution and death many times before and been delivered by the Lord (cf. 2 Cor. 11:22–33).

The lesson for the disciples was clear: they were to trust the Lord even in the most severe and threatening circumstances. They were, as Peter would later write, to cast all their anxiety on Him, knowing that He cared for them (1 Peter 5:7). Paul expressed his confident trust in the Lord's care when he wrote triumphantly, "For I am convinced that neither death, nor life, nor angels, nor principalities, nor things present, nor things to come, nor powers, nor height, nor depth, nor any other created thing, will be able to separate us from the love of God, which is in Christ Jesus our Lord" (Rom. 8:38–39). Summing up the lesson Jesus wants all believers to take from this incident, David Gooding writes,

> We live in a universe that is lethally hostile to human life: only the miracle of creation and divine maintenance preserves our planet and its wonderful adaptations and provisions for the propagation of human life. Within our earth itself wind, wave, lightning, storm, flood, drought, avalanche, earthquake, fire, heat, cold, germ, virus, epidemic, all from time to time threaten and destroy life. Sooner or later one of them may destroy us. The story of the stilling of the storm is not, of course, meant to tell us that Christ will never allow any believer to perish by drowning, or by any other natural disaster. Many believers have so perished. It does demonstrate that he is Lord of the physical forces in the universe, that for him nothing happens by accident, and that no force in all creation can destroy his plan for our eternal salvation or separate us from the love of God which is in Christ Jesus our Lord (see Rom. 8:38–39). (*According to Luke* [Grand Rapids: Eerdmans, 1987], 143)

Sometimes the Lord will bring a storm into believers' lives for chastening; other times to increase their faith. Jonah ended up in a storm because of his disobedience, while in this incident the disciples' obedience put them into the storm. In both cases God was there to deliver them.

EPILOGUE: THE STORM AFTER THE CALM

They were fearful and amazed, saying to one another, "Who then is this, that He commands even the winds and the water, and they obey Him?" (8:25b)

Having witnessed an astonishing, unparalleled display of super-natural divine power, the disciples understandably were **fearful and amazed.** The only thing they found more terrifying than the storm outside their boat was having the Creator and controller of the storm in it. The trauma of realizing that only God could do such a miracle caused them to say **to one another, "Who then is this, that He commands even the winds and the water, and they obey Him?"** (cf. 8:37, 47, 56). The obvious and only answer to that rhetorical question is the one they gave later after Jesus stilled another storm on the Sea of Galilee: "Those who were in the boat worshiped Him, saying, 'You are certainly God's Son!'" (Matt. 14:33). By then they had a firm answer to their question here.

In response to Christ's earlier miracle on the lake, Peter had exclaimed, "Go away from me Lord, for I am a sinful man, O Lord!" (Luke 5:8)—a response that is typical of those who experience God's presence. Abraham described himself as "dust and ashes" (Gen. 18:27); Job humbly said, "I have heard of You by the hearing of the ear; but now my eye sees You; therefore I retract, and I repent in dust and ashes" (Job 42:5–6); after encountering the preincarnate Christ in the person of the Angel of the Lord, Samson's father "Manoah said to his wife, 'We will surely die, for we have seen God'" (Judg. 13:22); exposed to God's presence on Mt. Sinai, the Israelites "trembled and stood at a distance. Then they said to Moses, 'Speak to us yourself and we will listen; but let not God speak to us, or we will die'" (Ex. 20:18–19); overwhelmed by a vision of God in His heavenly temple, Isaiah cried, "Woe is me, for I am ruined! Because I am a man of unclean lips, and I live among a people of unclean lips; for my eyes have seen the King, the Lord of hosts" (Isa. 6:5); Ezekiel fell on his face when he saw a vision of God (Ezek. 1:28); after seeing the glorified, exalted Christ, the apostle John "fell at His feet like a dead man" (Rev. 1:17).

This brief vignette of Christ's life reveals Him in His divine glory as the One who controls all of the natural forces of the universe. But not only does it reveal His power, but also His compassionate care for those who are His. This storm, as do all of life's storms for believers, served to increase the disciples' faith in His willingness and ability to deliver them from any situation, no matter how hopeless it may seem. Having experienced God's gracious care for him throughout his long and difficult ministry, the apostle Paul could say confidently as his life drew to a close, "The Lord will rescue me from every evil deed, and will bring me safely to His heavenly kingdom; to Him be the glory forever and ever. Amen" (2 Tim. 4:18).

The Maniac
Who Became
a Missionary
(Luke 8:26–39)

23

Then they sailed to the country of the Gerasenes, which is oppo-site Galilee. And when He came out onto the land, He was met by a man from the city who was possessed with demons; and who had not put on any clothing for a long time, and was not living in a house, but in the tombs. Seeing Jesus, he cried out and fell before Him, and said in a loud voice, "What business do we have with each other, Jesus, Son of the Most High God? I beg You, do not torment me." For He had commanded the unclean spirit to come out of the man. For it had seized him many times; and he was bound with chains and shackles and kept under guard, and yet he would break his bonds and be driven by the demon into the desert. And Jesus asked him, "What is your name?" And he said, "Legion"; for many demons had entered him. They were imploring Him not to command them to go away into the abyss. Now there was a herd of many swine feeding there on the moun-tain; and the demons implored Him to permit them to enter the swine. And He gave them permission. And the demons came out of the man and entered the swine; and the herd rushed down the steep bank into the lake and was drowned. When the herdsmen saw what had happened, they ran away and reported it in the

city and out in the country. The people went out to see what had happened; and they came to Jesus, and found the man from whom the demons had gone out, sitting down at the feet of Jesus, clothed and in his right mind; and they became frightened. Those who had seen it reported to them how the man who was demon-possessed had been made well. And all the people of the country of the Gerasenes and the surrounding district asked Him to leave them, for they were gripped with great fear; and He got into a boat and returned. But the man from whom the demons had gone out was begging Him that he might accompany Him; but He sent him away, saying, "Return to your house and describe what great things God has done for you." So he went away, proclaiming throughout the whole city what great things Jesus had done for him. (8:26–39)

A saying attributed to G. K. Chesterton, whose apologetic writings were instrumental in C. S. Lewis's conversion to Christianity, is that when people cease to believe in God they do not believe in nothing; they believe in anything. Having rejected the only true God, people today are fascinated with transcendent, alternative realities, science fiction, the legends of pagan mythology, or fictional beings with superhuman powers.

On a more sinister note, many are obsessed with the occult. Witchcraft, séances, Ouija boards, astrology, spiritism, fortune telling, palm reading, seers who allegedly predict the future, and even open worship of the devil are increasingly popular. The rise of interest in alternative realities, the paranormal, and the occult coincided with the declining influence of biblical Christianity in Western culture, as Os Guinness notes:

> Early hunters on safari in Africa used to build their fires high at night in order to keep away the animals in the bush. But when the fires burned low in the early hours of the morning, they would see all around them the approaching outlined shapes of animals and a ring of encircling eyes in the darkness. When the fire was high they were far off, but when the fire was low they approached again.
>
> As we have witnessed the erosion and breakdown of the Christian culture of the West, so we have seen the vacuum filled by an upsurge of ideas that would have been unthinkable when the fires of the Christian culture were high. (*The Dust of Death* [Downers Grove, Ill.: InterVarsity, 1973], 277)

People are inevitably drawn to the power and mystery that is just beyond their comprehension. But the fallen human race, compelled by demons, will never arrive at an accurate understanding of the supernatural realm. People on their own cannot get outside the space-time continuum and can only fantasize about it, while demons will only add their hellish deceptions to those fantasies. The Bible is the only source of accurate knowledge about the supernatural realm, and it is foolish and futile to seek such knowledge elsewhere:

> When they say to you, "Consult the mediums and the spiritists who whisper and mutter," should not a people consult their God? Should they consult the dead on behalf of the living? To the law and to the testimony! If they do not speak according to this word, it is because they have no dawn. (Isa. 8:19–20)

The Bible features insights into the character, purposes, and plan of God. It reveals His supernatural power to create and His purpose eventually to destroy the universe. But the primary supernatural event in Scripture is not God's creation or destruction of everything, as stupendous as that is. The central supernatural event in the Bible is the incarnation of the Lord Jesus Christ, God in human flesh, the one who perfectly reveals God to man (John 1:18; 14:9; Col. 1:15; Heb. 1:3).

Christ's coming to earth to "save His people from their sins" (Matt. 1:21) and to "destroy the works of the devil" (1 John 3:8; cf. Gen. 3:15; John 12:31; 16:11; Rom. 16:20; Col. 2:15; Heb. 2:14) touched off a frenzied outburst of demonic activity unlike anything that had come before. It should be noted, however, that the demons were not attacking Jesus; He was attacking them. There is only one recorded instance of demonic activity in the Old Testament (along with a few allusions to demons; e.g., Lev. 17:7; Deut. 32:17; Ps. 106:37), Genesis 6:1–4, where demon-possessed men cohabitated with women (cf. 2 Peter 2:4–5; Jude 6). Outside of the gospels and Acts, there are no references to demon possession in the New Testament. Only during the future time of the great tribulation will global, open demonic activity exceed that of the time of Christ's earthly ministry.

The rarity of overt demonic manifestation does not mean that the forces of hell are not always active. Those "deceitful spirits" (1 Tim. 4:1) prefer to remain anonymous, working behind the scenes disguised as angels of light (2 Cor. 11:14–15). But so great was their terror in the presence of the Lord Jesus Christ that they could not help revealing themselves. Earlier in Luke's account Jesus entered a synagogue in Capernaum and a demon-possessed man was there. Unable to control his fear, the demon blurted out, "Let us alone! What business do we have with each other, Jesus of Nazareth? Have You come to destroy us? I know who You are—the Holy One of God!" (Luke 4:34). Paul stated that the

Lord Jesus is "far above all rule and authority and power and dominion [angels]" (Eph. 1:21).

As God incarnate, Jesus Christ displayed the power to vanquish Satan that only God possesses. To the Jewish religious authorities, who blasphemously tried to explain away that power by claiming He was in league with the devil, Jesus replied,

> If I cast out demons by the finger of God, then the kingdom of God has come upon you. When a strong man, fully armed, guards his own house, his possessions are undisturbed. But when someone stronger than he attacks him and overpowers him, he takes away from him all his armor on which he had relied and distributes his plunder. (Luke 11:20–22)

As the Messiah and Son of God, Jesus defeated Satan and delivered His people from their bondage to him (Eph. 2:1–3; Col. 1:13; 1 John 5:19). The Lord demonstrated His power over the devil throughout His earthly ministry. The incident in this passage, presented by all three Synoptic Gospel writers, is the most dramatic and extreme encounter between Jesus and the forces of hell recorded in the Gospels. It tells the miraculous story of Christ's deliverance of a demon-plagued maniac, who became a most unlikely missionary. As the account unfolds, three forces are revealed: the destructive power of demons, the delivering power of Jesus, and the damning power of sin.

THE DESTRUCTIVE POWER OF DEMONS

Then they sailed to the country of the Gerasenes, which is opposite Galilee. And when He came out onto the land, He was met by a man from the city who was possessed with demons; and who had not put on any clothing for a long time, and was not living in a house, but in the tombs. Seeing Jesus, he cried out and fell before Him, and said in a loud voice, "What business do we have with each other, Jesus, Son of the Most High God? I beg You, do not torment me." . . . For it had seized him many times; and he was bound with chains and shackles and kept under guard, and yet he would break his bonds and be driven by the demon into the desert. (8:26–28, 29b)

This amazing demonstration of Jesus' divine power immediately follows another astonishing miracle. As the Lord and the disciples **sailed** across the northern section of the Sea of Galilee, a massive storm had arisen. Fearing for their lives, the disciples had awakened Jesus, who had instantly calmed the wind and the waves (see the exposition of 8:22–25 in the previous chapter of this volume). The powerful storm had undoubtedly blown them off course, and as a result it was probably daybreak by the time they made it to shore. Luke (along with Mark [5:1]) calls their destination **the country of the Gerasenes, which** was **opposite Galilee** on the eastern shore, while Matthew refers to it as "the country of the Gadarenes" (Matt. 8:28). Mark and Luke evidently referred to a small village (Gerasa; modern Kersa) near the shore of the Sea of Galilee, while Matthew referred to the larger town, Gadara, which gave its name to the region (and may have been its capital).

After Jesus and the disciples **came out** of the boats **onto the land,** they were **met by** the shocking sight of **a man from the city who was possessed with demons.** Matthew noted that there were two demon-possessed men (Matt. 8:28), while Luke and Mark focused on the one whom Jesus delivered. What happened to the other man is not recorded (although the use of the plural "demoniacs" in Matt. 8:33 suggests that he too was delivered). The demon-possessed **man** in Luke's account was literally a maniac, exhibiting extreme symptoms of wild, uncontrollable behavior.

As I wrote in the first volume of this commentary on Luke, Scripture uses four terms or phrases to describe demon possession:

> First, sixteen times such people are said to have a demon or evil spirit (4:33; 7:33; [8:27]; 13:11; Matt. 11:18; Mark 3:22, 30; 9:17; John 7:20; 8:48, 49, 52; 10:20; Acts 8:7; 16:16), indicating that a demon-possessed individual was indwelt, controlled, and tormented by the demon. The repeated phrases "entered him" ([8:]30), "cast out" (Matt. 8:16; 9:33; 12:24, 28; Mark 1:34), "came out" (Matt. 8:32), "come out" (Mark 5:8), and "coming out" (Mark 5:13) also indicate that demons indwell their victims. Demon possession is a supernatural phenomenon, not explicable in psychological or physical terms (though there can be physical symptoms associated with it; cf. [8:]27; Matt. 9:32; 12:22; 17:14–15; Mark 1:26; 5:5; [Luke] 9:42). It should be noted too that on no occasion when Jesus delivered an individual from demon possession was there a reference to forgiveness of sins. Nor did all those delivered repent and believe. The demon-possessed individuals whom Jesus delivered were not necessarily any more wicked than other sinners. The emphasis is on Jesus' power over the demons, not on the individuals being delivered. But after Jesus and the apostles passed from the scene, the only way to be delivered from demons is through saving faith in the Lord Jesus Christ.
>
> The second phrase translates the verb *daimonizomai,* which appears thirteen times in the New Testament ([8:]36; Matt. 4:24; 8:16, 28, 33; 9:32;

12:22; 15:22; Mark 1:32; 5:15, 16, 18; John 10:21), and is translated, "demon-possessed," or "demoniaics." Like the first phrase, it refers to someone indwelt and controlled by a demon or demons to the point that he cannot successfully resist, not to the general influence demons have in promoting false doctrine (1 Tim. 4:1), false worship (1 Cor. 10:20–21), immorality (1 Tim. 4:1–3), and attitudes of jealousy, divisiveness, and pride (James 3:13–16).

Third, the Bible speaks of those with an "unclean" spirit (Mark 1:23; 5:2) or having one (Mark 7:25). Those phrases also indicate that demons indwell their victims.

Finally, Acts 5:16 speaks of those "afflicted with unclean spirits," emphasizing the torment demon-possessed people suffer. (*Luke 1–5*, The MacArthur New Testament Commentary [Chicago: Moody, 2009], 283)

As those terms make clear and the present passage demonstrates, demon possession involves demons indwelling their victims and taking control of their minds, bodies, and voices. How the man in this story became demon possessed is not known, but all unbelievers are part of Satan's kingdom of darkness and hence vulnerable. Since this man was a Gentile, perhaps his idolatrous religion provided the entry point for the demons to enter him.

Having seized control of him, the demons compelled the man to behave in a bizarre manner. First, he **had not put on any clothing for a long time.** Shame has been associated with nakedness ever since the fall (Gen. 3:7; cf. Rev. 3:18; 16:15). Nakedness is also used in the Old Testament as a metaphor for sexual sin (Lev. 18:6–19; 20:11, 17–21). But not only was nakedness aberrant behavior, it was also physical torment for the man, who was exposed to all the extremes of weather and other dangers. Adding to the macabre nature of his existence, he **was not living in a house, but in the tombs.** He was so completely under the demons' dominion that he was more at home among the dead than the living. Furthermore he was a danger to himself. Mark 5:5 reveals that he was constantly gashing his body with sharp stones.

That violence was also directed toward others (Matt. 8:28) on an ongoing basis, as Luke's note that the demons **had seized him many times** indicates. He was such a threat that the people who lived nearby had done what they could to restrain him and his companion; **he was bound with chains and shackles and kept under guard.** And yet despite their best efforts, time and again his maniacal, demonic strength would cause him to **break his bonds and be driven by the demon into the desert.** The end result was that "no one was able to bind him anymore, even with a chain ... and no one was strong enough to subdue him" (Mark 5:3–4). The man and his partner remained a constant danger to that region.

On this particular morning, the two men spotted some potential victims coming ashore. In typical fashion, they raced down the hill toward them, shrieking and howling like banshees. But while the two men did not recognize the Lord, the demons indwelling them did. **Seeing Jesus,** the demon spokesman **cried out** using the man's voice in sheer panic and the man, expressing the demons' fear, abruptly **fell before Him** in a posture of submission. The last person the demons wanted to confront them was the Lord, who is sovereign over them and has already determined their eternal destiny.

Aware that he was in the presence of his divine judge, the demon **said in a loud voice, "What business do we have with each other, Jesus, Son of the Most High God?"** (cf. 4:34). It may seem strange for demons to give testimony affirming Jesus' true identity. But they, unlike their human victims, are all too aware of who He really is—God the Son, Lord of heaven and earth in human form. Even Satan, the leader of the demons, was forced to acknowledge that Jesus is the second person of the Trinity (Luke 4:3).

Specifically, this demon expressed his fear that Jesus was going to judge him before the appointed time (cf. Matt. 8:29). The demons understand biblical eschatology, and know that their final judgment does not take place at Christ's first coming. Therefore he pleaded with Him, **I beg You, do not torment me** before the designated time. The demons know their ultimate fate—eternal punishment in the lake of fire (Matt. 25:41; Rev. 20:10). They are aware that both their freedom and their power are restricted. In the presence of his executioner, the demon could only plead that the appointed time of his and his fellow demons' punishment had not yet arrived.

THE DELIVERING POWER OF JESUS

For He had commanded the unclean spirit to come out of the man. . . . And Jesus asked him, "What is your name?" And he said, "Legion"; for many demons had entered him. They were imploring Him not to command them to go away into the abyss. Now there was a herd of many swine feeding there on the mountain; and the demons implored Him to permit them to enter the swine. And He gave them permission. And the demons came out of the man and entered the swine; and the herd rushed down the steep bank into the lake and was drowned. When the herdsmen saw what had happened, they ran away and reported it in the

city and out in the country. The people went out to see what had happened; and they came to Jesus, and found the man from whom the demons had gone out, sitting down at the feet of Jesus, clothed and in his right mind; and they became frightened. (8:29a,30–35)

In a typically understated report of the astounding miracle of Jesus over the forces of hell, Luke reports that the Lord **commanded the unclean spirit to come out of the man.** Jesus addressed His command to **the unclean spirit** who was acting as the spokesman for all of the demons. That Jesus had the power to order the demons to leave this man is a mark of His deity, since only God is more powerful than angels. Angels are superior to humans in intelligence, power (2 Peter 2:11), influence (Dan. 10:13, 20), experience, since they are ageless and have lived throughout all of human history, and in nature, since they are spirits who live outside the realm of the physical.

Addressing the man, even though He knew the demon would answer, **Jesus asked him, "What is your name?"** No name for the man is given, and instead the spokesman for the demons, who had control over the man's voice, **said, "Legion."** That was an appropriate designation, **for many demons had entered him. Legion** is not a proper name, but a term referring to a unit of Roman soldiers, which could have as many as six thousand men. This poor, benighted, tormented soul was indwelt by literally thousands of demons; since there were two thousand pigs in the herd, there could have been that many demons indwelling the man and his companion.

The panicked demons **were imploring** Jesus **not to command them to go away into the abyss.** The *abussos* (**abyss**), or bottomless pit (Rev. 9:1–2) is a place where some demons are currently imprisoned. Some of these imprisoned spirits will be released for a brief time during the tribulation (Rev. 9:1–11); others, apparently those who indwelt men who then cohabited with women before the flood (Gen. 6:1–4; cf. Jude 6), are permanently bound (2 Peter 2:4). They will remain in the abyss until they are cast into the lake of fire. These demons were terrified, knowing that Jesus had the authority to imprison them in the **abyss** to await their final sentencing to eternal hell. In desperation, they proposed an alternative destination: **a herd of many swine that was feeding there on the mountain.** Their bizarre request reflects the demons' desire to continue to operate their corrupting plan in the physical world (cf. Matt. 12:43–45)—even, if need be, in animals.

After **the demons implored Him to permit them to enter the swine,** Jesus **gave them permission.** Here is further confirmation of Jesus' divine power over the demons; they could do nothing that He did not allow them to do. In an amazing scene **the demons came out of the man and entered the swine; and the herd,** acting with the same maniacal, self-destructive frenzy that had characterized the demon-possessed man, **rushed down the steep bank into the lake and was drowned.** This shocking development offered vivid, unmistakable proof that the demons had left the man. It also demonstrated Jesus' absolute authority over them, since they had no choice but to do so. Their destruction of the pigs also displayed the demons' evil propensity to kill and destroy.

After they recovered from their shock, **the herdsmen** who **saw what had happened ran away and reported it in the city and out in the country.** In response to their excited report, **the people went out to see what had happened.** Matthew notes that the entire city turned out (Matt. 8:34) to investigate. Having heard the eyewitness account of the herdsmen, **they came** looking for **Jesus.**

Some have argued that the people were upset at the loss of the pigs, and came to Jesus to hold Him accountable for their deaths and the economic loss. But the owners of the pigs are never mentioned in the gospel accounts, nor are the pigs the issue. The focus is on the sensational transformation of the formerly demon-possessed man and above all on Jesus, who transformed him. When the crowd arrived, they **found the man from whom the demons had gone out, sitting down at the feet of Jesus, clothed and in his right mind.** His radical change was complete, undeniable, and inexplicable from a human perspective. The man was clothed, not naked; seated at the feet of Jesus, not wandering aimlessly; away from the tombs, the realm of the dead, and in the presence of the Lord of life; quiet, not shrieking; calm and peaceful, not out of control and deadly; comforted, not tormented; in short, manifesting God-given sanity, not demon-inspired insanity. This is a magnificent picture of salvation transformation. No doubt Jesus had explained the gospel to him, telling him that He had come to save lost sinners (Luke 19:10), and the man had repented and been forgiven.

One would have expected the people to rejoice with the man over his deliverance, or at least to be relieved that he no longer posed any threat, but instead **they became frightened. Frightened** translates a form of the Greek word *phobeō,* which refers to extreme fear or terror (the related noun *phobos* is the root of the English word "phobia"). They realized that they were sinners in the presence of holy God (cf. Luke 8:25).

THE DAMNING POWER OF SIN

Those who had seen it reported to them how the man who was demon-possessed had been made well. And all the people of the

country of the Gerasenes and the surrounding district asked Him to leave them, for they were gripped with great fear; and He got into a boat and returned. But the man from whom the demons had gone out was begging Him that he might accompany Him; but He sent him away, saying, "Return to your house and describe what great things God has done for you." So he went away, proclaiming throughout the whole city what great things Jesus had done for him. (8:36–39)

In stark contrast to the delivered maniac, the response of the sane people tragically illustrates sin's power over the lost. It blinds them to the truth and causes them to hate it and reject all evidence of it. They obstinately cling to their false illusion of well-being because love of iniquity dominates them. Jesus had performed an undeniable miracle that clearly manifested His absolute power over the supernatural realm and to deliver people from the forces of hell.

The herdsmen, as noted above, **who had seen** Jesus cast the demons out of him and into the pigs, **reported to** the people **how the man who was demon-possessed had been made well** (or delivered). They heard the complete story in all its details. Some argue that sinners will be convinced if they see a powerful enough miracle, but here is proof that that is not necessarily the case. Before them was undeniable evidence of the saving power of the Lord Jesus Christ. It is hard to envision more dramatic, compelling proof than His casting thousands of demons out of the two maniacs. But so powerful was sin's hold on them that instead of believing in Jesus, all **the people of the country of the Gerasenes and the surrounding district asked Him to leave them.** Their hearts were like the hard-packed roadside soil in the parable of the sowers (cf. chap. 20 of this volume), which the seed of the gospel cannot penetrate.

Luke reiterates that the reason the people wanted Jesus to leave was that **they were gripped with great fear.** Knowing that they were in the presence of God, loving their sin (John 3:19) and blinded by Satan (2 Cor. 4:4), they wanted only to be rid of the one whose presence intimidated and terrified them. There was not a word of thanks for delivering them from the danger the man had posed; astonishingly, they saw Jesus as an even greater threat to their sinful lifestyle. Thus they preferred a maniac to the Son of God; to be terrified by Satan rather than offer reverence to God; to endure the presence of demonic danger rather than the presence of divine deliverance; the unholy to the holy; a tomb dweller to the Lord of life. David Gooding writes,

What a sad comment on man's fallen and unregenerate state it is, that man should feel more at home with demons, than with the Christ who has power to cast out demons.

Yet it is often so. Men who would try to help a criminal or a drunkard, or, if they should prove incorrigible, would want the one imprisoned and the other put into hospital, find it embarrassing and somewhat frightening if the criminal is saved by Christ and turned into a sane, wholesome, regenerate disciple. (*According to Luke* [Grand Rapids: Eerdmans, 1987], 146)

In a tragic reflection of their missed opportunity, Jesus **got into a boat and returned** to Capernaum. There is no record that He ever returned to their region.

But the story, mercifully, does not end there. **The man from whom the demons had gone out was begging** Jesus **that he might accompany Him.** His willingness to forsake all and follow Christ shows that he had been delivered from his sin as well as from the demons. Jesus was his Lord, Savior, and deliverer, and he naturally wanted to go with Him and learn from Him. But Jesus had a different plan and **sent him away, saying, "Return to your house and describe what great things God has done for you."** Since he knew enough to be saved, he knew enough to be a missionary. The priority for him was not further training, since he was the lone witness to the gospel in that region. Here is an example of God's grace in the face of man's rejection. Though they had rejected Him, Jesus had not totally rejected them. In obedience to the Lord's command, the man **went away, proclaiming throughout the whole city what great things Jesus had done for him.** Jesus had commanded him to tell others what God had done, and he told them what Jesus had done, since Jesus is God. As a result of his testimony to Jesus' power, everyone who heard him was amazed (Mark 5:20).

This remarkable story teaches several important truths. First and foremost, it reveals Christ's absolute authority over the demonic realm. It is also illustrates the truth that the good news of the gospel is for Gentiles, as well as Jews (cf. Matt. 12:18, 21). The passage also demonstrates that God graciously reaches out to those who reject Him. Finally, the story of the maniac who became a missionary illustrates that it is the responsibility of all Christians to tell others of how Jesus delivered them from the power of sin (Matt. 28:19–20).

Jesus' Compassionate Power (Luke 8:40–56)

24

And as Jesus returned, the people welcomed Him, for they had all been waiting for Him. And there came a man named Jairus, and he was an official of the synagogue; and he fell at Jesus' feet, and began to implore Him to come to his house; for he had an only daughter, about twelve years old, and she was dying. But as He went, the crowds were pressing against Him. And a woman who had a hemorrhage for twelve years, and could not be healed by anyone, came up behind Him and touched the fringe of His cloak, and immediately her hemorrhage stopped. And Jesus said, "Who is the one who touched Me?" And while they were all denying it, Peter said, "Master, the people are crowding and pressing in on You." But Jesus said, "Someone did touch Me, for I was aware that power had gone out of Me." When the woman saw that she had not escaped notice, she came trembling and fell down before Him, and declared in the presence of all the people the reason why she had touched Him, and how she had been immediately healed. And He said to her, "Daughter, your faith has made you well; go in peace." While He was still speaking, someone came from the house of the synagogue official, saying, "Your daughter has died; do not trouble the Teacher anymore." But

when Jesus heard this, He answered him, "Do not be afraid any longer; only believe, and she will be made well." When He came to the house, He did not allow anyone to enter with Him, except Peter and John and James, and the girl's father and mother. Now they were all weeping and lamenting for her; but He said, "Stop weeping, for she has not died, but is asleep." And they began laughing at Him, knowing that she had died. He, however, took her by the hand and called, saying, "Child, arise!" And her spirit returned, and she got up immediately; and He gave orders for something to be given her to eat. Her parents were amazed; but He instructed them to tell no one what had happened. (8:40–56)

Ever since the fall, life on the cursed earth has been subject to disease, disaster, and death. Tragedy, sorrow, misery, and suffering are woven into the fabric of human existence. Death is a universal experience, and all sophisticated modern medical technology can do is postpone the inevitable. Because of man's God-given capacity for love and relationships, sickness and death also produce intense grief and sadness.

Jesus understood the suffering associated with disease and death. He was, as Isaiah predicted, "A man of sorrows and acquainted with grief" (Isa. 53:3). As He observed the outpouring of sorrow and grief over the death of Lazarus, "He was deeply moved in spirit and was troubled" (John 11:33; cf. v. 38) and "wept" (v. 35). The Lord, of course, knew that He was about to raise Lazarus from the dead. But He grieved over the universally devastating impact of sin in a fallen world.

But despite the ruinous effects of sin, there is still hope. There is One coming who has the power to reverse the curse; to heal all diseases and restore paradise. He is the One promised by the Old Testament prophets; the Messiah, Savior, and King. He will set up the millennial kingdom, an Eden-like world where long life spans will be the norm (Isa. 65:20). After the millennial kingdom, the present earth and heaven will be destroyed (2 Peter 3:10), and the Lord will create a new heaven and a new earth from which disease, death, sorrow, and suffering will be forever banished (Rev. 21:1–5; cf. Isa. 65:17; 66:22).

The New Testament makes it unmistakably clear that only one person can accomplish those things—the Lord Jesus Christ. All other claimants are charlatans, fakes, and frauds (cf. John 10:7–8). The New Testament was written to establish that Jesus Christ is the Messiah, Lord, and Savior; the second person of the Trinity incarnate. He alone was born of a virgin, lived a sinless life, rose from the dead, and demonstrated absolute power over the natural realm and the spiritual realm.

This section of Luke's gospel presents two more illustrations of Jesus' supernatural power over disease and death. It is the story of one miracle, the raising of a synagogue ruler's daughter, sandwiched around another miracle, the healing of a woman with a hemorrhage. This account provides insight into the personal aspect of His ministry; what He was feeling. It takes us as far into the nature of the God-Man as the human mind can go, revealing that the Lord Jesus Christ not only had the power to heal, but also the compassionate desire to do so. As the story unfolds, eight aspects of Jesus' ministry to people become evident: His accessibility, availability, interruptibility, inexhaustibility, faithfulness, perspective, power, and priority.

HIS ACCESSIBILITY

And as Jesus returned, the people welcomed Him, for they had all been waiting for Him. And there came a man named Jairus, and he was an official of the synagogue; and he fell at Jesus' feet, and began to implore Him to come to his house; for he had an only daughter, about twelve years old, and she was dying. (8:40–42*a*)

As the story opens, Jesus had just **returned** from the region of Gadara, on the eastern shore of the Sea of Galilee. The Lord had gone there seeking relief from the ever-present throngs of people that followed Him wherever He went. On the voyage to Gadara, Jesus and the disciples had been caught in a powerful storm, which He miraculously calmed (see the exposition of 8:22–25 in chapter 22 of this volume). After they arrived, Jesus encountered two demon-possessed maniacs and cast the demons that infested them into a herd of swine (see the exposition of 8:26–39 in the previous chapter of this volume). The terrified inhabitants of the region then begged the Lord to leave, and He got into a boat and returned across the Sea of Galilee to the familiar town of Capernaum (8:37).

Upon His arrival, Jesus immediately was engulfed by a large crowd (Mark 5:21) who, in contrast to the people of Gadara, **welcomed Him, for they had all been waiting for Him.** Many in the crowd were crippled, blind, deaf, and plagued by various other diseases. They had been anxiously awaiting His return, hoping to be healed. Jesus was a hero for those already healed, and for some the ultimate celebrity. They were captivated by the miraculous signs He performed and further hoped that He would use His power to free them from the yoke of Roman occupation.

Unlike most religious leaders in Israel, who avoided the common people so as not to be defiled by them, Jesus secluded Himself only occasionally to rest, to give further insight and instruction to His disciples, or to spend time alone in communion with the Father. Apart from such occasions, His entire ministry was spent in public, mingling daily with the people in town and village streets, the fields, along the shore of the Sea of Galilee, and wherever else they gathered. Summarizing His ministry to Pilate, Jesus said, "I have spoken openly to the world; I always taught in synagogues [cf. Matt. 4:23; 9:35] and in the temple [cf. John 7:14, 28], where all the Jews come together; and I spoke nothing in secret" (John 18:20). That was consistent with His purpose in coming into the world—to proclaim the gospel message of repentance and forgiveness (cf. Mark 1:38).

Despite their eager welcome of Jesus, the crowd was fickle. Some, easily led by the hateful religious leaders, would eventually scream for His blood and cry out, "Crucify, crucify Him! ... His blood shall be on us and on our children!" (Luke 23:21; Matt. 27:25). Others were sign seekers (Luke 11:29) who would soon become disenchanted with Jesus and abandon Him (John 6:66). Only a few were enduring, true followers of Him (Matt. 7:14; 22:14; Luke 13:23–24).

Among those anxiously waiting for Jesus to return and resume His healing ministry were two very contrasting souls. One was a man, the other was a woman. One was rich, the other poor. One was a respected leader of society, the other a rejected outcast. But each had a desperate need that only Jesus could meet.

Luke introduced first **a man named Jairus, who was an official of the synagogue.** The Greek text includes the word *idou* ("see," "behold," "look"), which notes that his appearance was something unexpected or startling. As **an official of the synagogue** he was a respected leader, steeped in the Old Testament, and devoted to the religion of Judaism. He was one of those responsible for overseeing all activities in the synagogue, the focal point of Jewish religious life in his city. Jairus was a leading figure in Capernaum's religious establishment, which in turn was connected with national Judaism, which was mainly in the hands of Pharisees and scribes, who were hostile to Jesus and sought to destroy Him. For a local representative of the very leaders who hated Him to fall **at Jesus' feet, and . . . implore Him to come to his house** was a stunning development.

But Jairus did not come as a representative of the religious elite, but as a grief-stricken father whose **only** [cf. 7:12; 9:38] **daughter, about twelve years old, . . . was dying** (literally at the point of death [Mark 5:23]). He was no longer concerned about what his fellow leaders in the synagogue or the scribes and Pharisees might think of him. All that mattered to him was that he get to Jesus and bring Him to his daughter before it was too late.

Jesus had performed many miracles in Capernaum (cf. 4:38–40) one of which, His casting a demon out of a man in the synagogue

(4:33–35), Jairus, as a synagogue official, may have witnessed. Word of the Lord's raising a young man from the dead at Nain (7:11–15), only about twenty miles away, had certainly reached Capernaum, making Jairus aware of His power. Such information led him to believe that Jesus could heal his daughter. Perhaps, unlike the rich young ruler (18:18–23), he came to Jesus humbled by the reality of his own unworthiness, as he desperately sought help for his daughter. He must have been relieved and grateful to find Jesus, as always, accessible.

HIS AVAILABILITY

But as He went, (8:42*b*)

Jesus was not merely accessible in the crowd, but also was available to individuals. Having heard Jairus's desperate plea, **He went** with him. Despite the relentless demands of the crowds that constantly surrounded Him, the Lord spent time with individuals. The Gospels are filled with the stories of men, women, and even children (Matt. 19:13–14) to whom Jesus gave personal attention. As the Creator walked with people, He felt their pain and had compassion on them; He was a comforter and burden bearer. "Come to Me," He said, "all who are weary and heavy-laden, and I will give you rest. Take My yoke upon you and learn from Me, for I am gentle and humble in heart, and you will find rest for your souls. For My yoke is easy and My burden is light" (Matt. 11:28–30). Isaiah prophesied of Him, "Like a shepherd He will tend His flock, in His arm He will gather the lambs and carry them in His bosom; He will gently lead the nursing ewes. . . . A bruised reed He will not break and a dimly burning wick He will not extinguish" (Isa. 40:11; 42:3).

Of all the impressive miracles He could have done to prove that He was God, Jesus chose to do those that relieved people's suffering. Instead of flying off the pinnacle of the temple, He rescued His terrified disciples from a life-threatening storm. Instead of instantly creating a cow or a horse, He created food for thousands of hungry people. Instead of lifting up a mountain and casting it into the sea, He healed the sick and raised the dead. His choice of miracles revealed not only Jesus' deity, but also His divine compassion (Matt. 9:36; 14:14; Mark 1:41; 8:2; Luke 7:13).

Jairus's heart was breaking. Whatever he had thought about Jesus, or what the religious leaders might think of him for going to Him, was of no concern to him. His desperate need drove him to the compassionate, available Savior. Jesus responded to his weak faith and natural pain with a powerful demonstration both of His power and His compassion.

231

HIS INTERRUPTIBILITY

the crowds were pressing against Him. And a woman who had a hemorrhage for twelve years, and could not be healed by anyone, came up behind Him and touched the fringe of His cloak, and immediately her hemorrhage stopped. (8:42c–44)

As He endeavored to go with Jairus, the Lord found His way impeded by **the crowds** that **were pressing against Him.** The thick mass of bodies was immobile, all desperately wanting Jesus' attention. Jairus's anxiety and frustration at the delay in getting Jesus to his house must have been intense. Every passing moment brought his beloved daughter closer to death. Suddenly, to Jairus's dismay, the Lord's slow progress through the crowd was halted completely by an equally desperate person. **A woman who had a hemorrhage for twelve years, and could not be healed by anyone, came up behind Him and touched the fringe of His cloak.** The delay she caused could and would prove fatal to Jairus's daughter.

Jesus was used to being interrupted. Once while He was preaching a sermon, some men tore open the roof above Him and lowered a paralyzed man on a stretcher (Luke 5:17–19). On another occasion He was interrupted when "someone in the crowd said to Him, 'Teacher, tell my brother to divide the family inheritance with me'" (Luke 12:13). Despite the overwhelming demands, Jesus was never indifferent to individuals in need.

This woman had lived with a severe medical problem, a **hemorrhage, for twelve years**—as long as Jairus's daughter had been alive. While he and his family enjoyed watching their daughter grow up and looked forward to her future as a wife and mother, this woman had endured twelve years of misery and suffering. Her condition produced severe physical effects; continual bleeding, fatigue and lack of strength from the blood loss, fear that the condition might eventually prove fatal, and perhaps constant pain. But the social effects were even more severe. According to Leviticus 15:19–27, a woman with a bleeding problem like hers was ceremonially unclean for as long as the condition persisted. That meant that she could not go to the temple, or attend the synagogue. No one in her family could touch her or anything she touched or they too would become ceremonially unclean. She was an outcast, both in society and in her own family.

Her situation was hopeless, since like everyone else at that time she **could not be healed by anyone.** The woman's cure was beyond the limited medical knowledge of that day. All her desperate attempts to find relief had only increased her suffering; she had, as Mark records, "endured much at the hands of many physicians, and had spent all that she had and was not helped at all, but rather had grown worse" (Mark 5:26). Ancient, useless treatments prescribed for women with her condition were bizarre:

> One remedy consisted of drinking a goblet of wine containing a powder compounded from rubber, alum and garden crocuses. Another treatment consisted of a dose of Persian onions cooked in wine administered with the summons, "Arise out of your flow of blood!" Other physicians prescribed sudden shock, or the carrying of the ash of an ostrich's egg in a certain cloth. (William L. Lane, *Commentary on the Gospel of Mark*, The New International Commentary on the New Testament [Grand Rapids: Eerdmans, 1975], 192 n. 46)

Her money and hope gone, cut off from friends and family, she desperately and anxiously forced her way through the crowd to reach Jesus. Embarrassed and humiliated by her perpetually unclean condition and seeking to avoid disclosure, embarrassment, and resentment from the people, she **came up behind Him and touched the fringe of His cloak.** In the Old Testament law God had commanded the Jews, "You shall make yourself tassels on the four corners of your garment with which you cover yourself" (Deut. 22:12). Those tassels, on the **fringe** of their robes, served as a reminder of their obligation to obey God's commandments (Num. 15:37–41). The Greek verb translated **touched** suggests that the woman did not merely tap one of the Lord's tassels, but grabbed one and clutched it (the same verb is translated "clinging" in John 20:17). Matthew records that she kept "saying to herself, 'If I only touch His garment, I will get well'" (Matt. 9:21). After twelve years of suffering, Jesus was her only hope, so she literally and figuratively clung desperately to Him.

Jesus honored her faith, and as she grasped the tassel of His robe **immediately her hemorrhage stopped.** Jesus often healed those who had no faith, but never saved anyone who lacked it. This woman, her physical problem solved, was on the way to salvation.

His Inexhaustibility

And Jesus said, "Who is the one who touched Me?" And while they were all denying it, Peter said, "Master, the people are crowding and pressing in on You." But Jesus said, "Someone did touch Me, for I was aware that power had gone out of Me." When the woman saw that she had not escaped notice, she came trembling and fell down before Him, and declared in the presence of

all the people the reason why she had touched Him, and how she had been immediately healed. And He said to her, "Daughter, your faith has made you well; go in peace." (8:45–48)

There is an inexhaustible thoroughness in what Jesus did. Not content with restoring the woman physically, the Lord restored her socially by making her healing known publically. He also restored her spiritually to God.

After the woman grasped the tassel of His robe **Jesus said, "Who is the one who touched Me?"** Obviously, the omniscient Lord was not asking for information. He knew who had touched Him, and was calling for her to reveal herself. **And while they were all denying it, Peter said, "Master, the people are crowding and pressing in on You."** Following Peter's lead the rest of the disciples asked incredulously, "You see the crowd pressing in on You, and You say, 'Who touched Me?'" (Mark 5:31). The Lord's reply is one of the most profound things He ever said: **"Someone did touch Me, for I was aware that power had gone out of Me."** The power of God is not an impersonal force flowing from Him to people. He was fully aware of its action. No one ever receives the power of God into his or her life without acute awareness on His part.

Realizing that she could not hide, **when the woman saw that she had not escaped notice, she came trembling** in reverential fear **and fell down before Him** in homage and worship. She then **declared in the presence of all the people the reason why she had touched Him, and how she had been immediately healed.** Not content merely to restore her physically and socially, Jesus **said to her, "Daughter** (the only time in the Gospels that Jesus used that word to address a woman) **your faith has made you well; go in peace."** The phrase **made you well** translates a form of the verb *sōzō*, which is the common New Testament word for salvation. This same phrase in the Greek text appears in Luke 7:50, where it clearly refers to salvation from sin. It is also used in Luke 17:19 to describe one of the ten lepers who returned to worship Jesus. While all ten were healed, he alone was saved. Further, the Lord's calling her **daughter** indicates that He received her as a child of His kingdom (John 1:12). She was restored, physically, socially, and spiritually through the grace and personal power of the Lord Jesus Christ.

HIS FAITHFULNESS

While He was still speaking, someone came from the house of the synagogue official, saying, "Your daughter has died; do not trouble

the Teacher anymore." But when Jesus heard this, He answered him, "Do not be afraid any longer; only believe, and she will be made well." (8:49–50)

While Jesus **was still speaking** to the now-healed woman, Jairus received the news he had dreaded. **Someone came from** his **house** and told him, **"Your daughter has died; do not trouble the Teacher anymore."** The delay had proven deadly, and Jairus's worst fear was realized. While Jesus was ministering to a lowly outcast, the child of one of Capernaum's leading citizens had died. The unnamed messenger evidently did not believe Christ could raise the little girl from the dead. Therefore he saw no further need to keep Jesus from His ministry to others in the crowd. *Didaskalon* (**Teacher**) was a title of great respect. It was appropriate for Jesus since teaching, not performing miracles, was the primary focus of His ministry (cf. Mark 1:38).

Though Luke does not record it, at this point Jairus said to Jesus, "My daughter has just died; but come and lay Your hand on her, and she will live" (Matt. 9:18). Unlike the doubtful messenger, Jairus believed that Jesus had the power to raise his daughter from the dead as He had the young man at Nain.

When Jesus heard Jairus's report of his daughter's death **He answered him, "Do not be afraid any longer; only believe, and she will be made well."** Jesus was not making Jairus's faith a condition for resurrecting his daughter, but was encouraging and reassuring him. Although Jairus had faith that Jesus could resurrect her, his faith was mingled with fear (cf. Mark 9:24). The Lord exhorted him to stop being afraid and to keep believing in His promise that his daughter would **be made well** (cf. Matt. 17:19–20).

His Perspective

When He came to the house, He did not allow anyone to enter with Him, except Peter and John and James, and the girl's father and mother. Now they were all weeping and lamenting for her; but He said, "Stop weeping, for she has not died, but is asleep." And they began laughing at Him, knowing that she had died. (8:51–53)

After a significant delay in getting there (enough time had elapsed for the mourners to have gathered and the funeral to have started), Jesus finally **came to** Jairus's **house.** Since the Jews did not embalm, the mourners would have been put on notice that the girl was dying. By the time the Lord arrived, the funeral was in full swing. In contrast to modern funerals, which are usually quiet, somber, and sedate, a first-century Jewish funeral was a scene of barely-controlled chaos. The mourners, both the friends and family of the loved ones as well as the traditional hired female mourners, would be loudly screaming, wailing, and tearing their clothes. Others would be playing dissonant music on high-pitched flutes. The end result was a cacophony of confusion. Since Jairus was a well-respected leader in the community, the funeral for his daughter would have been even larger and louder than most.

Having arrived at the house, Jesus **did not allow anyone to enter with Him, except Peter and John and James** (here singled out from the rest of the disciples for the first time as they would often be in the future), **and the girl's father and mother.** The rest of the disciples and the crowd remained outside. Once inside the Lord witnessed "a commotion" (Mark 5:38), with "the flute-players and the crowd in noisy disorder" (Matt. 9:23) **all weeping and lamenting for** the dead girl. He abruptly ended the funeral by commanding the hired mourners to **"stop weeping, for she has not died, but is asleep."** Astonished, they **began laughing at Him, knowing that she had died.** But the Lord put the mocking mourners out (Mark 5:40).

Jesus' declaration that the girl had **not died, but** was **asleep** brought a revolutionary new perspective to death. By likening it to sleep, He redefined death as temporary; thus sleep is used in Scripture as a metaphor for the body in death (John 11:11–14; Acts 13:36; 1 Cor. 11:30; 15:6, 18, 20, 51; 1 Thess. 4:14–15; 5:10; 2 Peter 3:4). But while the body sleeps temporarily in death, the soul does not (cf. 16:19–31; 23:43; 2 Cor. 5:8; Phil. 1:23; Rev. 6:9–11).

HIS POWER

He, however, took her by the hand and called, saying, "Child, arise!" And her spirit returned, and she got up immediately; and He gave orders for something to be given her to eat. (8:54–55)

Having entered the room where the child's body lay (Mark 5:40), Jesus **took her by the hand and called** loudly **saying, "Child, arise!"** Jairus had asked Him to lay His hand on her and restore her to life (Matt. 9:18), and the Lord willingly did so. The Gospels were written in Greek, but Mark records the actual Aramaic words Christ spoke, "talitha kum" (5:41), which means, "Little girl, arise." Using the power by which He had created everything (John 1:1–3; Col. 1:15–16), Jesus commanded life into her.

Death's hold on the girl was shattered, **and her spirit returned.**

Life came back into her body—not just any life but her life, just as was the case with the widow's son (7:11–15), and would later be true of Lazarus (John 11:43–44). When her life was restored, **she got up immediately.** Like all of Jesus' healings, this was not a progressive healing; there was no rehabilitation and no recovery period. The Lord spoke and she was instantly and fully restored to life.

After the child got up, Jesus **gave orders for something to be given her to eat.** This again reveals His tender, compassionate care. It also shows that this was not an illusion but a real resurrection (cf. Luke 24:42–43). Her spirit had returned to her body and she had resumed living a normal life, sustained by food.

The resurrections the Lord performed during His earthly ministry demonstrated the power He will one day use to resurrect all people. In John 5:28–29 Jesus said, "An hour is coming, in which all who are in the tombs will hear His [Christ's] voice, and will come forth; those who did the good deeds to a resurrection of life, those who committed the evil deeds to a resurrection of judgment." The bodies of believers will be raised and reunited with their spirits to live forever in heaven; the bodies of unbelievers will be reunited with their spirits to experience everlasting punishment in hell. Believers need not fear death because they have put their faith in the One who conquered it.

HIS PRIORITY

Her parents were amazed; but He instructed them to tell no one what had happened. (8:56)

In addition to being overjoyed that their daughter was restored to life, **her parents were amazed. Amazed** translates a form of the verb *existēmi,* which literally means "to stand outside oneself," and is translated "He has lost His senses" in Mark 3:21. It signifies that the girl's parents were extremely astonished to the point of being terrified, as were the disciples (v. 25), the people of Gadara (v. 37), and the woman healed of a hemorrhage (v. 47) earlier in this chapter.

That the Lord **instructed them to tell no one what had happened** does not mean that He did not want people to know about the miracle. The news was impossible to keep secret (cf. Matt. 9:26), since everyone would see the resurrected girl. There were times when Jesus did not want the news of a miracle to be spread, because the resulting crowds of curiosity seekers would hinder His ministry (cf. Mark 1:40–45) or seek to make Him king by force (John 6:14–15), or as an act of judgment, hiding the truth from those confirmed in their rejection of Him

(Luke 9:21). As noted above, the news would spread on its own. The parents could enjoy being reunited with their daughter, and rejoice in Christ's goodness, grace, and mercy to them.

All of those matters could play a part in the restriction of silence Jesus put on them—but they are not the main reason. Our Lord frequently called for this kind of silence (Matt. 8:4; 9:30; 12:16; 17:9; Mark 1:25, 34, 44; 3:12; 5:43; 7:36; 8:26, 30; 9:9; Luke 4:41; 9:21). The real reason is given in Mark 8:30–31: "And He warned them to tell no one about Him. And He began to teach them that the Son of Man must suffer many things and be rejected by the elders and the chief priests and the scribes, and be killed, and after three days rise again." He did not want to be known as a healer or miracle worker—or even only as the Christ—those were true but incomplete. When He is proclaimed, it must be as the crucified and risen Savior. There is no gospel of Jesus Christ without the cross in all its meaning and the resurrection with all that it accomplished. Paul summed it up when he said he would only preach "Christ, and Him crucified" (1 Cor. 2:2) and proclaimed that salvation is for those who believe that God raised Him from the dead (Rom. 10:9–10).

This account of two of the countless miracles the Lord Jesus Christ performed reveals His personal, compassionate concern for hurting people. To the oppressed and burdened He offers rest (Matt. 11:28–30; for the troubled He provides peace (John 14:27; 16:33); and most important of all, to those enslaved by sin He offers salvation (Luke 4:16–21; 19:10) through the cross and resurrection to come.

A Profile of a Christian Messenger (Luke 9:1–9)

25

And He called the twelve together, and gave them power and authority over all the demons and to heal diseases. And He sent them out to proclaim the kingdom of God and to perform healing. And He said to them, "Take nothing for your journey, neither a staff, nor a bag, nor bread, nor money; and do not even have two tunics apiece. Whatever house you enter, stay there until you leave that city. And as for those who do not receive you, as you go out from that city, shake the dust off your feet as a testimony against them." Departing, they began going throughout the villages, preaching the gospel and healing everywhere. Now Herod the tetrarch heard of all that was happening; and he was greatly perplexed, because it was said by some that John had risen from the dead, and by some that Elijah had appeared, and by others that one of the prophets of old had risen again. Herod said, "I myself had John beheaded; but who is this man about whom I hear such things?" And he kept trying to see Him. (9:1–9)

This passage marks a significant transition for the Lord Jesus Christ. Approximately half of His three-year ministry is over, and His death on the cross is about eighteen months away. Up to this point, Jesus had ministered by Himself. He alone performed miracles, preached the gospel, answered questions, and handled conflicts with those who opposed Him. His ministry was isolated to wherever He was, since He was the only preacher, teacher, and healer. As a result, the crowds that followed Him all over Galilee grew larger and larger. In addition, the Lord's Galilean ministry was rapidly drawing to a close. As Luke 9:51 indicates, He was about to leave Galilee for Judea, adding time pressure to that from the increasing crowds.

Obviously, the one who created the universe in six days could have continued to minister effectively on His own. Instead, Jesus chose to multiply His ministry by using the twelve men whom He had called to be apostles (6:12–16). In an internship that would prepare them to minister later on their own without Him, the Lord sent the Twelve throughout Galilee to preach His kingdom. Up to this point they had been hearers and learners; now they needed to begin the transition to becoming preachers and messengers. The apostles needed to be trained to carry on Jesus' ministry after His death. They were ordinary, common men (cf. 1 Cor. 1:26), with no human credentials to qualify them for the most monumental task in human history. Even after three years of following Jesus and eighteen months of intensive training by Him, they all abandoned Him in His hour of need (Matt. 26:56) and cowered in hiding from the Jewish authorities after His death (John 20:19). It was not until the Holy Spirit filled them on the Day of Pentecost, empowering them for service (Acts 1:8) and bringing to mind all they had learned from Jesus (John 14:26), that they became the men who turned the world upside down (Acts 17:6).

Here as he occasionally did, Luke omitted events recorded elsewhere in the Gospels. He ended chapter 8 with the account of two miracles: the healing of a woman with an issue of blood, and the raising of Jairus's daughter. But in between those healings and the sending of the Twelve, Jesus made the second and final recorded trip to His hometown of Nazareth (Mark 6:1–6). Sadly, the people there rejected Him again, as they had the first time He ministered there (Luke 4:16–30). Though they could not deny His miraculous power over demons, disease, death, and the natural world, being consumed with self-righteous pride, they indignantly rejected His diagnosis of them as spiritually poor, prisoners, blind, and oppressed (4:18).

After leaving Nazareth, Jesus continued to travel around Galilee teaching in the villages (Mark 6:6) until He commissioned the Twelve. It is at that point that Luke picks up the narrative. Although they had already been named apostles, the Twelve had not yet been set apart from the larger group of Christ's followers and disciples. The Lord now **called the twelve together** to send them out, in keeping with His pledge to make them fishers of men (Matt. 4:19).

This was the penultimate stage in the Lord's calling of the apostles. The first phase was when He called them to saving faith (cf. 5:27–28; John 1:35–51). The second phase was their call to permanent, full-time discipleship (5:1–11). The third phase was their call to apostleship, as noted above. The short-term mission assignment described in this passage was the fourth phase. The final phase was the Great Commission when Jesus, just before His ascension, commanded them to "Go therefore and make disciples of all the nations, baptizing them in the name of the Father and the Son and the Holy Spirit, teaching them to observe all that I commanded you; and lo, I am with you always, even to the end of the age" (Matt. 28:19–20).

In a further act of grace and mercy, Jesus later sent seventy of His other disciples throughout Galilee on another preaching tour (10:1–20). They, however, were not apostles. Their ministry, though powerful (cf. vv. 9, 17), was temporary, a special one-time expansive mission to preach the gospel yet again to the hard-hearted Galileans. The apostles' ministry, on the other hand, was permanent. They were the foundation of the church (Eph. 2:20). Their teaching was authoritative (Acts 2:42) and they and their close associates were the human authors of the New Testament.

The reason the Lord chose twelve men to be His apostles instead of some other number was that twelve was symbolic of the twelve tribes of Israel. The number twelve's importance was reinforced by the addition of Matthias to take Judas's place (Acts 1:23–26), thus ensuring that the apostles would continue to be a twelve-man unit. Jesus' choice of these twelve men, none of them members of any part of the religious establishment, was an act of judgment, emphasizing the reality that Israel and its spiritual leadership were apostate.

One of the earliest official acts of Christ's ministry was His first cleansing of the temple (John 2:13–22), which highlighted the corruption, apostasy, and spiritual bankruptcy of the Jewish religious leaders and all who followed them. Their hostility toward Him had intensified over the intervening eighteen months. When the time came to choose His apostles, the Lord ignored the religious establishment. Instead, He chose twelve common, ordinary men to be the leaders of the new, true Israel of God—the redeemed, believing remnant. Jesus made that connection clear in Luke 22:29–30 when He told the Twelve that they would reign over Israel in the millennial kingdom: "Just as My Father has granted Me a kingdom, I grant you that you may eat and drink at My table in My kingdom, and you will sit on thrones judging the twelve tribes of Israel." Their names will also be emblazoned on the foundation stones of the New Jerusalem for all eternity (Rev. 21:14).

From Luke's inspired account of our Lord's commissioning of the Twelve, a profile of a messenger of Jesus Christ emerges. A Christian messenger proclaims salvation, manifests compassion, maintains trust, demonstrates contentment, and exercises discernment.

A CHRISTIAN MESSENGER PROCLAIMS SALVATION

And He sent them out to proclaim the kingdom of God (9:2*b*)

The Twelve's mission had a single purpose: they were **to proclaim the kingdom of God.** *Kērussō* (**proclaim**) refers to a herald's formal, authoritative, public announcement of important truth. In an era before mass media, that was how important messages were communicated to the public, just as town criers would do in later times. In town after town, the apostles publicly proclaimed that the kingdom of God was at hand because the Lord, Savior, and King had arrived. They also announced that entrance to the kingdom was through repentance (Mark 6:12), with confession of sin, and faith in the Messiah (John 1:12–13).

The preaching of the Twelve followed the pattern set by Jesus. In Luke 4:43 He announced, "I must preach the kingdom of God to the other cities also, for I was sent for this purpose." One of the proofs of His messiahship that He offered to the messengers from John the Baptist was that the "poor have the gospel preached to them" (7:22). At the beginning of chapter 8, Luke recorded that "He began going around from one city and village to another, proclaiming and preaching the kingdom of God" (8:1). As Luke noted in that same verse, "the twelve were with Him," learning from His example. When He sent them out, the Twelve preached the same message that Jesus did. The church today has that same responsibility to preach exactly what Jesus did without altering it. The church's message is not a social, political, philanthropic, or moral one. It is a message of sin, salvation, and forgiveness, which without being changed has been explained and enriched in the New Testament epistles.

The Lord narrowed the scope of the apostles' first preaching assignment by commanding them, "Do not go in the way of the Gentiles, and do not enter any city of the Samaritans; but rather go to the lost sheep of the house of Israel" (Matt. 10:5–6; cf. Rom. 1:16). The Jewish people, heirs of God's covenants, law, and promises (Rom. 9:4), were to have the gospel preached to them before it was widely proclaimed to the Gentiles and Samaritans. It would also be helpful for the Twelve if their first preaching assignment was to people of their own culture and not to the pagan Gentiles and half-breed Samaritans. But eventually, the gospel would be preached to the entire world (Matt. 28:19–20). Israel was never intended to be a cul-de-sac for the message of salvation, but rather a conduit through which it would flow to the world. Chosen to be God's witness nation, Israel's stubborn unbelief caused it to be temporarily set aside. The Lord chose a new people, the church, composed of believers from every people and nation. God has not permanently rejected Israel (Rom. 11:1–2, 25–26), and in the future the believing remnant will once again be His witnesses (Rev. 7:1–8).

A CHRISTIAN MESSENGER MANIFESTS COMPASSION

and gave them power and authority over all the demons and to heal diseases . . . and to perform healing. (9:1b, 2b)

The Twelve were granted **power and authority** the likes of which only Jesus (and briefly the seventy) ever possessed. If their message was to be validated and believed, there needed to be a way to attest its divine origin. Since the completion of the New Testament, a preacher's message can be measured against its inspired, infallible, inerrant standard. The Twelve's authenticity was verified by their God-granted ability to perform the same kind of miraculous signs that Jesus performed (cf. 4:36, 40–41; 6:17–18; 8:1–2).

Specifically, the Lord delegated to the apostles His **power and authority over all the demons,** giving them complete dominance over the supernatural realm of evil, fallen angels. They also received power **to perform healing,** and even to raise the dead (Matt. 10:8). The divine power they manifested proved that the apostles were preaching divine truth (cf. Rom. 15:18–19; 2 Cor. 12:12; Heb. 2:3–4). Such miraculous confirmation was no longer needed after the completion of the New Testament. Even by the end of the book of Acts, miracles were fading from the scene as the apostles disappeared. Paul healed people early in his ministry (cf. Acts 14:9–10; 19:11–12; 28:8), but toward the end of his life, he did not heal Trophimus (2 Tim. 4:20) and advised Timothy not to find a healer, but to treat his recurring stomach ailment with wine (1 Tim. 5:23).

But of the many ways the Lord could have shown His power through His messengers, He chose to have them, as He Himself did (cf. the discussion of 8:42 in the previous chapter of this volume), perform healing miracles that relieved human suffering. Those miracles reflect God's compassionate care for the needy and afflicted (Job 36:5–6; Pss. 9:18; 12:5; 35:10; 69:33; 140:12; Isa. 41:17), demonstrating that He is by nature a savior and deliverer, even on a temporal, physical level (cf. 1 Tim. 4:10).

In contrast to the compassionate, true servants of God, false teachers are portrayed in Scripture as merciless, abusive, and quick to take advantage of people (Isa. 56:10–12; Jer. 23:1–2; 50:6; Lam. 4:13; Ezek. 22:25; Mic. 3:5, 11; Matt. 7:15; 23:2–4; Mark 12:38–40; John 10:8, 10; Acts 20:29; 2 Cor. 2:17; Rev. 2:20). They lack the mercy, compassion, and kindness that marks a true messenger of Jesus Christ. They know nothing of Paul's passionate concern for the lost, which he expressed so eloquently in Romans 9:1–5:

> I am telling the truth in Christ, I am not lying, my conscience testifies with me in the Holy Spirit, that I have great sorrow and unceasing grief in my heart. For I could wish that I myself were accursed, separated from Christ for the sake of my brethren, my kinsmen according to the flesh, who are Israelites, to whom belongs the adoption as sons, and the glory and the covenants and the giving of the Law and the temple service and the promises, whose are the fathers, and from whom is the Christ according to the flesh, who is over all, God blessed forever. Amen.

That compelling concern drove Paul to literally beg sinners to be reconciled to Jesus Christ (2 Cor. 5:20).

A CHRISTIAN MESSENGER MAINTAINS TRUST

And He said to them, "Take nothing for your journey, neither a staff, nor a bag, nor bread, nor money; and do not even have two tunics apiece. (9:3)

Since the Twelve had been granted power to alleviate virtually all suffering, there was the potential to abuse that power for personal gain. Desperate people would have paid anything to have them heal diseases, cast out demons, and raise the dead—just as they do today to unscrupulous, fake healers, who cannot heal anyone.

The apostles, however, were not to enrich themselves at the expense of suffering people. Matthew records that Jesus commanded them, "Freely you received, freely give" (Matt. 10:8). Instead, they were to operate on faith and trust God to meet their needs. They were to **take nothing for** their **journey** other than the clothes on their backs; they were not to encumber themselves with extra baggage.

Specifically, the apostles were not to take a **staff** or a walking stick. Such staffs were helpful in negotiating the dirt roads of Israel, and could also be used in self-defense against robbers. Mark 6:8 records that the Lord "instructed them that they should take nothing for their journey, except a mere staff." Taken together, the two passages indicate that the Lord was forbidding them to take an extra staff. Nor were they to take a **bag** (perhaps a reference to a bag carried by beggars and itinerant teachers to hold the money they collected),since they were not to accumulate material things.There was no need for them to take **bread** or **money,** and they were not to"acquire gold,or silver,or copper for [their] money belts" (Matt. 10:9).Just as they were not to take an extra walking stick,they were **not even** to **have two tunics apiece** or an extra pair of sandals (Matt. 10:10).They were to trust dependently on the Lord's provision for their needs (cf.Matt.6:25–32;Phil.4:19).

That this austerity was temporary,for the purpose of the Twelve's training and not the norm,is clear from the Lord's reference to this event in the upper room.Reminding the apostles of His charge to them in this passage Jesus"said to them,'When I sent you out without money belt and bag and sandals,you did not lack anything,did you?'They said,'No,nothing'" (Luke 22:35).Then,establishing the pattern for their future ministry, the Lord "said to them, 'But now,whoever has a money belt is to take it along,likewise also a bag,and whoever has no sword is to sell his coat and buy one'" (v.36).The stringent rules the Lord enforced during this first training mission taught the apostles to trust and see the Lord provide.

A CHRISTIAN MESSENGER DEMONSTRATES CONTENTMENT

Whatever house you enter, stay there until you leave that city. (9:4)

In that day travelers stayed in people's homes. Hotels did not exist,and inns were dangerous and often little more than brothels.Wherever they traveled,**whatever house** they happened to be invited to stay in,the apostles were to **stay there until** they left **that city.** That would distinguish them from traveling false teachers,who moved from house to house collecting money from everyone they could.The apostles,and by extension all Christians, are to be content with their circumstances (cf.1 Tim.6:6–10).As the apostle Paul wrote to the Philippians,

> Not that I speak from want,for I have learned to be content in whatever circumstances I am.I know how to get along with humble means,and I also know how to live in prosperity; in any and every circumstance I have learned the secret of being filled and going hungry,both of having abundance and suffering need. (Phil.4:11–12)

A CHRISTIAN MESSENGER EXERCISES DISCERNMENT

And as for those who do not receive you, as you go out from that city, shake the dust off your feet as a testimony against them."

Departing, they began going throughout the villages, preaching the gospel and healing everywhere. Now Herod the tetrarch heard of all that was happening; and he was greatly perplexed, because it was said by some that John had risen from the dead, and by some that Elijah had appeared, and by others that one of the prophets of old had risen again. Herod said, "I myself had John beheaded; but who is this man about whom I hear such things?" And he kept trying to see Him. (9:5–9)

The Lord's last word of instruction covered the very important issue of how the Twelve should deal with **those who** would **not receive** them. In keeping with Jewish custom, Jesus told them that as they went **out from** the rejecting **city,** they were to **shake the dust off** their **feet as a testimony against them.** Underscoring the apostles' importance as His messengers, Jesus solemnly warned that "it will be more tolerable for the land of Sodom and Gomorrah in the day of judgment" than for those who rejected them and their message (Matt. 10:15). The Lord's command reflects the serious consequences of rejecting the gospel (cf. 1 Cor. 16:22; 2 Thess. 1:6–9).

To **shake the dust off** one's feet was a traditional Jewish gesture. When a Jew returned from traveling in a Gentile country, he would shake the dirt from that land off his clothes and sandals as a symbolic gesture of shaking off the pagan influences that could contaminate the Jewish people's lives and land. That act became an expression of disdain and rejection (cf. Acts 13:50–51; 18:6). The apostles were to treat the Jews who rejected their message as if they were no better than pagan, unclean Gentiles.

Turning away from hard-hearted rejecters was not only an issue of judgment, but also a question of priority. There is only so much time and opportunity available to evangelize, and that time is too precious to waste on those who have hardened themselves against the truth.

Jesus affirmed that principle in a shocking statement to His followers: "Do not give what is holy to dogs, and do not throw your pearls before swine, or they will trample them under their feet, and turn and tear you to pieces" (Matt. 7:6). "Dogs" in first-century Palestine were usually not domesticated pets but wild, dirty, and potentially dangerous scavengers. The thought of giving "what is holy," that is, a sacrifice offered to God, to a dog was shocking and unimaginable to the Jewish people. Throwing meat offered on the altar at the temple to dogs would have been an unspeakably blasphemous act of desecration. Throwing valuable pearls to pigs—the epitome of unclean animals—was equally unthinkable. Both would also be acts of supreme folly, since dogs have no appreciation of what is holy and pigs have no appreciation for what is precious.

In Christ's analogy, the dogs and swine represent those who permanently reject the gospel and treat it with utter disdain.What must have been even more surprising to the Twelve was the identity of the dogs and swine of whom the Lord warned them. Since, as noted above, the apostles were sent on this mission to the Jewish people, the dogs and swine were not unclean pagan Gentiles, but ultra-religious Jews.When faced with hard-hearted rejection of the truth, the apostles were to give them a warning of the judgment they faced and move on.

In obedience to all those instructions, the Twelve **began going throughout the villages, preaching the gospel and healing everywhere.** The details of their mission are not recorded, but the response they received highlighted their need for discernment. Galilee's response to their mission was symbolized by the reaction of its ruler, **Herod the tetrarch.** The **Herod** referred to here is Herod Antipas, a son of the notorious Herod the Great. Antipas ruled Galilee from 4 B.C. to A.D. 39, so his rule encompassed Jesus' entire ministry. **Tetrarch** refers to a ruler of a fourth of a region. After Herod's death in 4 B.C., his domain was divided among three of his sons, Archelaus, Antipas, and Philip, and a man named Lysanias (Luke 3:1), of whom little is known. Antipas was made ruler over the region of Galilee and nearby Perea and is the Herod referred to in the Gospels' accounts of Jesus' ministry. It was Antipas who imprisoned (Luke 3:20) and executed (9:9) John the Baptist.

When Herod **heard of all that was happening** in connection with the preaching ministry of the Twelve, **he was greatly perplexed.** The Twelve were giving all glory and credit for their powerful preaching and miracles to Jesus (cf. Acts 3:11–12). But who was Jesus? That **it was said by some that** He was **John** the Baptist **risen from the dead** was particularly troubling to Herod (see the discussion of v. 9 below). Adding to the confusion, it was being said by **some that Elijah had appeared, and by others that one of the prophets of old had risen again** (cf. v. 19; Matt. 16:14; 17:10).Yet Herod, haunted by his wrongful execution of John, whom even he acknowledged to have been "a righteous and holy man" (Mark 6:20), **said, "I myself had John beheaded."** According to Mark's account, Herod, plagued by his guilty conscience, "kept saying, 'John, whom I beheaded, has risen!'" (Mark 6:16). (For an account of Herod's execution of John, see the exposition of 7:18–23 in chapter 15 of this volume and the exposition of 3:19 in *Luke 1–5,* The MacArthur New Testament Commentary [Chicago: Moody, 2009], 231–32). Uneasily, Herod wondered, **"Who is this man about whom I hear such things?"**

That question of the identity of Jesus is the most important one ever asked and answered.The response each person gives to it will determine his or her eternal destiny, in hell or heaven. Because of its significance, Luke repeatedly recorded instances of people asking that question (cf. v. 18; 5:21; 7:20, 49; 8:25; 22:67, 70; 23:3). Tragically, most people then as now gave the wrong answer. But Peter, speaking for the disciples (Matt. 16:16), a Roman centurion at the cross (Mark 15:39), and doubting Thomas (John 20:28), among others, gave the correct answer: Jesus is God the Son, the Messiah, Savior, and Lord.

Driven by curiosity and fear, Herod **kept trying to see** Jesus. He was not an honest seeker, however. In Luke 13:31 some Pharisees warned Jesus, "Go away, leave here, for Herod wants to kill You." If Jesus was indeed John the Baptist risen from the dead as Herod feared, he intended to kill Him again. But Herod would not see Jesus until the Lord was sent to Him from Pilate as a prisoner (Luke 23:7). Even then Herod would not get the satisfaction of an answer from Jesus; "he questioned Him at some length; but He answered him nothing" (v. 9). The aftermath, which saw Herod and his soldiers mocking Jesus (v. 11), offered further evidence of Herod's insincerity.

The principles contained in Lord's charge to the Twelve are applicable to all believers in the Lord Jesus Christ. All Christ-honoring ministry consists of teaching the truth, demonstrating compassion, maintaining trust, being content with one's circumstances, and exercising discernment.

The
Compassionate
Lord
(Luke 9:10–17)

26

When the apostles returned, they gave an account to Him of all that they had done. Taking them with Him, He withdrew by Himself to a city called Bethsaida. But the crowds were aware of this and followed Him; and welcoming them, He began speaking to them about the kingdom of God and curing those who had need of healing. Now the day was ending, and the twelve came and said to Him, "Send the crowd away, that they may go into the surrounding villages and countryside and find lodging and get something to eat; for here we are in a desolate place." But He said to them, "You give them something to eat!" And they said, "We have no more than five loaves and two fish, unless perhaps we go and buy food for all these people." (For there were about five thousand men.) And He said to His disciples, "Have them sit down to eat in groups of about fifty each." They did so, and had them all sit down. Then He took the five loaves and the two fish, and looking up to heaven, He blessed them, and broke them, and kept giving them to the disciples to set before the people. And they all ate and were satisfied; and the broken pieces which they had left over were picked up, twelve baskets full. (9:10–17)

The Lord Jesus Christ performed countless miracles throughout His earthly ministry. In addition to the three dozen recorded in the Gospels, Jesus performed many other miracles on an almost daily basis (cf. Mark 6:2; Luke 19:37; John 2:23; 3:2; 6:2; 7:31; 11:47; 12:37; 20:30; 21:25; Acts 2:22). Throughout His ministry, Jesus constantly demonstrated His divine power over demons, disease, death, and nature.

The news of the Lord's miracles had spread all throughout Galilee. Galilee was a relatively small region, measuring about fifty miles from north to south and twenty-five miles from east to west. Its villages were mostly clustered around the Sea of Galilee, including Jesus' adopted hometown of Capernaum (Matt. 4:13). Jesus had grown up in that region, in the nondescript village of Nazareth, and He even returned there to preach the gospel but was viciously rejected (Luke 4:16–30). By ministering extensively in Galilee, the Lord was demonstrating His rejection of Israel's religious leadership, headquartered in the south in Jerusalem and Judea. Galilee was a region scorned by the religious leaders and other Judeans as an uncouth, backwater region, from which nothing good could come (John 1:46; 7:41, 52). Jesus' choice of it affirmed the apostasy of Israel's leadership.

As He neared the end of His Galilean ministry in the spring of A.D. 29, the Lord performed what was on a visible scale His most extensive miracle. Underscoring the significance of this incident, it is one of only two miraculous events recorded in all four Gospels, the other being Christ's resurrection. The feeding of five thousand men, along with surely an equal number of women and children, was the largest work of divine creative power since creation week and the restructuring of the earth after the flood (Gen. 6–8). It was also the highpoint and culmination of Christ's ministry in Galilee—and the last great opportunity for its people. The Lord would shortly depart Galilee to minister in the largely Gentile regions of Tyre and Sidon, and the Decapolis (where another such feeding miracle occurred; cf. Mark 8:1–8), then head south to Judea and Jerusalem. But after this undeniable demonstration of His divine power, only willful, stubborn, hard-hearted unbelief could explain why anyone in Galilee would continue to reject Him as Lord and Messiah—as they came to do in spite of momentary exuberance.

The miracle was so monumental in its impact and potential that the people wanted to make Jesus king by force (John 6:15). Their plan was for Him to topple Herod Antipas, install Himself as ruler in his place, and then oust the hated Roman occupiers. The result would be a welfare state with no sickness and all the free food they could eat. In fact, the day after the miracle, the crowd showed up in Capernaum, where Jesus had gone after the miraculous feeding (John 6:16–21), looking for breakfast (vv. 22–27).

But while our Lord's miraculous feeding of the multitude is an astounding display of His divine power, it is far more than that. As with all the miracles Jesus performed, this one is also a demonstration of God's tender, compassionate care, showing that His power cannot be divorced from His compassion. This miraculous provision of food on a massive scale is a striking exhibition of God's concern for even the most mundane issues of life. That Jesus fed people who would ultimately reject Him illustrates God's common grace, because of which "He causes His sun to rise on the evil and the good, and sends rain on the righteous and the unrighteous" (Matt. 5:45). It also previews Christ's power to usher in the blessings of the earthly millennial kingdom (cf. Isa. 25:6–9).

Luke's account of this miracle reveals Christ' sensitivity to five needs: the need for rest, the need for divine truth, the need for healing, the need for daily food, and the need for provision for His servants.

THE NEED FOR REST

When the apostles returned, they gave an account to Him of all that they had done. Taking them with Him, He withdrew by Himself to a city called Bethsaida. (9:10)

As noted in the previous chapter of this volume, Jesus had sent the Twelve on a preaching tour of Galilee. After **the apostles returned, they** met with Him, probably in Capernaum, and **gave an account to Him of all that they had done.** Recognizing that they were exhausted after their time of travel and ministry, Jesus took **them with Him** and **withdrew by Himself to a city called Bethsaida.** There they could rest and recover away from the crowds that kept them so busy that they did not even have time to eat (Mark 6:31). Jesus, the great high priest of His people, is aware of their weaknesses (Heb. 4:15) and sensitive to their every need. Having Himself experienced the fatigue that comes from extensive ministry (cf. Mark 4:38), Jesus understood the apostles' need for rest.

The exact location of **Bethsaida** is not precisely known, but its name means "house of fish," indicating it was one of many lakeside fishing villages. Bethsaida was perhaps located along the northeastern shore of the Sea of Galilee. (Some have suggested there may have been another village by the same name on the shore west of Capernaum [Mark 6:45].) This small village was important for a couple of reasons. First, it was the hometown of as many as four of the apostles: Peter and his brother Andrew (John 1:44; although they later moved to Capernaum [Luke 4:31,38]), Philip (John 12:21), and possibly Nathanael (John 1:45).

But on a more somber note, Bethsaida was singled out by the Lord, along with Chorazin, as being more deserving of judgment than Tyre and Sidon (Luke 10:13). Those two Gentile cities were symbols of paganism, idolatry, and evil to the Galilean Jews. The Old Testament records God's past devastating judgment on Tyre and Sidon for their unspeakable wickedness (Isa. 23:1–18; Ezek. 26–28; Amos 1:9–10; Zech. 9:3–4). They were headed for another destruction because they had rejected the Lord Jesus, who performed many miracles there (Luke 10:13). Undoubtedly some of the apostles (most likely the three or four who were from that village) also worked miracles in Bethsaida during their preaching tour. The massive miracle that occurred nearby only added more guilt to their rejection. Divinely granted privilege, when refused, leads to greater judgment; thus, as Jesus warned, "It will be more tolerable for Tyre and Sidon in the judgment than for [Chorazin and Bethsaida]" (Luke 10:14). The outwardly religious people of Bethsaida who rejected the truth will face a more severe judgment than pagans with less knowledge.

The Need for Divine Truth

But the crowds were aware of this and followed Him; and welcoming them, He began speaking to them about the kingdom of God (9:11*a*)

The Lord's departure for Bethsaida with the apostles did not go unnoticed; **the crowds were aware of this** development **and followed Him.** Literally, as Mark records, "The people saw them going, and many recognized them and ran there together on foot from all the cities, and got there ahead of them" (Mark 6:33). John records that the "crowd followed Him, because they saw the signs which He was performing on those who were sick" (John 6:2). They were thrill seekers, who eagerly followed Jesus as their king (v. 15) who could provide healing and free food. Their superficial, shallow-soil mentality drew a rebuke from Jesus (John 6:26–27).

Nonetheless, because of His compassionate concern for these shepherdless sheep (Mark 6:34), Jesus did not reject them out of hand. Instead, **welcoming them, He began speaking to them about the kingdom of God**—the constant theme of His preaching and teaching (4:43; 6:20; 8:1; 11:20; 17:20–21; 18:24–25; Mark 1:15; 4:11, 26–32; John 3:3; Acts 1:3). The Lord knew that although it was miracles that they sought, it was divine truth that they desperately needed. He had compassion on their souls as well as their bodies. Their shallowness, superficiality, and self-indulgence could not prevent Jesus from demonstrating the kindness of God.

THE NEED FOR HEALING

and curing who had need of healing. (9:11*b*)

Christ's compassion had constantly extended into the realm of human suffering caused by sickness, prompting Him again to cure **those who had need of healing.** Matthew 14:14 uses a form of the verb *splagchnizomai*, which refers to inner feelings, suggesting the physical effects of sympathy on the body, to describe the compassion Jesus felt. Human suffering truly caused Him pain, and moved Him to alleviate it. The Lord's healing, like His provision of food, foreshadows the blessings of the millennial kingdom (cf. Isa. 33:24; Jer. 30:17; Ezek. 34:16).

THE NEED FOR DAILY FOOD

Now the day was ending, and the twelve came and said to Him, "Send the crowd away, that they may go into the surrounding villages and countryside and find lodging and get something to eat; for here we are in a desolate place." But He said to them, "You give them something to eat!" And they said, "We have no more than five loaves and two fish, unless perhaps we go and buy food for all these people." (For there were about five thousand men.) And He said to His disciples, "Have them sit down to eat in groups of about fifty each." They did so, and had them all sit down. Then He took the five loaves and the two fish, and looking up to heaven, He blessed them, and broke them, and kept giving them to the disciples to set before the people. And they all ate and were satisfied; (9:12–17*a*)

Luke's narrative now turns to the actual miracle. His simple, unadorned account, framed in straightforward language, should not be allowed to obscure the staggering implications of this creative miracle.

As **the day was ending** (lit., "began to decline" after the the the sun reached its highpoint at noon) and the afternoon wore on, the apostles became concerned. Focused as they too often were on earthly things, **the twelve came** to Jesus **and** brashly, almost impertinently **said to Him, "Send the crowd away, that they may go into the surrounding villages and countryside and find lodging and get something**

to eat." They wanted the Lord to disperse the crowd before it got any later because, they informed Him, **"Here we are in a desolate place."** *Erēmos* (**desolate**) does not refer here to a desert, since there was abundant green grass (Mark 6:39), but rather to an uninhabited place. Evening was approaching, and there was nowhere for the crowd to acquire food.

The apostles' concern once again exhibited their lack of faith (cf. Matt. 8:26; 14:31; 16:8). They had a disconnect from all the miracles they had seen and they themselves had performed on the just-completed preaching tour. They might also have recalled that God had miraculously provided food in Israel's past:

> Now a man came from Baal-shalishah, and brought the man of God bread of the first fruits, twenty loaves of barley and fresh ears of grain in his sack. And he said, "Give them to the people that they may eat." His attendant said, "What, will I set this before a hundred men?" But he said, "Give them to the people that they may eat, for thus says the Lord, 'They shall eat and have some left over.'" So he set it before them, and they ate and had some left over, according to the word of the Lord. (2 Kings 4:42–44; cf. 1 Kings 17:10–16)

Incredibly, even after this amazing display of Christ's divine power, the apostles' faith was still weak. While Jesus, Peter, James, and John were on the mountain for the transfiguration, the nine who had not accompanied them were unable to cast out a demon because they failed to pray in faith (Luke 9:37–40). Exasperated by their continual lack of faith, Jesus sharply rebuked them, calling them an "unbelieving and perverted generation" (cf. Matt. 17:17). Rather than trust Jesus to deal with the obvious need for food, the apostles thought only of a human solution.

Jesus' response, **"You give them something to eat!",** seemingly detached from reality, must have amazed and surprised them. Incredulously they protested, **"We have no more than five loaves and two fish.** Andrew, anticipating the problem, had taken an inventory of what meager food the crowd possessed (John 6:8–9). Then somewhat sarcastically the apostles added, **"unless perhaps we go and buy food for all these people."** Perhaps playing off their remark, the Lord asked Philip, "Where are we to buy bread, so that these may eat?" (John 6:5). Aghast, "Philip answered Him, 'Two hundred denarii (nearly a year's pay for a common laborer) worth of bread is not sufficient for them, for everyone to receive a little'" (v. 7). As Luke's parenthetical note indicates, **there were about five thousand men** present. Including the women and children (Matt. 14:21), there could have been twenty to twenty-five thousand people present. The **five loaves** (small biscuits or crackers) **and two** small dried **fish** were obviously intended as a protest if not a mockery of the Lord's request.

Their amazement must have turned to complete shock when the Lord commanded the apostles to **"have them sit down to eat in groups of about fifty each."** Mark 6:40 notes that they "sat down in groups of hundreds and of fifties." Organizing the crowd like that would have made it easier to serve them. But the obvious question that would have arisen is, "Serve them what?" The apostles had just finished telling Jesus that they had nothing with which to feed them.

Despite their misgivings, the disciples obeyed the Lord **and had the people all sit down.** It was spring, just before Passover (John 6:4), and as previously noted there was plenty of green grass for the people to sit comfortably on. When all were seated, the Lord **took the five loaves and the two fish, and** then doing what every Jewish father did at a meal, **looking up to heaven, He blessed them.** By **looking up to heaven,** Jesus acknowledged God as the source of all provision. There was nothing mystical or spiritual that happened to the food by the Lord's blessing; *eulogeō* (**blessed**) simply means that He gave thanks to God.

Then, also doing what a father would do at a meal, Jesus **broke** the loaves and fish. But unlike any father had ever done, He **kept giving them to the disciples to set before the people.** In that understated way Luke described this astonishing display of Christ's power to create *ex nihilo*—the same power He used to create all things from nothing (John 1:3; Col. 1:16; Heb. 1:2). There was no doubt as to the source of the food; it was obvious to all who saw that it was being created in the Lord's hands and then given to the apostles to distribute to the crowd.

The people did not merely receive a minimal snack, but in keeping with God's bountiful grace, **they all ate and were satisfied. Satisfied** translates a form of the verb *chortazō*, which was originally used to describe fattening animals, who gorged themselves until they could eat no more (it is so used in Rev. 19:21). The people ate their fill until they were satiated.

The Need for Provision for His Servants

and the broken pieces which they had left over were picked up, twelve baskets full. (9:17*b*)

In His lavish provision of food, Jesus did not forget His own. After the meal was over, **the broken pieces** of the loaves and the fish (Mark 6:43) **which** the crowd **had left over were picked up** by the apostles. In the Lord's precision, nothing was wasted; the amount of leftover food was exactly enough to meet the needs of the Twelve.

There is a sad postscript to this remarkable story, which John records. The next day the crowds, thwarted in their attempt to make Him king, followed Jesus back to Capernaum (John 6:22–25). They expected Him to provide more food (v. 26), but when He refused and instead presented Himself as the Bread of Life come down from heaven (vv. 27–40), they rejected Him (vv. 41–66). So do all sinners who spurn God's generosity, compassion, and kindness (cf. Rom. 2:4–5).

Believers need to proclaim the Lord's power and mercy to those who need relief from life's physical and emotional struggles. But supremely, we must present to them the Savior who alone delivers from sin. It is our task to point them to the all-sufficient Bread of Life, the Lord Jesus Christ, the embodiment of God's compassion. Only through the salvation that He alone provides will lost sinners find eternal blessing and rest for their souls (Matt. 11:28–30).

Life's Most Important Question (Luke 9:18–22)

27

And it happened that while He was praying alone, the disciples were with Him, and He questioned them, saying, "Who do the people say that I am?" They answered and said, "John the Baptist, and others say Elijah; but others, that one of the prophets of old has risen again." And He said to them, "But who do you say that I am?" And Peter answered and said, "The Christ of God." But He warned them and instructed them not to tell this to anyone, saying, "The Son of Man must suffer many things and be rejected by the elders and chief priests and scribes, and be killed and be raised up on the third day." (9:18–22)

The question that the Lord Jesus Christ asked the apostles in verse 20, **"But who do you say that I am?"** introduces the most critical issue facing any person: the question of Jesus' identity (cf. 9:9). Where people spend eternity, either in heaven or in hell, depends on answering it correctly. Humanistic philosophy and secularism, as well as aberrant theological systems, cults, and false religions, inevitably reject the truth concerning the nature and work of Jesus Christ. The number of books, articles, papers, symposiums, lectures, and discussions advocating a false identity concerning Jesus Christ is seemingly endless. That plethora of supposedly scholarly and religious efforts to discover who Jesus is surely suggests to some that the question is a very complex, perhaps even unsolvable one. In reality, however, it is only difficult for those who reject the clear revelation of the Bible.

All four Gospels unambiguously present Jesus' true identity. Speaking for himself and the other gospel writers as well, the apostle John revealed the purpose for the inspired records of the life and labor of Jesus when on behalf of all four he wrote, "These have been written so that you may believe that Jesus is the Christ, the Son of God; and that believing you may have life in His name" (John 20:31). That statement is not obscure, but clear and precise: Jesus is the Messiah, God the Son incarnate, the only Savior, and faith in Him results in eternal life.

Like the other three historians, Luke clearly records the identity of Jesus Christ. The angel Gabriel said of Him, "He will be great and will be called the Son of the Most High; and the Lord God will give Him the throne of His father David; and He will reign over the house of Jacob forever, and His kingdom will have no end" (1:32–33). Later in chapter 1, Zacharias, the father of John the Baptist, testified that Jesus would fulfill all the promises of the Old Testament (1:68–69, 76–79). At His birth an angel said to the shepherds, "Do not be afraid; for behold, I bring you good news of great joy which will be for all the people; for today in the city of David there has been born for you a Savior, who is Christ the Lord" (2:10–11). Later Simeon (2:25–32) and Anna (2:36–38), testified that He was indeed the Messiah, the fulfillment of Old Testament prophecy. At the age of twelve, Jesus told His parents that He had to be in His heavenly Father's house (2:49). John the Baptist, His herald and forerunner, also identified Jesus as the Messiah (3:16–18). At His baptism the Holy Spirit anointed Jesus and the Father affirmed Him as His Son (3:21–22) as He did at the transfiguration (9:35). Even Satan had to acknowledge that Jesus is the Son of God (4:3), as did the demons (4:34, 41; 8:28).

The Twelve testified that Jesus was Messiah, Savior, and Lord. Recognizing that he was a sinner in the presence of holy God, Peter "fell down at Jesus' feet, saying, 'Go away from me Lord, for I am a sinful man, O Lord!'" (5:8). After Jesus stilled a raging storm on the Sea of Galilee, the apostles "were fearful and amazed, saying to one another, 'Who then is this, that He commands even the winds and the water, and they obey Him?'" (8:25). Immediately after the feeding in Galilee, the disciples were crossing the lake in a storm when Jesus appeared in the night, walking on the water. Matthew records that "those who were in the boat worshiped Him, saying, 'You are certainly God's Son!'" (Matt. 14:33). But it is here in Luke 9 that the Twelve made a clear, precise, and definitive affirmation that Jesus was the promised Messiah. It comes in Luke's narrative immediately after the climactic miracle of the Lord's Galilean ministry, the feeding of the multitude, although the two events did not actually take place in immediate sequence. In the intervening time, Jesus ministered in the largely Gentile regions of Tyre and Sidon and the Decapolis before returning briefly to Galilee. He then once again crossed to the eastern side of the Sea of Galilee (see Matt. 14:22–16:12, Mark 6:45–8:26). Some question why Luke failed to record those intervening events. But the vast amount of material available to the inspired gospel writers forced them to be selective (cf. John 21:25). Luke skipped the intervening material, recorded by Matthew and Mark, because doing so fit the thematic flow of this section of his gospel. In 8:25 Luke introduced the question of Jesus' identity when he recorded the disciples' fearful question, "Who then is this, that He commands even the winds and the water, and they obey Him?" Herod Antipas asked uneasily, "I myself had John beheaded; but who is this man about whom I hear such things?" (9:9). The people, influenced by their messianic expectations and their religious leaders, remained confused about who Jesus really was (see the exposition of v. 19 below). To insert material that would divert his readers from his focus on Jesus' identity did not serve Luke's purpose.

As the scene opened, Jesus **was praying** (cf. vv. 28–29; 3:21; 5:16; 6:12; 11:1; 22:41–45). It is instructive and challenging to note that the God-Man always made communion with the Father a priority in the face of the constant difficulties and demands people made on Him.

Though the Lord was praying **alone, the disciples were** nearby. By this time they had been with Him nearly two and a half years, observing His life and ministry, and being taught and discipled by Him. They had witnessed His power over demons, disease, nature, and death. They had seen overwhelming evidence that He is God, possessing divine power, knowledge, insight, and giving divine revelation. After all that they had seen and heard, the Lord's question to them in this passage amounted to their final exam.

The setting for this incident was Caesarea Philippi (Matt. 16:13; Mark 8:27), located north of the Sea of Galilee on the slopes of Mt. Hermon, about forty to fifty miles southwest of Damascus. It was near the extreme northern boundary of Old Testament Israel, not far from the city of Dan. It was originally named Panion, after the god Pan, whom Greek settlers, who entered the region after the death of Alexander the Great, worshiped in a nearby cave. Herod the Great built a temple there, and dedicated it to Rome and Augustus Caesar. Herod's son Philip the Tetrarch renamed the city Caesarea and appended his own name to it to distinguish it from the other Caesarea on the Mediterranean coast. At more than one thousand feet in elevation, this scenic region offered Jesus and the apostles some relief from the crowds in the lowlands. It was also farther from Jerusalem and the hostility of the Jewish leaders, and the threat of Herod Antipas.

The apostles'"final exam" consisted of two questions. The answer to the first one expressed human opinion concerning Jesus; the answer to the second one expressed divine revelation of His true identity.

THE ANSWER OF HUMAN OPINION

and He questioned them, saying, "Who do the people say that I am?" They answered and said, "John the Baptist, and others say Elijah; but others, that one of the prophets of old has risen again." (9:18b–19)

Addressing the Twelve Jesus **questioned them, saying, "Who do the people say that I am?"** *Ochlos* (**people**) is a word Luke used frequently to speak of the uncommitted mass of people who followed Jesus everywhere (cf. v. 37; 4:42; 5:1, 15; 7:11, 24; 8:4; 11:14, 29; 12:1, 54; 13:14, 17; 14:25). They never questioned the legitimacy of His miracles, having witnessed them firsthand (John 7:31; cf. 3:2; 9:16). Indeed, it was largely because of those miraculous signs that they followed Him (John 6:2). They also recognized that no mere human could exercise such supernatural power. Such unparalleled might and creative acts were beyond the realm of human capability, and thus Jesus had to be wielding the forces of heaven. But their ideas as to His specific identity were off target. Some, like Herod Antipas (Matt. 14:1–2), thought He was **John the Baptist** risen from the dead (cf. 9:7). Others opted for **Elijah** (cf. Mal. 4:5; Matt. 17:10); still others argued that another **one of the prophets of old** had **risen again.**

The correct answer to the Lord's question is clear in Scripture. He is the Son of Man (cf. 6:5; 9:26; 12:8, 10; 17:24, 26, 30; 18:8, 31; 19:10; 21:27, 36), a messianic title derived from Daniel 7:13–14. The angel Gabriel told Mary that He would be "the Son of the Most High" (1:32) and "the Son of God" (v. 35; cf. 22:70); another angel told the shepherds that He would be the Savior (2:11); even the demons were forced to acknowledge Him as "the Holy One of God" (4:34) and "the Son of God" (v. 41. See also the discussion of Christ's identity earlier in this chapter).

It seems incredible that the crowd, knowing what they knew, could come to any wrong conclusion about Jesus. At this point, though uncertain about His identity, the crowds had not yet turned against Jesus. They still hoped He would be the conquering messianic king, who would drive out the Romans, usher in His earthly kingdom and bring blessing and prominence to Israel (cf. John 6:14–15). Israel's ultimate rejection would not come until Passion Week under strong influence from the religious elite. Many of the Galileans would follow Jesus to Jerusalem and join the mammoth crowd hailing Him as the Messiah as He entered the city. Shockingly, by the end of the week, the crowds of pilgrims and residents would reject Him and scream for His blood. But for the time being, Jesus still maintained some popularity with the people.

John 12 reveals two significant reasons for the crowd's perplexing inability to correctly identify Jesus. Even during Passion Week, just days from His death, the crowd was still asking Him, "Who is this Son of Man?" (v. 34). Jesus replied that they were not lacking information; they already had the light, and needed to believe the truth that had been revealed to them (vv. 35–36). Having said that, Jesus "went away and hid Himself from them" (v. 36). The people knew the truth and rejected it, and as a result God judicially abandoned them:

> But though He had performed so many signs before them, yet they were not believing in Him. This was to fulfill the word of Isaiah the prophet which he spoke: "Lord, who has believed our report? And to whom has the arm of the Lord been revealed?" For this reason they could not believe, for Isaiah said again, "He has blinded their eyes and He hardened their heart, so that they would not see with their eyes and perceive with their heart, and be converted and I heal them." (vv. 37–40)

Tragically, their persistent rejection of the truth eventually brought God's judicial hardening so that they could not believe.

Another statement in John 12 reveals the second major reason that people fail to affirm Christ's true identity: "Nevertheless many even of the rulers believed in Him, but because of the Pharisees they were not confessing Him, for fear that they would be put out of the synagogue; for they loved the approval of men rather than the approval of God" (vv. 42–43). Here is a sobering illustration of the power of false religion—they knew the truth, but refused to act on it. Maintaining their façade of self-righteousness, being accepted by the Jewish religious authorities, and avoiding the trauma of being put out of the synagogue was more important to them than the truth. Like the fickle crowd, because they would not believe they eventually could not believe.

THE ANSWER OF DIVINE REVELATION

And He said to them, "But who do you say that I am?" And Peter answered and said, "The Christ of God." But He warned them and instructed them not to tell this to anyone, saying, "The Son of

Man must suffer many things and be rejected by the elders and chief priests and scribes, and be killed and be raised up on the third day." (9:20–22)

In light of the confusion and unbelief that His first question revealed, the Lord asked the Twelve, **"But who do you say that I am?** The word **you** is emphatic in all three gospel accounts of this incident (cf. Matt. 16:15; Mark 8:29). Who did they, in contrast to prevailing public opinion, believe Jesus to be?

The apostles' answer, voiced by their spokesman **Peter,** was the absolute antithesis of the crowd's suggestions. When the Twelve confessed Jesus to be **the Christ of God,** they did so with full knowledge of the alternative views of Him being proposed. To make their view of Him unmistakably clear, they added their affirmation that He is "the Son of the living God" (Matt. 16:16). *Christos* (**Christ**) is the Greek translation of the Hebrew word *mashiach.* Both words refer to the anointed one (cf. 4:18; Acts 10:38; Heb. 1:9), the one whom God Himself chose to be prophet, priest, and king, as the possessive phrase **of God** indicates (cf. 2:26; 23:35; Acts 3:18; 4:26; Rev. 11:15; 12:10). Anyone who rejects Jesus, God's Messiah, is cursed (1 Cor. 16:22) and deserving of the most severe punishment (Heb. 10:29).

The apostles knew Jesus was not merely another prophet, nor was He the political and military ruler that fit the expectation of the people. He was God's chosen, anointed Messiah and His beloved Son (Matt. 3:17; 17:5; Col. 1:13; 2 Peter 1:17), the king of Israel (John 1:49). The faith of the apostles would continue to waver at times between this confession and their Lord's death and resurrection. But despite the fluctuations in their trust, they would hold fast to their identification of Him. They would question His plan, especially when He spoke of His death. But never did they doubt His person.

Matthew's account records that Jesus also told Peter, and by extension the rest of the Twelve (except for the traitor, Judas Iscariot), "Blessed are you, Simon Barjona, because flesh and blood did not reveal this to you, but My Father who is in heaven" (Matt. 16:17). Spiritually dead people (Eph. 2:1–3) cannot be convinced that Jesus is God, Messiah, Savior, and King unless God awakens the mind, and gives understanding to the heart (1 Cor. 1:21; 2:10–14; 12:3). For that reason Jesus declared, "No one knows the Son except the Father; nor does anyone know the Father except the Son, and anyone to whom the Son wills to reveal Him" (Matt. 11:27) and, "No one can come to Me unless the Father who sent Me draws him" (John 6:44).

Since they had just confessed their belief in Him, this would seem to have been an appropriate time for the apostles to spread the word about Christ's true identity. They must have been puzzled when **He warned them and instructed them not to tell this to anyone.** The forceful terms *epitimaō* (**warned**) and *parangellō* (**instructed**) indicate that Jesus strongly, sternly commanded them not to spread the news that He was the Messiah. In John 12, this was a judicial act on the part of Jesus, hiding the truth from those who were already confirmed in their rejection of it, and the people, who had recently been thwarted in their attempt to make Jesus king (John 6:14–15), did not need to be incited to try again. But the reason for this prohibition was to instruct His followers that the message they were going to preach was not that Jesus was a healer or provider—but the Savior. They would never be sent out to preach permanently until after His death and resurrection. Those consummate achievements by the Lord Jesus would be the essential heart of the gospel they and all who followed them would preach. To show that this was His reason, He immediately spoke of it (cf. Matt. 16:20–23; Mark 8:30–33). On many occasions He restricted the proclamation of His power (Mark 1:25, 34; 3:12; 5:43; 7:36; 8:26, 30; 9:9). The Lord had no intention of starting a revolt against Rome—a revolt based on false expectations of Messiah's mission.

Instead, Jesus told the apostles, **"The Son of Man must suffer many things and be rejected by the elders and chief priests and scribes, and be killed and be raised up on the third day."** If His prohibiting them to spread the truth that He was the Messiah had puzzled the Twelve, this statement must have floored them. There was no mistaking the significance of Christ's words; the word **must** reveals that the Savior's death was part of God's unalterable plan. Jesus was, as Peter would later proclaim, "delivered over [to death] by the predetermined plan and foreknowledge of God" (Acts 2:23; cf. 3:18; 4:27–28; 13:27–28; Luke 9:31; 22:22, 37). What Isaiah predicted would infallibly come to pass:

Surely our griefs He Himself bore,
And our sorrows He carried;
Yet we ourselves esteemed Him stricken,
Smitten of God, and afflicted.
But He was pierced through for our transgressions,
He was crushed for our iniquities;
The chastening for our well-being fell upon Him,
And by His scourging we are healed.
All of us like sheep have gone astray,
Each of us has turned to his own way;
But the Lord has caused the iniquity of us all
To fall on Him.
He was oppressed and He was afflicted,
Yet He did not open His mouth;
Like a lamb that is led to slaughter,

And like a sheep that is silent before its shearers,
So He did not open His mouth.
By oppression and judgment He was taken away;
And as for His generation, who considered
That He was cut off out of the land of the living
For the transgression of my people, to whom the stroke was due?
His grave was assigned with wicked men,
Yet He was with a rich man in His death,
Because He had done no violence,
Nor was there any deceit in His mouth.
But the Lord was pleased
To crush Him, putting Him to grief;
If He would render Himself as a guilt offering. (Isa. 53:4–10)

The **many things** the Son of Man would suffer included the hatred of the Jewish leaders, the agony in Gethsemane, the betrayal by Judas, mockery, a brutal whipping, the crown of thorns, being **rejected by the elders and chief priests and scribes, and** being forsaken by the Father and **killed.** All of that must have dealt the apostles' messianic hopes a staggering blow. The plan was not that Jesus usher in the kingdom, but that He suffer death at the instigation of the rulers of the nation. Jesus came to be "made . . . sin on our behalf, so that we might become the righteousness of God in Him" (2 Cor. 5:21). Having accomplished redemption, Jesus would **be raised up** in triumph **on the third day.**

A Portrait of True Discipleship (Luke 9:23–26)

28

And He was saying to them all, "If anyone wishes to come after Me, he must deny himself, and take up his cross daily and follow Me. For whoever wishes to save his life will lose it, but whoever loses his life for My sake, he is the one who will save it. For what is a man profited if he gains the whole world, and loses or forfeits himself? For whoever is ashamed of Me and My words, the Son of Man will be ashamed of him when He comes in His glory, and the glory of the Father and of the holy angels." (9:23–26)

This brief passage is a diamond of truth, clear and brilliant, and it contains the heart of Jesus' invitation to sinners contemplating becoming one of His disciples. In His own words the Lord laid out what it means to be a genuine believer in Him; to be included in His salvation kingdom. It consequently reveals truth that is unsurpassed in importance.

What is most striking about the Lord's call to discipleship is that it demands radical self-denial, perhaps to the point of dying, while also living in complete obedience to His commands. That puts the true gospel, preached by Jesus, in sharp contrast with the contemporary pseudo-gospel of self-fulfillment popularly proclaimed and received by many who identify themselves as Christians. Such false teachers in effect view the Lord as little more than a utilitarian genie, who grants people whatever they wish. Some claim that Jesus wants people healthy and rich, and if they are not, it is because they have failed to claim their blessings. Others maintain that God's primary goal is to make people feel better about themselves by elevating their self-image (as if sinners had humility issues and needed more self-love) and eliminating their negative thinking. Some have even called for a "new reformation," abandoning biblical, God-centered theology in favor of an unabashedly man-centered theology of self-esteem. This "seeker-friendly" approach came along to replace the biblical gospel of salvation from sin with a set of psychological props to elevate people to fulfillment and higher life purpose. This quasi-Christian narcissism unabashedly promotes self-love, which characterizes the false teachers who preach it (2 Tim. 3:2) and focuses, as they do, on their satisfaction instead of God's glory.

A prayer from the pen of a godly saint of the past reveals the difference between today's man-centered false gospel and the attitude consistent with true saving faith:

> Lord, high and holy, meek and lowly …
> Let me learn by paradox
>   that the way down is the way up,
>   that to be low is to be high,
>   that the broken heart is the healed heart,
>   that the contrite spirit is the rejoicing spirit,
>   that the repenting soul is the victorious soul,
>   that to have nothing is to possess all,
>   that to bear the cross is to wear the crown,
>   that to give is to receive …
> Let me find thy light in my darkness,
>   thy life in my death,
>   thy joy in my sorrow,
>   thy grace in my sin,
>   thy riches in my poverty,
>   thy glory in my [humiliation].
> (Arthur Bennett, *The Valley of Vision* [Edinburgh: Banner of Truth, 1977], xv)

This is not an obscure passage that differs from Christ's normal teaching. Our Lord's teaching on the occasion of this passage is also recorded by Matthew (16:24–27) and Mark (8:34–38). The principles it contains are the same ones He repeatedly taught and modeled throughout His ministry. And since Jesus was the prototypical divine evangelist, He has given believers the pattern of how to evangelize. In Matthew 10:34–36 Jesus cautioned,

> Do not think that I came to bring peace on the earth; I did not come to bring peace, but a sword. For I came to set a man against his father, and a daughter against her mother, and a daughter-in-law against her mother-in-law; and a man's enemies will be the members of his household.

Believing in Him may actually make one's situation on earth worse. But instead of promising that their circumstances would improve, Jesus insisted that His followers be willing to pay whatever price is necessary for following Him:

> He who loves father or mother more than Me is not worthy of Me; and he who loves son or daughter more than Me is not worthy of Me. And he who does not take his cross and follow after Me is not worthy of Me. He who has found his life will lose it, and he who has lost his life for My sake will find it. (vv. 37–39)

The supreme goal for believers is not the development of their self-confidence by the betterment of their life perspective and situation, but following Christ no matter how severe the consequences.

Jesus encountered an important, wealthy young man eagerly seeking the answer to the crucial question of how to be saved. Mark records that he "ran up to [Jesus] and knelt before Him, and asked Him, 'Good Teacher, what shall I do to inherit eternal life?'" (Mark 10:17). Here was a seemingly sure-fire prospect. He had a felt need for salvation, went to the right person, and asked the right question. Yet in a manner that would have caused Him to fail any modern seeker-friendly course in evangelism, Jesus seemingly let him slip away. In fact, the Lord intentionally set the standard for eternal life far above what this tragic young man was willing to pay: "Looking at him, Jesus felt a love for him and said to him, 'One thing you lack: go and sell all you possess and give to the poor, and you will have treasure in heaven; and come, follow Me'" (v. 21). Crestfallen, "he went away grieving, for he was one who owned much property" (v. 22). He wanted Jesus on his terms, with his wealth intact. He had no interest in self-denying sacrifice.

Three incidents at the end of Luke 9 further reinforce the principle that following Jesus demands a willingness to give up everything if He asks. When a would-be disciple said to Him, "I will follow You wherever You go" (Luke 9:57), Christ replied, "The foxes have holes and the birds of the air have nests, but the Son of Man has nowhere to lay His head" (v. 58); in other words, following Him could be a homeless experience. More to the point, following Him promised nothing in this world. Jesus was not building an earthly kingdom of comfort and prosperity.

When Jesus challenged another man to follow Him, he replied, "Lord, permit me first to go and bury my father" (v. 59). The implication is that the man's father had not yet died, and he wanted to delay following the Lord until he received his inheritance. But Jesus replied, "Allow the dead to bury their own dead; but as for you, go and proclaim everywhere the kingdom of God" (v. 60). Again, this would-be disciple wanted to wait until his father had died so he could receive his inheritance. He would follow Jesus when he had all the earthly treasure coming to him.

Finally, "another also said, 'I will follow You, Lord; but first permit me to say good-bye to those at home'" (v. 61). Here was the same issue again. The man wanted to go home to negotiate some support from his family. Jesus and earthly possessions were his requirement. Jesus' reply, "No one, after putting his hand to the plow and looking back, is fit for the kingdom of God" (v. 62) confronted him with the true call to discipleship—let everything go and follow Me. Christ would later emphasize that a clean break with family may be required, since they are unbelievers. He said, "If anyone comes to Me, and does not hate his own father and mother and wife and children and brothers and sisters, yes, and even his own life, he cannot be My disciple" (Luke 14:26). Those who would be His followers must be desperate enough to be delivered from sin and hungry and thirsty enough to pursue righteousness radically.

The Lord's teaching in this brief but potent invitation may be expounded under three headings: the principle of true discipleship, the paradox of true discipleship, and the punishment of false discipleship.

THE PRINCIPLE OF TRUE DISCIPLESHIP

And He was saying to them all, "If anyone wishes to come after Me, he must deny himself, and take up his cross daily and follow Me. (9:23)

The good news Jesus preached is the truth that God offers forgiveness of all sin and the gift of eternal life to those who genuinely follow Him in faith. It calls for the total abandonment of self; as Paul wrote to the Galatians, "I have been crucified with Christ; and it is no longer I who live, but Christ lives in me; and the life which I now live in the flesh I live by faith in the Son of God, who loved me and gave Himself up for me" (Gal. 2:20).

That message is radically different than the "easy-believism" that is rampant in the church today. The Bible speaks of becoming a Christian as difficult. In Matthew 7:13–14 the Lord used the analogy of two gates to depict the choice facing every individual. The first is a wide gate, which is easy to enter. It opens into a broad, easily traversed path. That easy way, however, leads to eternal destruction (v. 13). The other gate is small and constricted, and the path it opens into is narrow and difficult. Yet that difficult way is the only one that leads to eternal life (v. 14).

Later "someone said to Him, 'Lord, are there just a few who are being saved?'" (Luke 13:23). Christ's reply reinforced the point He had made earlier in Matthew 7: "Strive to enter through the narrow door; for many, I tell you, will seek to enter and will not be able" (v. 24). In Matthew 11:12 Jesus again stated the difficulty of entering the kingdom, noting that "from the days of John the Baptist until now the kingdom of heaven suffers violence, and violent men take it by force" (cf. Luke 16:16), while Peter asked rhetorically, "If it is with difficulty that the righteous is saved, what will become of the godless man and the sinner?" (1 Peter 4:18). "You will seek Me and find Me," God declared, only "when you search for Me with all your heart" (Jer. 29:13). Sinners struggle mightily to come to true self-rejection, hatred of sin, and submission to Christ. And such a struggle ending in salvation is nothing less than energized by the power of the Holy Spirit operating in the sovereign purpose of God.

What makes the narrow gate so difficult to get through is the necessity for self-denial. Rejecting the Lord's call for him to forsake all and follow Him, the rich young ruler, as noted above, "was saddened, and he went away grieving, for he was one who owned much property" (Mark 10:22). Refusing Christ's call for extreme and absolute commitment to Him, "many of His disciples withdrew and were not walking with Him anymore" (John 6:66).

Because of the necessity for self-denial, Jesus challenged His would-be followers to consider what it might cost them to come to Him:

> For which one of you, when he wants to build a tower, does not first sit down and calculate the cost to see if he has enough to complete it? Otherwise, when he has laid a foundation and is not able to finish, all who observe it begin to ridicule him, saying, "This man began to build and was not able to finish." Or what king, when he sets out to meet another king in battle, will not first sit down and consider whether he is strong enough with ten thousand men to encounter the one coming against him with twenty thousand? Or else, while the other is still far away, he sends a delegation and asks for terms of peace. (Luke 14:28–32)

Then He applied the illustrations to His hearers: "So then, none of you can be My disciple who does not give up all his own possessions" (v. 33). The Lord was not, of course, teaching that salvation comes by impoverishing oneself. The self-denial in view is not merely of material things, but of anything that merits salvation (Rom. 7:18) or is more important to a person than God. His point is that coming to Him involves full submission to His lordship and willingness to abandon whatever He asks for His purpose. That is the point of the parables of the treasure hidden in the field, and the pearl of great price in which the treasure and the pearl were only acquired when the man sold everything (Matt. 13:44–46). The sinner is to understand the priceless value of eternal life and eagerly be rid of anything that would be a barrier to that everlasting joy.

As noted, the gospel is so contrary to fallen mankind's self-love, selfishness, and stubborn self-will that no one can come to faith in Christ apart from the convicting and regenerating work of the Spirit. The unregenerate, being dead in their sins, live lives totally controlled by personal desire driven by the lusts of the flesh (Eph. 2:1–3). By nature, they love the darkness of sin and hate the light of the truth (John 3:19–20), and are blinded by Satan so they cannot see that light (2 Cor. 4:4). Only when the Spirit convicts unbelievers of sin (John 16:8–11), draws them to Christ (John 6:44, 65) and gives them life (John 3:3–7) can salvation take place.

Having "summoned the crowd with His disciples" (Mark 8:34), Jesus began giving **to them all** this important teaching on genuine discipleship. A true commitment to Christ involves self-denial, cross bearing, and obedience.

SELF-DENIAL

he must deny himself, (9:23a)

Arneomai (**deny himself**) is a strong term, used to describe Peter's vehement denials that he knew Jesus (Matt. 26:70, 72), reprobates who permanently deny Christ (Luke 12:9; Titus 1:16; 1 John 2:22–23; Jude 4), and John the Baptist's insistence that he was not the messiah (John 1:20). It can even be translated "disowned," as it is in reference to Israel's rejection of Jesus (Acts 3:13–14; cf. 7:35). To be a follower of Jesus Christ is to disown one's natural, depraved, sinful self. It is to give up all dependence on and confidence in oneself and one's works to save.

No one had more impressive religious credentials than the apostle Paul. According to his own testimony, he was "circumcised the eighth day, of the nation of Israel, of the tribe of Benjamin, a Hebrew of Hebrews; as to the Law, a Pharisee; as to zeal, a persecutor of the church; as to the righteousness which is in the Law, found blameless" (Phil. 3:5–6). On trial before Herod, Paul testified that he had "lived as a Pharisee according to the strictest sect of our religion" (Acts 26:5). Looking back on his career before his salvation, Paul wrote, "I was advancing in Judaism beyond many of my contemporaries among my countrymen, being more extremely zealous for my ancestral traditions" (Gal. 1:14).

Yet when he met Christ on the road to Damascus, all of the zealous Pharisee's religious accomplishments became meaningless to him:

> For I know that nothing good dwells in me, that is, in my flesh; for the willing is present in me, but the doing of the good is not. (Rom. 7:18)

> But whatever things were gain to me, those things I have counted as loss for the sake of Christ. More than that, I count all things to be loss in view of the surpassing value of knowing Christ Jesus my Lord, for whom I have suffered the loss of all things, and count them but rubbish so that I may gain Christ. (Phil. 3:7–8)

> It is a trustworthy statement, deserving full acceptance, that Christ Jesus came into the world to save sinners, among whom I am foremost of all. (1 Tim. 1:15)

Paul exemplified the "poor in spirit" (Matt. 5:3), who acknowledge themselves to be destitute, impoverished, and spiritually bankrupt. Like the tax collector, they mourn over their sin and cry out, "God, be merciful to me, the sinner!" (Luke 18:13).

Like Paul, those who came face-to-face with God are overwhelmed with a sense of their own sinfulness. After God rebuked him, Job replied, "I despise myself, and repent in dust and ashes" (Job 42:6 ESV). Having seen the Angel of the Lord (the preincarnate Christ), Manoah, the father of Samson, exclaimed, "We will surely die, for we have seen God" (Judg. 13:22). When he saw a vision of God's glory in the temple, Isaiah, shattered by his sinfulness, cried out, "Woe is me, for I am ruined! Because I am a man of unclean lips, and I live among a people of unclean lips; for my eyes have seen the King, the Lord of hosts" (Isa. 6:5). After He miraculously created an enormous catch of fish for him and his partners, Peter "fell down at Jesus' feet, saying, 'Go away from me Lord, for I am a sinful man, O Lord!'" (Luke 5:8).

It is against that dark backdrop of sin and helplessness that the magnanimity of God's forgiving grace is manifested. Psalm 34:18 declares that "the Lord is near to the brokenhearted and saves those who are crushed in spirit." In his great prayer of contrition and confession David said, "The sacrifices of God are a broken spirit; a broken and a contrite heart, O God, You will not despise" (Ps. 51:17). "But to this one I will look," God declared, "to him who is humble and contrite of spirit, and who trembles at My word" (Isa. 66:2; cf. 57:15).

The law provides no hope for natural sinners. It was not given as a standard or means by which anyone could achieve salvation (Rom. 3:20, 28; 8:3; Gal. 2:16; 3:11). On the contrary, it was given to show sinfulness, to reveal helplessness, expose man's inability to gain salvation, and make clear the need for the Savior (Gal. 3:24). The law requires what is not possible—absolute, perfect obedience (Gal. 3:10; James 2:10) or God is angry, vengeful, and will punish the lawbreaker. In the Sermon on the Mount, Jesus attacked the Pharisaic religion, which was the most fastidious effort to keep the law. His message was designed to destroy their confidence in their superficial, hypocritical efforts at law keeping, and show how evil their hearts were (Matt. 5:17–48).

The realization that they are unable to satisfy the demands of God's law by their own efforts has always been what drives penitent sinners to the Lord (Isa. 55:6–7). Repentance is at the heart of the gospel message. Jesus came to call sinners to repentance (Luke 5:32), preached the necessity of repentance (18:13–14; Matt. 4:17; James 4:6–10), and commanded that His followers do the same (Luke 24:47).

The New Testament uses three Greek words to describe repentance. *Metanoeō* (Matt. 3:2; Matt. 4:17; Luke 10:13; 15:7, 10) expresses the mental aspect of repentance. It involves a reversal of one's thinking; a change of mind by which sinners see themselves as God sees them— fallen, depraved, and helpless to save themselves. *Metamelomai* (Matt. 21:29, 32) describes the emotional aspect of repentance, the regret and sorrow that a person's change of mind about themselves produces. Finally, *epistrephō* (Luke 17:4; 22:32; Acts 3:19; 9:35; 11:21; 2 Cor. 3:16) refers to the act of the will in changing one's direction in life; turning from sin to God (1 Thess. 1:9). Intellectually, repentance entails a recognition of sin's vileness. Emotionally, it produces an overwhelming sense of sorrow, remorse, and brokenness. Volitionally, the result is a change of direction in life away from sin to Christ.

It must be noted that repentance is not a meritorious human work. Sinners who are dead in their sins (Eph. 2:1), spiritually blind (Luke 4:18; cf. 2 Cor. 4:4) and trapped in Satan's domain of darkness (Col. 1:13) cannot repent of their own accord. Repentance comes when the Spirit of God uses the word of God to awaken sinners to their lost condition by convicting them of their sin (John 16:8–11). Acts 11:18 states that "God has granted to the Gentiles also the repentance that leads to life." Paul affirmed the divine choice to give such repentance when he instructed Timothy to "with gentleness [correct] those who are in opposition, if perhaps God may grant them repentance leading to the knowledge of the truth, and they may come to their senses and escape from the snare of the devil, having been held captive by him to do his will" (2 Tim. 2:25–26).

Sinners, then, are in no position to set the conditions by which they will come to Christ; they take Him on His terms, not theirs. The notable seventeenth-century English Puritan Thomas Watson described what it means to exhibit the self-denial that characterizes the poor in spirit:

The poor in spirit is content to take Christ upon his own terms. The proud sinner will article and indent with Christ. He will have Christ and his pleasure, Christ and his covetousness. But he that is poor in spirit sees himself lost without Christ, and he is willing to have him upon his own terms, a Prince as well as a Saviour: "Jesus my Lord" (Philippians 3:8). A castle that has long been besieged and is ready to be taken will deliver up on any terms to save their lives. He whose heart has been a garrison for the devil, and has held out long in opposition against Christ, when once God has brought him to poverty of spirit, and he sees himself damned without Christ, let God propound what articles he will, he will readily subscribe to them. "Lord, what wilt thou have me to do" (Acts 9:6). He that is poor in spirit will do anything that he may have Christ. He will behead his beloved sin. He will, with Peter, cast himself upon the water to come to Christ. (*The Beatitudes* [Reprint; Edinburgh: Banner of Truth, 1980], 47–48)

The following poem sums up in practical terms what self-denial means for a Christian:

When you are forgotten or neglected or purposely set at naught, and you don't sting or hurt with the insult or the oversight, but your heart is happy, being counted worthy to suffer for Christ—that is dying to self.

When your good is evil spoken of, when your wishes are crossed, your advice disregarded or your opinions ridiculed, and you refuse to let anger rise in your heart or even to defend yourself, but take it all in patient, loving silence—that is dying to self.

When you lovingly, patiently bear any disorder and irregularity, any impunctuality or any annoyance—when you come face to face with waste, folly, extravagance, spiritual insensibility—and endure it as Jesus endured it—that is dying to self.

When you are content with any food, any offering, any raiment, any climate, any society, any solitude, any interruption by the will of God— that is dying to self.

When you never refer to yourself in conversation, or to record your own good works, or itch after commendation, when you can truly love to go unknown—that is dying to self.

When you can see your brother or sister have his or her needs met and can honestly rejoice in spirit and can feel no envy nor question God, while your own needs are far greater and in more desperate circumstances—that is dying to self.

273

When you can receive correction and reproof from one of less stature than yourself and can humbly submit inwardly as well as outwardly, finding no rebellion or resentment rising up within your heart—that is dying to self.
(Bill Britton, "Dethrone the King: Dying to Self," *The Heartbeat of the Remnant*, July/August, 2002, 19)

CROSS BEARING

and take up his cross daily (9:23*b*)

In contemporary jargon one's cross has come to represent any difficult or unpleasant circumstance, no matter how trivial. Some argue that their job, boss, car, mother-in-law, or wayward teenager is their cross. Others view taking up their cross as identifying in some mystical sense with the crucifixion of Christ. That would not be a notion the followers of Jesus would have entertained, since though He had told them of His death, He had not yet told them He would be crucified. The Lord's hearers would be under no such illusions. To them, a **cross** represented only one thing—horrible suffering, pain, and death. Crucifixion was a common method of execution used by the Romans, and it was an all too familiar sight in first-century Palestine. Thus when the Lord declared that anyone who would follow Him had to **take up his cross daily** they understood perfectly what He meant. In the most graphic terms possible, Jesus was calling for a willingness to endure hatred, hostility, rejection, reproach, persecution, shame, even the most horrible death; to say no to self and no to safety for His sake (cf. 1 Peter 4:16). A sacrifice small when compared to the gift of eternal life.

Paul's farewell speech to the elders of the church at Ephesus reflected the apostle's willingness to suffer whatever was required of him for the cause of Christ:

> And now, behold, bound in spirit, I am on my way to Jerusalem, not knowing what will happen to me there, except that the Holy Spirit solemnly testifies to me in every city, saying that bonds and afflictions await me. But I do not consider my life of any account as dear to myself, so that I may finish my course and the ministry which I received from the Lord Jesus, to testify solemnly of the gospel of the grace of God. (Acts 20:22–24)

A short while later Paul said to those concerned about his safety if he went to Jerusalem, "What are you doing, weeping and breaking my heart? For I am ready not only to be bound, but even to die at Jerusalem for the name of the Lord Jesus" (Acts 21:13). "I die daily," he told the Corinthians

(1 Cor. 15:31), expressing the reality that he lived constantly on the brink of death (cf. Acts 20:19; 2 Cor. 11:22–33).

There is no crown without a cross. Eternal life is so precious that those who truly seek it are willing to give up everything to obtain it if the Lord wills and even suffer with joy (cf. 1 Peter 4:12–19). They can say with Paul, "Momentary, light affliction is producing for us an eternal weight of glory far beyond all comparison" (2 Cor. 4:17).

and follow Me. (9:23*c*)

The present tense of the verb translated **follow** indicates that a continual pattern of obediencc characterizes a true disciple of Jesus Christ. In the Sermon on the Mount, Jesus warned, "Not everyone who says to Me, 'Lord, Lord,' will enter the kingdom of heaven, but he who does the will of My Father who is in heaven will enter" (Matt. 7:21). In Luke 6:46 He asked the pointed question, "Why do you call Me, 'Lord, Lord,' and do not do what I say?" Speaking to the apostles in the upper room on the night before His death, Jesus emphasized that genuine saving faith will inevitably manifest itself in obedience:

> If you love Me, you will keep My commandments. (John 14:15)

> He who has My commandments and keeps them is the one who loves Me; and he who loves Me will be loved by My Father, and I will love him and will disclose Myself to him. . . . If anyone loves Me, he will keep My word; and My Father will love him, and We will come to him and make Our abode with him. He who does not love Me does not keep My words; and the word which you hear is not Mine, but the Father's who sent Me. (John 14:21, 23–24)

> If you keep My commandments, you will abide in My love; just as I have kept My Father's commandments and abide in His love. (John 15:10)

> You are My friends if you do what I command you. (John 15:14; cf. 1 John 2:5–6; 3:24; 5:3; 2 John 6)

As is the case with repentance (see the discussion above), self-denial, cross bearing, and obedience are not meritorious pre-salvation works that make a sinner acceptable to God. Nor are they chronological, sequential steps that lead to conversion, but rather the logical components of saving faith. Neither repentance nor saving faith can be produced under

human power; they are components of the divine work wrought by the
Spirit of God.

The Paradox of True Discipleship

**For whoever wishes to save his life will lose it, but whoever loses
his life for My sake, he is the one who will save it. For what is a
man profited if he gains the whole world, and loses or forfeits
himself?** (9:24–25)

Jesus further elaborated on the principle He had just given by
noting paradoxically that **whoever wishes to save his life will** in fact
**lose it, but whoever loses his life for My sake, he is the one who
will save it.** The only way for lost sinners to be saved from eternal punishment in hell is to experience the abandonment of everything for
Christ.

This clear call must have been a regular part of our Lord's preaching. Later in His ministry, He declared, "Whoever seeks to keep his life will
lose it, and whoever loses his life will preserve it" (Luke 17:33). Earlier, as
recorded in Matthew 10:39, He said, "He who has found his life will lose it,
and he who has lost his life for My sake will find it." John 12:25 states that
during Passion Week He repeated this call: "He who loves his life loses it,
and he who hates his life in this world will keep it to life eternal." Clearly,
the message is that those who focus on self-love, self-esteem, and fulfilling
all their desires, dreams, and ambitions in this life, even with a superficial
interest in Jesus, will lose their eternal soul (cf. Matt. 7:21–23). But those
who abandon their self-interests, deny themselves, hate their sinful condition, and give themselves wholly to Jesus Christ will be saved.

An important point to note is that Jesus was not investing all
forms of self-denial with any inherent nobility. He was not saying that
those who give their lives for social, political, or even religious causes will
benefit spiritually from doing so. The self-denial the Lord called for was
specifically, He said, **for My sake.**

Elaborating on His point, Jesus asked the rhetorical question, **For
what is a man profited if he gains the whole world, and loses or
forfeits himself?** Expressing the ultimate hyperbole, the Lord said in
effect, "Assume for the sake of argument that you could possess the whole
world—all that your passions hunger for, your eyes covet, and your pride
demands (cf. 1 John 2:16). What would that profit you if you forfeited
your eternal soul?" The obvious answer is "nothing." Nothing in the world
is of comparable value to a person's eternal soul.

THE PUNISHMENT OF FALSE DISCIPLESHIP

For whoever is ashamed of Me and My words, the Son of Man will be ashamed of him when He comes in His glory, and the glory of the Father and of the holy angels. (9:26)

Jesus identifies those who will not repent and believe in Him as those who are **ashamed** of Him and His **words** (cf. Matt. 10:32–33). To be **ashamed** in this context means to reject, despise, and find unaccept-able. Such people are proud of what they should be ashamed of; their "glory is in their shame" (Phil. 3:19). God said of sinful, unrepentant Israelites, "Were they ashamed because of the abomination they have done? They were not even ashamed at all; they did not even know how to blush" (Jer. 6:15). Despite the fact that He manifested the glory of God (John 1:14; Rev. 5:12), sinners reject Jesus (John 1:10–11). The message of the cross is foolish and offensive to those who want to hold on to their sin (1 Cor. 1:18, 23), who love the approval of men rather than the approval of God (John 12:43).

Those who are ashamed of Him will in turn find that **the Son of Man will be ashamed of** them **when He comes in His glory, and the glory of the Father and of the holy angels** (cf. 2 Thess. 1:7–9). Christ's words here reflect an Old Testament text with which His hearers would have been familiar. Daniel 7:9–10 describes the judgment also recorded in Revelation 20:11–15. Then verses 13 and 14 in Daniel de-scribe the appearance of the Son of Man, who will render judgment (cf. John 5:22, 27) and receive His eternal kingdom. At that time all who were ashamed of Him and rejected Him will be sentenced to eternal hell.

On the other hand, Christians are not ashamed of Christ or His word (Rom. 1:16; Phil. 1:20; 2 Tim. 1:12; 1 Peter 4:16). The promise to those who are ashamed of themselves and their sin, who boast only in the cross (Gal. 6:14; cf. Heb. 12:2), is that God will redeem them and grant them forgiveness and eternal life. The wonderful truth is that Jesus "is not ashamed to call them brethren" (Heb. 2:11) and "God is not ashamed to be called their God" (Heb. 11:16).

Previewing the Second Coming (Luke 9:27–36)

29

"But I say to you truthfully, there are some of those standing here who will not taste death until they see the kingdom of God." Some eight days after these sayings, He took along Peter and John and James, and went up on the mountain to pray. And while He was praying, the appearance of His face became different, and His clothing became white and gleaming. And behold, two men were talking with Him; and they were Moses and Elijah, who, appearing in glory, were speaking of His departure which He was about to accomplish at Jerusalem. Now Peter and his companions had been overcome with sleep; but when they were fully awake, they saw His glory and the two men standing with Him. And as these were leaving Him, Peter said to Jesus, "Master, it is good for us to be here; let us make three tabernacles: one for You, and one for Moses, and one for Elijah"—not realizing what he was saying. While he was saying this, a cloud formed and began to overshadow them; and they were afraid as they entered the cloud. Then a voice came out of the cloud, saying, "This is My Son, My Chosen One; listen to Him!" And when the voice had spoken, Jesus was found alone. And they kept silent, and reported to no one in those days any of the things which they had seen. (9:27–36)

One of the most glorious sections of Handel's masterpiece *Messiah* is the chorus "And the Glory of the Lord," which draws its text from Isaiah's prophecy. Speaking of the coming Messiah, Isaiah wrote, "Then the glory of the Lord will be revealed, and all flesh will see it together; for the mouth of the Lord has spoken" (Isa. 40:5). That text reveals that the Lord Jesus Christ is the glory of God manifest in the incarnation.

The Old Testament records many occasions when God revealed His attributes in visible, light-like glory. Glory appeared in the wilderness, in response to Israel's complaints about lack of food (Ex. 16:7, 10); in Leviticus 9:23 at the ordination of Aaron and his sons as priests; at Mt. Sinai at the giving of the law (Ex. 24:15–18); at the completion of the tabernacle (Ex. 40:34–35); in the wilderness in response to the nation's rebellion (Num. 14:10) and again after the rebellion of Korah, Dathan, and Abiram (Num. 16:19, 42); when the people complained about the lack of water at Meribah (Num. 20:6); at the completion of the temple (1 Kings 8:10–11); and to Ezekiel (Ezek. 1:28; 3:23; 10:4, 18; 11:23). Whenever the glory of the Lord appeared, it manifested the presence of God Himself.

The Old Testament manifestations of God were shrouded in mystery. "Behold, these are the fringes of His ways," Job declared, "and how faint a word we hear of Him! But His mighty thunder, who can understand?" (Job 26:14). Moses cried out to God, "I pray You, show me Your glory!" (Ex. 33:18). But God replied, "You cannot see My face, for no man can see Me and live!" (v. 20) and then told Moses, "And it will come about, while My glory is passing by, that I will put you in the cleft of the rock and cover you with My hand until I have passed by. Then I will take My hand away and you shall see My back, but My face shall not be seen" (vv. 22–23). The blazing fullness of God's glory would incinerate anyone who encountered it.

It is in the Lord Jesus Christ that the glory of God is most fully and clearly manifested. The writer of Hebrews began his book with a description of Christ's glory:

> God, after He spoke long ago to the fathers in the prophets in many portions and in many ways, in these last days has spoken to us in His Son, whom He appointed heir of all things, through whom also He made the world. And He is the radiance of His glory and the exact representation of His nature. (Heb. 1:1–3)

The apostle Paul called Him the "Lord of glory" (1 Cor. 2:8), and in 2 Corinthians 4:3–6 states,

> And even if our gospel is veiled, it is veiled to those who are perishing, in whose case the god of this world has blinded the minds of the unbelieving so that they might not see the light of the gospel of the glory of

> Christ, who is the image of God. For we do not preach ourselves but Christ Jesus as Lord, and ourselves as your bond-servants for Jesus' sake. For God, who said, "Light shall shine out of darkness," is the One who has shone in our hearts to give the Light of the knowledge of the glory of God in the face of Christ.

James referred to Him as "our glorious Lord Jesus Christ" (James 2:1). But the event that most powerfully and dramatically proved Jesus Christ to be the true glory of God, though veiled while He walked on earth, is the one recorded in this passage. The transfiguration is a preview of Christ's unveiled second coming, when He returns in full visible glory (Matt. 24:29–30; 25:31).

The last vision the world had of Jesus was of Him hanging on a cross; only His followers saw Him after the resurrection and witnessed His ascension. Crucifixion was from the Gentile standpoint the ultimate act of disdain toward society's most wretched people, while to the Jewish people it symbolized being cursed by God (cf. Gal. 3:13).

But that is not the final view the world will have of Jesus. While the world sees only His first coming, Jesus spoke often of His return (cf. Luke 9:26; 12:40; 17:24–30; 18:8; 21:27, 36). The two comings of Christ, the first in humility and the second in glory, are the two great themes of biblical prophecy.

Still, scoffers question why anyone should believe Jesus' promise to return. After all, nearly two thousand years have elapsed since His death. "Where is the promise of His coming?" they demand, "For ever since the fathers fell asleep, all continues just as it was from the beginning of creation'" (2 Peter 3:4). The same skepticism faced the Old Testament prophets when they predicted events in the distant future. But they also predicted near events, which dispelled skepticism when they came to pass, giving evidence that their future prophecies would also be fulfilled.

In this section Jesus followed the pattern of the Old Testament prophets. Having promised His glorious return in v. 26, which would not come in their day (see the discussion of that verse in the previous chapter of this volume), He promised an event to happen immediately to verify His believability. He told His hearers, **"But I say to you truthfully, there are some of those standing here** (identified in the next verse as Peter, John, and James) **who will not taste death** (a Hebrew colloquial expression for dying) **until they see the kingdom of God."** The preview glimpse they would receive of His divine nature to be fully revealed at His return was a gift to encourage their weak faith. Thus **some eight days after these sayings, He took along Peter and John and James, and went up on the mountain to pray.** Matthew (17:1) and Mark (9:2) place the transfiguration six days after the Lord spoke these words. There is no contradiction between their accounts and Luke's; the latter merely bookended the six days by adding the day Jesus made this statement and the actual day of the transfiguration.

Jesus **took along Peter and John and James** since those three men, along with Andrew, made up the innermost circle of the apostles (cf. 8:51; Mark 14:33). Jesus' choice of three men reflects the law's requirement that "on the evidence of two or three witnesses a matter shall be confirmed" (Deut. 19:15; cf. Matt. 18:16; 2 Cor. 13:1; 1 Tim. 5:19; Heb. 10:28). The apostles had been devastated by Jesus' prediction of His death (9:21–22) and the possibility of their own martyrdoms (vv. 23–24). Matthew (16:22–23) and Mark (8:32–33) tell us Peter rebuked Jesus for even suggesting such plans, for which he was severely rebuked by his Lord. It was extremely difficult to reconcile those unexpected and undesired predictions with their messianic views and the Lord's promised glory (v. 26). The amazing event that Peter, John, and James were about to witness was designed as a help to reinforce their faith in Jesus' glory and kingdom promises.

They had been waiting and hoping for the coming of the promised kingdom since they first began to follow Jesus. They had seen the power of the kingdom every time the King cast out demons, demonstrated control over nature, healed the sick, or raised the dead. They had also experienced divine power operating through them (9:1). But what Peter, James, and John were about to experience would go beyond merely observing the signs that point to the kingdom; they would actually briefly enter the kingdom itself.

In preparation for this glorious event, Jesus took the three apostles with Him and **went up on the mountain to pray.** On that unnamed mountain in Galilee, in the greatest revelation in His lifetime of who He truly is, Jesus' glory was manifested in four ways: the Son's transformation, the saint's association, the sleepers' suggestion, and the Sovereign God's revelation.

The Son's Transformation

And while He was praying, the appearance of His face became different, and His clothing became white and gleaming. (9:29)

As verse 32 indicates, Jesus alone **was praying;** the apostles were asleep. Suddenly, while they slept, **the appearance of His face became different** than it had ever been. As Matthew described it, "He was transfigured [*metamorphoō*, the source of the English word "metamorphosis"] before them; and His face shone like the sun" (Matt. 17:2). He who had been "found in appearance as a man" (Phil. 2:8) pulled back the veil of His flesh to reveal a brief glimpse of His divine glory—the shekinah glory of God that was manifested repeatedly in the Old Testament, as noted earlier in this chapter. The glory of Christ's divine shining nature radiated through His body so that **His clothing became white and gleaming.** The Greek word translated **gleaming** means "emitting light," and describes a brilliant, flashing light like lightning. Jesus will manifest that same blazing glory in its fullness at His second coming (Matt. 16:27; 25:31). It was Christ's divine glory that the three apostles would see when they woke up, along with two other glorious beings whom the narrative now introduces.

THE SAINTS' ASSOCIATION

And behold, two men were talking with Him; and they were Moses and Elijah, who, appearing in glory, were speaking of His departure which He was about to accomplish at Jerusalem. (9:30–31)

The phrase **and behold** introduces another startling aspect of this amazing scene. Jesus was not the only person from the eternal kingdom present; **two men were talking with Him; and they were Moses and Elijah, who** were also **appearing in glory;** that is, in the splendor of their glorified bodies (cf. Phil. 3:20–21). That the two were recognizable shows that people in heaven retain their identities. The choice of two men once again was in keeping with the law's standard for witnesses noted above. The topic of their conversation, Christ's **departure which He was about to accomplish at Jerusalem,** shows that His death was the fulfillment of God's eternal plan, not a breach of it. What was hard for the apostles to accept, Jesus' death, was in the divine plan and these Old Testament representatives understood that fact in their perfect knowledge. Moses and Elijah had been in the presence of God since their departures from this world, where they had known and worshiped Jesus and understood the plan of redemption.

Moses and Elijah were chosen to appear for at least three reasons. First, they both had unusual exits from the world. After Moses' death Michael the archangel and Satan fought over his body (Jude 9) and God buried him so that his body would never be found (Deut. 34:6). Elijah did not die, but as he and Elisha "were going along and talking, behold, there appeared a chariot of fire and horses of fire which separated the two of them. And Elijah went up by a whirlwind to heaven" (2 Kings 2:11).

Further, Moses and Elijah were two witnesses who would be trusted implicitly by Israel. Moses was the greatest and most revered leader in

283

the nation's history, the one who led them out of slavery in Egypt. Elijah was one of the greatest and most respected of the prophets. He also was one of only two men in the Old Testament, along with Enoch (Gen. 5:22–24) not to experience death but to be taken directly to heaven.

Finally, they represented the two great divisions of the Old Testament. Moses is identified with the law, which is commonly referred to as the law of Moses (e.g., Josh. 8:31; 1 Kings 2:3; 2 Kings 23:25; 2 Chron. 23:18; Ezra 7:6; Neh. 8:1; Dan. 9:11, 13; Mal. 4:4; Luke 24:44; John 7:23; Acts 13:39; Heb. 10:28). While Moses gave the law, Elijah guarded it. His strong stand against Israel's idolatrous rejection of the law culminated in his dramatic victory over hundreds of false prophets on Mount Carmel (1 Kings 18:19–40).

The question arises as to why the two men had visible bodies, since the Old Testament saints are described in Hebrews 12:23 as "the spirits of the righteous made perfect" and do not receive their glorified bodies until after the tribulation (Dan. 12:1–2). Evidently they either received the bodies they appeared in temporarily for that occasion, or God gave them their permanent resurrection bodies early.

THE SLEEPERS' SUGGESTION

Now Peter and his companions had been overcome with sleep; but when they were fully awake, they saw His glory and the two men standing with Him. And as these were leaving Him, Peter said to Jesus, "Master, it is good for us to be here; let us make three tabernacles: one for You, and one for Moses, and one for Elijah"—not realizing what he was saying. (9:32–33)

While this incredible scene was unfolding—Jesus' transfiguration and His dialogue with Moses and Elijah—**Peter and his companions had been overcome with sleep.** They were not uninterested, indifferent, or apathetic; the perfect passive participle translated **overcome** implies that their falling asleep was involuntary. And they had been asleep before the Lord's glory was revealed. Deeply saddened by Jesus' prediction of His rejection and death, the three apostles were sound asleep—as they would later be in Gethsemane (22:45).

But Jesus did not bring them there to sleep, but to witness His glory. They were awakened, groggy at first, perhaps rubbing their eyes and trying to make sense of the scene. **But when they were fully awake, they saw His glory and the two men standing with Him.** Obviously they would not have recognized Moses and Elijah unless the two men had introduced themselves, or been introduced by the Lord.

How long the glorious scene lasted is not known, but eventually Moses and Elijah began to leave. **And as these were leaving . . . Peter,** often impetuous and never afraid to speak his mind, **said to Jesus, "Master** (Matt. 17:4 and Mark 9:5 note that, overwhelmed by the glorious scene, Peter also called Him "Lord" and "Rabbi"). His first comment, **"It is good for us to be here,"** indicates that the revelation of the kingdom was what he had been waiting for. His suggestion, **let us make three tabernacles: one for You, and one for Moses, and one for Elijah,** reflects his desire to bypass the cross and make the current situation permanent.

A number of things prompted Peter's hope that what he was witnessing was the inauguration of the kingdom. First, the Feast of Tabernacles was being celebrated at that time. Since that feast celebrated Israel's exodus from Egypt, what better time could there be for Jesus' exodus from the world? Further, Peter knew from Zechariah 14:16–19 that the Feast of Tabernacles was to be celebrated in the millennial kingdom. He also knew that according to Malachi 3:1 and 4:5–6 that Elijah was associated with the coming of the kingdom.

Peter's brash suggestion shows astounding self-confidence. He was out of his element, the normal world of time and space, and in the supernatural realm of the divine. Yet he did not hesitate to offer suggestions to the Lord about what should be done. He was still trying to divert Jesus from His suffering and toward setting up His reign at that time (cf. Acts 1:6). Though well-meant and offered humbly, Peter's suggestion was off target; as was often the case, he spoke **not realizing what he was saying.** This was not the beginning of the kingdom; God's plan of redemption could not be short-circuited. Before the crown comes the cross; the path to the kingdom lies through Calvary. Before Jesus reigns as king, He must be the suffering servant of Isaiah 53. But the glorious vision they experienced that day would stay with the three apostles for the rest of their lives (2 Peter 1:16–18), reassuring them of the reality of the coming kingdom.

THE SOVEREIGN GOD'S REVELATION

While he was saying this, a cloud formed and began to overshadow them; and they were afraid as they entered the cloud. Then a voice came out of the cloud, saying, "This is My Son, My Chosen One; listen to Him!" And when the voice had spoken, Jesus was found alone. And they kept silent, and reported to no one in those days any of the things which they had seen. (9:34–36)

While Peter was interrupting the conversation between Jesus, Moses, and Elijah, God interrupted him. As he was offering his suggestion, a bright (Matt. 17:5) **cloud formed and began to overshadow them.** The cloud was a visible representation of God's presence in shekinah glory (cf. Ex. 13:21; 16:10; 24:16; 40:35; Num. 16:42; 1 Kings 8:11). It engulfed Jesus, Moses, and Elijah, leaving the apostles outside, since when they heard God's **voice** it **came out of the cloud.** Understandably, Peter, James, and John **were afraid,** and fell face down on the ground terrified because of the glorious presence of God (Matt. 17:6; cf. Isa. 6:5; Ezek. 1:28; Rev. 1:17).

As was the case at Jesus' baptism (Luke 3:22), the Father's declaration, **"This is My Son, My Chosen One,"** testified that as His Son, Jesus shared His nature, essence, and deity. He then commanded the terrified apostles to be silent and **listen to** Jesus, especially on the matter of His death.

There is a rather strange and unexpected epilogue to this incredible scene. After **the voice** of God **had spoken, Jesus was found alone.** The cloud representing God's presence had vanished, as had Moses and Elijah. Jesus raised the apostles up from the ground and calmed their fears (Matt. 17:7). But instead of immediately proclaiming the vision of the glorious Lord Jesus Christ they had just witnessed, **they kept silent, and reported to no one in those days any of the things which they had seen.**

Matthew reveals the reason for their silence: "As they were coming down from the mountain, Jesus commanded them, saying, 'Tell the vision to no one until the Son of Man has risen from the dead'" (Matt. 17:9). The Lord had brought them there to be witnesses; why then would He command them not to reveal what they had seen? There were several features to Christ's prohibition. First, what they had witnessed was so far removed from everyday reality that most people probably would not have believed the apostles' report. They would have been casting this precious pearl before swine (cf. Matt. 7:6). Further, speaking openly of the kingdom might have caused the Romans, ever on guard against the possibility of insurrection, to prematurely execute Jesus and the apostles. Additionally, news of the vision could easily have incited the Jews to try again to make Jesus the leader of a revolt against Rome (cf. John 6:14–15). But most important, they could not preach a glorified Christ without the truth of His death and resurrection. Only after the resurrection would Peter (2 Peter 1:16–18), John (John 1:14), and James testify to the glorious preview of the second coming they had seen, in its proper relation to the cross and empty grave.

The Significance of Faith
(Luke 9:37–45)

30

On the next day, when they came down from the mountain, a large crowd met Him. And a man from the crowd shouted, saying, "Teacher, I beg You to look at my son, for he is my only boy, and a spirit seizes him, and he suddenly screams, and it throws him into a convulsion with foaming at the mouth; and only with difficulty does it leave him, mauling him as it leaves. I begged Your disciples to cast it out, and they could not." And Jesus answered and said, "You unbelieving and perverted generation, how long shall I be with you and put up with you? Bring your son here." While he was still approaching, the demon slammed him to the ground and threw him into a convulsion. But Jesus rebuked the unclean spirit, and healed the boy and gave him back to his father. And they were all amazed at the greatness of God. But while everyone was marveling at all that He was doing, He said to His disciples, "Let these words sink into your ears; for the Son of Man is going to be delivered into the hands of men." But they did not understand this statement, and it was concealed from them so that they would not perceive it; and they were afraid to ask Him about this statement. (9:37–45)

The foundation of all spiritual life for Christians is faith in the Lord Jesus Christ. In perhaps the clearest statement of that truth in Scripture, Paul wrote, "For by grace you have been saved through faith; and that not of yourselves, it is the gift of God; not as a result of works, so that no one may boast" (Eph. 2:8–9; cf. John 1:12; Rom. 3:28; 5:1; Gal. 2:16; 3:8, 11, 24). Faith is also fundamental in sanctification. "I have been crucified with Christ;" Paul wrote, "and it is no longer I who live, but Christ lives in me; and the life which I now live in the flesh I live by faith in the Son of God, who loved me and gave Himself up for me" (Gal. 2:20). Faith is objective and expresses itself in confident confession of Jesus as Lord and obedience to the Word of God, which results in a progressive separation from sin and conformity to the Lord Jesus Christ until glorification, when faith is replaced by sight (cf. 2 Cor. 5:6–7).

But in today's postmodern world, faith has become subjective; a vague and ambiguous term. Faith is often viewed as a groundless, nonrational, contentless "leap in the dark" that is seen as virtuous and even impactful in and of itself. True biblical faith, however, is radically different. It may be defined simply as believing in who God is and what He has said because Scripture declares it to be true. Faith is not a nebulous, mystical experience, but is grounded in the nature of God as revealed in the Word of God. To believe the revelation of God in Scripture is always reasonable, because it is divinely inspired truth.

Hebrews chapter 11 contains the most extensive discussion of faith in the Bible; in fact, the word "faith" appears there twenty-five times. From the examples of godly men and women of the Old Testament, several truths about faith emerge. Verse 1 defines faith as "the assurance of things hoped for, the conviction of things not seen." Faith transports God's promises from the future into the present, giving substance to future reality. It is a substantial confidence that becomes an absolute, unshakable conviction.

Biblical faith is not natural, human faith. In that sense, everyone has faith, since everyone trusts in things, such as the safety of the water they drink and the edibility of the food they eat, the competence of those who maintain and fly the airplanes they travel on, and the effectiveness of the medicines they take. But, in all those examples, faith is based on human experience. Biblical faith trusts in what it has not experienced, based on its absolute confidence in the truth of God's promises in Scripture. Apart from such faith, it is impossible to please God (v. 6).

Theologians use three Latin words to delineate the elements of saving faith. *Notitia* (knowledge) refers to the intellectual element of faith, and "consists in a positive recognition of the truth, in which man accepts as true whatsoever God says in His Word" (Louis Berkhof, *Systematic Theology* [Grand Rapids: Eerdmans, 1976], 503). *Assensus* (assent) describes the emotional element of faith. Berkhof notes, "When one embraces Christ by faith, he has a deep conviction of the truth and reality of the object of faith, feels that it meets an important need in his life, and is conscious of an absorbing interest in it—and this is assent" (Berkhof, 504–505). Finally, *fiducia* denotes the volitional element of faith; it is an act of the will. Saving faith

> is not merely a matter of the intellect, nor of the intellect and the emotions combined; it is also a matter of the will, determining the direction of the soul ... this third element consists in a personal trust in Christ as Saviour and Lord, including a surrender of the soul as guilty and defiled to Christ, and a reception and appropriation of Christ as the source of pardon and of spiritual life. (Berkhof, 505)

Genuine faith inevitably results in a life of obedience to God; one cannot affirm Jesus as Lord without doing what He commands (Luke 6:46; cf. Matt. 7:21–23). Abel, Enoch, Noah, Abraham, Isaac, Jacob, Joseph, and the others mentioned in Hebrews 11 believed God's promises and obeyed Him, even though they all died without fully realizing what they had been promised. Saving faith overcomes death, endures torture, outlasts chains and prisons, withstands temptations, suffers martyrdom, and survives hardship (vv. 32–38). It is by such faith that people gain salvation and approval from God (v. 39).

In this section of Luke's gospel, the Lord Jesus Christ gave His followers a crucial lesson about faith. Verse 41 reveals that the point the Lord wanted to make is that a twisted, distorted view of the Word of God produces unbelief. This passage may be examined under four headings: demon possession, disciple perversion, divine power, and dazzling person.

Demon Possession

On the next day, when they came down from the mountain, a large crowd met Him. And a man from the crowd shouted, saying, "Teacher, I beg You to look at my son, for he is my only boy, and a spirit seizes him, and he suddenly screams, and it throws him into a convulsion with foaming at the mouth; and only with difficulty does it leave him, mauling him as it leaves. (9:37–39)

All three synoptic gospels place this incident **on the next day** after the transfiguration (cf. Matt. 17:14–21; Mark 9:14–29). After that amazing, dramatic experience of the eternal kingdom and Christ's divine glory, Jesus, Peter, James, and John returned to the harsh reality of life in a fallen, evil world. The contrasts between the two incidents are striking. One happened on a mountain, the other in a valley. There was glory on the mountain, tragedy in the valley. On the mountain Jesus Christ displayed His glorious majesty, while in the valley Satan displayed his ugly, cruel violence. Two sons are in view, one God-possessed, the other demon-possessed; one in whom His Father was well pleased, the other whose father was tortured with displeasure over his condition. One Son fulfilled the glorious plan of the ages, confirmed by both Old Testament and New Testament saints; the other son was disassociated, disconnected, demented, and chaotic, without purpose or value to anyone. One Son was the destroyer of demons; the other son was destroyed by demons. Both sons were given back to their fathers. The demon-possessed son was delivered and returned to his father; the Son of God was killed, rose from the dead, and ascended back to His Father.

When they came down from the unnamed **mountain** somewhere near Capernaum, Jesus, Peter, James, and John encountered a tragic situation. As was always the case, **a large crowd** was waiting for Jesus—including some scribes, who were arguing with the nine disciples who had remained behind (Mark 9:14).

One of the people in the crowd was desperate. His problem was an all too common one; his son was cruelly possessed by a demon. Jesus encountered demon possession throughout His ministry, when the greatest manifestation of demonic activity up to that point in history took place. He unmasked, exposed, and terrified the demons, as they faced the one who will ultimately cast them into the lake of fire prepared for them (Matt. 25:41). In this incident Jesus displayed His power over fallen angels in the most severe manifestation of demon possession in the New Testament. (For more information on demon possession, see *Luke 1–5*, The MacArthur New Testament Commentary [Chicago: Moody, 2009], 279–88.)

Having worked his way with his son through the crowd that surged forward to meet Jesus (Mark 9:15), the man fell to his knees before Him. He **shouted** to the Lord to make himself heard above the din of the crowd. Matthew's account reveals that he addressed Him as Lord (Matt. 17:15), likely in reference to His deity. Acknowledging that Jesus had divine power over demons, he said to Him, **"Teacher, I beg You to look at my son, for he is my only boy, and a spirit seizes him."** Though the father said the boy was epileptic (cf. Matt. 17:15, NKJV, ESV), he understood that his son's condition was not physiological, but demonic. Matthew adds that the demon repeatedly attempted to destroy the boy by throwing him into the open fires and pools or wells of water that were common in Israel (Matt. 17:15; cf. Mark 9:22). Mark notes that the demon had made the boy deaf and mute (Mark 9:17, 25), and that it that it had afflicted him since he was a child (v. 21). How, why or at what age the child became demon possessed is not revealed, so it is futile to speculate. God ultimately permitted it to happen, as He did in the case of the man born blind (John 9:1–3), for His glory in demonstrating Christ's power. The boy's condition also illustrates the reality that everyone who is outside the kingdom of God is under the power of Satan (Eph. 2:2). It is only a question of degree.

That the boy's father addressed Jesus as "Lord" (Matt. 17:15) and **teacher** suggests that he had faith not only in the person of Christ, but also believed that His teaching was the truth of God. He begged the Lord **to look** (*epiblepō;* to look upon with concern, have regard for [Luke 1:48], or to "pay special attention to" [James 2:3]) **at** his **son.** Adding to the poignancy of the situation, his father told Jesus, **"He is my only boy."** Only Luke notes the detail that the boy was his father's only son (cf. 7:12; 8:38).

The father then described his son's terrifying symptoms: **he suddenly screams** (exhibiting the demon's control of his physical faculties; cf. 4:33; 8:30), **and it throws him into a convulsion** and slams him to the ground (Mark 9:18) **with foaming at the mouth; and only with difficulty does it leave him, mauling him as it leaves.** That the demon only left the boy **with difficulty** signifies the relentless, prolonged, non-stop nature of the attacks. **Mauling** translates a form of the verb *suntribō,* which means, "to crush," "to shatter," or "to break in pieces," signifying the violence of the demon's assaults on this unfortunate boy— violent, sustained demonic assaults not unlike the bizarre behavior of the men in Gadara (see the exposition of 8:26–39 in chapter 23 of this volume).

DISCIPLE PERVERSION

I begged Your disciples to cast it out, and they could not." And Jesus answered and said, "You unbelieving and perverted generation, how long shall I be with you and put up with you? Bring your son here." While he was still approaching, the demon slammed him to the ground and threw him into a convulsion. (9:40–42*a*)

Anyone living in Israel at the time of Jesus would have identified the Jewish leaders and followers as extremely religious. They zealously observed religious laws, duties, ceremonies, rites, rituals, celebrations, and festivals. They lived lives of fastidious external morality, observing the rules and standards of conduct their religious culture demanded.

Indeed, it would be hard to imagine any society more religious than Israel in the time of Christ. Further, they worshiped the God of the Old Testament; the God of Abraham, Isaac, and Jacob, the giver of the covenants.

All of this religious activity had convinced the Jewish people that when the Messiah came, He would be pleased with their self-righteous religious achievements. They assumed that He would oust the Romans, establish His kingdom and usher them into it as a reward for all that they had achieved. But when the Messiah, Jesus, arrived He indicted them for their self-righteous hypocrisy and bankrupt religious activities. He warned them that they were not part of God's kingdom (Matt. 8:12), but rather the riff raff of society, the tax collectors and prostitutes, stood a better chance of entering it than they did (Matt. 21:31). Needless to say, they were shocked and outraged. Infuriated by Christ's unmasking of their hypocrisy and denunciation of their religious system as a worthless abomination, the religious elite had long been conspiring against Him and eventually murdered Him.

It was perfectly reasonable for this man to have brought his demon-possessed son to the **disciples to cast it out.** They had recently concluded an extended preaching tour during which they had cast out demons by the authority Christ had granted them (Matt. 10:1; cf. v. 8; Mark 6:13). But surprisingly on this occasion **they could not** cast out the demon plaguing the boy. After the Lord cast it out, the bewildered apostles "came to Jesus privately and said, 'Why could we not drive it out?' And He said to them, 'Because of the littleness of your faith'" (Matt. 17:19–20). The apostles did not lack power, experience, or authority; they lacked the faith to deal with this exceptionally powerful demon. (Evidently demons vary in strength just as humans do. For example in Daniel 10:12–14, a holy angel sent with a message for Daniel was held up by a stronger fallen angel until Michael the archangel intervened.) Having discerned the strength of the demon inhabiting this boy, the apostles should have sought God's help in believing prayer (Mark 9:29). If they had done so with even a tiny amount of faith—"faith the size of a mustard seed" (Matt. 17:20)—they could have handled even extreme difficulties (symbolized by the Lord's metaphorical statement, "you will say to this mountain, 'Move from here to there,' and it will move"). The word had been spoken, the promise given, the will of God made manifest. All the apostles needed to have done was to believe and ask God for the power. Unfortunately, in this instance they did not.

The Lord's rebuke, **"You unbelieving and perverted generation, how long shall I be with you and put up with you?"** encompassed the entire nation of Israel, whom He denounced on other occasions as a generation of "vipers" (Matt. 12:34; cf. 23:33), an "evil and adulterous generation" (Matt. 12:39; 16:4), a "wicked generation" (Luke

11:29), and an "adulterous and sinful generation" (Mark 8:38). They were acting as if they were no different from their fathers, whom Moses characterized as "a perverse and crooked generation" (Deut. 32:5). Deficient in their knowledge of the true and living God, the people of Israel had become perverse, twisted, and faithless—the ultimate manifestation of which was their rejection and murder of His Son.

Sadly, the specific targets of the Lord's rebuke on this occasion appear to have been His own apostles. Though not lacking in saving faith like the unbelieving crowd, their faith too was **perverted** in that they consistently failed to believe what He told them. His exclamation, **"How long shall I be with you and put up with you?"** reflects the disappointment and pain that their constant failure to believe and trust in what He told them caused Jesus.

Christ stepped in to do what the apostles could have done had they believed Him. Turning to the boy's father, the Lord commanded him, **"Bring your son here."** The man was going to get what he so desperately wanted. The demon, however, was going to get what he definitely did not want. He was about to come face-to-face with his sovereign, God the Son, who had thrown him out of heaven (Rev. 12:7–9) and will one day cast him into the lake of fire (Rev. 20:10; cf. Matt. 25:41). In desperation, **while** the boy **was still approaching, the demon** made one last attempt to kill him. As the father and son approached Jesus, the demon **slammed him to the ground and threw him into a** violent **convulsion.**

At this point Mark notes that his father, looking on in helpless anguish, cried out to Jesus, "If You can do anything, take pity on us and help us!" (Mark 9:22). The Lord replied, "If You can? All things are possible to him who believes" (v. 23). Jesus did not usually call for faith in those He healed. In this case, however, He intended to use this man as an illustration for the apostles of what even imperfect faith in Him can accomplish. In brutal honesty "the boy's father cried out and said, 'I do believe; help my unbelief'" (v. 24). Desperately, he pleaded for Jesus to give him whatever was lacking in his faith.

DIVINE POWER

But Jesus rebuked the unclean spirit, and healed the boy and gave him back to his father. (9:42*b*)

Without fanfare, in simple, matter of fact language, Luke records the boy's deliverance. Noting that a curious crowd was gathering and seeking to spare father and son any further embarrassment, **Jesus**

rebuked the unclean spirit. Authoritatively the Lord said to him, "You deaf and mute spirit, I command you, come out of him and do not enter him again" (Mark 9:25). That triggered one final, violent paroxysm as the demon, "after crying out and throwing him into terrible convulsions, . . . came out; and the boy became so much like a corpse that most of them said, 'He is dead!'" (v. 26). He was alive, however, **and** Jesus, having **healed the boy . . . gave him back to his father.** Once again the Lord exhibited the love, compassion, mercy, and kindness in the heart of God for those who suffer.

DAZZLING PERSON

And they were all amazed at the greatness of God. But while everyone was marveling at all that He was doing, He said to His disciples, "Let these words sink into your ears; for the Son of Man is going to be delivered into the hands of men." But they did not understand this statement, and it was concealed from them so that they would not perceive it; and they were afraid to ask Him about this statement. (9:43–45)

Luke's note that **they were all amazed at the greatness of God** provides a fitting climax to this story. *Ekplessō* (**amazed**) has the connotation of being driven out of one's senses with amazement. The crowd was astonished at the incomprehensible **greatness,** majesty (the noun translated **greatness** here is translated "majesty" in 2 Peter 1:16), and power Jesus displayed. The majesty Peter, James, and John witnessed on the mountain during the transfiguration was displayed in the valley as Jesus vanquished the demon. These verses reveal three reasons why Jesus was amazing: because of His power, sacrifice, and sympathy.

JESUS' AMAZING POWER

But while everyone was marveling at all that He was doing, (9:43b)

The people were **marveling** not only at Christ's deliverance of a young boy from a powerful and obstinate demon, but also **at all that He was doing.** That phrase indicates that as was typical of His ministry, Jesus had been performing other miracles (cf. 6:17–19; 7:21; 9:11; Matt. 4:23; 8:16; Mark 1:32–34; 3:10). *Thaumazō* (**marveling**) means to be filled with wonder and astonishment at something outside the realm of human explanation. The absolute sovereign authority Christ displayed over disease, death, demons, nature, and sin was inexplicable apart from it being the power of God at work. All of that authority was demonstrated on a limited basis during His incarnation, confined to His presence in Israel. But after the resurrection and ascension, His unlimited authority over all the created universe was restored (Matt. 28:18).

JESUS' AMAZING SACRIFICE

He said to His disciples, "Let these words sink into your ears; for the Son of Man is going to be delivered into the hands of men." (9:43c–44)

Jesus' demonstration of His power and authority over even a very strong demon heightened the disciples' fervent messianic expectations. Having been taught all their lives that Messiah would be a political and military deliverer, they found it difficult to let go of those deeply embedded hopes. But as He repeatedly made clear to them, in His first coming Jesus did not come as conqueror and ruler, but as Savior and sacrifice for sin.

Wanting to make certain that they did not cultivate and nurture any false expectations, the Lord once again **said to His disciples, "Let these words sink into your ears."** He exhorted them to listen; pay attention and understand what He was about to tell them. The homage of the crowd was fickle; the praise being offered to Him in wonder and awe at the greatness of God was trivial and temporary. In about six months the people would turn on Him, reject Him, and demand that He be crucified. At that time **the Son of Man** would **be delivered into the hands of men.** The individual by whom He would **be delivered** was, of course, Judas. But the Jews also were culpable for delivering Jesus to death. In Acts 3:13 Peter said, "The God of Abraham, Isaac and Jacob, the God of our fathers, has glorified His servant Jesus, the one whom you delivered and disowned in the presence of Pilate." Pilate also is to blame, because it was ultimately he who, in violation of the proud tradition of Roman justice, gave in to the threats and demands of the Jews and delivered Jesus to be crucified (Matt. 27:26).

But ultimately, it was God Himself who delivered His Son to be killed: "The Lord was pleased to crush Him, putting Him to grief" (Isa. 53:10). In Romans 8:32 Paul wrote that God "did not spare His own Son, but delivered Him over for us all." It is not true, as some skeptics claim, that Jesus intended to bring in the kingdom, but His plans went awry and He was killed. The plan of God from the beginning was that Jesus would offer Himself as a sacrifice for sin. He was, as Peter said, "delivered over by the predetermined plan and foreknowledge of God ... [and] nailed to a cross by the hands of godless men" (Acts 2:23). Therefore it was absolutely necessary for the Lord to "go to Jerusalem, and suffer many things from the elders and chief priests and scribes, and be killed, and be raised up on the third day" (Matt. 16:21). Before the kingdom came the cross. Jesus had to die; the plan of God could not be set aside (cf. Matt. 26:24, 54; Luke 24:25–26, 46).

JESUS' AMAZING SYMPATHY

But they did not understand this statement, and it was concealed from them so that they would not perceive it; and they were afraid to ask Him about this statement. (9:45)

The Lord's prediction of His death was too much for the disciples to **understand** (cf. 18:31–34). As noted above, the concept of Messiah as a political ruler and military deliverer was deeply ingrained in their thinking. They did not understand what Jesus was saying because it did not fit that concept. In addition, the precise details of that disturbing and upsetting truth were **concealed from them so that they would not perceive** them. Jesus, the tender, compassionate High Priest, knew what they could handle, and withheld information that He knew would devastate them. Nor did the apostles push the issue, because **they were afraid to ask Him about this statement.**

This passage emphasizes the centrality of faith in the Christian life, underscoring the importance of believing that God will do exactly what He said He will do. Those who have a twisted, perverted view of His person and promises as revealed in the Bible cannot expect to receive anything from God; He will not bless and honor the doubt of double-minded, unstable people (James 1:5–8). But He will honor the prayer of faith that cries out at the throne of grace to have its spiritual needs met (Heb. 4:16). Paul wrote that because of such believing prayer, "God will supply all your needs according to His riches in glory in Christ Jesus" (Phil. 4:19).

The Mark of
True Greatness
(Luke 9:46–50)

31

An argument started among them as to which of them might be
the greatest. But Jesus, knowing what they were thinking in their
heart, took a child and stood him by His side, and said to them,
"Whoever receives this child in My name receives Me, and whoever receives Me receives Him who sent Me; for the one who is
least among all of you, this is the one who is great." John
answered and said, "Master, we saw someone casting out demons
in Your name; and we tried to prevent him because he does not
follow along with us." But Jesus said to him, "Do not hinder him;
for he who is not against you is for you." (9:46–50)

This section stands at a critical juncture in Luke's gospel, as it
records the close of the Lord's Galilean ministry. Beginning in 9:51 and
continuing through 19:27 Luke records His final journey to Jerusalem.
While traversing the towns and villages of Judea for those months leading up to His death, Jesus focused on more intensive training of the
Twelve. This passage is also a crucial part of their preparation for future
ministry.
The overarching theme of these two incidents is the importance
of humility, set against the backdrop of the disciples' blatant pride. The

first incident finds them arguing among themselves about which one was the greatest; in the second one John confessed that they had attempted to hinder the ministry of someone outside of their group.

Nothing comes more naturally to fallen human beings than pride, manifesting itself in self-centeredness, self-love, self-promotion, and self-fulfillment. Pride is the defining sin of fallen human nature, the soil in which all other sins sprout, take root, and grow. It is the damning sin that produced angelic rebellion against God and sought to topple Him from His throne as the sovereign ruler of the universe. It produced the sin of Eve and Adam, plunging the race into corruption. That pride has been reclassified as a virtue throughout history and in contemporary society only reveals the depths of human depravity. Isaiah wrote of such a wicked reversal of reality, "Woe to those who call evil good, and good evil; who substitute darkness for light and light for darkness; who substitute bitter for sweet and sweet for bitter!" (Isa. 5:20).

In contrast to the pride that marks fallen humanity, those who come to Christ for salvation are transformed and become characterized by self-hate, self-denial, and self-abasement (see the discussion of 9:23 in chapter 28 of this volume). Only when pride is divinely overpowered by the conviction of one's sinfulness and wretchedness can a person truly repent and come to saving faith.

The apostle Paul's spiritual biography illustrates that truth. His resume, from a human perspective, was impressive (Phil. 3:5–6). He had adhered to all the rites, rituals, and traditions of Judaism, starting with his being circumcised when he was eight days old. Paul was not only an Israelite, but also a member of the tribe of Benjamin, one of the most noble of the twelve tribes. The zeal for the law that made him a Pharisee also made Paul a persecutor of the church. In terms of the external righteousness of the law, he was a blameless "Hebrew of Hebrews" (v. 5; cf. Gal. 1:14).

But when he was confronted by Christ and convicted by the Holy Spirit, Paul's view of himself was reversed. Those things that had been in the plus column he now wrote off as losses. So strongly did he repudiate the achievements of which he had once been proud that he described them as rubbish, or manure (Phil. 3:8). When through the convicting work of the Spirit, Paul understood that he was actually condemned because he was living as a consistent violator of God's law, he was brought face-to-face with the condition and consequences of his spiritual bankruptcy. As he explained in Romans 7:9–11:

> I was once alive apart from the Law; but when the commandment came, sin became alive and I died; and this commandment, which was to result in life, proved to result in death for me; for sin, taking an opportunity through the commandment, deceived me and through it killed me.

Although pride is broken at conversion, when the repentant sinner approaches God with what the Old Testament calls a "broken and contrite heart" (Ps. 51:17; cf. Isa. 57:15; 66:2), it is by no means permanently defeated. Even after his salvation, Paul still struggled with the sins that flow from pride:

> For what I am doing, I do not understand; for I am not practicing what I would like to do, but I am doing the very thing I hate. But if I do the very thing I do not want to do, I agree with the Law, confessing that the Law is good. So now, no longer am I the one doing it, but sin which dwells in me. For I know that nothing good dwells in me, that is, in my flesh; for the willing is present in me, but the doing of the good is not. For the good that I want, I do not do, but I practice the very evil that I do not want. But if I am doing the very thing I do not want, I am no longer the one doing it, but sin which dwells in me. I find then the principle that evil is present in me, the one who wants to do good. For I joyfully concur with the law of God in the inner man, but I see a different law in the members of my body, waging war against the law of my mind and making me a prisoner of the law of sin which is in my members. Wretched man that I am! Who will set me free from the body of this death? (Rom. 7:15–24)

Sanctification is the progressive triumph of humility over pride in the power of the Holy Spirit (Rom. 8:1–14). That pride is not easily defeated is evident from the experience of the disciples. Even after the Lord confronted their pride on this occasion, it continued to surface even in the most shocking and unlikely of circumstances. At the Last Supper, just after the Lord had made His dramatic announcement that one of them would betray Him, the apostles "began to discuss among themselves which one of them it might be who was going to do this thing" (Luke 22:23). Incredibly, the discussion degenerated into "a dispute among them as to which one of them was regarded to be greatest" (v. 24)—the same selfish argument that prompted the Lord's teaching on this occasion.

It must be noted that sinners' humbling themselves in repentance is not a pre-salvation work by which they prepare their hearts for God to save them; the unaided human will has no capacity to be humble. Those who are spiritually dead (Eph. 2:1), blind (2 Cor. 4:4), and unable to understand spiritual truth (1 Cor. 2:14) are not able to debase themselves, repent, and bring themselves to saving faith and spiritual life. Only the Spirit of God, using the Word of God, can penetrate the stubborn, proud heart, humble it, and make it contrite and penitent.

Throughout the Bible God promises to bless the humble. He will strengthen them (Ps. 10:17), teach them (Ps. 25:9), save them (Ps. 76:9), give grace to them (Prov. 3:34; James 4:6), revive them (Isa. 57:15), give them the blessings of His kingdom (Matt. 5:3–5), and exalt them (Luke 14:11; 1 Peter 5:6). Humility is the ground that receives the refreshing rain of God's richest blessing; it is the soil in which all the other Christian virtues grow. Believers must strive with all their strength against remaining pride in dependency on the Holy Spirit to gain the humility that honors God and brings His blessing. The battle is relentless all through life, since pride is powerful and resistant in the heart.

There is no greater teacher of humility than the Lord Jesus Christ, who is "gentle and humble in heart" (Matt. 11:29). No one has ever been more exalted and no one has ever gone lower. Jesus,

> although He existed in the form of God, did not regard equality with God a thing to be grasped, but emptied Himself, taking the form of a bond-servant, and being made in the likeness of men. Being found in appearance as a man, He humbled Himself by becoming obedient to the point of death, even death on a cross. (Phil. 2:6–8)

The "Lord of glory" (1 Cor. 2:8) went from the glory of heaven to the shame of the cross. He is the example for believers to follow as they fight pride. Paul exhorted believers to do "nothing from selfishness or empty conceit, but with humility of mind regard one another as more important than [themselves and] not merely look out for [their] own personal interests, but also for the interests of others" (Phil. 2:3–4). By doing so they will have the same "attitude [of humility] in [themselves] which was also in Christ Jesus" (v. 5).

The disciples' quarrel over which of them was the greatest reflected the prevailing prideful attitude in their religious culture. That was particularly true of the leaders of Judaism, who exhibited their pride openly as a symbol of their spirituality by enlarging the tassels of their robes and their phylacteries (Matt. 23:5), and making a public spectacle of their fasting (Matt. 6:16), praying (Luke 20:47), and almsgiving (Matt. 6:2), as well as in their disdain for all the common people beneath them (Matt. 23:4). They knew nothing of humble servant leadership (Matt. 20:26–28).

The geographical setting for this lesson on humility was Capernaum (Mark 9:33). Located at the northern tip of the Sea of Galilee, Capernaum had been Jesus' headquarters during His Galilean ministry (Matt. 4:13). The incidents took place in a house (Mark 9:33), possibly Peter's (cf. Matt. 8:5, 14). Jesus used the apostles' proud quarrel and John's confession to clarify six characteristics of pride. Pride ruins unity, raises relativity, reveals depravity, rejects deity, reverses reality, and reacts with exclusivity.

PRIDE RUINS UNITY

An argument started among them (9:46*a*)

Jesus' warning of His impending suffering and death (9:44) and their need to be willing to suffer (9:23–26) had not sunk in with the apostles (9:45–46). They still were focused on the crown instead of the cross; on the glory, not the suffering. Still anticipating the imminent arrival of the kingdom, **an argument started among them** as to their place in it. Ironically, while Jesus spoke of His personal suffering, they argued about their personal glory.

This was a disturbing and potentially disastrous development. These men were the first generation of gospel preachers, and would be the leaders of the soon to be founded church. With so much riding on them and so much opposition from the hostile world, they needed to be unified and supportive of each other. The danger revealed here is that pride ruins unity by destroying relationships. Relationships are based on loving sacrifice and service; on selfless deferring to and giving to others. Pride, being self-focused, is indifferent to others. Beyond that, it is ultimately judgmental and critical, and therefore divisive. Because of that, pride is the most common destroyer both of relationships and churches. It plagued the Corinthian church, causing Paul to ask, "For since there is jealousy and strife among you, are you not fleshly, and are you not walking like mere men?" (1 Cor. 3:3; cf. 2 Cor. 12:20). Knowing that pride is the wedge Satan uses to split churches and splinter relationships, the Lord stressed to the disciples the crucial necessity of humility.

PRIDE RAISES RELATIVITY

as to which of them might be the greatest. (9:46*b*)

Pride results in thinking oneself superior and ranking others lower in an arbitrary fashion. The apostles were arguing about **which of them might be the greatest,** no doubt touting what they had accomplished during their recent preaching and healing tour (9:1–6). Such an obvious manifestation of carnal immaturity (cf. 1 Cor. 3:1–9) must have saddened Jesus. The apostles were like those of whom Paul wrote, "When they measure themselves by themselves and compare themselves with themselves, they are without understanding" (2 Cor. 10:12). Anything they had accomplished in their ministries was not because of their abilities, but solely through the power granted them by Jesus (9:1).

The endless sorting of people in petty fashion to make some feel superior to others, as the apostles were doing, merely pours gas on the fires of pride and burns through the fabric of unity.

PRIDE REVEALS DEPRAVITY

But Jesus, knowing what they were thinking in their heart, took a child and stood him by His side, (9:47)

As always, **Jesus** went beyond the outward manifestation of sinful behavior to the deeper issue. In His omniscience, the Lord knew **what they were thinking in their heart** (cf. 5:22; 7:39–40; John 2:25). The apostles' argument flowed from sinful hearts (the noun translated **thinking** is the same one translated "argument" in v. 46). The singular form of the noun translated **heart** indicates it is being used in a collective sense. They were all thinking the same evil thoughts.

The depraved heart (Jer. 17:9; Rom. 2:5) is the source of all the defiling speech that flows out of the mouth, since the "mouth speaks from that which fills [the] heart" (Luke 6:45). In Mark 7:14–15 Jesus, "after He called the crowd to Him again … began saying to them, 'Listen to Me, all of you, and understand: there is nothing outside the man which can defile him if it goes into him; but the things which proceed out of the man are what defile the man.'"

Mark notes that at this point Jesus confronted the apostles by asking them about what He already knew in His omniscience had happened. He said to them, "What were you discussing on the way?" (Mark 9:33). Embarrassed, "they kept silent, for on the way they had discussed with one another which of them was the greatest" (v. 34). According to Matthew's account of this incident, the disciples, apparently committed to the nobility of their debate, asked Jesus to settle their dispute and declare which of them was the "greatest in the kingdom of heaven" (Matt. 18:1). To illustrate the inappropriateness of their ridiculous hassling and to overturn their legitimizing of pride, Jesus **took a child** (perhaps one of Peter's children) **and stood him by His side.** The Lord chose a child to illustrate humility because children were the lowliest in society. Darrell L. Bock writes, "In Judaism, children under twelve could not be taught the Torah, and so to spend time with them was considered a waste" (*Luke 1:1–9:50* (Grand Rapids: Baker, 1998), 894–95).

Having taken up the child in His arms (Mark 9:36), Jesus said, "Truly I say to you, unless you are converted and become like children, you will not enter the kingdom of heaven. Whoever then humbles himself as this child, he is the greatest in the kingdom of heaven" (Matt. 18:3–4). Instead of touting their supposed achievements, the apostles (like all who would enter the kingdom) needed to humble themselves and acknowledge that they had no rank and no achievements that merited entrance into or elevation in God's kingdom; that they could contribute nothing to their salvation. Since all who enter the kingdom are considered the greatest in it, there is no spiritual ranking; greatness in the kingdom is absolute, not relative (cf. Luke 18:15–17). Jesus used the most insignificant of all to teach what it really is to be the greatest of all.

PRIDE REJECTS DEITY

"Whoever receives this child in My name receives Me, and whoever receives Me receives Him who sent Me; (9:48*a*)

Jesus' next statement indicates the severest consequence of pride: **Whoever receives this child,** symbolic of believers, **in My name receives Me.** The Lord spoke here of His union with those who are His. Paul expressed that principle when he wrote that "the one who joins himself to the Lord is one spirit with Him" (1 Cor. 6:17). Therefore those who reject believers are also rejecting Jesus (cf. Matt. 25:41–45; Acts 9:4–5). Further, since **whoever receives** Jesus **receives** the Father **who sent** Him, those who reject other Christians are not only rejecting Jesus, but the Father as well (cf. John 5:23). So strongly does Jesus identify with believers that He declared that those who lure them into sin are deserving of the most horrifying death imaginable: "Whoever causes one of these little ones who believe in Me to stumble, it would be better for him to have a heavy millstone hung around his neck, and to be drowned in the depth of the sea" (Matt. 18:6). As the Lord solemnly warned, "See that you do not despise one of these little ones, for I say to you that their angels in heaven continually see the face of My Father who is in heaven" (v. 10). How believers treat each other is how they treat the Son and the Father. To demean or show disdain toward one of the Lord's own is to seriously dishonor Him.

PRIDE REVERSES REALITY

for the one who is least among all of you, this is the one who is great." (9:48*b*)

Pride drives people to exalt themselves, push their agendas, fulfill their ambitions, and receive praise from others. But how fallen minds think is the reverse of spiritual reality since, as Jesus told the apostles, **the** one who is least among all of you, this is the one who is great (cf. Matt. 23:11–12). Spiritual wisdom, which equates greatness with humility, is counterintuitive; it is the opposite of the way the world, both secular and religious, thinks. The truly great in the heavenly kingdom are not those who claw their way to the top and seek for people to give them honor, but those who humbly defer to others, considering them more important than themselves and looking out for their interests (Phil. 2:3–4). It is the humble, not the proud, that God will exalt (1:52; 14:11; 18:14; Matt. 23:5–12; James 4:10; 1 Peter 5:6).

PRIDE REACTS WITH EXCLUSIVITY

John answered and said, "Master, we saw someone casting out demons in Your name; and we tried to prevent him because he does not follow along with us." But Jesus said to him, "Do not hinder him; for he who is not against you is for you." (9:49–50)

This second incident reveals that **John** at least was beginning to understand the Lord's message. In light of Jesus' warning in verse 48 John wondered whether the apostles had acted properly in an earlier incident, and feeling some guilt decided to ask Jesus about it. **"Master,** he said, **"we saw someone casting out demons in Your name; and we tried to prevent him because he does not follow along with us."** Since this incident is not recorded in the Gospels, the identity of this man is not known. That he was not a phony exorcist like the sons of Sceva (Acts 19:13–14) is clear, since he was successfully **casting out demons in** Christ's **name;** that is, consistent with His authority and power. It was not an empty claim such as that in Matthew 7:21–23:

> Not everyone who says to Me, "Lord, Lord," will enter the kingdom of heaven, but he who does the will of My Father who is in heaven will enter. Many will say to Me on that day, "Lord, Lord, did we not prophesy in Your name, and in Your name cast out demons, and in Your name perform many miracles?" And then I will declare to them, "I never knew you; depart from Me, you who practice lawlessness."

Whoever he was, the apostles, pridefully jealous of their exclusive position, **tried to prevent him** from carrying on his ministry **because he** did **not follow along with** them. In other words, he was not one of their group. Why Jesus permitted him to do what he did is also not clear. It may be that he would later be included as one of the seventy, who would have such power (Luke 10:17). In any case, he provided another object lesson for Jesus to use to teach the disciples humility.

Jesus confirmed John's doubt about how they had handled the situation, and **said to him, "Do not hinder him."** The Lord removed any doubt that this man was a genuine disciple, since He would never have forbidden the apostles to rebuke a false teacher.

Pride promotes exclusivity, but humility promotes unity. We cannot embrace those who claim to be Christ's but do not preach the truth of Christ. However we must embrace all who both name the name of Christ and also speak His truth, whatever organization they belong to. Christians must have the attitude of Paul, who rejoiced when the truth was proclaimed—even when those preaching it were cruelly hostile to him (Phil. 1:15–18).

Jesus closed this section with the axiomatic statement, **"He who is not against you is for you."** There is no middle ground between truth and error; between sound doctrine and heresy. Every person is either for Christ, or against Him. Later in Luke's gospel, the Lord repeated this saying, this time relating it directly to Himself: "He who is not with Me is against Me; and he who does not gather with Me, scatters" (11:23). Only those who teach the truth can be embraced as fellow servants of the Lord Jesus Christ.

Pride is not a virtue, but the source of all sin. It must not be excused or justified, nor can its heinousness be downplayed. The sobering truth is that "everyone who is proud in heart is an abomination to the Lord; assuredly, he will not be unpunished" (Prov. 16:5), since "a proud heart ... is sin" (Prov. 21:4). But the blessed promise is that although "God is opposed to the proud, [He] gives grace to the humble" (James 4:6).

A Mission of Mercy (Luke 9:51–56)

32

When the days were approaching for His ascension, He was determined to go to Jerusalem; and He sent messengers on ahead of Him, and they went and entered a village of the Samaritans to make arrangements for Him. But they did not receive Him, because He was traveling toward Jerusalem. When His disciples James and John saw this, they said, "Lord, do You want us to command fire to come down from heaven and consume them?" But He turned and rebuked them, and said, "You do not know what kind of spirit you are of; for the Son of Man did not come to destroy men's lives, but to save them." And they went on to another village. (9:51–56)

Mercy is a word filled with loveliness. To say that someone is merciful is to pay them the highest of compliments; it is to characterize them as loving, compassionate, tender, forgiving, selfless, caring, and protective. In contrast merciless people are vicious, vengeful, deadly, destructive, hate others, and wish them only evil.

Both the Old Testament and the New Testament extol the value of mercy. Proverbs 3:3 ranks mercy with truth—which God has magnified according to His name (cf. Ps. 138:2). While divine truth is of supreme value, it must be balanced with mercy. God is truth (Ps. 31:5; Isa. 65:16), but He exalts mercy to the degree that truth is exalted. If that were not true, His truth would instantaneously crush sinners. Reflecting God's mercy, believers are charged to speak the truth, not harshly or impatiently, but in love (Eph. 4:15). Scripture also emphasizes the importance of mercy by linking it with justice (Hos. 12:6 NKJV; Zech. 7:9 NKJV).

Mercy is also beneficial. Solomon noted that "the merciful man does himself good, but the cruel man does himself harm" (Prov. 11:17). David expressed that same principle when he wrote, "How blessed is he who considers the helpless; the Lord will deliver him in a day of trouble" (Ps. 41:1). Daniel counseled King Nebuchadnezzar, "Break away now from your sins by doing righteousness and from your iniquities by showing mercy to the poor, in case there may be a prolonging of your prosperity" (Dan. 4:27). In the Beatitudes Jesus said, "Blessed are the merciful, for they shall receive mercy" (Matt. 5:7).

To show mercy is to imitate God (cf. Eph. 5:1), who is merciful. David called Him "a God merciful and gracious" (Ps. 86:15). Zechariah, the father of John the Baptist, spoke of "the tender mercy of our God" (Luke 1:78). Paul described God as "the Father of mercies" (2 Cor. 1:3), who is "rich in mercy" (Eph. 2:4), while the writer of Hebrews described the Lord Jesus Christ as "a merciful and faithful high priest" (Heb. 2:17).

Christians are commanded to show mercy. In Luke 6:36 Jesus instructed believers, "Be merciful, just as your Father is merciful," while James cautioned that those who fail to show mercy will face God's judgment, since "judgment will be merciless to one who has shown no mercy; mercy triumphs over judgment" (James 2:13).

Mercy may be defined as unconditional love reaching out to meet a person's need without thought of whether he or she deserves it. It is compassionate kindness that does good to people simply because they are in need. Mercy is activated by the suffering of others, and grants them loving-kindness because of their desperate condition. The supreme New Testament illustration of mercy is the story of the prodigal son. After squandering his inheritance by his profligate, sinful living, he was forgiven and welcomed home by his merciful father and extended mercy to relieve his terrible condition. In an Old Testament illustration of mercy, 2 Kings 6:11–23 recounts the story of some Aramean soldiers whom Elisha struck with blindness and led captive into the city of Samaria. The king of Israel wanted to execute them, but instead Elisha commanded him to prepare a feast for the soldiers and then set them free (vv. 22–23). In a world where vengeance is considered a virtue, the people of God must be characterized by mercy.

This passage records the first incident on the Lord's lengthy journey to Jerusalem (see the discussion below). Jesus seized the opportunity provided by a Samaritan village's rejection of Him to teach His disciples a riveting and unforgettable lesson on mercy. It is the perfect follow-up to the lesson on humility He had taught them in the previous section (see the discussion of 9:46–50 in chapter 31 of this volume), since only the humble are merciful. Though this is a brief narrative account that never mentions the word mercy, it is implicit in our Lord's attitude that He has come to extend this priceless treasure to those in desperate need, but do not deserve it. As Jesus heads toward Jerusalem, it is to provide mercy by His death; as He enters a Samaritan village, it is also to extend mercy.

MERCY MADE AVAILABLE

When the days were approaching for His ascension, He was determined to go to Jerusalem; (9:51)

The phrase **when the days** signifies that an indefinite period of time had passed since the incident recorded in 9:46–50. However this incident probably did not take place too long afterward. It marks a major turning point in Luke's narrative of Christ's life and ministry. Up to this point, Luke has focused on Jesus' coming, detailing the angelic announcement of His birth to Mary, the account of His birth, the incident in the temple when He was twelve, His baptism by John, His temptation by Satan, and the first two and a half years of His ministry as Messiah, reaching its pinnacle at the transfiguration.

But at this point, the whole tenor of Luke's gospel changes. The focus is no longer on Jesus' coming, but on His going. The Galilean ministry is over, and He is on His way for the final time to His passion in Jerusalem. Although the Lord would, in the few intervening months of His Judean ministry, make brief return visits to Galilee (e.g., 17:11–37), Galilee was no longer His base of operations. Much of the material in this travelogue (cf. vv. 52, 57; 10:1, 38; 13:22, 33; 17:11; 18:35; 19:1, 11, 28–29) of Christ's final journey to the cross (9:51–19:27) is unique to Luke's gospel. Of the other gospel writers, only John records features from the months in Judea (John 7–11).

Immediately after the revelation of His glory and majesty at the transfiguration, the Lord warned His disciples, "Let these words sink into your ears; for the Son of Man is going to be delivered into the hands of men" (9:44). From the exaltation of the transfiguration, Jesus took the Twelve through the valley of humiliation that culminated in His death. Although Jerusalem was only a couple of days' walk from Galilee, Jesus did not go directly there. But although He took months to traverse the region of Judea with a final stop in Perea (Luke 18; cf. Matt. 19–20; Mark 10), all the while He was inexorably focused on arriving in Jerusalem at Passover—the appointed time for the Lamb of God's sacrificial death. Along the way, Christ's primary focus was not on the crowds, but on training the first generation of gospel preachers, the apostles whom He had chosen to carry on His ministry after He departed for heaven.

Sumplēroō (**approaching**) literally means, "to be fulfilled," or "completed." God's plan of redemption was to be fulfilled by Christ's going to Jerusalem to die as a sacrifice for sin, and He always operated on a divinely prewritten timetable (cf. Luke 13:31–33; John 7:8, 30; 8:20). In Gethsemane Jesus rebuked Peter for his valiant but wrongheaded attempt to prevent His arrest, asking him, "How then will the Scriptures be fulfilled, which say that it must happen this way?" (Matt. 26:54; cf. v. 56; Luke 22:37). On the road to Emmaus after His resurrection, Jesus reminded two of His disciples, "All things which are written about Me in the Law of Moses and the Prophets and the Psalms must be fulfilled" (Luke 24:44). Peter declared to the Jewish people that "the things which God announced beforehand by the mouth of all the prophets, that His Christ would suffer, He has thus fulfilled" (Acts 3:18), while Paul told the Gentiles in Pisidian Antioch, "Those who live in Jerusalem, and their rulers, recognizing neither [Jesus] nor the utterances of the prophets which are read every Sabbath, fulfilled these by condemning Him" (Acts 13:27).

Some limit **ascension** (lit., "lifting up") to Jesus' death on the cross, connecting this passage with His declaration, "As Moses lifted up the serpent in the wilderness, even so must the Son of Man be lifted up" (John 3:14; cf. 8:28; 12:32). But while the noun *analēmpsis* (**ascension**) appears only here in the New Testament, the related verb *analambanō* is used of Christ's ascension in Acts 1:2, 11, 22, and 1 Timothy 3:16. It seems that Luke's use of the term here encompasses the entire sequence of events from the cross, through the resurrection, to the actual ascension into glory (Acts 1:9–11).

Sterizō (**determined**) describes something that is fixed, immovable, or firmly established. It expresses Christ's unshakable, unwavering resolve **to go to Jerusalem** and endure the shame of the cross with its suffering, rejection, and bearing of God's wrath against sin. In the words of the writer of Hebrews, Jesus "for the joy set before Him endured the cross, despising the shame, and has sat down at the right hand of the throne of God" (Heb. 12:2; cf. Phil. 2:9–11).

The heart of the Lord Jesus Christ's mission was mercy, which Jude described as "the mercy of our Lord Jesus Christ to eternal life" (Jude 21). He was on a mission of mercy to Jerusalem to die as the only way undeserving sinners could receive divine mercy to redeem them from sin and eternal hell.

MERCY EXTENDED TO ALL

and He sent messengers on ahead of Him, and they went and entered a village of the Samaritans to make arrangements for Him. But they did not receive Him, because He was traveling toward Jerusalem. When His disciples James and John saw this, they said, "Lord, do You want us to command fire to come down from heaven and consume them?" But He turned and rebuked them, and said, "You do not know what kind of spirit you are of; for the Son of Man did not come to destroy men's lives, but to save them." And they went on to another village. (9:52–56)

In contrast to Matthew, whose focus is primarily on Jesus' ministry to the Jewish people, Luke is much more expansive. He described the universal scope of redemption and emphasized that salvation was available to everyone, not just the Jews, but also the Gentiles (cf. Acts 10:34–48; 14:24–27; 15:12–19). He himself was a Gentile, and he wrote to Theophilus, (1:3), who was also a Gentile. Not only did Luke view the gospel as being for all ethnic groups, including Jews, Samaritans, and Gentiles, but also for all types of people within those groups, including women (even prostitutes), outcasts (including lepers), those possessed by demons, even despised tax collectors (cf. 7:36–50; 10:25–37; 15:11–32; 16:19–31; 8:2, 27–38; 17:11–19; 19:1–10). Luke's emphasis on the gospel's universal appeal is also evident in his genealogy of Jesus. Matthew began his genealogy with Abraham, the father of the Jewish people, but Luke traced Christ's genealogy all the way back to Adam, the father of the entire human race.

Jesus needed to teach His disciples the inclusive character of the gospel of mercy, and the first incident on their journey to Jerusalem provided such a teaching opportunity. Surprisingly, the Lord chose to travel through Samaria, which most Jews took great pains to avoid doing. Jews traveling from Galilee to Judea would cross to the east side of the Jordan River, travel south through Perea, and then recross the river at Jericho and go up into Judea. Those who did travel through Samaria carried their own food so as not to have to eat food defiled by the unclean and despised Samaritans.

The animosity between the Jews and the Samaritans dated back several centuries before the time of Christ. After the northern kingdom (Israel) was defeated by the Assyrians, the ten northern tribes of

> Israel [were] carried away into exile from their own land to Assyria . . . [and] the king of Assyria brought men from Babylon and from Cuthah and from Avva and from Hamath and Sephar-vaim, and settled them in the cities of Samaria in place of the sons of Israel. So they possessed Samaria and lived in its cities. (2 Kings 17:23–24).

Those Gentile foreigners intermarried with the Jews who had not been deported, forming a mixed race known as the Samaritans (the name derives from the region and capital city of the northern part of the divided kingdom, both called Samaria). The new arrivals brought their idolatrous false religion with them (2 Kings 17:29–31), which became mixed with the worship of the true God (vv. 25–28, 32–33; 41). Eventually the Samaritans abandoned their idols and worshiped Yahweh alone, after their own convoluted fashion (for example, they accepted only the Pentateuch as canonical Scripture, and worshiped God on Mt. Gerizim, not at Jerusalem). This is the background of our Lord's encounter with the Samaritan woman, recorded in John 4:7–42.

When the Jewish exiles returned to Jerusalem under Ezra and Nehemiah, their first priority was to rebuild the temple. Claiming to be loyal to Israel's God, the Samaritans offered to help (Ezra 4:1–2). But the Jews bluntly rejected their offer (Ezra 4:3), which enraged the Samaritans, who then became their bitter enemies (Ezra 4:4ff.; Neh. 4:1–3, 7ff.). Barred from worshiping at Jerusalem, the Samaritans built their own temple on Mt. Gerizim (c. 400 B.C.). The Jews later destroyed that temple during the intertestamental period, which further worsened relations between the two groups.

Centuries of mistrust produced a deep animosity between the Jews and the Samaritans. The writer of the apocryphal book of Ecclesiasticus expressed the scorn and contempt the Jews felt for the Samaritans when he derisively referred to them as "the stupid people living at Shechem" (50:25–26). The Jewish leaders of Jesus' day exhibited that same prejudice. The worst insult they could think of to hurl at Jesus was to call Him a Samaritan (John 8:48). The Samaritans, of course, reciprocated the Jews' hostility, as in this encounter.

But the Lord's mission of saving mercy transcended all racial and cultural boundaries. He was willing to go to where the hate-filled Jewish religious leaders would kill Him, and to go to a Samaritan town that those same leaders would never dream of going to. Therefore **He sent messengers on ahead of Him, and they went and entered a village of the Samaritans to make arrangements** for food and lodging **for Him** and those who accompanied Him. The Lord Jesus Christ was mercy incarnate, reaching out even to people despised by His fellow Jews to offer the hope of salvation.

Not surprisingly, the Samaritan village **did not receive** Jesus. But that rejection was not of Him personally; they knew nothing of His miraculous power and divine teaching. They did not even reject Him solely because He was Jewish. Instead, the Samaritans rejected Jesus **because He was traveling toward Jerusalem** to worship at the temple. As noted above, the Maccabean ruler John Hyrcanus had destroyed the

Samaritan temple on Mt. Gerizim during the intertestamental period, and it had never been rebuilt. The Samaritans, clinging to their own religious system despite the lack of a temple, refused to recognize the Jerusalem temple as a proper place of worship. Thus, they rejected all who worshiped there.

Incensed at this blatant insult to their Master, **when His disciples James and John saw this, they said, "Lord, do You want us to command fire to come down from heaven and consume them?"** The two brothers, to whom Jesus "gave the name Boanerges, which means, 'Sons of Thunder'" (Mark 3:17) because of their volatile nature, wanted to incinerate the Samaritan village. What prompted them to propose that method of destruction is that Elijah had done something similar in that very region. King Ahaziah of the northern kingdom of Israel sent a company of fifty men to arrest him. However Elijah called down fire from heaven, which consumed them. A second company of fifty met the same fate. Finally, the commander of the third company begged Elijah to spare his life and the lives of his men. The prophet went with him to the king, upon whom he pronounced God's judgment (2 Kings 1:9–16). James and John wanted to do the same to this insolent village.

Jesus, however, **turned and rebuked them** for their merciless attitude. To want to destroy those who reject the truth is not gospel ministry. The words **and said, "You do not know what kind of spirit you are of; for the Son of Man did not come to destroy men's lives, but to save them"** are not in the oldest manuscripts, indicating that somewhere in later history a scribe wanted to clarify the rebuke and borrowed from other texts. Nonetheless, the principle that Jesus came to save the lost is clearly taught in those borrowed passages (Luke 19:10; John 12:47).

Unlike His overly zealous disciples, the Lord Jesus Christ grants mercy to hostile, ignorant sinners, like the apostle Paul had been before his conversion (1 Tim. 1:13). As noted above, the Samaritans did not know who Jesus was or what He taught. They rejected Him not because He claimed to be Lord, Savior, and Messiah, but merely because He was a Jew traveling to the temple at Jerusalem. Mercy was the right response there, and judgment gives way to mercy on those who cease their hostility toward the truth. But when that hostility is continually fixed and persistent, mercy is withdrawn. For example, when He sent them out to preach the gospel, Jesus commanded the seventy,

> But whatever city you enter and they do not receive you, go out into its streets and say, "Even the dust of your city which clings to our feet we wipe off in protest against you; yet be sure of this, that the kingdom of God has come near." I say to you, it will be more tolerable in that day for Sodom than for that city. (Luke 10:10–12)

Then He Himself pronounced judgment on hard-hearted rejecters of the truth:

> Woe to you, Chorazin! Woe to you, Bethsaida! For if the miracles had been performed in Tyre and Sidon which occurred in you, they would have repented long ago, sitting in sackcloth and ashes. But it will be more tolerable for Tyre and Sidon in the judgment than for you. And you, Capernaum, will not be exalted to heaven, will you? You will be brought down to Hades! (vv. 13–15)

But this was not the time of judgment for this village, so Jesus and those traveling with Him merely left and **went on to another village.** Because the Lord in His mercy spared them, perhaps some of these villagers later repented at the preaching of Philip the evangelist (Acts 8:6–8) and Peter and John (v. 25) and were saved.

Although it must never compromise the truth or tolerate sin, the church must show the same mercy to the lost as Jesus did. Whenever those claiming to represent Jesus Christ have wielded the right to pronounce temporal judgment, the results have been disastrous. The Inquisition, the Crusades, the execution of those thought to be witches, and the persecution of the Anabaptists by Reformed Protestants and Catholics alike have been a blight on the name of Jesus Christ. The church must confront sin and call for repentance, but leave the final judgment to God (that is the point of the parable of the wheat and the tares [Matt. 13:24–30] and the indictment of Jesus on the Jewish leaders [Matt. 7:1–3]). Mercy is at the heart of redemptive ministry, and is to be extended to all without regard to race, gender, age, or cultural background. The God who delights in mercy (Mic. 7:18 NKJV) delights in merciful Christians (cf. 2 Cor. 4:1).

Barriers to True Discipleship (Luke 9:57–62)

33

As they were going along the road, someone said to Him, "I will follow You wherever You go." And Jesus said to him, "The foxes have holes and the birds of the air have nests, but the Son of Man has nowhere to lay His head." And He said to another, "Follow Me." But he said, "Lord, permit me first to go and bury my father." But He said to him, "Allow the dead to bury their own dead; but as for you, go and proclaim everywhere the kingdom of God." Another also said, "I will follow You, Lord; but first permit me to say good-bye to those at home." But Jesus said to him, "No one, after putting his hand to the plow and looking back, is fit for the kingdom of God." (9:57–62)

During His earthly ministry, the Lord Jesus Christ repeatedly called people who were attracted to Him to follow Him permanently as Messiah and Lord. Some singularly responded to His call and became His true disciples; others rejected it when His demands were stringent and left Him (John 6:60–66). Whenever Jesus called people, such as Matthew (Matt. 9:9; Mark 2:14; Luke 5:27), Philip (John 1:43), Peter (John 21:19, 22), as well as the rest of those who became His disciples (Matt. 16:24; Mark 8:34; Luke 9:23; John 12:26), He used the same word, *akoutheō* ("to follow," "to accompany," "to be a disciple"). He always employed that verb in the present imperative tense, to indicate He was not seeking a momentary following, but a continuous, lifelong commitment.

The Lord's approach is very different from contemporary evangelism, which views becoming a Christian as an emotional and even impulsive decision; a feeling-induced act to which people are led by fiery preaching, heartrending stories, and emotion-stirring music. The goal of contemporary evangelistic methodology is to induce people to seize the moment, pray a prayer, and make a decision to accept Christ. But Jesus never tried to move people emotionally into a moment of crisis in which they would accept Him. There is no record in the New Testament of Jesus or the apostles counseling someone to make such a momentary choice, or pray a prayer in order to be saved. When the Lord invited a person to receive forgiveness and salvation by faith in Him, He did not want the emotion of a moment's feeling of guilt, fear, or desire for a better life, but a carefully thought out (cf. Luke 14:28–33) lifetime commitment to Himself as Lord. To Jesus, and the apostles as well, following Christ salvifically was not an event, but a way of life. Martin Luther captured the essence of that principle in the very first of his famed Ninety-five Theses: "When our Lord and Master, Jesus Christ, said 'Repent,' He called for the entire life of believers to be one of penitence" (cited in John Dillenberger, *Martin Luther, Selections from His Writings* [Garden City, N.Y.: Anchor, 1961], 490).

In keeping with that principle, Jesus often made things extremely difficult for superficial followers. In His conversations, He would deliberately put up barriers between them and salvation. Like those in John 6, many exposed as uncommitted false disciples "withdrew and were not walking with Him anymore" (John 6:66). In the present text, Jesus confronted three would-be disciples. In each case He put up an insurmountable barrier that uncovered their lack of genuine faith and insincere commitment to Him. And in each case, the demands drove them away.

The setting of this account is not clear; Luke merely places it on a road along which Jesus and those accompanying Him were traveling. Matthew, however, places the Lord's conversations with the first two individuals near Capernaum, as He was getting ready to cross the Sea of Galilee to Gadara (Matt. 8:18–22). Luke may have included the incident here because it fit thematically into the Lord's training of the Twelve, which is a major theme of His journey to Jerusalem. In 9:46–50 Jesus gave them a lesson in humility; in verses 51–56 He gave them a lesson on mercy; in this section He gave them a lesson on the cost of discipleship. As has been noted in previous chapters of this volume, it is not unusual for Luke to arrange his material topically rather than chronologically.

As always, the crowd accompanying Jesus ranged across the

spectrum from genuine disciples who, by the Holy Spirit had repented of their sins and affirmed Jesus as the Son of God and Messiah, to the other extreme, those who hated Him and sought to kill Him. In the middle were the rest, who were at varying levels of non-committal interest. Matthew's reference to the second individual as "another of the disciples" (Matt. 8:21) places him in that large group. But as this incident makes clear, he and the other two individuals did not demonstrate saving faith. They sought not forgiveness and salvation, but self-fulfillment as they looked for the things they desired. When Jesus confronted them with what is required of those who truly follow Him as Lord—self-denial, self-sacrifice, and submission to His authority—that was not acceptable to them.

The passage illustrates three things that hinder people from following Jesus: desire for personal comfort, desire for personal riches, and desire for personal relations.

DESIRE FOR PERSONAL COMFORT

As they were going along the road, someone said to Him, "I will follow You wherever You go." And Jesus said to him, "The foxes have holes and the birds of the air have nests, but the Son of Man has nowhere to lay His head." (9:57–58)

Somewhere in the vicinity of Capernaum **as they were going along the road, someone said to Him, "I will follow You wherever You go."** Matthew identifies this man as a scribe (Matt. 8:19). Scribes were highly esteemed experts in the Mosaic and rabbinic law, which they interpreted authoritatively for the common people. Scribes were qualified and authorized by the Jewish religious leaders, and were hostile to Jesus (Matt. 9:3; 12:38–42; 15:1–2; 16:21; 20:18; 21:15–16; 23:1–36; 26:57; 27:41; Mark 2:6–7, 16; 3:22; 12:38; 14:1, 43; Luke 6:7; 15:2; 20:19; 23:10).

Given that hostility was so common among them, it is surprising that this scribe approached Jesus and said to Him, **"I will follow You wherever You go."** Having no doubt witnessed the miracles recorded in Matthew 8:5–18, he was attracted to Jesus and eager to attach himself to such an unparalleled teacher. Traveling rabbis frequently had groups of students that accompanied them and learned from them. This scribe acknowledged Jesus as his rabbi and wanted to join His entourage. According to Matthew's account, he addressed Jesus as "Teacher," thus offering himself as a willing pupil of the miracle worker from Nazareth. Moreover, his willingness to follow Jesus wherever He went suggests that there was the notion of long-term loyalty in his decision. And even though he knew that Jesus condemned the narrow legalism of the scribes, He was nonetheless the most impressive teacher this scribe had ever met and was thus worthy of his devotion.

Seemingly a prize convert, this respected scholar would appear to be a welcome defector from a group that was openly hostile to Christ. To have a converted scribe as a follower would seem to have been quite a coup for Jesus. But as He does with all men (John 2:23–25), Jesus saw beneath the outer veneer of enthusiasm to his heart and refused to embrace his eager offer. The Lord knew that the scribe, having seen the crowds and the miracles and having heard Jesus' incomparable teaching, wanted to be associated with the one in the center of all the action, who had an unequalled potential future of elevation.

Jesus shattered the man's ambitious expectations with His surprising response, **"The foxes have holes and the birds of the air have nests, but the Son of Man has nowhere to lay His head,"** which must have been puzzling to the scribe. The Lord saw through his professed commitment driven by his desire for comfort and confronted him with reality. Even the foxes that were common in Israel (cf. Judg. 15:4–5; Ps. 63:10; Song 2:15; Lam. 5:18; Ezek. 13:4) had **holes** to sleep in, while the ubiquitous **birds of the air** had **nests.** But **the Son of Man** (Jesus' favorite title for Himself), the Messiah, God incarnate, had **nowhere to lay His head.** The Creator had fewer creature comforts than the animals He had created.

The Lord raised this issue because He knew that self-denial was a barrier for this man. He viewed following Jesus in terms of what he would gain rather than the reception of forgiveness of sins at any cost. He lacked the desperation from fear of judgment that characterizes the penitent poor in spirit (Matt. 5:3) who hunger and thirst for righteousness (v. 6); who, in fear of divine punishment, want grace, forgiveness, and eternal life so badly that they put no conditions on it—even the kind of rejection Jesus experienced.

In the previous passage, Jesus had been denied lodging by a Samaritan village (9:51–53). Even though He had cast the demons out of a maniac who had terrorized their region, "all the people of the country of the Gerasenes and the surrounding district asked Him to leave them, for they were gripped with great fear" (Luke 8:37). The people of His hometown of Nazareth "drove Him out of the city, and led Him to the brow of the hill on which their city had been built, in order to throw Him down the cliff" (Luke 4:29). Capernaum, where He settled after leaving Nazareth (Matt. 4:13), also rejected Christ, causing Him to declare, "And you, Capernaum, will not be exalted to heaven, will you? You will be brought down to Hades!" (Luke 10:15). Eventually the nation as a whole would reject Jesus and the crowds would scream, "Crucify Him!" (Matt. 27:22) and, "His blood shall be on us and on our children!" (v. 25).

His followers could expect no better. When He sent the Twelve out to preach the gospel, Jesus warned them of the hostility and opposition they would face:

> Behold, I send you out as sheep in the midst of wolves; so be shrewd as serpents and innocent as doves. But beware of men, for they will hand you over to the courts and scourge you in their synagogues; and you will even be brought before governors and kings for My sake, as a testimony to them and to the Gentiles. But when they hand you over, do not worry about how or what you are to say; for it will be given you in that hour what you are to say. For it is not you who speak, but it is the Spirit of your Father who speaks in you. Brother will betray brother to death, and a father his child; and children will rise up against parents and cause them to be put to death. You will be hated by all because of My name, but it is the one who has endured to the end who will be saved. (Matt. 10:16–22)

Then in verse 25 He added, "It is enough for the disciple that he become like his teacher, and the slave like his master. If they have called the head of the house Beelzebul, how much more will they malign the members of his household!"

This man typified the rocky soil, which symbolizes people "who, when they hear the word, immediately receive it with joy; and they have no firm root in themselves, but are only temporary; then, when affliction or persecution arises because of the word, immediately they fall away" (Mark 4:16–17). Ultimately, he was not prepared to "deny himself, and take up his cross daily and follow" the Lord (Luke 9:23). He wanted to be in on the benefits of following Jesus, but not the sacrifices.

DESIRE FOR PERSONAL RICHES

And He said to another, "Follow Me." But he said, "Lord, permit me first to go and bury my father." But He said to him, "Allow the dead to bury their own dead; but as for you, go and proclaim everywhere the kingdom of God." (9:59–60)

This second incident immediately followed the first one. Turning to **another** man, who had probably overheard His conversation with the first one, Jesus challenged him, **"Follow Me." But he,** too, was only willing to follow Christ on his own terms, so he **said, "Lord, permit me first to go and bury my father."** At first glance, this seems to be a reasonable request. It was every son's duty to make sure that his father was properly cared for in death (cf. Gen. 25:9; 35:29; 49:29–50:13); only the high priest (Lev. 21:10–11) and those who had taken a Nazarite vow (Num. 6:6–7) were excused from their father's funeral, since they were forbidden to go near a dead person.

The problem with the man's excuse was that his father was not yet dead! Since the Jews did not embalm, Jewish custom dictated that burial take place immediately after death. A comparison of John 11:1, 6, and 17 reveals that Lazarus was buried the same day that he died (one day for the messenger from Mary and Martha to reach Jesus, Jesus delayed two more days, then arrived on the fourth day to find that Lazarus had been buried four days earlier). Both Ananias (Acts 5:6) and Sapphira (v. 10) were buried immediately after they died.

What this man was really saying was that he wanted to delay following the Lord until his father died and he received his inheritance. He knew that Jesus was moving out of the area, and to leave now might cause him to lose out on his share of his father's estate. Unlike the Twelve (cf. Matt. 19:27; Luke 5:11, 28), he was not willing to leave everything and follow Jesus. He was an example of "the seed which fell among the thorns, these are the ones who have heard, and as they go on their way they are choked with worries and riches and pleasures of this life, and bring no fruit to maturity" (Luke 8:14).

Jesus replied with a proverbial saying that was a rebuke of this man's wrong priorities: **"Allow the dead to bury their own dead."** That does not mean that believers are forbidden to attend funerals or care for their dead relatives' affairs. To say that the spiritually **dead** can **bury their own dead** is to say that there are issues that are priorities to the spiritually dead, but not to those who are alive in Christ. Jesus challenged this individual to leave temporal, earthly matters to worldly people and not make them his overriding priority. Secular people are preoccupied with secular matters, but he was to **go and proclaim everywhere the kingdom of God** no matter what doing so might cost him. But like the rich young ruler, he was more committed to personal riches than spiritual truth. It is impossible to serve both God and riches (Luke 16:13), and when forced to choose the men both chose riches.

DESIRE FOR PERSONAL RELATIONS

Another also said, "I will follow You, Lord; but first permit me to say good-bye to those at home." But Jesus said to him, "No one, after putting his hand to the plow and looking back, is fit for the kingdom of God." (9:61–62)

Another man, probably following up on the Lord's discussion with the previous individual, also volunteered to follow Jesus. **"I will follow You, Lord"** he promised, **"but first permit me to say good-bye to those at home."** Unlike the man the Lord had just spoken with, this third individual was willing to leave his inheritance behind. He had only one request, which seemed reasonable enough: He wanted to delay joining Christ long enough to go home and say good-by to his loved ones.

But as was the case with the other two, the Lord, knowing what was in his heart, rejected this man's proposal. Perhaps he wanted to do a little quick fundraising among his family and friends before leaving on his mission trip with Jesus. More likely, however, there was a deeper issue involved. His words revealed that his family ties were too strong for him to break away from them. Jesus knew that if he returned home, the impulse of the moment would die and he would never be able to leave. Like many people, fear of being away from or ostracized by his family would keep him from following the Lord. That is why Jesus cautioned the crowds that followed Him, "If anyone comes to Me, and does not hate his own father and mother and wife and children and brothers and sisters, yes, and even his own life, he cannot be My disciple" (Luke 14:26).

Jesus replied by adapting a popular proverb that dates back to the eighth-century B.C. Greek poet Hesiod: **"No one, after putting his hand to the plow and looking back,** He declared, **is fit for the kingdom of God."** This saying pictures complete dedication to the task at hand, since one could hardly plow a straight furrow while looking backwards. It is impossible to follow Christ with a divided heart, as this man's was. He was not fit for the kingdom of God because he was holding on to the kingdom of this world. "Do you not know that friendship with the world is hostility toward God?" James asked. "Therefore whoever wishes to be a friend of the world makes himself an enemy of God" (James 4:4; cf. 1 John 2:15–17).

Though the text does not describe what ultimately became of these three men it is obvious that they, like the rich young ruler, abandoned Christ to hold on to earthly things. The issue in view in all three of these encounters was not fitness for service by those in the kingdom, but saving faith by which one enters the kingdom. Those unwilling to part with something—comfort, riches, relationships, or anything else—cannot enter the kingdom of God; salvation is for those who have come to complete self-denial. "If anyone wishes to come after Me, he must deny himself, and take up his cross daily and follow Me," Jesus declared, because "whoever wishes to save his life will lose it, but whoever loses his life for My sake, he is the one who will save it" (Luke 9:23–24).

Essential Elements for Evangelism (Luke 10:1–16)

34

Now after this the Lord appointed seventy others, and sent them in pairs ahead of Him to every city and place where He Himself was going to come. And He was saying to them, "The harvest is plentiful, but the laborers are few; therefore beseech the Lord of the harvest to send out laborers into His harvest. Go; behold, I send you out as lambs in the midst of wolves. Carry no money belt, no bag, no shoes; and greet no one on the way. Whatever house you enter, first say, 'Peace be to this house.' If a man of peace is there, your peace will rest on him; but if not, it will return to you. Stay in that house, eating and drinking what they give you; for the laborer is worthy of his wages. Do not keep moving from house to house. Whatever city you enter and they receive you, eat what is set before you; and heal those in it who are sick, and say to them, 'The kingdom of God has come near to you.' But whatever city you enter and they do not receive you, go out into its streets and say, 'Even the dust of your city which clings to our feet we wipe off in protest against you; yet be sure of this, that the kingdom of God has come near.' I say to you, it will be more tolerable in that day for Sodom than for that city. Woe to you, Chorazin! Woe to you, Bethsaida! For if the miracles had

been performed in Tyre and Sidon which occurred in you, they would have repented long ago, sitting in sackcloth and ashes. But it will be more tolerable for Tyre and Sidon in the judgment than for you. And you, Capernaum, will not be exalted to heaven, will you? You will be brought down to Hades! The one who listens to you listens to Me, and the one who rejects you rejects Me; and he who rejects Me rejects the One who sent Me. (10:1–16)

Most of Christ's followers were motivated by self-interest and eventually abandoned Him (cf. Matt. 7:14; 19:25–26; Luke 13:23–24; John 6:66). There were, on the other hand, His true disciples who refused to leave (cf. John 6:67–69). This passage introduces seventy of them, the first kingdom missionaries, who were sent by the King to announce His presence. The seventy were willing to deny themselves, take up their crosses daily, and follow Him. Like the Twelve they were ordinary men, chosen for an extraordinary task.

The message the seventy proclaimed was that the kingdom of God had come near because the King, the Lord Jesus Christ, was present—the same message proclaimed by John the Baptist (Matt. 3:2), Jesus (Matt. 4:17, 23; 9:35; Luke 4:43), and the apostles (Matt. 10:7). A kingdom is a realm, sphere, or territory ruled by an absolute monarch who functions with absolute authority. In the kingdom of God, He is the "blessed and only Sovereign, the King of kings and Lord of lords" (1 Tim. 6:15). In a general sense, all creation is included under His sovereign rule in His universal kingdom (Ps. 103:19), but the kingdom of salvation is the theme of all gospel preaching. Those who enter that aspect of His kingdom through faith in the Lord Jesus Christ submit themselves completely to His authority and receive all the benefits of eternal life. The rest of humanity is in the kingdom of the world (Rev. 11:15), under the rule of Satan (John 12:31; 14:30; 16:11; Acts 26:18; 2 Cor. 4:4; Eph. 2:2); there are no free agents. The gospel is the good news that sinners can be forgiven, delivered from the kingdom of darkness into "the kingdom of His beloved Son" (Col. 1:13), and thereby reconciled to God, who gives them permanent peace, comfort, and joy both in time and eternity.

The phrase **after this** indicates that the sending of the seventy took place subsequent to the events of chapter 9, which marked the close of the Lord's Galilean ministry and the beginning of His journey to Jerusalem. That journey would last for several months, and take place mainly in Judea and east of the Jordan in Perea. It would end with Christ's arrival in Jerusalem for the events of Passion Week, which would culminate in His death, resurrection, and ascension. Early in that journey, **the Lord appointed** these **seventy** messengers (some translations read "seventy-two"; the manuscript evidence is not clear as to which reading is correct).*Anadeiknumi* (**appointed**) appears elsewhere in the New Testament only in Acts 1:24, where it refers to the Lord's choice of Matthias to replace Judas as an apostle. Jesus sovereignly chose the seventy, just as He did the twelve apostles. Why the Lord chose seventy is not revealed, but it may have been a parallel to Moses' choice (at God's direction) of seventy elders to help him govern Israel (Num. 11:16–17, 24–25).

After choosing these seventy men, Jesus **sent them in pairs ahead of Him to every city and place** in Judea **where He Himself was going to come.** The question arises as to why He diluted their impact by having them travel in pairs (as He had earlier done with the Twelve [Mark 6:7]). First, the Lord in His wisdom knew they would be able to support and encourage each other, a principle Solomon stated in Ecclesiastes 4:9–12:

> Two are better than one because they have a good return for their labor. For if either of them falls, the one will lift up his companion. But woe to the one who falls when there is not another to lift him up. Furthermore, if two lie down together they keep warm, but how can one be warm alone? And if one can overpower him who is alone, two can resist him. A cord of three strands is not quickly torn apart.

Second, and more important, the Old Testament law required that "on the evidence of two or three witnesses a matter shall be confirmed" (Deut. 19:15). Thus the testimony these men gave about Jesus in the towns and villages would conform to the law's requirements.

The Lord's instruction to the seventy provides insight for believers today, who are all called to distribute the good news of salvation. Three requirements rise from His charge to the seventy: all who proclaim salvation in Christ must be content with the Lord's provision, faithful to the Lord's message, and diligent to declare judgment.

CONTENT WITH THE LORD'S PROVISION

And He was saying to them, "The harvest is plentiful, but the laborers are few; therefore beseech the Lord of the harvest to send out laborers into His harvest. Go; behold, I send you out as lambs in the midst of wolves. Carry no money belt, no bag, no shoes; and greet no one on the way. (10:2–4)

The attitude Jesus expected of the seventy is composed of five elements, all of which are transferable to believers today. Luke's record of what **He was saying to** them is most likely only a rich summary of our Lord's instruction. As is the case in all the records of His teaching, we assume He said much more on the matters that are only briefly referred to by the writers. This section presents aspects of dependence on the Lord.

SHARING HIS COMPASSION

The harvest is plentiful, but the laborers are few; (10:2*b*)

Since we do not naturally care for souls and do not fully understand hell's horrors, we must borrow from the Lord's compassion expressed in this statement. That it is a statement flowing from compassion becomes clear from another text. In Matthew 9:37, just prior to commissioning the Twelve, He said, "The harvest is plentiful, but the workers are few." In verses 35 and 36 Matthew shows that compassion prompted Christ's remark: "Jesus was going through all the cities and villages, teaching in their synagogues and proclaiming the gospel of the kingdom, and healing every kind of disease and every kind of sickness. Seeing the people, He felt compassion for them, because they were distressed and dispirited like sheep without a shepherd." Throughout His ministry the Lord continually demonstrated His deeply felt sympathy for desperate and despairing sinners. In Matthew 14:14 "He saw a large crowd, and felt compassion for them and healed their sick." Before feeding the four thousand "Jesus called His disciples to Him, and said, 'I feel compassion for the people, because they have remained with Me now three days and have nothing to eat; and I do not want to send them away hungry, for they might faint on the way'" (Matt. 15:32). Similarly just before the feeding of the five thousand "Jesus ...saw a large crowd, and He felt compassion for them because they were like sheep without a shepherd" (Mark 6:34). "Moved with compassion" for two blind men, "Jesus touched their eyes; and immediately they regained their sight and followed Him" (Matt. 20:34). Mark 1:41 records that after a leper pleaded with Him to be healed, Jesus was "moved with compassion [and] stretched out His hand and touched him, and said to him, 'I am willing; be cleansed.'" Near the village of Nain the Lord's compassion prompted Him to dramatically interrupt a funeral procession:

> As He approached the gate of the city, a dead man was being carried out, the only son of his mother, and she was a widow; and a sizeable crowd from the city was with her. When the Lord saw her, He felt compassion for her, and said to her, "Do not weep." And He came up and touched the coffin; and the bearers came to a halt. And He said, "Young man, I say to you, arise!" The dead man sat up and began to speak. And Jesus gave him back to his mother. (Luke 7:12–15)

The word translated "compassion" in those verses, *splangnizomai*, derives from the noun *splangnon*, which literally refers to the internal organs (it is translated "intestines" in Acts 1:18). The verb reflects the reality that intense emotions can have physical effects, like the English expression "to feel it in the pit of one's stomach." Isaiah's prophetic description of Jesus as a "man of sorrows and acquainted with grief" (Isa. 53:3), is reflected in the strong emotions He displayed at the tomb of Lazarus (John 11:33, 35, 38), and when He wept over lost, unbelieving Jerusalem (Luke 19:41).

Jesus, of course, understood perfectly the doctrines of the sovereignty of God, predestination, and election. He knew that all those who would believe had their names "written from the foundation of the world in the book of life of the Lamb who has been slain" (Rev. 13:8; cf. 3:5; 17:8; 20:12, 15; 21:27; Phil. 4:3). But that did not keep Him from grieving over the lost, who of their own volition rejected Him (cf. Matt. 23:37; John 1:11; 3:19; 5:40; 12:37). God's sovereignty in salvation does not cancel out human responsibility, and it must not be allowed to rob believers of their evangelistic zeal. The same apostle Paul, who strongly emphasized God's sovereignty (Rom. 9:14–24), cried out passionately concerning the lost, "I am telling the truth in Christ, I am not lying, my conscience testifies with me in the Holy Spirit, that I have great sorrow and unceasing grief in my heart. For I could wish that I myself were accursed, separated from Christ for the sake of my brethren, my kinsmen according to the flesh" (Rom. 9:1–3).

The Lord's compassion was prompted by His knowledge of what awaits those who refuse to repent; the **harvest** of which He spoke was not one of bringing people into the kingdom of God. It was the gathering of sinners for their final judgment (cf. Joel 3:12–14; Matt. 13:30, 39–43; Rev. 14:14–15). Compounding the matter, although the **harvest is plentiful . . . the laborers are few.** The mass of humanity moving inexorably toward divine judgment and eternal hell, while only few are working to reach them with the saving truth of the gospel, moved the heart of the Savior as it should move us. True evangelism begins with a proper assessment of the plight of sinners; with an awareness of their desperate condition and with the realization that they all face the terrifying reality of eternal punishment.

SEEKING HIS RESOURCES

therefore beseech the Lord of the harvest to send out laborers into His harvest. (10:2c)

In light of the impending harvest of divine judgment, believers are commanded to pray for the salvation of the unregenerate. In Romans 10:1 Paul wrote, "Brethren, my heart's desire and my prayer to God for them [unbelieving Israelites] is for their salvation." But the prayer in view here is that God would raise up people to evangelize the lost; that **the Lord of the harvest** would **send out laborers into His harvest** to rescue people from the coming judgment.

The Lord of the harvest is the Lord Jesus Christ, to whom the Father has committed all judgment (John 5:22, 27–29; cf. 2 Thess. 1:5–10). The compassionate Lord seeks to rescue people from His wrath and judgment through the prayers of believers. This is the paradox and wonder of the gospel. The judge commands His people to pray that more sinners be saved from His judgment; more than that, that more evangels be sent to those sinners, because the judge and executioner was Himself executed to save others from being executed by Him.

OBEYING HIS COMMAND

Go; (10:3a)

The present imperative form of the verb *hupagō* (**go** and keep going) reflects the urgency of the Lord's command. There was no time for delay or extensive training; the cross was only a few months away and there were many villages that needed to hear the message and be prepared to receive Jesus when He came. Since the seventy were themselves part of the kingdom of salvation, they knew enough to tell others how to be as well. While specific training in evangelism and apologetics is helpful, the lack of it is no excuse for believers, from the moment of their conversion, not to bring to other sinners the gospel truth they have believed.

A rich illustration of evangelistic urgency by a new believer is found in our Lord's command to the transformed Gerasene demoniac (see the exposition of 8:26–39 in chapter 23 of this volume): "Return to your house and describe what great things God has done for you." In response, with only a childlike knowledge of Christ's salvation, "he went away, proclaiming throughout the whole city what great things Jesus had done for him" (v. 39).

TRUSTING HIS POWER

behold, I send you out as lambs in the midst of wolves. (10:3b)

By likening the seventy to **lambs in the midst of wolves,** Jesus stressed the reality of the threats that awaited gospel witnesses and their need both for innocence and vigilance. Like innocent, helpless **lambs** in the midst of a wolf pack, the seventy had no strength of their own and were only as safe as the strength of their Shepherd. As He did the apostles (cf. Matt. 10:16–18; John 16:1–4, 33), Jesus warned them of the hostility, hatred, and danger they would face. All of the apostles faced persecution, and as far as is known, all were martyred except for John. The seventy also would face persecution in the synagogue courts, by religious and secular authorities, and even from their own families, and perhaps a number of them were martyred as well. But they were all protected by the power and strength of their Shepherd until their work was done.

ACCEPTING HIS PROVISION

Carry no money belt, no bag, no shoes; and greet no one on the way. (10:4)

As He had done with the Twelve (Luke 9:1–3), the Lord did not allow the seventy to take any extra provisions for their journey, such as a **money belt, bag, and shoes.** Nor were they to **greet** anyone **on the way.** Jesus was not referring to giving a polite greeting in passing, but rather to stopping and indulging in the elaborate greetings that were part of the culture (cf. Ex. 18:5–12). They were not to establish relationships from which they could expect support. Nor was doing so essential to this mission of evangelizing people; people would be saved by the power of the gospel, not the power of friendship. This mission was to be a time of training, of learning to trust God to supply all their needs (cf. Phil. 4:19). The seventy were not only to trust the Lord to protect them from the wolves, as noted above, but also to supply their basic necessities.

As was the case with the apostles, this austerity was for temporary training purposes and not permanent, as Jesus' later reference to His sending the Twelve indicates: "When I sent you out without money belt and bag and sandals, you did not lack anything, did you?" They said, 'No, nothing'" (Luke 22:35). But the pattern for future ministry would be different, Jesus told them: "But now, whoever has a money belt is to take it along, likewise also a bag, and whoever has no sword is to sell his coat and buy one'" (v. 36). The rigorous rules the Lord enforced during the initial training of both the apostles and the seventy were relaxed after it was completed.

FAITHFUL TO THE LORD'S MESSAGE

Whatever house you enter, first say, 'Peace be to this house.' If a man of peace is there, your peace will rest on him; but if not, it will return to you. Stay in that house, eating and drinking what they give you; for the laborer is worthy of his wages. Do not keep moving from house to house. Whatever city you enter and they receive you, eat what is set before you; and heal those in it who are sick, and say to them, 'The kingdom of God has come near to you.' But whatever city you enter and they do not receive you, go out into its streets and say, 'Even the dust of your city which clings to our feet we wipe off in protest against you; yet be sure of this, that the kingdom of God has come near.' (10:5–11)

The message the seventy were charged to preach would inevitably divide people based on one of two responses: acceptance bringing peace, or rejection bringing punishment.

PEACE

Whatever house you enter, first say, 'Peace be to this house.' If a man of peace is there, your peace will rest on him; but if not, it will return to you. Stay in that house, eating and drinking what they give you; for the laborer is worthy of his wages. Do not keep moving from house to house. Whatever city you enter and they receive you, eat what is set before you; and heal those in it who are sick, and say to them, 'The kingdom of God has come near to you.' (10:5–9)

These itinerant evangelists from Galilee would be strangers in virtually every Judean town and village that they entered. In His instructions to the Twelve, Jesus had told them, "Whatever city or village you enter, inquire who is worthy in it, and stay at his house until you leave that city" (Matt. 10:11). In other words, they were to look for someone receptive to the gospel message, a true Jew who was one inwardly (Rom. 2:29); who was waiting for the Messiah as Simeon was (Luke 2:25). The seventy were likewise to look for those who were ready, eager, and divinely prepared to hear the gospel.

Then the Lord gave them specific instructions as to how to find such a person, **"Whatever house you enter, first say, 'Peace be to this house.'"** They were to seek out a **house** where there was an interest in the message of **peace** with God that Messiah, the "Prince of Peace"

(Isa. 9:6; cf. Luke 1:79) would bring. This saying was more than merely a polite greeting since, as Jesus went on to say, **"If a man of peace is there, your peace will rest on him"**; in other words, the gospel message would find a home with him. The phrase **man of peace** literally reads "son of peace." In Jewish vernacular, to say that someone was a son of something meant that person had a disposition or nature consistent with it. A son of peace would be receptive to the message of eternal peace with God and entrance into His kingdom that comes only through the Messiah, the Lord Jesus Christ (cf. Rom. 5:1). On the other hand, Jesus told them that **if** the message is **not** accepted **it will return to** them, an expression signifying rejection. In that case the seventy, like the Twelve (Matt. 10:13), were not to waste any more time with the rejecters, but to go somewhere else (cf. Matt. 7:6).

When they were welcomed into the house of a man of peace, they were to **stay in that house, eating and drinking what they** were given, since **the laborer is worthy of his wages** (cf. Matt. 10:10; 1 Cor. 9:14; 1 Tim. 5:17–18). The seventy were strictly forbidden to **keep moving from house to house** seeking nicer accommodations or better food. This was the same charge that the Lord gave the Twelve when He sent them out to preach (Luke 9:4). The point was to distinguish the true preachers of the gospel from greedy false teachers. The latter were constantly looking to stay in the most comfortable and wealthy homes for a while and then move on, seeking to take advantage of as many people as possible. Obeying Christ's command would demonstrate the integrity, sincerity, and honesty of His messengers and their message, as opposed to the false teachers.

Broadening the scope of His instructions, Jesus then told the seventy, **"Whatever city you enter and they receive you, eat what is set before you."** In contrast to the false teachers, they were not to put a price on their ministry by demanding certain living arrangements or quality of food. Nor did they need to be concerned even about the Jewish dietary laws should they stay in a Gentile home, since Jesus had already declared all foods clean (Mark 7:18–19).

Finally, the Lord charged the seventy to **heal those** in each city they visited **who are sick.** Verse 17 indicates that they also received power to cast out demons. Those miraculous powers, which may have been granted only for the duration of their mission, served to authenticate their message as it did the apostles (Luke 9:6) in the time before the completion of the inspired New Testament. The message they proclaimed, as noted above, was that **the kingdom of God** had **come near** because the King was present.

DILIGENT TO DECLARE JUDGMENT

**But whatever city you enter and they do not receive you, go out
into its streets and say, 'Even the dust of your city which clings to
our feet we wipe off in protest against you; yet be sure of this,
that the kingdom of God has come near.' I say to you, it will be
more tolerable in that day for Sodom than for that city. Woe to
you, Chorazin! Woe to you, Bethsaida! For if the miracles had
been performed in Tyre and Sidon which occurred in you, they
would have repented long ago, sitting in sackcloth and ashes. But
it will be more tolerable for Tyre and Sidon in the judgment than
for you. And you, Capernaum, will not be exalted to heaven, will
you? You will be brought down to Hades! The one who listens to
you listens to Me, and the one who rejects you rejects Me; and he
who rejects Me rejects the One who sent Me.** (10:10–16)

The seventy could not expect to find a favorable reception in
every **city** they visited; the Lord Himself had just been rejected by an
entire Samaritan village (9:52–53). When a city did **not receive** them,
they were not to slip away quietly, but **go out into its streets and say,
"Even the dust of your city which clings to our feet we wipe off in
protest against you; yet be sure of this, that the kingdom of God
has come near."** This was a public pronouncement of judgment on
those who rejected the King and His kingdom. Wiping off the dust from
one's feet was a demonstrative expression of disdain in Jewish culture
(cf. the exposition of 9:5 in chapter 25 of this volume). This was a final
call to those who had rejected the King, graphically warning them that
they themselves were being rejected by Him. Despite their rejection, they
could **be sure of this, that the kingdom of God** had **come near.** God's
kingdom moves inexorably through history and those who are not swept
up into it are crushed by it.

Understanding the good news of the gospel is predicated on
understanding the bad news about what happens to those who reject it.
To be faithful to the Word of God, a gospel presentation must include not
only the promise of heaven, but also the threat of judgment and hell (Ps.
96:13; John 5:28–29; Acts 17:31; 24:25; Rom. 2:5; 2 Thess. 2:12; 2 Tim. 4:1;
Heb. 9:27; 2 Peter 2:9; 3:7; Rev. 20:11–15).

In the conclusion of His charge to the seventy, the Lord Jesus
Christ emphasized the reality of comparative judgment. Those who rejected the message the seventy proclaimed will face a severer judgment
than those who have never heard the truth. Jesus gave the seventy the
principle of comparative judgment, some examples of comparative judgment, and then personalized the principle of comparative judgment.

THE PRINCIPLE OF COMPARATIVE JUDGMENT

I say to you, it will be more tolerable in that day . . . it will be more tolerable (10:12a, 14a)

The Lord's emphatic declaration **I say to you** (cf. Matt. 5:18, 20, 22, 26, 28, 32, 34, 39, 44) indicates the importance of this truth. The warning given here is not hearsay or inference, but firsthand information straight from the judge's mouth. The Lord listed six cities, three Jewish and three Gentile, and then shockingly proclaimed that the Jewish cities would face a severer judgment **in that day. It will be more tolerable** refers to the degree of punishment dropped on the unbelieving sinners at the Great White Throne judgment, the final sentencing of the lost to the lake of fire (Rev. 20:11–15). In that place of unceasing torment there will be different levels of punishment. To be exposed to the gospel of Jesus Christ and reject it is to incur greater guilt and punishment.

But while all who reject the gospel and refuse to repent of their sins will face eternal punishment in hell, the degree of their punishment will depend on the amount of knowledge they had. The severest punishment belongs to those who had the most knowledge of the truth. The writer of Hebrews expressed that principle when he wrote, "How much severer punishment do you think he will deserve who has trampled under foot the Son of God, and has regarded as unclean the blood of the covenant by which he was sanctified, and has insulted the Spirit of grace?" (Heb. 10:29; cf. Luke 12:47–48).

THE EXAMPLES OF COMPARATIVE JUDGMENT

I say to you, it will be more tolerable in that day for Sodom than for that city. Woe to you, Chorazin! Woe to you, Bethsaida! For if the miracles had been performed in Tyre and Sidon which occurred in you, they would have repented long ago, sitting in sackcloth and ashes. But it will be more tolerable for Tyre and Sidon in the judgment than for you. And you, Capernaum, will not be exalted to heaven, will you? You will be brought down to Hades! (10:12–15)

To illustrate His point, Jesus gave three examples of cities whose judgments would be different based on their level of exposure to the truth. All three of the examples He gave would have shocked the Jewish people. First, the Lord declared that **it will be more tolerable in that day for Sodom than for that city.** The unspecified city is any city that rejected the seventy and their message about Christ (v. 10). That Sodom would face a lesser judgment than any city in Israel was incomprehensible. The appalling evil of Sodom, especially its gross homosexual sin, would seem to merit the most severe judgment. God Himself declared of Sodom and its sister city Gomorrah, "The outcry of Sodom and Gomorrah is indeed great, and their sin is exceedingly grave" (Gen. 18:20). Yet Jesus declared that any city that rejected the gospel would face a more severe judgment than Sodom.

The second example contrasts the Old Testament cities of **Tyre** and **Sidon** with **Chorazin** and **Bethsaida.** Chorazin was a small village near Capernaum, the headquarters of Jesus' Galilean ministry. Bethsaida, the hometown of Andrew, Peter, and Philip (John 1:44), was another village near Capernaum. The two cities' proximity to Capernaum ensures that the people of Chorazin and Bethsaida were familiar with Jesus' miracles and His message. Their rejection of Him prompted the Lord to pronounce **woe** (i.e., judgment) on them, and then to reveal the shocking truth that **if the miracles had been performed in Tyre and Sidon which occurred in** Chorazin and Bethsaida **they would have repented long ago.** Tyre and Sidon were seaports on the Phoenician coast. The two cities epitomized evil in the Old Testament, and both Isaiah 23 and Ezekiel 28 prophesied the judgment that fell on them. Yet if they had had the information that the inhabitants of Chorazin and Bethsaida had, they would have put on **sackcloth and ashes,** a symbol of deep mourning and contrition (1 Kings 21:27; 1 Chron. 21:16; Neh. 9:1; Est. 4:1,3; Job 42:6; Jer. 6:26; Dan. 9:3; Jon. 3:5–9), to demonstrate the sincerity of their repentance.

If the Jewish people had been asked to name the most evil people in history, those two cities and Sodom would have been at the top of the list. Yet because of their stubborn rejection of the truth and refusal to repent and trust Jesus Christ, the Jewish people faced a more severe judgment than those wicked Gentile cities who had never heard from God.

The Lord then turned His attention to **Capernaum** which, He warned, **will not be exalted to heaven** as its self-righteous inhabitants imagined, but **will be brought down to Hades!** Like the people of Chorazin and Bethsaida, their religious pride would plunge the people of Capernaum into punishment. **Hades** is a general word for the place of the dead, but when used in contrast to heaven it can only refer to hell (cf. Luke 16:23–24). Capernaum had been the Lord's headquarters throughout His Galilean ministry. Its people had heard His teaching and repeatedly witnessed the countless miracles He performed. There is no record in the Gospels of any overt hostility to Jesus on the part of that city; its inhabitants never persecuted Him, mocked Him, ridiculed Him, or tried to run Him out of town. They merely tolerated Him. But indifference to Christ is just as damning as outright rejection since, as Jesus said, "He who is not with Me is against Me; and he who does not gather with Me scatters" (Matt. 12:30).

THE PERSONALIZATION OF COMPARATIVE JUDGMENT

The one who listens to you listens to Me, and the one who rejects you rejects Me; and he who rejects Me rejects the One who sent Me. (10:16)

This statement brings the issue down from the city level to the personal one. Because the seventy represented Him, Jesus told them, **"The one who listens to you listens to Me, and the one who rejects you rejects Me."** When His faithful messengers proclaim the message of the gospel, the Lord speaks through them. Each gospel writer records this truth that Jesus reiterated in John 13:20, "Truly, truly, I say to you, he who receives whomever I send receives Me; and he who receives Me receives Him who sent Me" (cf. Luke 9:48; Matt. 10:40; Mark 9:37). When those who hear the message respond to it in faith, they are listening to Him; but when they refuse to listen, they are rejecting Him. Furthermore, the one **who rejects** Jesus **rejects the One who sent** Him. The idea that someone can honor God while rejecting Jesus Christ is a damning lie. In John 5:23 Jesus said to the hostile Jews, "He who does not honor the Son does not honor the Father who sent Him," while in John 8:42 He added, "If God were your Father, you would love Me, for I proceeded forth and have come from God, for I have not even come on My own initiative, but He sent Me." In John 15:23 Jesus told the apostles, "He who hates Me hates My Father also." The apostle John wrote, "Whoever denies the Son does not have the Father; the one who confesses the Son has the Father also" (1 John 2:23), and "Anyone who goes too far and does not abide in the teaching of Christ, does not have God" (2 John 9).

Evangelism, when done in dependence on the Lord, with loyalty to the gospel message, and strong in words of warning about the judgment of hell, will follow the pattern set on this occasion with the seventy.

Joy at the Seventy's Return (Luke 10:17–24)

35

The seventy returned with joy, saying, "Lord, even the demons are subject to us in Your name." And He said to them, "I was watching Satan fall from heaven like lightning. Behold, I have given you authority to tread on serpents and scorpions, and over all the power of the enemy, and nothing will injure you. Nevertheless do not rejoice in this, that the spirits are subject to you, but rejoice that your names are recorded in heaven." At that very time He rejoiced greatly in the Holy Spirit, and said, "I praise You, O Father, Lord of heaven and earth, that You have hidden these things from the wise and intelligent and have revealed them to infants. Yes, Father, for this way was well-pleasing in Your sight. All things have been handed over to Me by My Father, and no one knows who the Son is except the Father, and who the Father is except the Son, and anyone to whom the Son wills to reveal Him." Turning to the disciples, He said privately, "Blessed are the eyes which see the things you see, for I say to you, that many prophets and kings wished to see the things which you see, and did not see them, and to hear the things which you hear, and did not hear them." (10:17–24)

When they consider God and His attributes, most people think of characteristics like holiness, sovereignty, omniscience, omnipresence, immutability, justice, wrath, love, grace, and mercy. Rarely considered, however, is God's joy. In 1 Chronicles 16:27 David said of Him, "Strength and joy are in His place." The prophet Zephaniah declared to Israel, "The Lord your God is in your midst, a victorious warrior. He will exult over you with joy, He will be quiet in His love, He will rejoice over you with shouts of joy" (Zeph. 3:17). Jeremiah records God's promise to Israel, "I will rejoice over them to do them good and will faithfully plant them in this land with all My heart and with all My soul" (Jer. 32:41), while in Isaiah 62:5 God said to His people that in the future, "As the bridegroom rejoices over the bride, so your God will rejoice over you" (cf. 65:19; Deut. 30:9).

God's joy is the ultimate purpose for which all His attributes function; it is the all-glorious displaying of them that brings Him the fullest joy. God's attributes ensure not only His eternal joy, but also that of all the inhabitants of heaven. There "He will wipe away every tear from their eyes; and there will no longer be any death; there will no longer be any mourning, or crying, or pain" (Rev. 21:4). The dominant reality of heaven is unmixed joy forever, which is why the Lord said that those who enter heaven "enter into the joy of [their] master" (Matt. 25:21) and Jude gave the benediction, "Now to Him who is able to keep you from stumbling, and to make you stand in the presence of His glory blameless with great joy" (Jude 24).

It is true that the Lord Jesus Christ was, in the familiar words of Isaiah's prophecy, a "man of sorrows and acquainted with grief" (Isa. 53:3). He wept at the grave of Lazarus (John 11:35; cf. vv. 33, 38) and over the city of Jerusalem (Luke 19:41). In Gethsemane He "began to be grieved and distressed" (Matt. 26:37) and said to Peter, James, and John, "My soul is deeply grieved, to the point of death" (v. 38). Reflecting on that experience, the writer of Hebrews said of Him, "In the days of His flesh, He offered up both prayers and supplications with loud crying and tears to the One able to save Him from death" (Heb. 5:7). The unfathomable sorrow the Savior experienced on the cross was expressed when He cried out, "My God, My God, why have You forsaken Me?" (Matt. 27:46).

But while the Bible says much about Christ's sorrow and grief, this passage is the only one that pictures Him rejoicing during His life on earth. It is a unique treasure, providing insight into the joy experienced by the Man of Sorrows. It comes at a critical transition in our Lord's earthly ministry. The early days of amazement, wonder, and fascination with His miraculous power and authoritative teaching were coming to an end. He was facing increasing apathy and indifference, which would soon turn to rejection and opposition leading to His murder. Christ's Galilean ministry, which had lasted a little more than a year, was over. He had done many miracles throughout the region, demonstrating His divine power over disease, death, demons, and nature. He had proclaimed the gospel of the kingdom, the message of forgiveness and salvation, and had sent the Twelve out to do the same. Yet the Galileans had provided a meager response to Christ's monumental ministry among them; when He returned to Galilee after His resurrection, only 500 believers met Him there (cf. 1Cor 15:6). But as this passage reveals, Jesus rejoiced despite circumstances that were disappointing from a human perspective; the Man of Sorrows was at the same time the God of joy.

Like Jesus, believers are to be joyful no matter what the circumstances. In Philippians 4:4 Paul wrote, "Rejoice in the Lord always; again I will say, rejoice!" (cf. 3:1; 1 Thess. 5:16). Despite his appalling situation, Paul nevertheless could write from prison, "I rejoiced in the Lord greatly" (Phil. 4:10). His joy was constant, imperturbable, and unaffected by circumstances (cf. vv. 11, 12), because it was rooted not in the vagaries of those circumstances, but in the unchanging reality of God's faithfulness. Believers rejoice because of God's goodness (Ex. 18:9; 2 Chron. 7:10), salvation (1 Sam. 2:1; Hab. 3:18), love (Pss. 13:5; 31:7), strength (Ps. 21:1), word (Ps. 119:14, 162), and truth (1 Cor. 13:6).

The successful completion of their ministry prompted both the seventy and Jesus to rejoice. This passage reveals three reasons for the seventy's joy, followed by three reasons for the Savior's joy.

REASONS FOR THE SEVENTY'S JOY

The seventy returned with joy, saying, "Lord, even the demons are subject to us in Your name." And He said to them, "I was watching Satan fall from heaven like lightning. Behold, I have given you authority to tread on serpents and scorpions, and over all the power of the enemy, and nothing will injure you. Nevertheless do not rejoice in this, that the spirits are subject to you, but rejoice that your names are recorded in heaven." (10:17–20)

The **seventy** had obeyed Christ's call to self-denial (9:23–24) and in return they received full and complete joy. As noted above, there were three reasons for that joy: divine power over Satan's kingdom, divine protection from Satan's kingdom, and divine preservation in God's kingdom.

DIVINE POWER OVER SATAN'S KINGDOM

The seventy returned with joy, saying, "Lord, even the demons are subject to us in Your name." And He said to them, "I was

watching Satan fall from heaven like lightning. (10:17–18)

When the **seventy returned** to Jesus after completing their evangelistic mission, they immediately gave the first reason for their **joy, saying** to Him, **"Lord, even the demons are subject to us in Your name."** All of the angels were originally created holy, but Satan, corrupted by pride and desiring to be equal with God, chose not to submit to Him. Joined by one third of the angels (Rev. 12:4), Satan led an unsuccessful rebellion against God. The Bible describes him as the ruler of this world (John 12:31), the prince of the power of the air (Eph. 2:2), the god of this world (2 Cor. 4:4), a murderer and the father of lies (John 8:44), a deceiver (Rev. 12:9), the accuser of believers (Rev. 12:10), and the evil one (1 John 5:19). The choice of the **demons,** the angels who followed Satan, is irrevocable; they are unredeemable and one day will be cast into the lake of fire (Matt. 25:41) along with their leader (Rev. 20:10). Like Satan, they are the enemies of God, Christ, the Holy Spirit, and God's people. They deceive unbelievers (2 Cor. 4:4), and use false teachers to spread demonic doctrines that twist and pervert the Scriptures (1 Tim. 4:1).

The demons' activity reached its zenith during Christ's earthly ministry as they desperately but futilely fought to keep Him from "destroy[ing] the works of the devil" (1 John 3:8). They failed, and through His death and resurrection Jesus disarmed and defeated them (Eph. 1:20–21; Col. 2:15; 1 Peter 3:22). The task of evangelism is to deliver souls from the clutches of Satan through the power of Christ. It is a rescue operation against the forces of hell, invading the domain of darkness (Col. 1:13) and freeing lost souls held captive under the deceiving influence of Satan and his demon hosts (2 Cor. 4:4).

The Jewish people believed in the existence of Satan and the demons. They understood that Messiah would have to defeat Satan's kingdom before He could establish His own (cf. Gen. 3:15). Thus, anyone claiming to be the Messiah would have to demonstrate his power over Satan and the demonic realm—which Jesus did especially at His temptation and repeatedly by casting out demons (4:33–35,41; 8:2,27–33).

As He had earlier done with the apostles (9:1), Jesus delegated His power over Satan and the demons to the seventy. Whether the seventy had the added authority to cast out demons like the apostles did, or it was the Spirit's power through their gospel preaching that delivered those who responded in saving faith is not clear. In any case, **the demons** were **subject to** them in the **name** of Christ. There is no human power that can defeat them, as some phony exorcists at Ephesus found out the hard way. When they tried to invoke the name of Jesus as if it were a magical incantation, the demon scornfully replied, "I recognize Jesus, and I know about Paul, but who are you?" (Acts 19:15). He then used the man he inhabited to administer a severe beating to the would-be exorcists (v. 16). But the seventy had ministered in the power of Christ, and were overwhelmed with joy by the great reality that through their preaching souls were freed from Satan's domain.

In response to the seventy's joyous exclamation, Jesus **said to them, "I was watching Satan fall from heaven like lightning."** Commentators have offered various interpretations of what the Lord meant by this saying. Some argue that it refers to Satan's original fall (Isa. 14:12), but that incident has nothing to do with the immediate context. Others have suggested several other possibilities: that Christ had in mind His vanquishing of Satan at His temptation; or that He referred to Satan's subjection to Him by virtue of His own ministry of casting out demons; or the crushing of Satan's head at the cross, or Satan's future sentencing to the lake of fire. But the imperfect tense of the verb translated **I was watching** suggests a continual process rather than a one-time event such as those offerings. Although they were truly triumphs of Christ over Satan, the vivid imagery of **lightning,** which repeatedly flashes brilliantly and then is gone, suggests a different explanation. The picture here is of Jesus rejoicing as He observed Satan's kingdom being destroyed one rescued soul at a time through the seventy's evangelistic ministry. That would continue to be true throughout all the history of the church as God and the holy angels rejoice every time one lost and damned soul is recovered from Satan's domain (cf. Luke 15:7, 10).

DIVINE PROTECTION FROM SATAN'S KINGDOM

Behold, I have given you authority to tread on serpents and scorpions, and over all the power of the enemy, and nothing will injure you. (10:19)

Demons strongly resist when believers invade Satan's kingdom and attempt to snatch brands from the fire (Jude 23). They would like to thwart the work of God by destroying those faithful witnesses who proclaim the gospel and halting their work. But the seventy, and by extension all who faithfully evangelize the lost, need not fear the opposition of the forces of hell. **Behold** introduces an important or startling truth: **I have given you,** Jesus promised, **authority to tread on serpents and scorpions, and over all the power of the enemy, and nothing will injure you.** The perfect tense of the verb translated **I have given** indicates a past action with continuing effects. The Lord has permanently given believers **authority,** or power, over Satan and the demons, depicted metaphorically here as **serpents** (cf. Rev. 12:9; 20:2) **and scorpions** (Rev. 9:3,5,10).

Not by their own power or wisdom, but because believers are in Christ (Rom. 8:1; 1 Cor. 1:30; 2 Cor. 5:17; 1 Peter 5:14), they triumph over the forces of hell through Him. They need not fear Satan and the demons, since "the God of peace will soon crush Satan under [their] feet" (Rom. 16:20), "the Lord is faithful, and He will strengthen and protect [them] from the evil one" (2 Thess. 3:3), and "greater is He who is in [them] than he who is in the world" (1 John 4:4).

DIVINE PRESERVATION IN GOD'S KINGDOM

Nevertheless do not rejoice in this, that the spirits are subject to you, but rejoice that your names are recorded in heaven. (10:20)

Satan may, if God permits, bring trials into our lives as he did to Job (Job 1:6–12; 2:1–7), Peter (Luke 22:31), and Paul (2 Cor. 12:7). But he can never take away our salvation or separate us from God's love (John 10:27–29; Rom. 8:28–39; Jude 24–25). The cause for that confidence lies in the final reason for the seventy's rejoicing.

Although they rejoiced in the power over and protection from Satan's kingdom of darkness the Lord had granted them, there was a far more significant reason for the seventy to rejoice. Jesus exhorted them **not** to **rejoice** merely because **the spirits** were **subject to** them, **but** rather **that** their **names are recorded in heaven.** They would not only experience God's power and protection in this life, but also His blessing forever.

The wondrous reality that the seventy were genuine disciples was the supreme cause of their joy. Success in evangelism and power over Satan's kingdom are for this life only. Believers' knowledge that their **names are recorded in heaven,** never to be blotted out (cf. Dan. 12:1; Phil. 4:3; Rev. 3:5; 13:8; 17:8; 20:12, 15; 21:27), far surpasses all earthly joys.

REASONS FOR THE SAVIOR'S JOY

At that very time He rejoiced greatly in the Holy Spirit, and said, "I praise You, O Father, Lord of heaven and earth, that You have hidden these things from the wise and intelligent and have revealed them to infants. Yes, Father, for this way was well-pleasing in Your sight. All things have been handed over to Me by My Father, and no one knows who the Son is except the Father, and

who the Father is except the Son, and anyone to whom the Son wills to reveal Him." Turning to the disciples, He said privately, "Blessed are the eyes which see the things you see, for I say to you, that many prophets and kings wished to see the things which you see, and did not see them, and to hear the things which you hear, and did not hear them." (10:21–24)

Three realities **at that very time** of the seventy's return prompted Jesus to **rejoice greatly** (lit.,"overflow with joy") **in the Holy Spirit** (i.e.,in keeping with His person,purpose,and power):the sovereign pleasure of the Father,the supreme power of the Son,and the surpassing privilege of the saints.

THE SOVEREIGN PLEASURE OF THE FATHER

"I praise You, O Father, Lord of heaven and earth, that You have hidden these things from the wise and intelligent and have revealed them to infants. Yes, Father, for this way was well-pleasing in Your sight. (10:21*b*)

What produced the ultimate joy for Jesus was the satisfaction of God.The Lord expressed that joy here in the form of a prayer of praise and adoration, the passion of which is evident from the phrases **O Father,** and **Yes, Father.** By calling God His Father,Jesus was claiming to share His essence.John 5:18 records that"for this reason therefore the Jews were seeking all the more to kill Him, because He not only was breaking the Sabbath, but also was calling God His own Father, making Himself equal with God." So that there can be no question as to whom He was referring,Jesus identified His Father as the **Lord of heaven and earth** (cf.Acts 17:24)—a traditionally Jewish designation of the supreme and only God of the universe (cf.Gen.14:19,22;Ezra 5:11;Isa.66:1).

Jesus rejoiced that God's sovereignty meant that He always did what **was well-pleasing in** [His] **sight.** *Eudokia* (**well-pleasing**) refers to what brings God perfectly satisfying pleasure. Despite the opposition and rejection Jesus had encountered, His mission was not a failure; it was unfolding exactly the way the Father planned it.The Lord found joy in the reality that His Father,who rules the universe,does exactly what He purposes and plans to do for His holy joy.

The central reality for which Jesus praised His Father was that He had **hidden these things from the wise and intelligent and . . . revealed them to infants.** The antecedent of **these things** is the revelation of everything concerning Jesus, including His deity, messiahship, the miracles He performed, the gospel, the kingdom—in short, all the features of Christ's life, ministry, and mission. The Father had sovereignly determined to whom those truths should be revealed, and from whom they should be hidden, and operated within that determination to reveal to the elect what was otherwise not discernable through human wisdom or intelligence.

Jesus rejoiced that His Father had not devised a plan of salvation that only the **wise and intelligent** could comprehend. Salvation is not restricted to the spiritual elite, the worldly wise and the intelligent, such as the well-educated scribes and Pharisees of Jesus' day, or those claiming elevated, esoteric, secret knowledge, like the Gnostics and the followers of the mystery religions. God has **hidden** spiritual truth so that it is not discoverable by the most elevated human wisdom apart from His self-revelation in Scripture and regenerating work of the Holy Spirit in minds:

> For the word of the cross is foolishness to those who are perishing, but to us who are being saved it is the power of God. For it is written, "I will destroy the wisdom of the wise, and the cleverness of the clever I will set aside." Where is the wise man? Where is the scribe? Where is the debater of this age? Has not God made foolish the wisdom of the world? For since in the wisdom of God the world through its wisdom did not come to know God, God was well-pleased through the foolishness of the message preached to save those who believe. For indeed Jews ask for signs and Greeks search for wisdom; but we preach Christ crucified, to Jews a stumbling block and to Gentiles foolishness, but to those who are the called, both Jews and Greeks, Christ the power of God and the wisdom of God. Because the foolishness of God is wiser than men, and the weakness of God is stronger than men. For consider your calling, brethren, that there were not many wise according to the flesh, not many mighty, not many noble; but God has chosen the foolish things of the world to shame the wise, and God has chosen the weak things of the world to shame the things which are strong, and the base things of the world and the despised God has chosen, the things that are not, so that He may nullify the things that are, so that no man may boast before God. But by His doing you are in Christ Jesus, who became to us wisdom from God, and righteousness and sanctification, and redemption, so that, just as it is written, "Let him who boasts, boast in the Lord." And when I came to you, brethren, I did not come with superiority of speech or of wisdom, proclaiming to you the testimony of God. For I determined to know nothing among you except Jesus Christ, and Him crucified. I was with you in weakness and in fear and in much trembling, and my message and my preaching were not in persuasive words of wisdom, but in demonstration of the Spirit and of power, so that your faith would not rest on the wisdom of men, but on the power of God. (1 Cor. 1:18–2:5)

That is a critical portion of Scripture where the wisest of the world are fools and the fools of the world made wise because they are "chosen"and"by His doing"brought into Christ (cf.James 3:15–18). The contrast is not between being educated and being uneducated, but between being able and unable. In contrast to the notion that these profound truths are only for the elevated elite, Jesus' chose **infants** as an illustration of those who understood. As noted in the exposition of 9:47 in chapter 31 of this volume, young children have nothing to boast of; they have not yet achieved anything in life, they are not educated, and they have no exposure to the world's wisdom or knowledge. Only those who humbly admit their inability to know God in their own wisdom and knowledge apart from His revelation of Himself can be saved. Jesus was pleased with that truth because it gives all glory to God (cf. 1 Cor. 1:29, 31). Salvation belongs not to the intelligent, wise, proud, conceited, and boastful (1 Cor. 2:14), but rather to those who are admittedly ignorant and foolish, humble, broken, and contrite (Isa.57:15;66:2).

THE SUPREME POWER OF THE SON

All things have been handed over to Me by My Father, and no one knows who the Son is except the Father, and who the Father is except the Son, and anyone to whom the Son wills to reveal Him. (10:22)

Jesus rejoiced not only in God's sovereign plan, but also in His role in that plan. In the perfect harmony of the Trinity, **all things**—every circumstance in the universe, whether in heaven, earth, or hell, involving angels, men, or demons—have been **handed over to** Jesus by His **Father** (Matt. 28:18; John 3:35; 13:3; 17:2). The Father's sovereign purpose set the plan of redemption in motion, and He has given the Son supreme power to bring that purpose to pass through the instrumentality of the Holy Spirit.

In keeping with the Father's sovereign design, **no one knows who the Son is except the Father.** No one would know who the Son is if the Father, who along with the Holy Spirit, has perfect knowledge of the Son, had not chosen to reveal Him by sending Him into the world. Conversely, no one knows **who the Father is except the Son.** Because of that Jesus alone can reveal Him. In John 1:18 the apostle John wrote,"No one has seen God at any time; the only begotten God who is in the bosom of the Father, He has explained Him." Jesus is "the Word [who] became flesh, and dwelt among us, and we saw His glory, glory as of the only begotten from the Father, full of grace and truth" (v. 14);"the Son of

God [who] has come, and has given us understanding so that we may know Him who is true" (1 John 5:20). Jesus Himself said to Philip, "He who has seen Me has seen the Father; how can you say, 'Show us the Father'?" (John 14:9).

As noted above, spiritual truth is not discernible through unaided human reason. Therefore only those **to whom the Son wills to reveal Him** can come to know the Father. It is clear in the Bible that God predetermined before the foundation of the world those who would be saved and to whom He would reveal Himself. Jesus said in John 6:44, "No one can come to Me unless the Father who sent Me draws him," and then repeated it: "For this reason I have said to you, that no one can come to Me unless it has been granted him from the Father" (v. 65; cf. v. 37). Anticipating the objection based on a human sense of justice corrupted by the fall, Paul writes,

> What shall we say then? There is no injustice with God, is there? May it never be! For He says to Moses, "I will have mercy on whom I have mercy, and I will have compassion on whom I have compassion." So then it does not depend on the man who wills or the man who runs, but on God who has mercy. For the Scripture says to Pharaoh, "For this very purpose I raised you up, to demonstrate My power in you, and that My name might be proclaimed throughout the whole earth." So then He has mercy on whom He desires, and He hardens whom He desires. (Rom. 9:14–18)

To those who would protest, "Why does He still find fault? For who resists His will?" (v. 19), the apostle answers,

> On the contrary, who are you, O man, who answers back to God? The thing molded will not say to the molder, "Why did you make me like this," will it? Or does not the potter have a right over the clay, to make from the same lump one vessel for honorable use and another for common use? What if God, although willing to demonstrate His wrath and to make His power known, endured with much patience vessels of wrath prepared for destruction? And He did so to make known the riches of His glory upon vessels of mercy, which He prepared beforehand for glory, even us, whom He also called, not from among Jews only, but also from among Gentiles. (vv. 20–24)

Writing to the Corinthians, Paul expressed the practical outworking of God's sovereignty in evangelism: "I planted, Apollos watered, but God was causing the growth. So then neither the one who plants nor the one who waters is anything, but God who causes the growth" (1 Cor. 3:6–7).

Apart from God's sovereign choice and regenerating power, no one would be saved. There is no capacity in fallen, sinful human beings to see the light of the gospel and believe savingly on their own. Those who are dead in their trespasses and sins (Eph. 2:1, 5), blinded by Satan (2 Cor. 4:4), unable to understand spiritual truth (1 Cor. 2:14) and unable to please God (Rom. 8:8) cannot save themselves.

But while the Bible clearly and unambiguously teaches God's sovereignty in salvation, it also proclaims human responsibility. In the same context in which He declared that no one can come to Him unless drawn by the Father, Jesus said, "All that the Father gives Me will come to Me, and the one who comes to Me I will certainly not cast out" (John 6:37). Matthew 11:28 records the Lord's invitation, "Come to Me, all who are weary and heavy-laden, and I will give you rest." Isaiah 55:1 records an Old Testament invitation to salvation: "Ho! Every one who thirsts, come to the waters; and you who have no money come, buy and eat. Come, buy wine and milk without money and without cost." The familiar words of John 3:16 express the universal nature of God's invitation to salvation: "For God so loved the world, that He gave His only begotten Son, that whoever believes in Him shall not perish, but have eternal life." The great doctrine of election is always balanced by God's universal call to responsible sinners to repent and believe the gospel.

THE SURPASSING PRIVILEGE OF THE SAINTS

Turning to the disciples, He said privately, "Blessed are the eyes which see the things you see, for I say to you, that many prophets and kings wished to see the things which you see, and did not see them, and to hear the things which you hear, and did not hear them." (10:23–24)

Turning to the disciples after praising the Father, Jesus addressed them **privately.** What He was about to say applied only to His genuine followers; the Twelve, the seventy, and the other true believers. The Lord rejoiced greatly over the truth that had been revealed to them, finding joy in their joy over such blessed privilege.

That **blessed** joy was not only for those whom Jesus addressed that day, but for all who would believe in Him, as the phrase **the eyes which see the things you see** indicates. The **things** they were privileged to **see** and understand include the great truths that the Messiah had come, the salvation of God had been revealed, the work of redemption accomplished, the promised kingdom offered, all the Old Testament prophecies, promises, and covenants fulfilled in Christ, who would make the final offering for sin. Satan had met his conqueror, demons were completely dominated, disease vanquished, nature submissive, death defeated through Christ, and forgiveness and eternal life granted to all who believe.

The little flock (Luke 12:32) of genuine followers were blessed to see it all and enabled to understand it by the Holy Spirit. They were the humble, broken, contrite, self-denying, cross-bearing, obedient ones, chosen by the Father, to whom the Son revealed Himself through the Holy Spirit. The blessings they received are available to all who accept the Savior's invitation, "Come to Me, all who are weary and heavy-laden, and I will give you rest" (Matt. 11:28).

Just how privileged believers are to have the knowledge they have been granted is evident from the closing statement of the Lord's discourse: **"Many prophets and kings wished to see the things which you see, and did not see them, and to hear the things which you hear, and did not hear them."** Even the most prominent of the Old Testament saints were not blessed with the knowledge given to believers under the New Covenant:

> As to this salvation, the prophets who prophesied of the grace that would come to you made careful searches and inquiries, seeking to know what person or time the Spirit of Christ within them was indicating as He predicted the sufferings of Christ and the glories to follow. It was revealed to them that they were not serving themselves, but you, in these things which now have been announced to you through those who preached the gospel to you by the Holy Spirit sent from heaven— things into which angels long to look. (1 Peter 1:10–12)

The Old Testament heroes of faith, including Abel, Enoch, Noah, Abraham, Sarah, Isaac, Jacob, Joseph, Moses, Rahab, Gideon, Barak, Samson, Jephthah, David, Samuel, and the prophets, "died in faith, without receiving the promises, but having seen them and having welcomed them from a distance" (Heb. 11:13). Although they "gained approval through their faith, [they] did not receive what was promised, because God had provided something better for us, so that apart from us they would not be made perfect" (vv. 39–40). New Covenant believers have been granted the privilege of knowing the mysteries of the kingdom of God—the New Testament revelation of all the things kept secret in the Old Testament. That privilege, granted by God's sovereign pleasure, brought joy to Jesus and the seventy, and should bring joy to all believers.

Finding Eternal Life (Luke 10:25–37)

36

And a lawyer stood up and put Him to the test, saying, "Teacher, what shall I do to inherit eternal life?" And He said to him, "What is written in the Law? How does it read to you?" And he answered, "You shall love the Lord your God with all your heart, and with all your soul, and with all your strength, and with all your mind; and your neighbor as yourself." And He said to him, "You have answered correctly; do this and you will live." But wishing to justify himself, he said to Jesus, "And who is my neighbor?" Jesus replied and said, "A man was going down from Jerusalem to Jericho, and fell among robbers, and they stripped him and beat him, and went away leaving him half dead. And by chance a priest was going down on that road, and when he saw him, he passed by on the other side. Likewise a Levite also, when he came to the place and saw him, passed by on the other side. But a Samaritan, who was on a journey, came upon him; and when he saw him, he felt compassion, and came to him and bandaged up his wounds, pouring oil and wine on them; and he put him on his own beast, and brought him to an inn and took care of him. On the next day he took out two denarii and gave them to the innkeeper and said, 'Take care of him; and whatever more you spend, when I return I

will repay you.' Which of these three do you think proved to be a neighbor to the man who fell into the robbers' hands?" And he said, "The one who showed mercy toward him." Then Jesus said to him, "Go and do the same." (10:25–37)

Of all the questions that could be asked, none is more important than the one in this passage: "What shall I do to inherit eternal life?" That question's significance is rooted in the reality that every human soul is immortal. Annihilationism, materialism, reincarnation, and any other view that denies that people will continue to be the persons that they are forever is false. The question is not if people will live forever, but where they will live forever—in heaven, or in hell.

As this story unfolds, Jesus was in the final months of His earthly ministry, journeying slowly to Jerusalem and blanketing Judea's towns and villages with the message of eternal life while calling people to be His true disciples (cf. Luke 9:23). But despite His powerful preaching and miraculous signs, only a very small number of people savingly believed and embraced the gospel. Most rejected His call to humble themselves, repent of their sin and self-righteousness, receive complete forgiveness, and in faith enter the kingdom of God. They would not accept Christ's message because they would not acknowledge themselves to be wretched sinners on their way to eternal destruction. Having rejected the diagnosis, they denied themselves the only cure.

That the Lord ministered not only to the crowds, but also often to individuals, is evident in this passage. Although it took place in a public setting, this was a personal conversation between Jesus and this man. He was a member of the religious establishment, the highly educated, prominent, powerful, and influential people who made up Judaistic apostate religion, hostile to Jesus. This unnamed scribe had a rare privilege whose value is beyond estimation—having a conversation about eternal life with the One who is Himself eternal life (1 John 5:20). In a tragic example of missed opportunity that rivals Judas, the scribe, despite asking the right question of the right person and receiving the right answer, he turned away to face eternal death.

Despite its outcome, this incident provides a valuable lesson on doing personal evangelism the way Jesus did it. Those who would have the opportunity to receive eternal life will have to grasp the truth regarding the nature of eternal life, the motivation for eternal life, the complexion of eternal life, and the acquisition of eternal life.

THE NATURE OF ETERNAL LIFE

The supremely important question of how to obtain or inherit eternal life was also asked by the rich young ruler (18:18; Matt. 19:16; Mark 10:17). Implicit in his and the scribe's question was the Jewish belief in immortality. The Jews recognized that God had promised an eternal kingdom of blessing, joy, peace, and fulfillment. If the scribe had not shared that common belief, this conversation would never have taken place. There would have been no reason for him to ask Jesus how to inherit eternal life unless he already believed in its actuality. He knew that Adam's fall had caused the human race to forfeit that eternal life, and he wanted to know how to personally recover it.

In today's postmodern world, dominated by naturalism, evolution, and humanism, Christians can no longer assume that the people they evangelize understand that they will live forever. The enemy loves to propagate the lie that the present life is all there is, so there is nothing better than to "eat and drink, for tomorrow we die" (1 Cor. 15:32). Yet God has set eternity in the heart of man (Eccl. 3:11), and even those who deny its reality still feel its pull in their hearts. That universal sense of eternity has been expressed in various rituals and traditions involving burying the dead throughout history.

But general revelation was not the reason the scribe believed in the immortality of the soul. As an expert in the Mosaic Law, he knew that was the clear teaching of the Old Testament. Job understood that after he died he would personally see God (Job 19:26–27). David rejoiced in the knowledge that "in [God's] right hand there are pleasures forever" (Ps. 16:11), and after the tragic death of his newborn son, he was comforted by the knowledge that he would see him again: "I will go to him, but he will not return to me" (2 Sam. 12:23). Daniel's prophecy notes that "the saints of the Highest One will receive the kingdom and possess the kingdom forever, for all ages to come" (Dan. 7:18), and that at the time of the end, "Many of those who sleep in the dust of the ground will awake, these to everlasting life, but the others to disgrace and everlasting contempt" (12:2; cf. 2:44; Ps. 21:4).

It may seem strange that a member of the religious establishment would ask this question. After all, the Jewish people were convinced that as Abraham's children (Matt. 3:9; John 8:39), "to whom belongs the adoption as sons, and the glory and the covenants and the giving of the Law and the temple service and the promises, whose are the fathers" (Rom. 9:4–5a), they were guaranteed entrance into God's eternal kingdom. But their Jewish heritage would not save those whose religion was shallow, superficial, hypocritical, and external (Luke 3:8; Rom. 2:28–29). The question about inheriting eternal life kept coming up because of the doubts and fears caused by a nagging conscience and a discontented heart. Like this lawyer, many knew that they were not right with God; that their veneer of religious activities merely served as whitewash, covering a tomb "full of dead men's bones and all uncleanness" (Matt. 23:27). The question asked both by the rich young ruler and by the scribe reflected their fear that they might miss out on eternal life despite all their outward show of religious zeal.

In the scribe's mind, Jesus was a logical person to ask about eternal life, because it was the constant theme of His preaching (Matt. 25:46; Mark 10:29–30; John 4:36; 5:24, 39; 6:27, 40, 47, 54, 68; 10:28; 12:25, 50; 17:2–3; cf. Acts 13:48; Rom. 2:7; 5:21; 1 Tim. 1:16; Titus 1:2; 1 John 1:2; 2:25; 3:15; 5:11, 13, 20; Jude 21). It is here that much modern evangelism is deficient. Talking about eternal life and especially about hell is considered uncouth, and some who profess to be evangelicals question or even openly deny hell's existence. Jesus, however, described hell in terrifyingly graphic language (Matt. 8:12; 22:13; 24:51; 25:30; Mark 9:43–48) and said more about it than He did about heaven. Heaven, surprisingly, is also an unpopular topic, since the emphasis is on making things better in the present life. To that end, contemporary evangelism seeks to discover people's felt needs and then present Jesus to them as the cure for all that is dysfunctional in their lives.

But the Bible does not guarantee that a person's circumstances will improve after salvation. In fact, they may even become worse (Acts 14:22; Rom. 8:17; 1 Thess. 3:4; 2 Tim. 3:12; 1 Peter 4:12–16). Salvation does bring supernatural peace (John 14:27), strength to endure trials and suffering (2 Thess. 3:3; 1 Peter 5:10), and comfort (2 Cor. 1:3–5) that turns sorrow into joy (Ps. 30:5; John 15:11). But the focus of biblically-based evangelism is not on the comforts of the present life, but on the reality of eternity; on getting people's attention off this temporary world and onto the everlasting existence by explaining in biblical detail the joys of heaven and the horrors of hell.

THE MOTIVATION FOR ETERNAL LIFE

And a lawyer stood up and put Him to the test, saying, "Teacher, what shall I do to inherit eternal life?" (10:25)

The NASB leaves untranslated the particle *idou* ("behold"), which indicates that the question asked by the **lawyer** was a surprising development. But as noted above, he was motivated to ask this question by concern that he not miss out on eternal life. A **lawyer** (*nomikos*), or scribe, was an expert in the interpretation and application of the Mosaic

Law and the rabbinical traditions that had been formed over the centuries. Scribes are frequently seen in the Gospels accompanying the
Pharisees and seeking ways to discredit Jesus (Matt. 12:38; 15:1; Mark
2:16; Luke 5:21; 6:7; 11:53; 15:2; John 8:3). This one, however, was apparently asking this question on his own, since he wanted to know what he, not
people in general, needed to **do to inherit eternal life.** His question
indicates that the emphasis on corporate salvation in Judaism had not
negated the concepts of individual salvation and human responsibility.

That he **stood up** and interrupted Jesus was not a sign of disre-
spect, since he addressed the Lord courteously as **teacher.** While the
phrase **put Him to the test** could often imply evil intent on the ques-
tioner's part (cf. Mark 10:2), for this lawyer it may have been merely an
effort to determine whether Jesus knew the answer for which he felt a
great need.

THE COMPLEXION OF ETERNAL LIFE

**And He said to him, "What is written in the Law? How does it
read to you?" And he answered, "You shall love the Lord your
God with all your heart, and with all your soul, and with all your
strength, and with all your mind; and your neighbor as yourself."
And He said to him, "You have answered correctly; do this and
you will live."** (10:26–28)

The Master responded to the lawyer's question by asking one of
His own: **"What is written in the Law?"** Christ's question affirms His
commitment to the Law (cf. Matt. 5:18–19)—the very thing the scribes
and Pharisees accused Him of violating (cf. Matt. 15:2). The **Law** to which
Jesus referred was the law of God given to Moses, which the Jews had
embellished, but not forgotten. The Lord's second question, **"How does
it read to you?"** could mean, "How do you understand it?" But it is better to translate the Lord's question, "How do you recite it?" Jesus was referring to the Jewish profession of faith known as the *Shema* (Deut. 6:4–5),
which was recited twice daily. The first part of the lawyer's answer, **"You
shall love the Lord your God with all your heart, and with all
your soul, and with all your strength, and with all your mind,"**
comes from the *Shema.* The additional clause, **"and your neighbor as
yourself"** is quoted from Leviticus 19:18. When He was asked to name
the most important of the commandments, Jesus gave the same answer
as the lawyer did (Mark 12:28–31), so his answer was correct.

The command calls for total commitment to selfless **love**
(*agapaō;* the highest kind of love) involving all human faculties, including

the **heart, soul, strength,** and **mind.** These two commands sum up the Ten Commandments, the first half of which describes how to love God, while the second half describes how to love one's neighbor. Only those who practice such self-denying love (cf. Luke 9:23) can receive eternal life.

Because the lawyer's answer was the right one, Jesus **said to him, "You have answered correctly; do this and you will live"** (cf. Lev. 18:5; Deut. 6:25; Neh. 9:29; Ezek. 20:11, 13, 21). Since he knew the answer, the lawyer was accountable. But like everyone who has ever lived, he was not able to keep the law by perfectly loving God and other people. To do so is impossible, "because by the works of the Law no flesh will be justified in His sight; for through the Law comes the knowledge of sin" (Rom. 3:20) and, "For as many as are of the works of the Law are under a curse; for it is written, 'Cursed is everyone who does not abide by all things written in the book of the law, to perform them'" (Gal. 3:10; cf. Deut. 27:26). As a result, "all have sinned and fall short of the glory of God" (Rom. 3:23), so that "there is none righteous, not even one" (Rom. 3:10; cf. 5:12; Gal. 3:22).

Jesus, of course, was not saying that there were some people somewhere who could be saved by keeping the law. On the contrary, He was pointing out the absolute impossibility of doing so, since the law demands the impossible—perfect and complete obedience (James 2:10), and promises physical, spiritual, and eternal death to those who disobey it (Ezek. 18:4, 20; Rom. 6:23). Those realities put sinners in a hopeless situation. They are required to keep the law perfectly, but are not able to do so, and as a consequence face death. The only way out of that frightening dilemma is to acknowledge one's sin (Ps. 32:5; Prov. 28:13; 1 John 1:9), cry for mercy (Luke 18:13), and through faith alone (John 3:16, 36; 5:24; Acts 15:9; Rom. 3:20–30; 4:5; 5:1; Gal. 2:16; Eph. 2:8–9; Phil. 3:9; 1 Peter 1:9) embrace the Lord Jesus Christ as the Savior and only sacrifice for sin (Eph. 5:2; Heb. 9:24–28; 10:12). For such penitent believers God made His Son, "who knew no sin to be sin on [their] behalf, so that [they] might become the righteousness of God in Him" (2 Cor. 5:21).

THE ACQUISITION OF ETERNAL LIFE

But wishing to justify himself, he said to Jesus, "And who is my neighbor?" Jesus replied and said, "A man was going down from Jerusalem to Jericho, and fell among robbers, and they stripped him and beat him, and went away leaving him half dead. And by chance a priest was going down on that road, and when he saw him, he passed by on the other side. Likewise a Levite also, when he came to the place and saw him, passed by on the other side. But

a Samaritan, who was on a journey, came upon him; and when he saw him, he felt compassion, and came to him and bandaged up his wounds, pouring oil and wine on them; and he put him on his own beast, and brought him to an inn and took care of him. On the next day he took out two denarii and gave them to the innkeeper and said, 'Take care of him; and whatever more you spend, when I return I will repay you.' Which of these three do you think proved to be a neighbor to the man who fell into the robbers' hands?" And he said, "The one who showed mercy toward him." Then Jesus said to him, "Go and do the same." (10:29–37)

At this point in the discussion, the scribe should have acknowledged his inability to love as God required and cried out for mercy like the tax collector in Luke 18:13 did. But backed into a corner from which there was no escape, his wretched pride and self-righteousness took over, like the Pharisee's had (vv. 11–12). By **wishing to justify himself,** he failed to deny himself. He refused to confess the reality of his sinful heart, but disdaining the conviction of sin that he surely felt rising internally, he adamantly reaffirmed his external self-righteousness and worthiness.

Sadly, this was familiar behavior, Paul would later note, typical of the nation of Israel as a whole. In Romans 2:23–29, the apostle rebuked his fellow Jews for keeping the law superficially and externally:

You who boast in the Law, through your breaking the Law, do you dishonor God? For "The name of God is blasphemed among the Gentiles because of you," just as it is written. For indeed circumcision is of value if you practice the Law; but if you are a transgressor of the Law, your circumcision has become uncircumcision. So if the uncircumcised man keeps the requirements of the Law, will not his uncircumcision be regarded as circumcision? And he who is physically uncircumcised, if he keeps the Law, will he not judge you who though having the letter of the Law and circumcision are a transgressor of the Law? For he is not a Jew who is one outwardly, nor is circumcision that which is outward in the flesh. But he is a Jew who is one inwardly; and circumcision is that which is of the heart, by the Spirit, not by the letter; and his praise is not from men, but from God.

In Romans 10 the apostle explained why the Jewish people were in that lost condition:

Brethren, my heart's desire and my prayer to God for them is for their salvation. For I testify about them that they have a zeal for God, but not in accordance with knowledge. For not knowing about God's righteousness and seeking to establish their own, they did not subject themselves to the righteousness of God. (vv. 1–3)

Underestimating God's righteousness, they imagined Him to be more tolerant of sin than He is, and thus less holy than He is. That made them think they were more righteous than they were. As a result, Israel failed to realize their need for a Savior, and did not understand the truth that "Christ is the end of the law for righteousness to everyone who believes" (v. 4), since "what the Law could not do, weak as it was through the flesh, God did: sending His own Son in the likeness of sinful flesh and as an offering for sin, He condemned sin in the flesh" (Rom. 8:3). Far from being a means of salvation, "the Law has become our tutor to lead us to Christ, so that we may be justified by faith" (Gal. 3:24. See also the verses listed in the previous section).

In his attempt to justify himself, the scribe ignored the issue of loving God perfectly, thus implying that he believed he did. He also believed that he was loving his neighbors perfectly, unless Jesus had a different definition of neighbor. Seeking to clarify the Lord's definition he asked Him, **"And who is my neighbor?"** The Lord replied with one of His most memorable and powerful illustrations, the story of the Good Samaritan.

This dramatic tale is widely used to teach the importance of helping those in need. In fact, the term "Good Samaritan" has become an idiom for those who demonstrate unusual, sacrificial kindness toward others. But while it is important to help the needy, that is not the point of the story. It is in reality a story about how one inherits eternal life, because that is the question that initiated the conversation to which this story is the conclusion.

The Lord offered this story in answer to the scribe's question, with its somewhat cynical implication that he did love all those whom he considered to be his neighbors. Jesus graciously gave him one more unforgettable, inescapably clear insight into his wretchedness; one more opportunity to acknowledge his sinfulness and cry for mercy.

As the story opens **a man was going down from Jerusalem to Jericho.** Although it is less than fifteen miles from Jerusalem, **Jericho,** at about nine hundred feet below sea level, is nearly 3,500 feet lower in elevation. Thus the road **going down from Jerusalem to Jericho** was steep and dangerous—all the more so because its caves and rock formations provided hideouts for robbers and highwaymen. Unfortunately for this man the predictable happened, and he **fell among robbers,** who **stripped him,** repeatedly **beat him, and went away leaving him half dead.** The man's situation was desperate. He was stranded on a lonely road in critical condition and in need of immediate medical attention. Yet there was no guarantee when or if anyone would care to help him.

Having described the man's dire situation, Jesus immediately introduced a ray of hope, noting that **by chance a priest was going down on that road.** This would appear to have been the best possible news. A **priest** was a servant of God by definition, one who offered sacrifices for the people's sins, expected to be a paragon of spiritual virtue and the best, godliest, and most righteous of men. He would be intimately familiar with the Old Testament law and committed to living out its principles, one of which was the requirement to show mercy. In Leviticus 19:34 God commanded the people of Israel, "The stranger who resides with you shall be to you as the native among you, and you shall love him as yourself, for you were aliens in the land of Egypt; I am the Lord your God." According to Exodus 23:4–5 they were to rescue an enemy's donkey if it wandered off, or collapsed under its load—how much more the man himself.

The hope the Lord introduced was short-lived, however. Instead of stopping to assist the wounded and helpless man, the priest **passed by on the other side.** Commentators have offered many suggestions as to why the priest avoided the injured man. But all such speculation is pointless, since he was not a real person, but merely a character in the Lord's story. The point Jesus was making is that because he knew the law's requirements, he would have been expected to stop and aid the injured man. Nor is this an indictment on Israel's priesthood for lacking compassion, though that was often true; the priest in this story merely functions as someone who would have been expected to help, but did not.

Fortunately for the desperate man, another traveler appeared on the stretch of road. This man was **a Levite,** one of those who assisted the priests. He, too, would have been very familiar with the Old Testament law and its requirements to show mercy to those in need. But incredibly **when he came to the place and saw** the injured man, the Levite also refused to stop and help him, but like the priest had, he **passed by on the other side.** Despite their circumcision, knowledge of God's law, and involvement in the religious system, both he and the priest proved themselves unqualified for eternal life. They did not love God, since they did not keep His commandments. Nor did they love their neighbor, since both passed up an opportunity to demonstrate that love.

At this point the story takes a surprising and unexpected twist. When all seemed lost, help arrived from the most unlikely of sources. **A Samaritan, who was on a journey, came upon** the wounded man. Given the hostility between Jews and Samaritans, this man would seem to be the most indifferent to the injured man. As noted in the exposition of 9:52 in chapter 32 of this volume, the hatred between Jews and Gentiles had existed for centuries. The Samaritan could hardly have been expected to help this man; in fact, he may even have finished what the robbers had started. But amazingly, **when he saw** the beaten, helpless man, **he felt compassion** for him. His heart went out to the man in sadness, grief, and sympathy. Instead of passing him by as the other two men had, he **came to him** and assessed the situation. Noting his traumatic injuries, the Samaritan **bandaged up his wounds, pouring oil and wine on them.** Since the robbers had stripped their victim, the Samaritan would have had to tear up some of his own spare clothes to make the bandages. He also used some of his own provisions to treat the wounds before bandaging them. **Pouring oil and wine on** the wounds served to sanitize them and soften them, thus relieving the pain and helping them to heal. This was generous, lavish care, certainly unexpected for one who was his enemy.

But the Samaritan was not through. Instead of being content to treat the man's wounds and then leaving, **he put him on his own beast** (perhaps a donkey or a mule) **and brought him to an inn and took care of him.** Inns offered meager fare at best, and at worst were places of prostitution and robbery. Innkeepers were often unscrupulous, evil, and without compassion. But in this case there was no choice; the wounded man needed shelter, food, water, and rest. Having negotiated a place to stay, the Samaritan took the man in and continued to care for him throughout the night, since he did not leave until **the next day.**

When he left the next morning, the Samaritan **took out two denarii and gave them to the innkeeper and said, "Take care of him."** Depending on the quality of the inn, that amount would have paid for the injured man's room and board for anywhere from three weeks to two months. Here was still another example of the Samaritan's generous, compassionate love. But he still was not finished. He promised the innkeeper, **"Whatever more you spend, when I return I will repay you."** In effect, he gave him a blank check. His generosity knew no bounds. He cared for the injured stranger the way most people care for themselves. That is the kind of limitless love that it takes to earn one's way into God's kingdom. The scribe did not love like that.

Jesus then asked the scribe, **"Which of these three do you think proved to be a neighbor** to the man who fell into the robbers' hands?" He replied with the obvious answer, **"The one who showed mercy toward him."** Driving home the point of the story, **Jesus said to him, "Go and do the same."** The idea is that only by continuously, perfectly loving God and every neighbor on every occasion—even his worst enemy—could the scribe satisfy the first and second commandments and obtain eternal life. Obviously, Christ's point is that neither the scribe nor anyone else is capable of such love. This is an indictment of the whole of fallen humanity, and the only proper response was for him to acknowledge his inability to save himself, and plead with God for mercy and forgiveness. Jesus, God incarnate, stood before him ready to extend forgiveness, grace, and mercy to him. But there is no indication that the lawyer did so; his pride and self-righteousness held him captive and he likely forfeited eternal life.

The Christian's Priority (Luke 10:38–42)

37

Now as they were traveling along, He entered a village; and a woman named Martha welcomed Him into her home. She had a sister called Mary, who was seated at the Lord's feet, listening to His word. But Martha was distracted with all her preparations; and she came up to Him and said, "Lord, do You not care that my sister has left me to do all the serving alone? Then tell her to help me." But the Lord answered and said to her, "Martha, Martha, you are worried and bothered about so many things; but only one thing is necessary, for Mary has chosen the good part, which shall not be taken away from her." (10:38–42)

The record of this unique and wonderful event appears nowhere else in the Gospels. Despite its brevity, it occupies an important place in the flow of Luke's gospel and conveys an essential truth by revealing the highest priority of the Christian life, that of loving God. It makes a fitting follow-up to the story of the Good Samaritan, which stressed the importance of loving one's neighbor as evidence of loving God.

The word "priority" is a commonly used one today. Books and seminars purporting to teach people how to get their lives in order by understanding and setting their priorities abound. As people's lives become more frenetic, frantic, disjointed, and disconnected, they battle to stay focused on what should be their priorities. A priority is by definition a matter that ranks above all others in importance. David said in Psalm 27:4, "One thing I have asked from the Lord, that I shall seek," while in the New Testament Paul wrote, "One thing I do" (Phil. 3:13). David's single focus was on beholding and meditating on the beauty of the Lord, and Paul's was on pursuing Him so as to be conformed to His likeness. Both are illustrations of the highest priority for believers—the deep, transforming knowledge of God.

This story sets the stage for the last phase of Jesus' ministry. As noted in previous chapters of this volume, Luke covers Jesus' final journey to Jerusalem in 9:51–19:27. That period between the end of His Galilean ministry and His triumphal entry into Jerusalem found the Lord traveling extensively in Judea and occasionally east of the Jordan River in Perea. His primary emphasis during that peripatetic journey was not on performing miraculous signs, but on teaching His disciples. He covered subjects such as prayer, Satan, demons, divine judgment, hypocrisy, persecution, suffering, the Holy Spirit, greed, contentment, money, giving, stewardship, unity, righteousness, holiness, divine justice, humility, pride, the cost of loyalty to Him, the kingdom of God and how to enter it, heaven's joy over repentant sinners, divorce, hell, penitence, forgiveness, and faith. Luke's focus on the content of Jesus' teaching to His disciples during those months is the reason the locations are vague. For example, in verse 38 he writes that Jesus "entered a certain village" (NKJV); in 11:1 that He was praying "in a certain place"; in 13:22 that "He was passing through from one city and village to another"; and in 17:11–12 that "He was passing between Samaria and Galilee" and "entered a village."

Always Christ's teaching was a radical departure from the conventional Jewish wisdom of His day. It was not only cogent, powerful, and urgent, but true and thus life changing, because when He spoke God was speaking. In John 7:16 He declared, "My teaching is not Mine, but His who sent Me." "I have many things to speak and to judge concerning you," Jesus said, "but He who sent Me is true; and the things which I heard from Him, these I speak to the world" (John 8:26). In verse 28 He added, "When you lift up the Son of Man, then you will know that I am He, and I do nothing on My own initiative, but I speak these things as the Father taught Me." To those who sought His life He said, "You are seeking to kill Me, a man who has told you the truth, which I heard from God" (v. 40). He told the apostles in the upper room, "No longer do I call you slaves, for the slave does not know what his master is doing; but I have called you friends, for all things that I have heard from My Father I have made known to you" (John 15:15). In His high-priestly prayer Jesus said to the Father, "The words which You gave Me I have given to them; and they received them and truly understood that I came forth from You, and they believed that You sent Me" (John 17:8).

As this passage illustrates, the supreme priority for believers is to hear the revealed Word of God. It is foundational to the other spiritual duties, all of which are motivated, informed, and defined by Scripture. Don Whitney writes,

> No Spiritual Discipline is more important than the intake of God's Word. Nothing can substitute for it. There simply is no healthy Christian life apart from a diet of the milk and meat of Scripture. The reasons for this are obvious. In the Bible God tells us about Himself, and especially about Jesus Christ, the incarnation of God. The Bible unfolds the Law of God to us and shows us how we've all broken it. There we learn how Christ died as a sinless, willing Substitute for breakers of God's Law and how we must repent and believe in Him to be right with God. In the Bible we learn the ways and will of the Lord. We find in Scripture how to live in a way that is pleasing to God as well as best and most fulfilling for ourselves. None of this eternally essential information can be found anywhere else except the Bible. Therefore if we would know God and be Godly, we must know the Word of God—intimately. (*Spiritual Disciplines for the Christian Life* [Colorado Springs, Colo.: Navpress, 1991], 24)

As the story begins Jesus and those accompanying Him **were traveling,** as they would do throughout Judea. Where this incident fits chronologically into the Lord's journey to Jerusalem is not known, but Luke placed it here for a specific purpose. His intent was to put his readers in the position of students, ready to absorb the teaching of the Lord Jesus Christ in the chapters to follow. Though he does not name the **village** Christ **entered,** John tells us it was Bethany, where Martha and Mary, and their brother Lazarus lived (John 11:1; 12:1–3). According to John 11:18, Bethany "was near Jerusalem, about two miles off," so Jesus was in the vicinity of Jerusalem, though not for the last time. As the Lord entered the village, He met **a woman named Martha.** Luke's introduction of her as **a woman** suggests that Jesus had not yet met her. This may have been the first of many times He stayed in the home she shared with Mary and Lazarus.

Neither Jesus nor His messengers always received a welcome in the villages they visited (cf. 9:51–53; 10:10–12). But in this case **Martha** enthusiastically **welcomed Him into her home** and entertained Him as a highly-prized guest. **Martha** is an Aramaic name that means "mistress" (i.e., a female head of a household), which suits her character and position. She may well have been a widow, since there is no mention of her husband and Luke describes the place as **her home.** Since she is usually mentioned first when the sisters are named together (John 11:29–30; 12:2–3), Martha was probably the older of the two. Along with her sister, Martha evidently was a believer in Jesus, since she called Him "Lord" (v. 40).

As the story unfolds it reveals the different reactions of the two sisters (and also common among believers) to the teaching of Jesus: Mary was devoted, but Martha was distracted.

MARY DEVOTED

She had a sister called Mary, who was seated at the Lord's feet, listening to His word. (10:39)

Luke does not mention Martha's brother Lazarus, but does reveal that **she had a sister called Mary.** Although Martha was mentioned first, Mary is the central figure in the story and an example for all believers to follow. After He entered the house, she **was seated at the Lord's feet, listening to His word.** Her position, as close to Him as she could get, indicates Mary's intense interest in His teaching. Though this was a typical position for students of a rabbi, in first-century Judaism rabbis did not take women as students. The imperfect tense of the verb translated **listening** suggests a continual hearing on her part. Mary's attention was riveted to the most powerful, clear, truthful teacher who ever spoke.

Mary demonstrated the attitude of a true believer. In Luke 6:47 Jesus defined a genuine disciple as one "who comes to Me and hears My words and acts on them," in contrast to those who "call [Him], 'Lord, Lord,' and do not do what [He says]" (v. 46). In Luke 8:21 Jesus defined His true spiritual brethren as "these who hear the word of God and do it," and later said, "Blessed are those who hear the word of God and observe it" (11:28). In the parable of the soils, He declared that "the seed in the good soil, these are the ones who have heard the word in an honest and good heart, and hold it fast, and bear fruit with perseverance" (8:15). James exhorted his readers to "prove yourselves doers of the word, and not merely hearers who delude themselves" (James 1:22). Paul was confident that the Thessalonians' faith was genuine, because "when [they] received the word of God ... [they] accepted it not as the word of men, but for what it really is, the word of God, which also performs its work in [those] who believe" (1 Thess. 2:13). Mary understood that the highest priority for a believer is to hear the truth that has come from heaven (cf. John 8:43–47).

MARTHA DISTRACTED

But Martha was distracted with all her preparations; and she came up to Him and said, "Lord, do You not care that my sister has left me to do all the serving alone? Then tell her to help me." But the Lord answered and said to her, "Martha, Martha, you are worried and bothered about so many things; but only one thing is necessary, for Mary has chosen the good part, which shall not be taken away from her." (10:40–42)

Unfortunately, even genuine believers can lose their focus on what really matters. Unlike her sister, **Martha was distracted** from hearing the Lord's teaching, being preoccupied **with all her preparations.** The verb translated **distracted** literally means, "to be dragged away." She allowed **her preparations** (lit., "much serving"), such as fixing a meal for the guests and making arrangements for where they would sleep, to keep her from the priority of listening to the Lord teach.

There is certainly nothing wrong with showing hospitality; in fact, Scripture commands it. Paul wrote that believers are to be constantly "practicing hospitality" (Rom. 12:13). The writer of Hebrews exhorted, "Do not neglect to show hospitality to strangers, for by this some have entertained angels without knowing it" (Heb. 13:2), while Peter commanded, "Be hospitable to one another without complaint" (1 Peter 4:9). Showing hospitality marks both elders (1 Tim. 3:2; Titus 1:8) and godly women (1 Tim. 5:10). But in the process of doing that, Martha got her priorities twisted; she was fussing and fretting, trying to get everything arranged to her satisfaction, maybe to make an impression on Jesus. As a result, she failed to take advantage of a rare and priceless opportunity—to hear in person the Lord of the universe teach and be impressed profoundly by Him.

Her misguided priorities finally caused Martha to lose the joy of serving. She became more and more flustered, agitated, and frustrated, until finally she became angry. The target of her anger was her sister who, instead of helping with the chores, was sitting there listening to Jesus. Finally, in exasperation, Martha **came up to** Jesus and interrupted Him. Her irritation and anger caused her to lose control and make the unthinking accusation, **"Lord, do You not care?"** To so rebuke the one who is "compassionate and gracious" (Ex. 34:6; 2 Chron. 30:9; Neh. 9:17, 31; Pss. 103:8; 111:4; 116:5; Joel 2:13; Jonah 4:2) and cares for His people (1 Peter 5:7; cf. Ps. 34:15; Matt. 6:26–30) is one of the most foolish and graceless statements anyone ever made to Jesus.

Specifically, Martha accused Jesus of not caring **that** her **sister** had **left** her **to do all the serving alone.** And if He did care, **then** He should **tell her to help** bear the burden of serving. After falsely accusing Him of not caring, Martha then presumed to tell the Lord exactly what to do, implying that her will and her plans were more important than His. She had lost her perspective; she was totally out of control; her view of reality was severely skewed. Martha was worried about the bread that feeds the body, while Mary's focus was on the Bread of Life that feeds the soul (cf. John 6:33, 35, 48, 51).

Demonstrating the gentle, compassionate care that Martha had unthinkingly questioned, **the Lord answered and said to her, "Martha, Martha.** Repeating her name as a sign of intensified emotion (cf. 6:46; 8:24; 13:34), Jesus said to her, **"You are worried and bothered about so many things."** Martha was unduly concerned and troubled about temporal things to the point that she had forgotten that **only one thing is necessary**—listening to the Word of God. Far from rebuking her as Martha had demanded, Jesus commended Mary for understanding that reality. **"Mary has chosen the good part** (lit., "what is best"), He told Martha, **which shall not be taken away from her."**

All too often Christians, like Martha, allow their lives to be regulated by what is not necessary. Faithfulness on the job, in the home, and in the church has a place, but must not be allowed to replace faithfulness to divine truth. "Man does not live by bread alone, but man lives by everything that proceeds out of the mouth of the Lord" (Deut. 8:3). Only by making that their highest priority can believers behold the beauty of the Lord, as David did, and know Christ, as was Paul's supreme passion. To that end they must "commend [themselves] to God and to the word of His grace, which is able to build [them] up and to give [them] the inheritance among all those who are sanctified" (Acts 20:32; cf. Col. 3:16; Eph. 6:17; 1 Tim. 4:6; 1 Peter 2:2; 1 John 2:14).

Thus, in this account, the necessity of being a student of the Divine Teacher is established, and the lessons from His lips will unfold through the subsequent chapters.

Bibliography

Bock, Darrell L. *Luke 1:1–9:50.* Baker Exegetical Commentary on the New Testament. Grand Rapids: Baker, 1994.

Bruce, Alexander B. "The Synoptic Gospels," in W. Robertson Nicoll, ed. *The Expositor's Greek Testament.* Vol. 1. Reprint. Peabody, Mass.: Hendrickson, 2002.

Carson, D. A., Douglas J. Moo, and Leon Morris. *An Introduction to the New Testament.* Grand Rapids: Zondervan, 1992.

Ellis, E. Earle. *The Gospel of Luke.* The New Century Bible Commentary. Grand Rapids: Eerdmans, 1974.

Gooding, David. *According to Luke.* Grand Rapids: Eerdmans, 1987.

Guthrie, Donald. *New Testament Introduction.* Revised edition. Downers Grove, IL: InterVarsity, 1990.

Hendriksen, William. *Exposition of the Gospel According to Luke.* New Testament Commentary. Grand Rapids: Baker, 1978.

Hiebert, D. Edmond. *An Introduction to the New Testament.* Vol. 1, *The Gospels and Acts.* Chicago: Moody, 1975.

Lenski, R. C. H. *The Interpretation of St. Luke's Gospel.* Minneapolis: Augsburg, 1961.

Liefeld, Walter L., and David W. Pao. "Luke," in Tremper Longman III and David E. Garland, eds. *The Expositor's Bible Commentary.* Vol. 10. Revised edition. Grand Rapids: Zondervan, 2007.

Marshall, I. Howard. *The Gospel of Luke.* The New International Greek Testament Commentary. Grand Rapids: Eerdmans, 1978.

Morris, Leon. *The Gospel According to St. Luke.* The Tyndale New Testament Commentaries. Grand Rapids: Eerdmans, 1975.

Plummer, Alfred. *The Gospel According to St. Luke.* The International Critical Commentary. Edinburgh: T. & T. Clark, 1969.

Stein, Robert H. *Luke.* The New American Commentary. Nashville: Broadman & Holman, 1992.

Indexes

Index of Greek Words and Phrases

abussos, 222
adelphos, 202
agapaō, 353
agora, 164
akantha, 189
akoloutheō, 315
alēthōs, 60
analēmpsis, 310
anadeiknumi, 325
analambanō, 310
anepsios, 202
anoia, 10
apostolos, 17
arneomai, 270
autos, 126

brechō, 173

charizomai, 175
chortazō, 97, 255
Christos, 262

daimonizomai, 219
didaskalon, 235
dokos, 115
doulos, 125

ekplessō, 294
entimos, 125
epiblepō, 291
epistrephō, 272
epitimaō, 263
erēmos, 254
eudokia, 343
euangelizō, 180
existēmi, 237

genea, 163

hamartōloi, 107
hupagō, 328

idou, 230, 352

kērussō, 180, 242
kai idou, 172
kalōs, 104
kalaphileō, 173
kaphos, 115
katabainō, 209

lailaps, 209
laos, 87

makarios, 95
malakos, 154
martureō, 49
mathētēs, 15, 208
megas, 209, 211
metamelomai, 272
metanoeō, 272
mikros, 69

nomikos, 352

ochlos, 260
ouai, 95

pais, 125

parabolē, 114,187
parangellō, 263
paratēreō, 7
peirasmos, 192
petros, 25
phobeō, 223
phobos, 223
plēn, 99
prōtos, 25
ptōchos, 95
ptōssō, 95

sōzō, 234
samplēroō, 310
seismos, 209
skullō, 127
splangnon, 327
sterizō, 310
sumplēroō, 310
suntribō, 291

thaumazō, 294

zēlōtēs, 70

Index of Scripture

Genesis		45:7	14	32:1–24	21
1:1	142	45:9	14	34:6	365
2:2	3	45:26	14	34:6–7	136
3:7	220	49:29–50:13	319		
3:15	82,205,340	50:20	14	Leviticus	
6:1-4	222			9:23	280
6:12	189	Exodus		15:19–27	232
9:20–21	20	3:6	138	18:5	354
12:12	21	4:10	45	19:34	357
13:2-22	143	8:15	190	21:10–11	320
16:7–13	143	13:21	286	24:9	6
18:4	176	17:2	53		
18:27	213	18:5–12	329	Numbers	
25:9	319	18:9	339	6:2-4	154
25:30–33	21	20:8–11	3,6	15:37–41	233
26:7	21	20:18–19	213	20:2–5	53
29:13	176	23:4–5	357	20:6	53
41:39–44	14	25:30	5	20:7–8	53

20:10–12	21	14:15	39	**Psalms**		
20:12	54	14:20–23	39	1:1–3	147	
34:11	208	14:45–46	39	7:9	200	
		21:1–6	5	9:18	243	
Deuteronomy		25:40–42	17	10:17	299	
7:7–8	45			18:2	120	
13:5	112	**2 Samuel**		23:5	173	
18:15–18	139	11:1–4	21	25:9	299	
18:15–19	143	11:14–15	21	32:5	354	
19:15	325	12:23	351	34:15	365	
22:12	233	23:1	21	34:18	96	
23:25	5			40:7	142	
27:16	161	**1 Kings**		41:1	308	
30:9	338	11:26ff.	74	41:9	79	
34:6	283	18:17–40	38	51:17	128,299	
		19:1–3	21	63:1	97	
Joshua		21:1–16	54	65:5–7	210	
8:31	284	21:27	334	75:7	63	
9:3–27	21			76:9	299	
12:3	208	**2 Kings**		111:4	137	
24:2	14	1:9–12	42	116:5	136–37	
		2:11	283	138:2	307	
Judges		10:16	42			
6:1–6	38	10:31	42	**Proverbs**		
7:2	38	14:18–20	74	1:22	188	
7:3	38	17:14	191	3:3	307	
7:6–8	38			3:34	300	
7:12	38	**2 Chronicles**		6:6–12	106	
7:16–25	38	36:22–23	135	11:17	308	
13:22	213			11:18	308	
15:15–20	38	**Ezra**		11:31	172	
19:21	176	5:11	343	15:5	161	
				16:5	305	
Ruth		**Nehemiah**		16:9	134	
1:6	138	9:1	334	18:14	191	
4:1–11	135	9:17	365	19:17	96	
		9:29	191,354	19:26	161	
1 Samuel				21:1	134	
13:5	38	**Esther**		21:4	305	
13:6	39	2:21–23	74	23:23	2	
13:7	39	4:1	334	24:29	106	
13:7–14	38	4:3	334	29:15	161	
13:14	21					
13:19–22	38	**Job**		**Ecclesiastes**		
14:11	39	19:26–27	351	3:11	351	
14:13–14	39	26:14	280	4:9–12	325	

9:8	173	14:13	113	Micah	
12:14	200	14:15	112	3:5	112,244
		17:9	302	7:18	314
Song of Solomon		29:13	269		
2:15	318	30:17	253	Zephaniah	
		32:41	338	3:17	338
Isaiah					
1:10	198	Lamentations		Zechariah	
1:11–17	8–9	2:14	113	7:9	308
5:20	298	3:22	137	9:9	61
6:5	21,271	5:18	318	12:10	135
7:14	207			14:16–19	285
11:6	206	Ezekiel		14:16–21	85
14:12	341	1:28	280		
25:6–9	251	13:4	318	Malachi	
26:4	120	13:9	100	3:1	156,285
26:19	148	17:24	63	4:4	284
33:22	157	20:11	354		
33:24	253	34:16	253	Matthew	
40:3	154			1:5	14
40:3–5	155	Daniel		1:20	84
40:5	280	4:27	308	1:21	139,203,205
40:11	231	7:9–10	277	1:23	144
41:8	14	7:13–14	260	3:1	154
41:17	243	7:18	206,351	3:1–2	158
51:2	14	7:27	206	3:2	272,324
53	228,285	9:3	334	3:4	14,165
53:3	327	10:13	222	3:5–6	162
53:4–10	264	10:20	222	3:7	152
53:10	295	12:1	342	4:2	128
55:1	347			4:13	25,123,126
55:11	133	Joel		4:17	84,88,94,158,
56:10–12	244	2:13	137		180,181,272
56:11	112	2:21–27	206	4:18	25,39,40
57:15	299,345	3:4	87	4:19	40
58:6–14	9	3:12–14	327	4:21	40
61:2–3	97			4:22	40
61:10	192	Amos		4:23	294
65:17	228	2:2	75	4:25	41
66:1	343	3:6	135	5:1	86
66:2	271,299			5:3	318
		Jonah		5:14–16	199
Jeremiah		1:1–2	21	5:17	71
1:5	45	1:15–17	21	5:18	93,333
5:21	114	3:1–3	21	5:40	106
6:15	277	4:1–3	21	5:43	103
10:12	206	4:2	137	5:45	93,108,251
11:4	198			5:48	24

6:2	162	10:15	246	14:31	20,29
6:26–30	365	10:16–18	329	14:33	213,258
6:30	129,144,211	10:16–22	319	15:14	162,179
7:1–3	314	10:27	200	15:15	28
7:6	246,286,331	10:34–36	136,266	15:15–16	182
7:13–14	268	10:37–39	267	15:16	19
7:14	186,324	11:11	14	15:24	179
7:15	98,116	11:14	155	15:32	326
7:15–20	3,191	11:19	167	15:32–38	16
7:21	119,275	11:28	347,348	16:8	20,211
7:21–23	289,304	11:28–30	4,231,	16:9–11	19
7:28	122		238,256	16:13	146,259
7:28–29	16,88	12:1	188	16:16	30,64,
8:4	238	12:7	6,7		69,132
8:5	207	12:14	10	16:16–17	30,31
8:6	126	12:18	225	16:17	25,31,262
8:11–12	100,129	12:21	225	16:17–19	30–31
8:12	292	12:30	335	16:21	31
8:18–22	316	12:33	117	16:22	31
8:21	317	12:34	292	16:23	30,31
8:24	210	12:38	353	16:24	315
8:25	20	12:38–42	148	16:24–27	266
8:26	20,182	12:39	292	16:35	31
8:28	219	12:43–45	222	17:1	39,47,281
8:29	221	13:2	187	17:4	285
8:32	219	13:8	189	17:5	285
8:33	219	13:12–13	190	17:6	286
8:34	223	13:15	116	17:14–21	289
9:3	317	13:21	192	17:15	290,291
9:9	65	13:22	194	17:17	254
9:10	66	13:23	195	17:19	20
9:10–13	172	13:24–30	120,314	17:19–20	235
9:11	166	13:31–32	187	17:25	33
9:14	145	13:34	187	17:26	33
9:15	166	13:37	190	17:27	34
9:18	235	13:44–46	181,194	18:6	303
9:21	233	13:55	25,202	18:21	28
9:26	237	14:12	49	19:4	5
9:32	219	14:14	89,236	19:13–14	231
9:36	231	14:14–21	16	19:27	28,320
10:1–5	18	14:21	57	20:20–21	20
10:2	25,39	14:25–32	16	20:20–28	35
10:2–4	16	14:25–34	29	20:24	43
10:3	71	14:26	29	20:25–28	43
10:5–6	179,242	14:27	29	20:33	43
10:7	324	14:28	29	21:19	122
10:8	244	14:29	29	21:26	152
10:9	245	14:30	29	21:31	292

21:42	5	1:29	26,39	7:31	41
22:31	5	1:30	26	8:1–8	250
23:1–33	94	1:32–34	294	8:9	86
23:1–36	3	1:38	235	8:17	19
23:4	4	1:41	231,326	8:27	259
23:5	300	2:6-7	317	8:29	262
23:6	8,43	2:16	107	8:34–38	266
23:11	24	2:27	6	9:1–10	50
23:13	127	3:2	7	9:14	290
23:15	114,162	3:5	10	9:14–29	289
23:27	162	3:6	10	9:22	290,293
23:28	116	3:10	294	9:24	235
24:13	192	3:14	17	9:29	292
24:38	165	3:16–17	42	9:32	19
25:1–12	164	3:16–19	16	9:33	300
25:31	281	3:17	42,313	9:33–34	20,42
25:41	221,290	3:19	75	9:35	35
25:41–45	303	3:21	203,237	9:36	302
25:46	352	3:22	317	9:37	335
26:6	78	3:31–35	202	10:6	92
26:6–13	171	4:8	189	10:17	267
26:31–32	31	4:10–13	182	10:22	269
26:33	31	4:11–12	188	10:37	43
26:48	80	4:13	19	11:25	110
26:56	29,240	4:16–17	319	12:10	5
26:69–74	32	4:20	195	12:28–30	181
26:69–75	20	4:35	207	12:28–31	353
27:3	81	4:37	209	12:39	8
27:26	295	4:38	210,251	13:3	28
27:41	317	4:39	211	14:3	25
27:46	338	5:5	220	14:10–11	79
27:55–56	43	5:20	41,57	14:33	39,282
27:56	183	5:21	229	14:37–38	27
28:7	27	5:31	234	14:50	20
28:10	32	5:37	39	15:21	25
28:18	295,345	5:40	236	15:39	124,248
28:19	200	6:2	250	15:40	43,69
28:19–20	103,159,	6:6	123,240	15:47	183
	225,242	6:7	325		
		6:17–18	145	**Luke**	
Mark		6:31	251	1:15	146,153,
1:5	152	6:33	252		154,165
1:14	7	6:39	254	1:17	155
1:15	93	6:45–8:26	259	1:41–45	85
1:16	39	6:52	30	1:44	39
1:20	41,184	7:18–19	331	1:54	260
1:21	39	7:24–31	87	1:68	138
1:25	263	7:25	220	1:73	14

1:80	14	5:27–28	16, 18	8:6–7	157
2:25	40, 330	5:27–29	170	8:12	198
3:1	247	5:29	66	8:14	320
3:7	152	5:30	15, 65	8:16	199
3:8	117, 165, 351	5:32	181	8:19–21	202
3:9	148, 165	5:36–39	3	8:22–25	205
3:14	105	6:1–5	3	8:25	223
3:17	148, 165	6:1–11	1, 16	8:37	229
3:18	7	6:2	15	8:45	29
3:20	247	6:7	15, 317	8:45–48	234
4:14	126	6:11	15	8:49–50	235
4:14–15	7	6:12	15	8:54–55	236
4:15	2	6:12–13	13	8:56	237
4:16–30	240	6:13a	15	9:1	16
4:18	7	6:13b	17	9:1–6	301
4:18–21	7	6:14a	23	9:4	331
4:22	122	6:14b	39	9:5–9	246
4:29	318	6:14b, c	37	9:9	247, 257
4:31	7, 25	6:14c	41	9:10	251
4:32	86	6:14d	45	9:18–22	257
4:34	217, 221	6:14e, f	53	9:20	257
4:38	25, 26	6:15	25	9:23	268, 315,
4:38–39	25	6:15–16a	63		319, 350
4:41	238	6:16b	73	9:23–24	321
4:42	2	6:17–19	83	9:23–26	265
4:43	242	6:20–26	91	9:24–25	276
4:44	7	6:27–38	101	9:26	277, 281
5:1	208	6:39–49	111–12	9:29	282
5:1–11	40	6:41–42	115	9:32–33	284
5:3	26	6:45	302	9:34–35	285
5:4–9	16, 207	6:46	289	9:37–39	289
5:5	26	6:47	364	9:40–42a	291
5:6–11	18	7:1	87	9:43c–44	295
5:8	127, 271	7:1–10	121	9:44	309
5:8–11	16	7:11–16	164	9:45	19
5:10	26, 41, 47	7:11–17	131	9:46	35
5:11	40, 64	7:12–15	326	9:46–48	20
5:15	2, 7	7:13	89, 231	9:47	302
5:16	15	7:14	186	9:49–50	304
5:17	2, 7, 15	7:18–20	145	9:51	42, 133, 240,
5:17–19	232	7:22	7		297, 309
5:17–26	7	7:24–25	153	9:51–19:27	362
5:21	15, 171, 353	7:32	164	9:52	42
5:22	2, 8, 175	7:33	157	9:52–56	311
5:23	5	7:34	172	9:53	42
5:24	7	7:36–50	25, 183	9:54	42
5:26	2	7:37–38	172	9:55–56	42
5:27	65	7:50	234	9:57	209, 267

9:57–58	317	16:25	99	1:35–42	17
9:57–62	315	17:4	272	1:35–51	18
9:59	209	17:19	234	1:36	40
9:61	209	18	310	1:37–39	40
9:61–62	320	18:13	127,355	1:40	39
9:62	209	18:18–25	194	1:41	40
10:1–16	323–324	18:28–30	19,184	1:42	25,40
10:5–11	330	18:34	19	1:43	56,59,315
10:7	184	19:7	166,172	1:44	25,39
10:10–12	313	19:10	42,92,171,	1:45	147,251
10:10–16	332			1:45–51	59
10:12–15	333		223,313	1:46	250
10:13	252	19:27	297	2:1–10	164
10:17	304	19:41–44	139	2:12	202
10:17–24	337	20:1	7	2:13–22	241
10:25	352	20:3-4	5	2:16	276
10:25–37	349–350	20:20	7	2:23	163
10:26	5	20:24	5	2:23–25	87
10:26–28	353	20:46	8	2:24–25	61
10:38–42	361	21:27	281	2:25	302
10:39	364	21:36	281	3:3	48
10:40–42	365	22:22	77	3:3-7	270
11:14	260	22:24	20,35,43	3:5	117
11:17	8	22:29–30	16	3:14	310
11:19	166	22:31	27,35,342	3:16	51
11:20–22	218	22:31–32	20	3:19	191,224
11:29	179	22:32	35	3:22	76
11:43	8	22:35	245,329	3:35	50
11:46	4	22:49	29	4:4	133
12:1	16,260	22:51	29	4:6	128
12:32	348	22:61	32	4:7	208
12:37	97	22:62	32	4:9	42
12:41	28	23:7	248	4:39–42	170
12:47–48	333	23:21	230	5:9	176
13:1–5	94	23:34	105,110	5:22	328
13:23	269	23:41	146	5:23	303
13:28	100	23:55	183	5:24	95,176
13:31	248	24:12	122	5:28–29	237
13:33	133,179	24:25	142	5:35	157
14:1	7	24:44	71	6:1	208
14:1–12	145	24:45	19	6:1–13	193
14:11	63	**John**		6:2	252
14:26	268,321	1:3	255	6:4	255
14:28–32	269	1:12	234,288	6:5	40,254
15:7	341	1:14	61,143,286	6:7	40
15:10	341	1:16	201	6:8	39
16:16	269	1:18	217	6:9	40
16:23–24	334	1:21	155	6:14–15	237,260,263

6:22–25	256	12:26	315	20:9	10
6:26–27	252	12:31	340	20:20	68
6:33	366	12:34	261	20:24	68
6:38	92	12:36	261	20:24–25	144
6:44	56	12:37	88	20:25	66
6:53–65	16,30	12:37–40	261	20:27	69
6:59	180	12:47	313	20:28	132
6:60–66	315	13:1–15	20	20:30–31	20
6:64	76	13:6–10	35	20:31	258
6:66	16,20,230	13:9	35	21	35,36
6:67	30	13:10–11	79	21:2	60,67
6:70	16	13:18	16,77,79	21:3	27,32
6:71	25	13:20	17,335	21:4–7	32
7–11	309	13:34–35	35,102	21:5–11	16
7:5	203	14:2	275	21:9	32
7:14	230	14:6	58,118	21:15–17	27,32
7:15	60	14:7–9	132	21:18	33,36
7:30	179	14:22	72	21:19	33,36
7:33	68	14:23–24	275	21:20–22	28
7:41	180	14:26	30	21:25	259
7:46	16,163	14:27	238		
7:49	156	14:31	50	**Acts**	
8:3	353	15:2	195	1:2	310
8:12	114	15:11	352	1:3	19
8:24	132	15:12–13	35	1:6	71,76,146
8:26	362	15:14	275	1:8	18,20,90,240
8:43–47	364	15:15	362	1:13	16
8:44	93	15:16	16,24,195	1:14	202
8:46	174	15:17	35,104	1:23–26	16,241
8:48	312	16:1–4	329	1:24	325
8:56	14	16:2	104,105	1:25	78
9:20–22	262	16:8	195	2:14–40	29,31
10:8	162	16:13–14	30	2:22	250
10:25	49	16:16–21	250	2:23	77,263
11	67	17:4	178	2:38	84
11:1	363	17:8	363	2:42	18,241
11:11–14	236	17:11–26	20	3:1–11	51
11:16	67	17:12	81	3:12–26	29
11:18	67	17:17	186	3:13–14	270
11:33	327	18:2	80	4:8–12	29
11:43	137	18:10	29	4:12	58,118,139
11:43–44	237	18:11	29,34	4:13	14,30,180
12:1–3	25	18:20	180	4:18–20	36
12:1–8	171,184	19:21	189	4:19–20	29
12:16	19	19:25	43	5:27–29	36
12:20	41	19:28	128	5:29–33	29
12:21	41	20:1–18	183	5:37	70
12:22	41	20:4–6	29	5:41	99

6:1	56	2:23–29	355	3:3	301
6:5	59	2:24	127	3:6–7	346
7:23	14	2:29	330	3:22	25
7:30	14	3:10	108	4:9–13	46
7:59–60	110	4:16	14	4:16	19
8:6–8	314	5:1	186,331	4:17	55
8:9–24	25	5:5	48	5:10	103
8:12	181	5:8	107	6:9–11	170
9:16	98	7:9–11	298	6:17	303
9:22–24	54	7:15–24	299	9:5	25
9:43	25	7:18	269,271	11:1	19
10:1–48	31	8:3	356	11:30	236
10:22	57	8:8	347	13:6	339
10:32	27	8:32	295	13:12	89
10:34–48	311	8:38–39	212	15:5	25
10:43	85,186	9:14–18	346	15:9	21,46
10:44–48	124	10:1–3	355	15:10	32,45
11:18	272	10:2	42	15:31	275
12:1–2	43	10:2–3	129	15:32	351
13:50–51	246	10:9	119		
14:15	201	10:9–10	238	**2 Corinthians**	
15:5	11	10:14–15	103	4:1	314
15:10	4	11:3	99	4:3–6	280
17:6	24	11:26	147	4:4	224,340
17:11	49,144	12:3	31	4:7	21,24
17:24	343	12:13	365	4:17	275
17:31	332	12:19	104	5:6–7	288
20:17–20	159	14:17	96	5:8	236
20:22–24	274	15:19	19,45	5:17	167
20:29	55			5:19	159
20:32	366	**1 Corinthians**		5:21	264,354
21:8	59	1:12	25	10:12	301
21:13	274	1:18	24,167,	11:24	105
25:12	54		206,277	12:7–9	193
25:21–27	54	1:18–2:5	344	12:9	24
26:5	270	1:20–29	13–14	12:12	19,243
26:18	199	1:21	252	13:1	282
26:23	199	1:23	277		
26:24	46	1:26	240	**Galatians**	
27:1	124	1:29	345	1:8–9	112
		1:31	345	1:14	298
Romans		2:4–5	24	2:9	25
1:16	24,58,242	2:8	280	2:16	176,288
2:4	109	2:12–16	198	2:20	268
2:4–5	256	2:14	102,190,	3:7	14
2:5	302,332		345,347	3:22	354
2:7	352	2:16	159	3:24	356
2:16	200	3:1–9	301	4:14	17

5:6	184	4:14–15	236	13:7	24
		5:16	339		
Ephesians				**James**	
1:11	78	**2 Thessalonians**		1:2–4	193
2:1	299,347	2:9	75	1:8	26
2:1–3	270	3:10	106	1:22	119,203,364
2:2	291			2:13	308
2:5	347	**1 Timothy**		3:13–16	220
2:10	167	1:3-7	55	4:10	64,304
2:14	176,272	1:13	313	5:17	24,173
2:20	18,46,241	1:15	11,21,107,271		
3:5	18,19	1:16	32	**1 Peter**	
3:8	45	1:20	80	1:2	119
4:11–12	18	2:5	61	1:4	186
4:11–15	47	3:2–7	23–24	1:6	98
4:32	175	4:1	113	1:10–12	348
5:1	108	5:19	282	1:22	35
6:6	41	5:20	109	1:23	190
6:17	366	6:9	194	2:2	366
				2:4	125
Philippians		**2 Timothy**		2:5–8	120
1:11	201	1:6	55	2:12	34
1:15–18	305	2:25–26	272	2:13–18	34
2:3–4	300	3:2	266	2:17	35
2:5–8	15	4:20	243	2:21–23	34
2:6-8	300			3:9	104
2:8	282	**Titus**		3:14–15	36
2:9–11	310	1:6–9	53	4:3–4	170
3:2	112	1:9–16	55	4:8	35
3:5–6	270	3:5	117	4:16	274,277
3:7–8	181,271			5:3	35
3:8	201,273	**Hebrews**		5:5–6	35
3:20–21	283	1:1–3	280	5:6	300,304
4:3	327	1:2	255	5:7	212
4:10	339	2:3–4	19,243	5:8–10	35–36
4:11–12	245	2:14	217	5:14	342
4:19	245	2:17	308		
		3:14	192	**2 Peter**	
Colossians		4:15	137,148	1:1	27
1:13	218	5:7	338	1:7	35
1:23	192	10:28	284	1:12–15	33
2:13	175	10:29	333	1:17	262
4:10	202	11:13	348	2:4	222
		11:16	277	3:4	281
1 Thessalonians		11:31	14	3:10	228
1:6	19	11:39–40	158	3:18	36
1:8	199	12:2	277		
2:13	364	13:1	102		

1 John		10	109	2:20–23	112
1:19	193			2:23	201
2:15–17	194,321	3 John		7:1–8	243
2:18	48	9	43	9:1–11	222
2:20	158			11:3–12	156
2:27	158	Jude		11:15	205,262,324
3:2	115	6	217	12:9	49,340
3:8	217	9	283	13:8	327
4:1–6	49	21	310,352	14:14–15	327
4:4	342	24	338	19:21	255
5:20	350			20:10	221
		Revelation		20:11–15	277,332
2 John		1:1	84	21:1–5	228
5	51	1:17	213,286	21:12–14	19
9	335	2:20	244	21:14	18,241

Apocryphal Works

Acts of Philip — 59

Ecclesiasticus
50:25–26 — 12

Ancient Texts

Against Heresies
(Irenaus)
3.3.4 — 51

Agriculture (Varro)
1.17 — 125

Analects
(Confucius)
XV.24 — 107

Antiquities (Josephus)
18.1.6 — 70

Ecclesiastical History
(Eusebius)
II.9 — 43

Ethics (Aristotle)
1161b — 125

Histories (Polybius)
vi.xix-xlii — 124

Institutes (Gaius)
1.52 — 125

Nicocles (Isocrates)
3.60 — 106–107

Index of Subjects

Aaron, 21, 143
Abel, 84, 85
Abraham, 20, 60, 99, 142–44, 213
Absalom, 74
abyss, 222
Adam, 84, 142
Aeneas, 36
Ahab, 54, 75
Ahasuerus, 74
Ahaziah (king), 54, 74, 313
Ahimelech (priest), 5, 6
Ahithophel, 74

Alamo, 38
Alcibiades, 73
Alexander the Great, 259
Alphaeus, 69
amazement, 122–23, 213
Amaziah, 74
Amon's servants, 74
analogies, 187
Ananias, 36, 320
"And the Glory of the Lord" (*Messiah* chorus), 280

Andrew,25,39,251
  choosing of,16,17
  as missionary,40,41,58
  significance,18,47,55,282
Anna,60,183,258
anti-semitism,126
Antwerp,Belgium,37
apostles,17,144,251
  See also Twelve apostles
apostleship,241
Aramaic,94,236
Archelaus,247
Aristotle,125
Arnold,Benedict,74
Artemis,54
ascension,309,310
Athaliah,74
Athens,54,73
authenticity,200,243
authority,88,92,93,294–95

Baasha,74
banquets,172
baptism,152,156
Bartholomew (Nathanael),16,18,55,
  59–61,251
Bastogne,Belgium,38
Bathsheba,21
Battle of San Jacinto,38
Battle of Thermopylae,37
Beatitudes,93
Belgium,37,38,56
Bereans,49,144,147
Bethany,67,171
Bethlehem,60,144
Bethsaida,25,39,40,57,251,252,334
Bible,83,84,93
Bigthan (Persian official),74
bleeding problem (hemorrhage),232,
  233
blessed/blessing,84–85,95–99,102
blindness,114
Boanerges,42,313
boats,207
Boaz,143
borrowing/lending,106
Bowie,James,38

boy possessed by demon,290–94
brats,161,162,164–67
bread,244,245
bread of life,256
brothers,202,203

Caesarea,259
Caesarea Philippi,259
Cain,84
calming the storm miracle,209–10,
  212,213
Capernaum,86,123,208,231
  Christ's hometown,250
  humility lesson in,300
  location,25
  Peter and Andrew in,40
  punishment for,334
  synagogue in,126,230
centurions,123,124–29,248
Cephas,25
Cerinthus,51
Chesterton,G.K.,216
children,161,164,167,302,303
Chinneroth (Sea of Galilee),208
Chorazin,252,334
Christ,262
  See also Jesus Christ; Messiah
Christian culture,216
Christian life,268
  See also discipleship
church,242,243,301,314
Chuza (Herod's steward),183
clothing,154
cohorts,124
"Come Thou Long Expected Jesus"
  (hymn),141–42
commitment,187,316
common grace,108,251
comparative judgment,332–35
compassion,9,35,89–90,136–37,
  326–27,358
Confucius,107
contentment,245
contributions (financial),184
Corinth,170
corn,measuring of,110
courage,36

cousins, 202
covenants, 18, 21, 151, 348
creation, 206, 255
Crockett, Davy, 38, 122
cross, 238, 268, 270, 274, 275
crowds
    in Capernaum, 229–31, 290
    danger of, 203
    groups in, 93–94
    Jesus's identity and, 260, 261
    motivation of, 187, 229, 230
    size of, 86, 87, 118, 290
crucifixion, 274, 281
curiosity, 28
the cursed, 99–100
Cyrus, 134–35

Damascus, 54
Daniel, 144, 259
D'Aquino, Iva Ikuko Toguri ("Tokyo
    Rose"), 74
David, 5, 6, 14, 21, 74, 75, 143
Dead Sea, 145, 208
death, 135, 137–38, 228, 236–37, 281,
    319–20
Decapolis, 57, 250
deity, 92, 132, 133, 139
demon possession, 165, 166, 183,
    217–21, 290–94
demons
    believers' power over, 341–42
    Christ and, 217–19, 340
    Christ's power over, 88–89, 218,
        221–23, 225
    Gerasene demoniac, 165, 328, 370
    power of, 218–21
depravity, 302
"Dethrone the King: Dying to Self"
    (poem), 273–74
devil, 191, 218
    See also Satan
Diaspora, 17
Didymus. *See* Thomas (Didymus)
Diotrephes, 43
discernment, 109
disciples, 15, 16, 40, 87, 113, 123, 209
discipleship, 241, 268–77
diseases, 87, 88, 228

disobedience, 161–62
divine compassion, 136–137
divine power, 137–38
divine providence, 134–35
divine purpose, 133–34
dogs, 246, 247
Dorcas, 36
doubt, 144–49, 163, 296
"Doubting Thomas," 66
    See also Thomas

Elah, 74
Elijah, 21, 144
    Christ and, 139, 260
    in Christ's transfiguration, 283–86
    fire from heaven and, 54, 313
    John the Baptist as, 155
Elisha, 133, 139
Elizabeth, 144, 183
Emmaus, 310
emotions, 136, 157, 327
enemies, 102–4
Epaphroditus, 125
Ephesus, 51, 54
era of fulfillment, 158–59
Esau, 21
Essenes, 70
eternal life
    aquiring, 350, 354–59
    the law and, 353–54
    motivation for, 352–53
    nature of, 351–52
eternal punishment, 327, 333
    See also hell
evangelism, 186, 195, 199–200, 266, 316,
    335
Eve, 84, 142
evil, 116, 117
exclusivity, 304–5
Expected One, 142–46, 152
    See also Messiah
experiences. *See* life experiences
Ezekiel, 213

faith
    of apostles, 254, 262
    of centurion, 128–29
    elements of, 288–89

fear and, 235
heroes of, 348
imperfect, 292, 293
of Peter, 132, 248, 262
prayers of, 296
salvation and, 176
See also saving faith
false prophets, 100, 284
false religion, 3, 8, 9, 10, 261
false teachers
    characteristics of, 113–17, 243–44
    God's attitude toward, 112
    methods of, 48, 49, 266
fear, 223, 224, 286
Feast of Tabernacles, 285
feeding of five thousand, 57, 250–55
fig trees, 61
forgiveness, 110, 175, 176
foundations, 119–20
fruitfulness, 194–96, 201
funerals
    attending, 320
    children and, 164, 165
    Christ and, 138, 326
    Jewish customs regarding, 134–35,
        137, 235–36

Gabriel, 144, 258, 260
Gadara, 219, 229
Gaius, 125
Galilean ministry, 324, 338
Galileans, 14, 60, 64, 75, 179, 339
Galilee, 124, 133, 145, 152, 171, 240
    Christ's return to, 339
    description of, 188, 250
    Herod Antipas ruler of, 247
    Jesus's ministry in, 2, 40, 171, 179, 240
    Judean view of, 177, 180
    Sea of Galilee in, 208
    the Twelve's ministry in, 240
garden of Eden, 84
generation, 163, 292, 293
generosity, 110, 126–27
Gennesaret, Lake. *See* Sea of Galilee
Gentiles
    centurion, 124, 126
    Jewish people and, 129, 147, 242
    Judaism's attitude toward, 103

Philip (apostle) and, 57, 58
    salvation of, 85, 311
Gerasa, 208, 219
Gerasene demoniac, 165, 170, 328
Gerizim (Mount), 42, 312, 313
Gethsemane, 27, 29, 80, 284, 310
Gideon, 38, 39, 144
Gillars, Mildred Elizabeth ("Axis
    Sally"), 74
Girty, Simon, 73–74
God
    love of, 45
    power of, 206–13
    See also kingdom of God; Jesus
        Christ; Holy Spirit
Golan Heights, 208
Golden Rule, 106–7
Gomorrah, 334
Good Samaritan, 357–58
good soil, 189
governments, 105
grain fields, 5
Great Commission, 241
Great White Throne judgment, 333
greatness, 294, 301–3
Greece, 37
Greek (language), 236
Greek philosophy, 106–7
Greeks, 41, 57, 94
greetings, 329

Hades, 334
harvest, 327, 328
hatred, 97, 98, 104
healings
    demonstrating Christ's power, 88
    of Jairus's daughter, 230, 234–35
    of man with withered hand, 6–10
    need for, 253
    of woman with hemorrhage, 232–33
heart, 186–87, 191, 302
heaven, 89, 112, 118–19, 237, 334, 342
Hebraism, 163
hell, 81, 276
    degrees of punishment in, 333
    demons sentenced to, 89, 222
    false prophets and, 112, 132
    forces of, 218, 340

nature of,100,237
hemorrhage (bleeding problem),
232–33
Herod Agrippa,199
Herod Antipas,124,183,248,260
on Jesus's identity,259
Jewish people and,157,250
John the Baptist and,145,152,153,
247
Herod Philip I,145
Herod the Great,70,247,259
Herodians,10
Herodias,145,149
heroes of faith,348
Hillel (Jewish rabbi),107
Hitler,Adolf,37
Holy Spirit,92,144,158,240,343,348
Hosea,144
humility
of centurion,126–28
God's blessing of,299–300
God's demand for,63,65,301
greatness and,304
Peter and,34–35
hymns,120,141,142
hypocrites/hypocrisy,115–16,165,172,
201,292

immortality,350
imprisonment,145,146
inclusiveness,118
infants,343,345
initiative,28–29
Isaac,21,143
Isaiah,21,143–44,213,263–64,271
Islam,132
isolation,102
Israel,177,179

Jacob,21
Jairus,230–32,235
James (John's brother),26
ambition,43
choosing of,40
importance of,16–18,39
martyrdom of,98
occupation,41,47
personality,42,313

at transfiguration,282,286
James the son of Alphaeus,16,17,18,
69
Jehovah's Witnesses,132
Jehu,42
Jericho,170,311,356
Jeroboam,74
Jerusalem,42,57,87,179–80,309–10,
312,324,356
Jesus Christ
compassion of,89–90
deity of,92,132,133,139
the Father and,344–47
glory of,280,281,283
identity of,247–48,257–64,260,261
Lord of the Sabbath,6
popularity of,86–87
power of,88–89,206,207,228,234,
345–46
in prophecy,85
scope of ministry,178–84
See also God;Messiah
Jews,126,147,295,311
Jezebel,54
Joanna,183
Joash,74
Job,99,213,271
Joel,144
John,39
background of,47–48
characteristics of,47,313
choosing of,40
commitment to truth,48
importance,16–18,42
occupation,26,41
Peter and,36
at transfiguration,282,286
John Hyrcanus,312–13
John the Baptist,40,47,105,163
Antipas's execution of,149,247
greatness of,152–57
ministry of,165
questioning of Christ,145–48
on repentance,181
Jonah,21,212
Jonathan,38,39
Jordan River,152,162,208
Jordan Valley,208

Joseph,14,143
Joseph (brother of James the Son of Alphaeus),69
Joseph (Mary's husband),144,203
Joseph of Arimethea,99
Joshua,21
joy,98,192,338,339,342,343
Joyce,William ("Lord Haw Haw"),74
Judah,142
Judaism,93,126,127
  Christianity and,118
  Messianic misconceptions in,146
  national,230
  Paul's position in,270
  pride and,300,302
  Sabbath regulations of,3,4
Judas Iscariot,14,16,36
  betrayal of Christ,18,74,79–82,144
  disillusionment,78–80,184
  lessons from life of,81–82
  Matthias replacing,16,36,241
  motives,76–78
  name,75–76
Judas the Galilean,70
Judas the son of James (Thaddeus), 16,18,71–72
Judea,133,309,310,324
judgment,84,112,120,147–48,165, 332–35

Kerioth,75
Kersa,Israel
  See also Gerasa
kindness,109
kingdom of God
  Christ's teachings on,96,182
  forms of,157–58
  as kingdom of heaven,181
  love of,103–9
  mysteries of,190
  nearness of,332
  proclaiming,180–81,242,252
  at the transfiguration,282
kingdoms,324
kissing,173,174

lambs,329
lamps,199

law,106,271,272,317,352–56
lawyers,156,352,353,359
  See also scribes
Lazarus,67–68,139,171
leadership,23–24,28–30,45,57
Lebanon,87
Lebbaeus,71
legalism,2–6
legion,222
lending/borrowing,106,108
Leonides I (of Sparta),37,73
Levi.*See* Matthew (Levi)
Levites,357
Lewis,C.S.,216
life experiences,30
light,199,200
listening
  with authenticity,200–201
  with evangelical purpose,199–200
  with obedience,202–4
  with productivity,201–2
  value of,197–98
loans,108
Lord of the harvest,328
love
  apostle John and,46,47
  of centurion,125,127
  for enemies,102–3
  of God,45
  John's commitment to,50–52
  as kingdom love,103–9
  self-denying,353–54,358
Luther,Martin,32,316
Lysanias,247

Machaerus,145
Magdala,183
Maimonides,103
Malachi,155,156
man of peace,331
Manaen,183
manna,143
Manoah,213,271
market place,164
Martha (Mary's sister),139,184
martyrdom,41,43,69,98
Mary Magdalene,173,183
Mary (Martha's sister),171,184

Mary (mother of James the son of Alphaeus),69
Mary (mother of Jesus),144,183,202, 203
Matthew (Levi),14,16–18,65–66,71, 166,170
Matthias,16,36,241
mauling,291
McAuliffe,Anthony (American General), 38
Mediterranean Sea,87,208
Melchizedek,142
Menahem,74
mercy,9,109,307
    definition,308
    inclusiveness of,311–14
    as Jesus's mission,310
    kindness and,9,109
    value of,307
Messiah
    as Christ's identity,258,262,263
    doubts regarding,144–46,153,157, 163
    messianic kingdom of,148
    predictions regarding,155
    Satan's kingdom and,340
Messiah (Handel),280
Micah,144
Michael (archangel),132,283,285
Midrash,163
milennial kingdom,148,241
ministry,167,230
miracles
    boy possessed by demon,290–94
    calming the storm,209–10,212,213
    evidencing kingdom inauguration, 148
    feeding of five thousand,57,250–55
    number of,250,338–39
    See also healings
missionaries,40,41,58,225
money,244,245,329
Mordecai,74
Mormonism,132
Mosaic law,106,317,352–53
Moses,55,213
    assertiveness of,53,54
    Christ's transfiguration and,283–86

God's glory and,280
Messianic predictions of,142,143
    qualifications,14,21,45,63
Mozambique,208
Mt.Gerizim,42,312,313
multiplication (of ministry),179,182
mysteries,158,190

Nadab,74
Nain,133,134,135,326
nakedness,220
narrow gate,269
Nathanael.*See* Bartholomew (Nathanael)
Nazareth,60,126,177,240,250
Nazirite vow,154,165
neighbor,356,358
New Covenant,18,21,348
New Jerusalem,241
New Testament,84,85,241,243
Nicodemus,99,180
Ninety-five theses,316
Noah,20,84
Noah's ark,143

obedience,119,198,203,204,275,289
Old Testament,66,84,85,157–58
Olivet Discourse,165
Onesimus,175
Open Theism,134
outcasts,232
Owen,John,195–96

Palestine,164
Panion,259
parables,114,163,187,188,270,357–58
Passion Week,261,324
Passover,57,79,255,310
Patmos (island),51
Patton,George (General),38
Paul,144
    courage of,54–55
    on ministry,182
    religious credentials of,11,270,298
    self-assessment of,21,32,45–46
    during storm,212
    suffering and,99
peace,330–31

pedophilia, 125
Pekah, 74
Pekahiah, 74
Peloponnesian War, 73
Pentecost, 240
Perea, 145, 247, 310, 311, 324, 362
perfume, 173
persecution, 98, 329
perseverance, 192, 195
Persia, 134–35
pessimism, 68
Pétain, Henri, 74
Peter, 39, 77, 213
  faith of, 132, 248, 262
  as leader, 24, 28–30, 33, 36
  life experiences of, 30–33, 56, 251
  naming of, 25–28, 40
  occupation, 47
  primary position of, 16–18, 25, 41, 42, 55
  during transfiguration, 281–86
  virtues of, 33–36
Peter's mother-in-law, 184
Pharaoh, 190
Pharisees, 43, 70, 270
  Christ's condemnation of, 117, 162
  hostility to Jesus, 7, 10, 15
  Jesus dining with, 171–76
  in Judaism, 230
  legalism/ritualism and, 2
  Sabbath regulations and, 3, 5–7
  spiritual blindness of, 114
Philemon, 175
Philip (apostle), 41, 251
  choosing of, 16, 56
  at feeding of five thousand, 40
  ministry of, 59, 61
  personality, 55, 57
  priority of, 18, 56
  in upper room, 58
Philip (evangelist), 58, 59, 314
Philip (Herod Antipas's brother), 145
Philip the Tetrarch, 56, 147, 259
Philippi, 54, 99
Philistines, 38, 39
Phoenicia, 87
pigs, 222, 223, 246, 247
Pilate, 122, 248, 295

place of honor, 43
playgrounds, 164
Polybius, 124
Polycarp, 51
Pontius Pilate, 122, 248, 295
poor/poor in spirit, 95, 96, 271–73
possessions, 267, 268
power, 88, 137–38, 206, 207, 243
prayer, 15, 105, 259, 328
preaching, 180, 181, 242
prejudice, 60
pride, 298–305
priesthood, 143
priests, 5, 263, 264, 357
proclaiming, 180, 181, 199, 242
prodigal son, 308
prophecies, 77, 152, 153, 281
prophets
  Elijah and, 156
  false, 100, 284
  Jewish tradition on, 146
  John the Baptist and, 145, 152–55
  Moses on, 139
prostitutes, 14, 172
proverbs, 114
providence, 134–35
punishment, 327, 333, 334

Quirinius, 70
Quisling, Vidkun, 74

rabbis, 172, 183
Rahab, 14
rebelliousness, 198
redemption plan, 83–84
regulations, 3–6
rejoicing, 339, 342
  See also joy
religions, 118
remorse, 80–81
repentance, 97, 156, 181, 272, 299
resurrections, 238
revenge, 103, 104, 106
riches, 320
  See also wealth
ritualism, 2–6
"Rock" (Peter's nickname), 25, 26, 27
rocky soil, 189, 192

Rome, 263
Ruth, 143

Sabbath
    Jesus Lord of, 6
    rabbinic restrictions on, 3–5, 7–9
    regulations, 3–6
sacrifices, 143
Sadducees, 70
Salome, 47
salvation
    blessings of, 186
    by faith, 176
    obedience and, 119, 289
    sin and, 195–96, 234
    transformation, 223
    See also saving faith
salvation wisdom, 167
Samaria, 133, 311, 312
Samaritan woman, 133, 170
Samaritans, 42, 47, 179, 242, 311–12,
    357–58
Samson, 38, 39
sanctification, 299
Sanhedrin, 80
Santa Anna, Antonio Lopez de, 38
Sapphira, 36, 320
Sarah, 20, 144
Satan, 31, 283
    Christ's power over, 88–89, 142, 218,
        340
    emissaries of, 112, 113
    Jesus's identity and, 221, 258
    Judas Iscariot and, 80
    methods of, 75
    protection from, 341–42
    See also demons
Saul (apostle), 170
Saul (king), 38
saving faith
    elements of, 289–90
    of Gentiles, 129
    indicators of, 192
    obedience and, 119, 275
    self-denial and, 321
    See also faith

scribes, 43, 318
    Christ's condemnation of, 114, 162,
        179
    functions of, 317
    hostility of to Christ, 2, 7, 10
Scripture, 83, 84, 85, 93
Sea of Chinnereth (Sea of Galilee), 208
Sea of Galilee, 15, 183
    calming of storm on, 207, 210–13,
        218–19, 229
    description, 208
    fishing occupations on, 41, 47, 210
Sea of Tiberias (Sea of Galilee), 208
sectarianism, 50
"seeker-friendly" approach, 266
self-control, 34
self-defense, 105
self-denial, 265, 269–74, 276, 318, 319,
    321
self-love, 266
self-righteousness, 99, 100, 115, 179, 261
Sermon on the Mount, 86, 94, 117–18,
    123
serpent in the wilderness, 143
the seventy, 241, 324–25, 329–32, 335,
    339–41
shaking the dust off, 246
Shallum, 74
shame (ashamed), 277
Sheba, 74
Shunem, 133
Sidon, 87, 250, 252, 259, 334
Silas, 99, 144
silence, 237, 238, 286
Simeon, 61, 258
Simon, 25, 26, 27, 40
Simon Barjona, 25
Simon Iscariot, 75, 171
Simon Magus, 36
Simon Peter, 25, 26, 171
    See also Peter
Simon the leper, 171
Simon the magician, 171
Simon the Pharisee, 171–76, 183
Simon the tanner, 25, 171
Simon the Zealot, 16–18, 25, 70–71, 171

sin,84,85,127–28,156,355
sinners,107,108,156,166–67,172
skepticism,58,66,68,144,281
　　See also doubt
slaves,125
sleeping,208,236,284
Sodom,334
soil,188–96,319
"The Solid Rock"(hymn),142
Son of Man,166,260,263,264,295
sons,134,135,290,291
sons of Sceva,304
"Sons of Thunder,"42,313
sovereignty,327,344–47
sowers,190
Sparta,73
spiritual brats,161,162,164–67
spiritual deficiency,96
staff (walking stick),244
Stalin,Joseph,103
standards,23–24,24
Stephen,98
storms,207,210–13,218–19,229
submission,33–34
suffering,99
Susanna,183
swine,222,229,246,247
sympathy,326
　　See also compassion
synagogues,6,7,126–27,180,230
Syria,208
Syro-Phoenician woman,179

Tabernacles,Feast of,285
Talmud,3,103
tax collectors,65,166
teachers,115,235
teaching,88
temple,312,313
temptation,192
Teresh (Persian official),74
testing.*See* trials
tetrarch,247
Texas,38
Thaddeus.*See* Judas the son of James
　　(Thaddeus)
theft,106

Thomas (Didymus),16,18,66–69,132,
　　248
thorns,189,193–94
Tiberias,208
Tiberias,Sea of.*See* Sea of Galilee
Timothy,55,182,243
tolerance,162
Torah,302
training,182,184,329
traitors,73–75
transfiguration,47,50,86,198,281
trials,192,193
tribunes,124
Trophimus,243
trust,128,129
　　See also faith
truth,45,305
　　Jesus's proclamation of,2–3
　　John's commitment to,46–48
　　mercy and,307–8
Twelve apostles,47,162,241
　　choosing,15–17,46
　　commitment,64
　　importance,18–21
　　preaching,240,247
　　sending,17–18
　　training,182,184,297
　　weaknesses,19–21,24,182
Tyre,87,250,252,259,334

unbelievers,105,107,108,144
unclean spirits,220
　　See also demon possession
upper room,58,201,245

vengeance,103,104,106
virginity,202

Watson,Thomas,272–73
weaknesses,19–21
wealth,99,267,320
weddings,164,166
weeds,189
Wesley,Charles,141,142
Western Allies,37–38
widow at Nain,184
wilderness,152–54,165

women, 183, 184
  Samaritan woman, 133, 170
  woman with hemorrhage, 232–33
Word of God, 83
  See also Scripture
World War 2, 37–38

Xenophon, 73

Yam Kinneret (Sea of Galilee), 208
young man from Nain, 131–39

Zaccheus, 166, 170
Zacharias, 144, 258
Zealots, 70, 103
Zebedee, 41, 47
Zechariah, 144
Zimri, 74

MOODY
Publishers™

From the Word to Life

Lift your study to new heights with the *complete* MacArthur New Testament Commentary series.

Respected Bible scholar and author John MacArthur opens up the wonder of the New Testament, offering verse-by-verse analysis, theological insights, and points of application. These works are sure to enrich your study of the Bible, and indeed your faith.

The MacArthur New Testament Commentary series includes:

Matthew 1–7
Matthew 8–15
Matthew 16–23
Matthew 24–28
Mark 1–8
Mark 9–16
Luke 1–5
Luke 6–10
Luke 11–17
Luke 18–24
John 1–11
John 12–21
Acts 1–12
Acts 13–28
Romans 1–8
Romans 9–16
First Corinthians
Second Corinthians
Galatians
Ephesians
Philippians
Colossians & Philemon
First & Second Thessalonians
First Timothy
Second Timothy
Titus
Hebrews
James
First Peter
Second Peter & Jude
First–Third John
Revelation 1–11
Revelation 12–22

www.MoodyPublishers.com | 1-800-678-6928